KOVELS' AMERICAN COLLECTIBLES

1900 TO 2000

BOOKS BY RALPH AND TERRY KOVEL

American Country Furniture 1780–1875

A Directory of American Silver, Pewter, and Silver Plate

Kovels' Advertising Collectibles Price List

Kovels' American Antiques: 1750 to 1900

Kovels' American Art Pottery

Kovels' American Silver Marks: 1650 to the Present

Kovels' Antiques & Collectibles Fix-It Source Book

Kovels' Antiques & Collectibles Price List

Kovels' Bid, Buy, and Sell Online

Kovels' Book of Antique Labels

Kovels' Bottles Price List

Kovels' Collector's Guide to American Art Pottery

Kovels' Collector's Guide to Limited Edition Plates, Figurines, Ingots, Paperweights, Etc.

Kovels' Collectors' Source Book

Kovels' Depression Glass & American Dinnerware Price List

Kovels' Depression Glass & Dinnerware Price List

Kovels' Dictionary of Marks—Pottery and Porcelain: 1650 to 1850

Kovels' Guide to Selling, Buying, and Fixing Your Antiques and Collectibles

Kovels' Guide to Selling Your Antiques & Collectibles

Kovels' Illustrated Price Guide to Royal Doulton

Kovels' Know Your Antiques

Kovels' Know Your Collectibles

Kovels' New Dictionary of Marks—Pottery & Porcelain: 1850 to the Present

Kovels' Organizer for Collectors

Kovels' Price Guide for Collector Plates, Figurines, Paperweights, and Other Limited Editions

Kovels' Quick Tips: 799 Helpful Hints on How to Care for Your Collectibles

Kovels' Yellow Pages: A Collector's Directory

Kovels' Yellow Pages: A Resource Guide for Collectors

The Label Made Me Buy It: From Aunt Jemima to Zonkers—The Best-Dressed Boxes, Bottles, and Cans from the Past

KOVELS' AMERICAN COLLECTIBLES
1900 TO 2000

by Ralph and Terry Kovel

RANDOM HOUSE
REFERENCE
New York

Kovels' American Collectibles

by Ralph and Terry Kovel

This book is available for special discounts for bulk purchases for sales promotions or premiums. Special editions, including personalized covers, excerpts of existing books, and corporate imprints, can be created in large quantities for special needs. For more information, write to Special Markets/Premium Sales, 1745 Broadway, MD 6-2, New York, NY, 10019 or e-mail specialmarkets@randomhouse.com.

Please address inquiries about electronic licensing of reference products for use on a network, in software or on CD-ROM to the Subsidiary Rights Department, Random House Reference, fax 212-572-6003.

Visit the Random House Web site: www.randomhouse.com

Cover and interior design by Geraldine Sarmiento

Photos on front cover:
1. Studebaker pedal car (James Julia)
2. Gouda pticher (Treadway)
3. Eames LCW plywood chair (Treadway)
4. Sterling silver candelabra (Treadway)

Photo on spine
1. Moriage vase (Jackson's)

Photos on back cover, left to right:
1. Pewabic covered bowl (Ralph and Terry Kovel)
2. Handel lamp (James Julia)
3. Scheier vase (Raph and Terry Kovel)
4. Kalo Shop brooch (Skinner)

Library of Congress Cataloging-in-Publication Data is available.

Printed in China

First Edition

0 9 8 7 6 5 4 3 2 1

July 2007

ISBN: 978-0-609-80891-7

Dedicated to

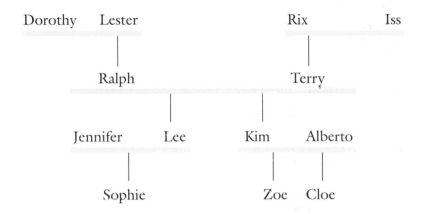

Dorothy   Lester   Rix   Iss

Ralph   Terry

Jennifer   Lee   Kim   Alberto

Sophie   Zoe   Cloe

Who lived in the twentieth century and
had these collectibles when they were new.

The past is always with you.

Try to understand it.

TABLE OF CONTENTS

PREFACE

Kovels' American Collectibles is about the furnishings, decorative and useful objects, jewelry, and even toys that could be found in a home or office in the United States from 1900 to 2000. Included is everything from eggbeaters to expensive chairs made or used in America, as well as products from other countries that influenced American design, like Scandinavian and Italian furniture. This book is for the general reader who is curious about twentieth-century decorative arts, and it is for the collector, both the beginner and the old-timer. It is also for the researcher who wants details on names, dates, and biographical information. It is a history of everyday objects made since 1900, and it is a study of the artists who moved "out of the box" to create new styles with new materials.

We are proud of some of the book's special features. *Kovels' American Collectibles* includes information about historic changes in lifestyles that led to new designs for collectibles; for example, new eating habits led to new types of tableware—cocktail parties in the 1930s required cocktail shakers, and buffets in the late

1940s needed chip 'n' dip dishes. This book not only identifies and dates objects, but also focuses on how the objects fit into the lives of the people who originally owned them. And there is an emphasis on somewhat neglected subjects, such as mid-twentieth-century enameled metal and artistic ironwork. Definitions for technical terms, like *cameo glass* or *pâte-de-verre*, are included. There are charts with names, dates, and marks that we found after searching many sources; hints about dating marks; and clues to the values and prices of important pieces.

Research took us to old store catalogs, museum show catalogs, old reference books, historical societies, memories of those who used many of these items, movies, the Internet, and more. Calls were made to companies and ex-employees to learn details of products and their history. Dealers told us what they had learned. Artists added information about contemporaries who had died. We used stock market information about company mergers and government sources for dates of laws, rates of postage, and requirements for imports and exports.

Especially significant is the book's emphasis on the decorative arts of the last twenty years of the twentieth century. Although these objects are still in stores and can be seen in decorating magazines, only a few collectors have begun to consider the possibility that they will become collectible and rise in value.

Our years of writing about antiques have shown us that tastes change rapidly—this year's kitsch is next year's find. Great collections are created by those who understand the value of seemingly unimportant objects. So our book does not ignore giveaway dishes like carnival glass and calendar plates, and does not leave out the so-called dated resin furniture and silver jewelry of the 1950s. To take what we've learned one step further, yesterday's trash can become tomorrow's treasure. Nineteenth-century liquor flasks are now in museums as examples of quality glasswork of their day. Old handmade quilts by anonymous housewives are featured as authentic folk art.

This is our second book discussing the decorative arts in America. The first, *Kovels' American Antiques*, focuses on the years from 1750 to 1900. The present volume covers the years 1900 to 2000. We hope readers find both books easy to read, historically accurate, and filled with information. We trust that the history, descriptions, marks, and photographs will make antiques and collectibles easier to recognize and understand.

We have chosen to picture a wide range of items. Some represent museum-quality work. Others are everyday furnishings. Masterpieces alone cannot explain the decorative arts, so you will find both the finest Tiffany lamp worth thousands of dollars and inexpensive kitchen gadgets. Any judgments about artistic value are based on the opinions of other experts—we like *everything* in the book.

Thousands of facts, marks, and pictures are included in *Kovels' American Collectibles*, and each one was checked and rechecked. Heidi Makela had the difficult job of gathering all of the information from those who helped with research and editing and bringing it all together. She also edited, wrote, and kept us all working, making it possible to finish nearly on time. The pictures we used came from many sources, and our picture editor, Karen Kneisley, made sure they were the best possible. Her talent with computers and her understanding of collectibles, especially glass, made it all possible. Marcia Goldberg was our last word on anything to do with grammar, punctuation, correct usage, spelling—all the things hurried writers might ignore. Kim Kovel and Alberto Eiber, who live with the designs of the late twentieth century and are friends of many of the designers, helped steer the selections of which artists to include. Liz Lillis and Linda Coulter worked on the tables and lists and unearthed marks for each of the makers. Lisa Bell, Grace DeFrancisco, Gay Hunter, Katie Karrick, Tina McBean, Nancy Saada, June Smith, Julie Seaman, and Cherrie Smrekar also helped with our researching quests.

We consulted a number of outside experts who solved special problems. Thanks to Lars Christoffersen (Danish Porcelain Imports), Josephine Lynn Dillon (Royal Copenhagen Porcelain, USA), Linda Edward (United Federation of Doll Clubs), Diane

Frager (Ohio Art Company), Jeffrey Herman (Society of American Silversmiths), Bernard Jazzar (Long Beach Museum of Art), Mark McDonald (twentieth-century dealer-expert), David Meaders (Meaders family member), Jill Thomas-Clark (Corning Museum), and Helen Zagar (Royal Doulton USA Inc.). The pictures came from many sources. Most have not been published before. We are grateful for all of them and have listed complete photo credit information at the end of the book.

Random House Information Group made this book a reality and even made it match our vision. Thanks to Mark LaFlaur, our editor whose comments and attention to detail improved our work, and to Elizabeth Bennett, the publishing director, who carried it even further. Rahel Lerner completed the last of the editing. Beth Levy and Patricia Dublin, managing editors, and Oriana Leckert, editorial assistant, also worked on text and technical production problems. Thanks to all of them and to the production staff, Lisa Montebello, production manager, and Lisbeth Dyer, production editor. Fabrizio La Rocca, creative director, designed pages that blended pictures and text to make our meaning clear and even made lengthy tables look attractive. Geraldine Sarmiento, designer, and Tigist Getachew, art director, are also part of the reason the book has turned out so well. David Naggar, president of Random House Information Group, and Sheryl Stebbins, vice president and publisher of Random House Reference, have been working with us for many years, and their support has made many of our books possible. We thank all of them and share the credit with them for helping us with this, our ninety-fifth book about antiques and collectibles, all with the same publisher.

Ralph Kovel
Terry Kovel
October 2006

Introduction

Wallace Nutting, whose hand-tinted pictures and furniture reproductions are prized by collectors, wrote in 1933 in Volume III of his *Furniture Treasury,* ". . . no furniture built after 1830 is worth having or classing as antique." In the 1930s, only restrained designs made before 1850 were thought of as "artistic" and "worthy." But by the 1950s, a few adventurous collectors were searching for the Victorian furniture, colored glass, and highly decorated ceramics of the late nineteenth and early twentieth centuries, even though decorating magazines were featuring the look of Colonial Williamsburg or the knotty pine "Early American" style with its cobbler's-bench coffee tables. Younger "antiques"—only fifty to a hundred years old—were becoming popular.

Collectors before the 1950s wanted to furnish a house with a recognizable period look, perhaps Chippendale or "Colonial." Today collectors think more in terms of history, artistic value, and personal statement. Some seek the Arts and Crafts look of 1900. Others want the "mid-century modern" lines of 1950s furniture. Many remember their own childhoods with nostalgia and treasure lunch boxes, radios, and toys from their younger days. Decorators who work with collectors have had to add storage and display units for these collections. A room filled with blue and white plates or plastic purses is now considered an expression of individuality, not an eccentricity.

Consider the everyday ceramics of the twentieth century. Collectors like amusing ceramics, figural salt and peppers, egg timers, reamers, cookie jars, and mixing bowls, as well as dishes by important artists like Eva Zeisel and Russel Wright. All of these are collectible, most are inexpensive, and some are already in museums.

In the twentieth century, people started appreciating the beauty in products of technology—the case and workings of a radio, the structure of a plastic chair—on their own merits, not as later versions of an inlaid music box or a carved Chippendale chair.

Before the nineteenth century, a chair or vase was usually designed and made by hand at a single workshop. With the

Industrial Revolution, goods could be mass-produced once they were designed, so experts did the designing. The best of them had artistic talent as well as engineering skill, and knew which production techniques lowered costs. In 1919 the term *industrial designer* was coined by American Joseph Sinel, a designer of trademarks and typefaces, but it was not until the 1920s—probably 1927 with the redesign of the Model A Ford—that the designation *industrial designer* came into general use.

To stimulate sales during the Depression, commercial artists were asked to become industrial designers and improve the appearance and manufacturing costs of many everyday items. New materials—chrome, stainless steel, and plastics—were used, and smooth, streamlined forms evolved. Industrial designers created new shapes for dishes, electric fans, chairs, teapots, cigarette packages, kitchen gadgets, printing presses, cars, trains, and almost any other commercial object, large or small. They improved designs to make better use of space and materials and to create more useful, less expensive, more attractive products.

These designers changed the look of America's home furnishings, cars, and industrial machinery.

Designers also became stars. Henry Dreyfuss, Norman Bel Geddes, Raymond Loewy, Viktor Schreckengost, Walter Darwin Teague, Russel Wright, Eva Zeisel, and others became so well known their names helped to sell products. Yet many unmarked examples of their work can still be found at low prices.

Many industrial designers are featured throughout this book. If an artist or designer worked in several fields, we have included biographical information in the chapter that focuses on the talent for which the designer is best known. For example, special attention is given to Russel Wright's work in the Tableware chapter. Wright is also mentioned in the Furniture chapter and the Silver and Other Metals chapter.

VIKTOR SCHRECKENGOST
INDUSTRIAL DESIGNER
A Twentieth-Century Phenomenon

A talented industrial designer could improve a product's looks and lower its cost. Well-known potter Viktor Schreckengost (see page 71) was also an industrial designer. One day, walking through the design area at Sears where a group was working on kitchen cabinets, he noticed that the cabinet handle stuck out just enough to require a larger shipping box. He drew a six-inch circle at the center of the two cabinet doors, had it cut a half inch into the wood, and put the handle in the hole so it was flush with the front of the door. The smaller shipping carton required was less expensive and took up less space, so more units could be loaded on the same truck. This minor change meant major savings, and the attractive circular handle became a feature on many Sears products.

Kovels' American Collectibles examines the decorative arts, tools, and everyday utensils of the twentieth century. It explains how things were made, why they were different from earlier examples, what technology did to change construction methods, and how wars, radio, television, and the Internet made the arts international. It is written not to instruct experts, but to see the world through the eyes of a collector or amateur historian. Dates, marks, and methods of identification are in every chapter to help place objects in the proper location and time frame.

In developing its collection, a museum considers "connoisseurship": what is rare, important, and artistic; how a particular piece represents culture and good taste; and why an art historian might consider a piece significant. A look back through the last two centuries shows that these criteria are not absolutes. Mission furniture was being discarded by the 1930s, and Victorian style was in poor taste in the 1950s. Museums deaccessioned the ceramics of Taxile Doat and the University City Pottery of St. Louis in the 1940s, but pay high prices for the same vases today. George Ohr pottery from Biloxi, Mississippi, was unwanted in the 1970s, but now is being honored with its own museum. Using information available in books and museums and on the Internet, collectors have formed their own ideas of what is exceptional art or important design. They could be acquiring the museum exhibits of the future.

Chapter 1

American Pottery and Porcelain

AMERICAN ART POTTERY, 1876 TO 1950

ART POTTERY WAS made in America from the late 1870s to the 1950s. The term *art pottery* can have several meanings. To the scholar and researcher, it is pottery that was handmade or primarily handmade and produced before the 1940s in the spirit of the Arts and Crafts movement. The Arts and Crafts movement started in England as a rebellion against the machine age and the excessive decoration of the Victorian era. It encouraged handcraft and traditional design. The company that produced art pottery may also have made industrial or florist wares at the same time.

Collectors define *art pottery* a little differently. For them, the term refers to any pottery made by companies that produced art pottery during the 1876–1950 era. Sometimes it includes commercial and florist wares like those by Roseville; sometimes it includes studio potters' work from the 1920s

Collectors have expanded the meaning of art pottery to include not only the handmade artistic pottery made from 1876 to the 1950s, but also some commercial and florist wares made during those years. These vases were made by Brush Pottery.

through the 1940s. California potteries were founded much later than those on the East Coast, so collectors sometimes call pottery made in the West as late as the 1950s "art pottery."

The first American art pottery was made soon after the Centennial Exhibition in Philadelphia in 1876. The latest French and British ceramic designs and techniques were on display in Philadelphia. Haviland and Company exhibited pottery with underglaze designs made at its Auteuil studio near Paris. Doulton and Company of London displayed salt-glazed stoneware and faience with underglaze designs. The exotic, unfamiliar ceramics exhibited by the Japanese were another important influence. The critics considered the American pieces on display—primarily porcelain and white ware by potteries like Ott and Brewer, New York City Pottery, Union Porcelain Works, and Laughlin Brothers Pottery—inferior, not as artistic or imaginative as the work by the English, French, and Japanese. The Exposition's Women's Pavilion showed off the pottery and other art done by women working in the United States. A display of ceramics by a group of women working in Cincinnati, Ohio, was included. The women used mineral painting over the glaze, a technique that was new in America. The critics were impressed, not by the artistic quality of the pottery but by the possibility that women could be employed making ceramics for sale. Many of the art potteries started in the next fifty years were established to teach women a marketable skill so they could support themselves in an "honorable" job.

Mary Louise McLaughlin experimented with many types of ceramics. This rare, carved Losanti porcelain vase was part of a group of 1,239 pieces made from 1900 to 1906. McLaughlin never exhibited her porcelain in the United States. (Photo: Rago)

Mary Louise McLaughlin, one of the Cincinnati potters, saw French Haviland pottery at the 1876 Centennial Exhibition, and the next year, after experimenting, she began making pottery with similar decorations. Others soon discovered this new style. In 1880 Cincinnati potter Maria Longworth Nichols founded the Rookwood Pottery (1880–1967), which became a successful commercial enterprise. Other Cincinnati-area potteries included Cincinnati Art Pottery

Company (1879–1891), Matt Morgan Art Pottery (1883–1884), and Avon Pottery (1886–1888). Some of the potters who trained at Rookwood left to found other companies, such as the Pauline Pottery (1883–1893) of Chicago, Illinois, and Edgerton, Wisconsin; and Valentien Pottery (1911–1914) of San Diego, California, and the Van Briggle Pottery (1901–present) of Colorado Springs, Colorado.

Other firms that took advantage of the natural assets and potters available in Ohio included the Cowan Pottery (1913–1931), Lonhuda Pottery (1892–1895), Roseville Pottery (1892–1954), and Weller Pottery (1872–1948). At the same time, potteries were operating in other parts of the country. New England potters had seen the same Haviland pieces at the Centennial, and soon art potteries like Chelsea Keramic Art Works (1875–1889), Dedham (1895–1943), Low Art Tile Works (1877–1902), and Volkmar (1879–1911) were founded.

Eventually the art pottery movement spread to all parts of the United States. George Ohr's Biloxi pottery (1883–1909) in Biloxi, Mississippi, made Ohr's unique style of crumpled vases. Newcomb Pottery (1895–1939) in New Orleans perfected a matte glazed ware with carved stylized floral decoration. Grueby (1894–1911) pottery, made in Boston, was decorated with a matte green glaze that became so popular it was copied at lower prices and the company was forced to close. Other art potteries opened in Michigan, Illinois, and California.

Some companies found the problems of making high-quality artistic ware too difficult and simply closed. Others kept making more and better designs while enlarging their plants. By the 1920s many of the firms, especially in Ohio, were making both art pottery and commercial-quality wares to sell to florists and gift shops for reasonable prices. Gradually the quality of the work suffered as pricing became more important, and by the late 1920s most of the firms that had produced art pottery had either closed or discontinued their art lines. Crafts people who wanted to make pottery worked alone in small shops and became known as "studio potters."

IMPORTANT AMERICAN ART POTTERIES

Fulper Pottery

The Fulper Pottery, established in Flemington, New Jersey, in 1860, to make utilitarian items, began making its art ware line, *Vasekraft*, in 1909. The pottery had classical and oriental shapes and several kinds of glazes, including the expensive rose shades; *Mirror Glaze*, a high-gloss, crystalline glaze; and *Mission Matte*, a brown-black glaze with shaded greens. After a 1929 fire at the Flemington plant, all operations moved to Trenton, New Jersey. Art ware was made on a small scale until 1935. J. Martin Stangl bought the firm in 1930, and production shifted to dinnerware marked with the *Stangl* name, then to bird figurines. The company's name was not officially changed to Stangl Pottery until 1955.

Red Wing Stoneware Company/Red Wing Union Stoneware Company/Red Wing Potteries, Inc.

The Red Wing Stoneware Company opened in Red Wing, Minnesota, in 1878. The company went through several mergers until 1908, when it reincorporated as Red Wing Union Stoneware Company. At first it made pottery flowerpots and vases with a green stain over a tan background. Red Wing made art pottery from the 1920s. From 1932 to 1937, it also made pottery for George Rumrill, who sold it as Rum Rill pottery. Red Wing began making contemporary-style dinnerware in the 1930s. It changed its name to Red Wing Potteries, Inc., in 1936 and continued working until 1967.

Rookwood Pottery

Maria Longworth Nichols had been decorating china since 1873 when, after seeing pottery at the Philadelphia Centennial Exhibition in 1876, she began making her own vases at the Dallas Pottery in Cincinnati, Ohio. In 1880 she started the Rookwood Pottery, which made white graniteware tableware and yellow clay pieces. Nichols and her friends also fired their art pottery at

This is the Iris bowl, no. 500 in Fulper's Vasekraft catalog. Fulper made several unusual vases with figural feet like this one held by strange birds.

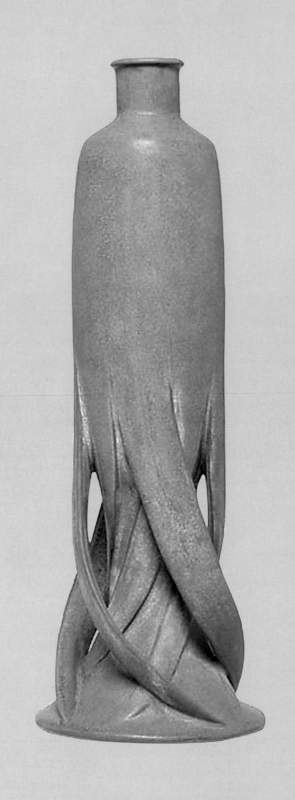

Rookwood. By 1881 Rookwood Pottery pieces were decorated with underglaze blue or brown prints, and some Japanese-inspired art ware was also produced. In 1883 the popular Rookwood Standard Glaze was developed. Rookwood made some pottery with added silver overlay. It also made novelties, wall plaques, and vases. Rookwood made decorative architectural tiles from 1901 until the 1940s. Rookwood tiles were used in the New York City subways in the early 1900s and can still be seen in some stations.

Rookwood used local Ohio clays in the early years. The matte glaze and Tiger Eye glaze are among the most famous finishes. Rookwood's art pottery was top quality and won many international prizes. The artist Kataro Shirayamadani, who joined the staff in the 1880s, made vases that are now considered masterpieces. (In 2004 a Rookwood vase by Shirayamadani, decorated with flying cranes and electroplated copper and silver overlay of lotus blossoms, sold for $350,750.) After Nichols retired in 1890, new lines were added and new artists joined the pottery. The company had money problems and was bought and sold several times. In 1960 operations moved to Starkville, Mississippi. Pottery was made until 1966. The plant closed in 1967, and the molds and formulas were purchased in 1973. A limited number of pieces have been made from the molds since 1984. New owners who purchased the Rookwood Pottery in 2005 announced they will manufacture new pottery in the tradition of the old wares, some from original molds with original glazes. New marks will be used.

Teco/Gates (American Terra Cotta and Ceramic Company)

Teco is the name used today by collectors to refer to the pottery made by William D. Gates. He founded the Spring Valley Tile Works in Terra Cotta, Illinois, in 1881. He renamed it the Terra Cotta Tile Works in 1885, and changed the name again to the American Terra Cotta and Ceramic Company in 1887. It was sometimes called the Gates Pottery. The company made architectural terra-cotta bricks, drain tile, and pottery. After 1887 it began experimenting with art pottery, and in 1901 Teco potters started making molded ceramics. The name Teco (from *te* in *terra*

Opposite Page: The most sought-after Teco vases are tall, slender, and often have unusual cutout shapes. The vase was usually molded, then finished by hand. Matte glaze, usually green, was preferred. This 18½-inch-high vase has a cutout swirled base.
(Photo: Treadway)

and *co* in *cotta*) was used on experimental pieces as early as 1895. Vases and, later, tea ware and tiles were made with silvery green glaze, simple shapes, and no added decoration. After 1909 a few new colors were introduced. Most admired today are the unusual-shaped vases with a single-color matte glaze. The company was sold and renamed American Terra Cotta Corporation in 1930 and then made mainly architectural terra-cotta and ornamental pottery. It closed in 1966.

The art deco influence is seen in this piece of Roseville Pine Cone pottery, the most successful of Roseville's patterns. It was made in seventy-five shapes and three colors: blue, brown, and green. This 7¼-inch-high vase was made after 1935.

Roseville Pottery

Roseville Pottery was founded in Roseville, Ohio, in 1892. The company made stoneware jars and flowerpots in Roseville and at an additional factory in Zanesville, Ohio. By 1910 all Roseville pottery was being made in Zanesville. The company started making art pottery in 1900. Its first line of handmade art pottery was an underglaze and slip-decorated, dark brown ware called Rozane. The designs were usually hand-painted portraits or flowers. By 1920 Roseville had stopped making handmade art ware and was instead producing machine-made, commercial pottery. Patterns with molded, raised decorations, especially flowers and fruits in natural colors, were the most popular. Only a few dinnerware patterns were made. Production ended in 1954. Since 1990 Roseville pottery has been the most popular pottery collected in the United States.

Green Grueby pottery with applied handles or added tendrils or pieces featuring several colors are the most expensive today.

Grueby Faience Company/Grueby Pottery Company/Grueby Faience and Tile Company

William Henry Grueby started working at Boston-area potteries as a boy. He founded an architectural tile company in 1884 before opening his own Grueby Faience Company ten years later. The company made architectural tiles and art pottery. Most of it had a matte green glaze created by a special method of firing. The pottery was made by hand, thrown on a wheel, then modeled by a group of young artists. Raised designs were natural shapes such as leaves, tulips, or grasses. The veining on a leaf was added as a thin spaghettilike piece of clay, and some incised (cut-in) lines were also used. Because the pieces were hand tooled, the surface of the vase appears rough. The glaze was thick and usually green, but it might also be pink, yellow, brown, blue, gray, graying purple, or white. Sometimes a flower was glazed in a different color, such as a yellow flower on a green or blue ground.

The leaves on this Grueby vase were sculpted. Sometimes Grueby potters added leaves, then carved them to make a more interesting decoration. The 7½-inch vase is covered with Grueby's typical matte green glaze. (Photo: Treadway)

Grueby Pottery Company, created as an art pottery division around 1898, was incorporated in 1907 and closed about 1911. Grueby Faience went bankrupt in 1909, and William Grueby started Grueby Faience and Tile Company to make architectural tiles. The company was bought in 1919 by Calvin Pardee and production continued until 1920.

Newcomb Pottery

In 1895 Ellsworth Woodward, on the staff at Sophie Newcomb College, a women's college in New Orleans, persuaded the college to start a pottery class and sell the students' products. Woodward believed the class would provide vocational training for the women and increase their appreciation of arts and crafts. Joseph Fortune Meyer was chief potter; Paul Cox was technician. George Ohr taught there briefly.

For the first fifteen years, designer Mary G. Sheerer and Joseph Meyer were the main artistic influences at Newcomb. Between 1900 and 1910, most wares were blue-green with incised decoration emphasized with black. From about 1910 to 1930, low molded relief designs and matte glaze were used. Newcomb Pottery made vases, mugs, tea sets, candlesticks, and lamps. Designs reflected the landscape of the South with trees dripping moss and large full moons.

Sadie Irvine is one of the best-known Newcomb Pottery artists. This carved and painted vase is decorated with Spanish moss-laden trees. It is 8¼ inches high. (Photo: Treadway)

Newcomb's art pottery era ended in 1931. Limited production and exhibitions continued for a few years, but by 1939 the college had the pottery only for teaching purposes. Students' and alumnae's works marked with a new label, The Newcomb Guild, continued to be sold into the 1940s.

Van Briggle Pottery/Van Briggle Pottery and Tile Company/Van Briggle Art Pottery Company

Artus Van Briggle worked as a decorator at the Rookwood Pottery in Ohio until he had to move west for his health. He opened the Van Briggle Pottery in Colorado Springs, Colorado, in 1901. When he died in 1904, his wife, Anne, who had also been a decorator at Rookwood, took over management of the pottery. The company was reorganized in 1910 and renamed the Van Briggle Pottery and Tile Company. In 1931 the name was changed to the Van Briggle Art Pottery Company. It is still working.

Artus Van Briggle used art nouveau designs and colors associated with the Southwest. The pottery made a variety of pieces, including vases, bowls, lamps, candleholders, and tiles. Marks were usually incised by hand, so each one is slightly different. The famous *AA* mark (for Artus and his wife, Anne) is usually in a rectangle or trapezoid. Some pottery is marked only *Van Briggle,* and some pieces made from 1955 to 1968 with a glossy finish are marked *Anna Van.* Most pieces made between 1900 and 1907 and from 1912 to 1919 have a mark that includes the date. Marks include the words *Colorado Springs* or *Colo Sprgs.*

A brass top with a citrine handle was made to fit this 6½-inch-diameter Pewabic bowl. The thick iridescent glaze has run on the bottom, almost covering the impressed mark.

Pewabic Pottery

Mary Chase Perry and her neighbor Horace James Caulkins began making pottery tiles, vases, and cosmetic jars in 1903. Pewabic Pottery's famous Persian or Egyptian blue glaze was used by 1911. The Detroit, Michigan, pottery was known for its building friezes, mosaics, tiles, and other architectural decorations. It also made vases,

Artus Van Briggle designed a group of art nouveau vases featuring nudes when he started his pottery. This 16-inch-high turquoise Despondency *vase is in the line, which has been made since 1903.*

fountains, and even church altars. Perry continued working until her death in 1961. Pewabic employees Ira and Ella Peters then made pottery in their home studio using Pewabic glazes until 1969. Their pieces were marked with a circle, the letters *PP*, and the word *Detroit*, which was the old Pewabic mark without the factory name.

Green and black glaze emphasizes the molded fruit and leaves on this melon-ribbed Tiffany pottery vase. It is marked LC Tiffany Favrile Pottery. (Photo: James Julia)

Tiffany Studios

Louis Comfort Tiffany began experimenting with pottery in 1898 but didn't sell his creations until 1904. His firm, Tiffany Studios in Corona, New York, made vases and pottery lamp bases for its Favrile glass shades. Very little art pottery was produced. Some pieces were thrown on a wheel, but most were cast in molds. Vases were decorated with plants—lotuses, poppies, jack-in-the-pulpits, ferns, mushrooms, branches, and leaves—birds, and insects. Early wares were a deep ivory shaded to brown. Later, green shades in varicolored glaze were applied on the outside of the vases. The insides were glazed green, blue, or brown. Matte, crystalline, and iridescent glazes were also tried, as were blue, red, and dull bronze. Pottery production ended between 1917 and 1920. The pottery and glassware were both marked with the initials of Louis Comfort Tiffany.

Paul Revere Pottery

About 1906 the librarian Edith Guerrier started offering a pottery class at the Boston Public Library to teach immigrant teenage girls a trade. By 1912 more than two hundred girls, members of the Saturday Evening Girls Club, worked at the pottery, named *Paul Revere Pottery*. It made mostly children's dishes and tiles. Glazes were solid colors with matte or glossy finish. Children's sets were decorated with incised chickens, rabbits, scenes from nursery rhymes, ducks, roosters,

Immigrant girls learning to make pottery as a trade decorated bowls like this, marked SEG *(Saturday Evening Girls). Children's dishes were stock items and also made to order with names and dates in the design. The duck border was a popular design.* (Photo: Treadway)

boats, flowers, trees, windmills, or cats. Special orders included names, birth dates, or initials as part of the design. Decorations were outlined in black and filled with color. Some pieces were marked with a paper label, *Bowl Shop*, *S.E.G.* Others had a round stamped mark picturing a man on horseback with the words *Paul Revere Pottery*. The pottery closed in 1942.

This University City vase is covered with a rare purple, green, and ivory drip glaze. It is 5½ inches high and marked #117B.
(Photo: Treadway)

University City Pottery

In 1907 Edward Gardner Lewis founded the American Woman's League in University City, Missouri, to educate women. In 1909 Taxile Doat, the famous French potter from Sèvres, came to the United States to organize, teach, and work at the league's pottery. Other well-known artists at University City Pottery included Adelaide Alsop Robineau, Frederick Hürten Rhead, and Edward Dahlquist. Pieces were often covered with crystalline glazes, and Doat's pâte-sur-pâte technique was also used. Production at the pottery stopped by 1915, and Doat returned to France. When the pottery closed, all the remaining inventory went to the St. Louis Art Museum. The museum deaccessioned most of the collection in the 1940s, and it was sold by a New York City store at bargain-basement prices. Today any important piece by University City or by Taxile Doat sells for thousands of dollars.

Cowan Pottery is best known for the Jazz bowl ordered by Eleanor Roosevelt for her husband, the president. It is considered the best piece of American art deco pottery. Cowan also made commercial pieces like these Push-me, Pull-me elephant bookends.

Cowan Pottery Studio/ Cowan Potters, Inc.

R. Guy Cowan opened his Cowan Pottery Studio in Cleveland, Ohio, in 1913. Early Cowan pieces were terra-cotta and buff clay that was

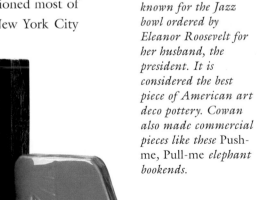

lead-glazed. The studio closed during World War I, and in 1920 Cowan built a new pottery in Rocky River, Ohio. In 1921 he began large-scale production of art wares. Cowan used a high-fired porcelain body and colorful glazes. The company made molded figurines, vases, dishes, candlesticks, bookends, and tiles. Products ranged from limited-edition, art-deco-inspired art pottery to inexpensive commercial pottery ashtrays and bowls. Cowan Pottery Studio was reorganized and renamed Cowan Potters, Inc., in 1930. It closed in December 1931.

Pisgah Forest Pottery

Walter B. Stephen first made pottery with his mother in Tennessee. In 1913 he moved to Pisgah Forest, North Carolina, where he founded the Pisgah Forest Pottery in 1926. He made fire-vitrified ware. He was well known for his turquoise and crystalline glazes and his cameo ware, which featured American scenes of Indians and wagon trains. The company was renamed Stephen's Pottery from 1940 to 1941 and then returned to the Pisgah Forest name. When Stephen died in 1961, the business continued. It is operated on a limited basis by Tom Case, Stephen's grandson

It is hard to miss the Pisgah Forest pottery decorated with a raised "cameo" design of Indians and wagon trains. This teapot, marked Stephen *in ink, is 5½ inches high.* (Photo: Craftsman Auctions)

American Art Potteries

Art pottery was made at these potteries, sometimes for only a short time.

Rookwood vase by Kataro Shirayamadani (Photo: Treadway)

Pottery and Location	Dates	Mark
Alberhill Pottery Alberhill, California	1912–1914	**ALBERHILL**
Albery Novelty Pottery Evanston, Illinois	1913–1915	**ALBERY**
American Art Clay Company/AMACO Indianapolis, Indiana (Art pottery 1930–1937)	1919–present	AMERICAN ART CLAY Co. AMACO INDIANAPOLIS, IND
Arc-en-Ciel Pottery/Brighton Pottery Zanesville, Ohio	1903–1907	ARC-EN-CIEL POTTERY
Arequipa Fairfax, California	1911–1918	AREQUIPA CALIFORNIA
Avon Works/Faience Pottery Company Tiltonville, Ohio	1900–1905	AVON
Edwin Bennett Baltimore, Maryland	1845–1936	E.BENNETT 1896. POTTERY Co
Brouwer Pottery (See Middle Lane Pottery.)		Brouwer
Brush Guild New York, New York	c.1897–1908	HFC
Brush Pottery Zanesville, Ohio (There were two different companies named Brush Pottery, both organized by George Brush.)	1906–1908 1925–1982	BRUSH ART STUDIOS
Brush-McCoy Pottery Roseville and Zanesville, Ohio (Formerly J. W. McCoy Pottery)	1911–1925	THE BRUSH-McCOY POTTERY Mitusa ZANESVILLE

Pottery and Location	Dates	Mark
Buffalo Pottery Buffalo, New York	1901–1956	
Byrdcliffe Woodstock, New York	1903–1928	
Camark Pottery Camden, Arkansas (art pottery 1926–1933)	1926–1982	
Cambridge Art Pottery Cambridge, Ohio	1900–1909	
Clewell Pottery Canton, Ohio	c.1906–1955	
Clifton Art Pottery Clifton, New Jersey	1905–1914	
Cliftwood Art Potteries Morton, Illinois	1920–1940	
Cowan Pottery Cleveland, Ohio	1913–1931	
Craven Art Pottery East Liverpool, Ohio	1905–1908	
Dedham Pottery East Dedham, Massachusetts (Formerly Chelsea Pottery U.S.)	1895–1943	
Denver Art Pottery Denver, Colorado	1909–1955	White Denver
Denver China and Pottery Company Denver, Colorado	1901–1905	
Durant Kilns Bedford Village, New York	1910–c.1930	DuranT

Pottery and Location	Dates	Mark
Edgerton Art Clay Works Edgerton, Wisconsin (Formerly American Art Clay Works. Became Norse Pottery in 1903.)	1895–1899 1902–1903	SAMSON BROS. & CO. American Art Clay Works Est'd 1892 Edgerton, Wis.
Edgerton Pottery Edgerton, Wisconsin (Formed by shareholders of bankrupt Pauline Pottery.)	1894–1902	Rock Pottery, Edgerton,Wis.
Florentine Pottery Company Chillicothe, Ohio	1901–1905	FLORENTINE CHILLICOTHE
Fulper Pottery Flemington, New Jersey Trenton, New Jersey (Became Stangl Pottery in 1955.)	1860–1929 1929–1955	FULPER
Grand Feu Pottery Los Angeles, California	1912–1918	GRAND FEU POTTERY L. A., CAL.
Grueby Faience/Grueby Pottery Boston, Massachusetts	1894–1911	GRUEBY FAIENCE CO. BOSTON.U.S.A.
Haeger Potteries Dundee and Macomb, Illinois	1871–present	H Haeger
Halcyon Art Pottery Halcyon, California	1910–1913 1931–1940	HALCYON CAL.
Hampshire Pottery Keene, New Hampshire	1871–1923	HAMPSHIRE POTTERY
Handicraft Guild of Minneapolis Minneapolis, Minnesota	1904–1919	Handicraft Guild of Minneapolis
D. F. Haynes and Son Baltimore, Maryland	1896–1924	276
Herold China and Pottery Company Golden, Colorado	1910–1920	J.H. J·H·

Pottery and Location	Dates	Mark
Hull Pottery Crooksville, Ohio	1905–1986	
Iowa State Pottery Ames, Iowa	1924–1930	
Jalan Pottery San Francisco and Belmont, California	1920–early 1940s	*JALAN*
Jervis Pottery Oyster Bay, New York	1908–1912	
Jugtown Pottery Jugtown, North Carolina	1921–present	
Kenton Hills Pottery Erlanger, Kentucky	1939–1945	
Knowles, Taylor and Knowles Company East Liverpool, Ohio	1870–1929	
J. W. McCoy Pottery Roseville and Zanesville, Ohio (Became Brush-McCoy Pottery in 1911.)	1899–1911	**LOY-NEL-ART** **McCOY**
Marblehead Pottery Marblehead, Massachusetts	1904–1936	
Markham Pottery Ann Arbor, Michigan National City, California	c.1905–1913 c.1913–1921	*Markham*
Merrimac Pottery Company Newburyport, Massachusetts	1902–1908	*MERRIMAC*
Middle Lane Pottery Long Island, New York (Usually called the Brouwer Pottery after 1903)	1894–1946	

Pottery and Location	Dates	Mark
Moravian Pottery and Tile Works Doylestown, Pennsylvania	c.1898–present	
Muncie Clay Products Company **Muncie Potteries, Inc.** Muncie, Indiana	1919–1931 1931–1939	
Newcomb Pottery New Orleans, Louisiana	1895–1939	
Niloak Pottery Benton, Arkansas	c.1911–1947	
Norse Pottery Edgerton, Wisconsin Rockford, Illinois	1903–1904 1904–1913	
North Dakota School of Mines Grand Forks, North Dakota	1909–present	
George E. Ohr (Biloxi Pottery) Biloxi, Mississippi	1883–1909	
Ouachita Pottery Hot Springs, Arkansas	1906–1908	
Overbeck Pottery Cambridge City, Indiana	1910–1955	
Owen China Company Minerva, Ohio (Founded by Ted Owen)	1902–1932	
Owens Pottery Company Zanesville, Ohio (Founded by John B. Owens)	1891–1907	
Paul Revere Pottery Boston, Massachusetts	c.1906–1942	

Pottery and Location	Dates	Mark
Peters & Reed Pottery Zanesville, Ohio	1897–1921	Pottery not marked
Pewabic Pottery Detroit, Michigan	c.1904–1969	
Pisgah Forest Pottery Pisgah Forest, North Carolina	1926–present	
Poillon Pottery Woodbridge, New Jersey	c.1903–c.1928	
A. Radford Pottery Broadway, Virginia Tiffin, Ohio Zanesville, Ohio Clarksburg, West Virginia	1890–c.1893 c.1893–1898 1903 1904–1912	RADFORD JASPER
Red Wing Stoneware Company **Red Wing Union Stoneware Company** **Red Wing Potteries, Inc.** Red Wing, Minnesota	1878–1906 1906–1936 1936–1967	
Redlands Redlands, California	1902–1908	
Rhead Pottery Santa Barbara, California	1914–1917	
Robertson Pottery Los Angeles, California	1934–1952	F. H. R. Los Angeles
Robineau Pottery Syracuse, New York (A. A. Robineau worked at University City Pottery from 1910 to 1911.)	1903–1910 1911–1928	
Roblin Pottery San Francisco, California	1898–1906	

Pottery and Location	Dates	Mark
Rookwood Pottery Cincinnati, Ohio	1880–1967	
Rose Valley Rose Valley, Pennsylvania	1904–1905	
Roseville Pottery Roseville and Zanesville, Ohio	1892–1954	
Saturday Evening Girls (See Paul Revere Pottery)		
Shawsheen Pottery Billerica, Massachusetts, and Mason City, Iowa	1906–1911	
Stangl Pottery Trenton, New Jersey	1955–1978	
Stockton Terra Cotta/ **Stockton Art Pottery** Stockton, California	1891–1902	
Teco-Gates Terra Cotta, Illinois	1887–1930	
Tiffany Studios Corona, New York	1904–c.1920	
University City Pottery University City, Missouri	1909–1915	
Valentien Pottery San Diego, California	1911–1914	
Van Briggle Pottery Colorado Springs, Colorado	1901–present	

Pottery and Location	Dates	Mark
Volkmar Pottery Greenpoint, Tremont, Brooklyn, and Corona, New York; Menlo Park and Metuchen, New Jersey	1879–1911	VOLKMAR KILNS. METUCHEN.N.J.
W. J. Walley West Sterling, Massachusetts	1898–1919	W J W
Wahpeton Pottery Company Wahpeton, North Dakota	1940–1961	Rosemeade
Walrath Pottery Rochester, New York	1904–1921	Walrath Pottery
Wannopee Pottery New Milford, Connecticut	1892–1903	W
Weller Pottery Zanesville, Ohio	1872–1948	WELLER
Wheatley Pottery Company Cincinnati, Ohio	1903–1927	T J Wheatley
Zane Pottery Zanesville, Ohio	1921–1941	ZANEWARE MADE IN USA
Zanesville Art Pottery Zanesville, Ohio	1900–1920	LA MORO

A FEW IMPORTANT ART POTTERS

John Lessell

John Lessell (sometimes spelled *Lassell*) (1871–1926) moved to the United States from Mettlach, Germany. He worked for at least eight American potteries from 1888 to 1926 and developed several important glazes and lines of pottery. An iridescent gold luster glaze and other metallic glazes are the best known. While Lessell was at the Owen China Company in Minerva, Ohio, the company made Swastika Keramos. This line of art pottery, produced from 1906 to 1908, was made with metallic bronze, brass, or copper glazes. Lessell made art ware with copper and bronze glazes at Lessell Art Ware Company in Parkersburg, West Virginia, from 1911 to 1912. At the Weller Pottery in Zanesville, Ohio, where he was art director from 1920 to 1924, Lessell designed the LaSa and LaMar lines, both featuring a metallic overglaze. In 1926 Lessell moved to Camden, Arkansas, to be art director at Camark Pottery. At Camark he developed lines similar to those he produced for Weller and Owen. Lessell died shortly after the start of production at the Camden plant.

John Lessell created metallic glazes for at least four potteries. This Camark lamp base, signed Lessell, *was made shortly before his death.* (Photo: Treadway)

Frederick Hürten Rhead

Frederick Hürten Rhead (1880–1942), born in England, was the son of Frederick Alfred Rhead (1856–1933), who was well known in the ceramics industry. He worked with his father before moving to the United States in 1902. In America Rhead worked at the Vance/Avon Faience Pottery (1902–1903), Weller Pottery (1904), Roseville Pottery (1904–1908), Jervis Pottery (1908–1909), University City Pottery (1909–1911), and Arequipa Pottery (1911–1913). Rhead moved to Santa Barbara, California, and opened

Frederick Hürten Rhead worked in at least ten different potteries. This jardinière, 12 inches in diameter, was made by Vance/Avon about 1903. It is decorated with "squeezebag" trees, leaves, and pinecones, a technique he later used at other potteries. (Photo: Treadway)

Iridescent metallic glazes were popular, so Weller hired Frenchman Jacques Sicard to share his glaze secret. He created the Sicardo line for Weller, but left after six years and took the secret of his glaze with him. This vase is signed Sicardo.

Rhead Pottery, which operated from 1914 to 1917. At Rhead Pottery, he made art pottery vases, tiles, ceramic lighting fixtures, bowls, and dinnerware. Much of his work was inspired by Chinese, Egyptian, and art nouveau designs. Decorations were incised and inlaid. Rhead's favored glazes were the high-gloss *Mirror Black* and a matte black. He also used metallic brown and white glazes. After his pottery closed, Rhead worked for American Encaustic Tiling Company in Zanesville, Ohio. In 1927 he became art director of the Homer Laughlin China Company in Newell, West Virginia, where he designed Fiesta, the company's most famous dinnerware line. He worked at Homer Laughlin until his death in 1942.

Jacques Sicard

Jacques Sicard (1865–1923) worked at Clement Massier Pottery in Golfe Juan near Cannes, France, for a number of years before he immigrated to the United States in 1901. He soon found a job at Weller Pottery in Zanesville, Ohio, and he developed the metallic luster used on pieces known as *Sicardo* ware. Sicardo ware was usually signed *Weller-Sicard* or *Sicardo*. Sicard returned to France in 1907 and opened a successful pottery in Golfe Juan.

AFTER AMERICAN ART POTTERY— THE STUDIO POTTER

The art pottery movement in the United States gradually disappeared during the 1930s. A few "studio potters" had started working about 1915 making a very limited number of handmade pottery pieces. The studio potter was usually a single person or at most a group of fewer than five people. Some were artists who had worked for the larger art potteries in their waning days. Little has been written about the smaller potteries, so collectors who become acquainted with local studio potters should be able to find bargains in the works of "undiscovered artists." A few, however, are already well known to collectors.

Studio potters became more and more creative from the 1970s to the present. Italian, American, and Japanese potters were the most inventive. Potters searching for new ways to work made slab construction vases, teapots, and abstract sculptures from thick clay.

Teapots no longer looked like teapots; it was difficult to determine where the handle and spout were. Vases were often geometric towers or strange asymmetrical shapes. Wheel-thrown vases were distorted into strange forms, then combined with hand-thrown or modeled shapes. Glazes were often shaded earth tones or had the flaws and iridescence of raku. Some vases had geometric or tribal-looking decorations. It would seem that the most well known of the late-twentieth-century potters made sculptures, not useful wares, and even the sculptures are rarely recognizable objects but rather abstract constructions with unexpected decorations and colors.

F. Carlton Ball

F. Carlton Ball (1911–present) is best known for making huge pots, some six feet high. He developed a method of making cylindrical vases on the wheel, then adding coils of clay and reworking the vase until the huge piece was finished. His works were limited only by the size of his kiln. Ball used the Japanese technique of wax-resist decoration popular in the 1950s. He also used sgraffito decorations, made by scratching or cutting a design through slip or glaze before a piece is fired, revealing the ground color underneath. Ball taught at Mills College in Oakland, California, from 1939 to 1950 and at the University of Puget Sound, Washington, from 1968 until he retired in 1977.

F. Carlton Ball made huge pots and many smaller ones like this 13¼-inch-high vase with a decoration of nudes balancing on horses. He did the potting; Aaron Bohrod did the sgraffito decoration.
(Photo: Rago)

Rose Cabat

Rose Cabat (1914–present) is best known for her porcelain vessels called *feelies*, small round or oval vases with narrow necks and satin matte glazes. Rose was born in the Bronx, New York, in 1914. She and Erni Cabat (1914–1994) grew up in the same neighborhood, married in 1936, and moved to Tucson, Arizona, in 1942. Rose had little formal training in ceramics. She first made earthenware and stoneware, but by the late 1950s she was making porcelain pieces. Erni, an artist, helped Rose develop special glazes, and he sometimes decorated her pieces. For years, the Cabats experimented with shapes and glazes until they developed the feelie, a shape with a finish that not only appeals to the eye, but also feels good when it is cupped in the hand. After Erni died in 1994, Rose continued to create feelies, bowls, and other pieces at her Tucson studio.

Waylande DeSantis Gregory

Waylande Gregory (1905–1971) was one of many artists who worked at the Cowan Pottery in Cleveland, Ohio. He started there in 1928 after working with ceramics, especially architectural pieces, in the Chicago area. At Cowan he created figurines and statues. After Cowan closed in 1931, he worked at Cranbrook Academy of Art in Bloomfield Hills, Michigan, then Cooper Union in New York City, and then he started his own studio in Bound Brook, New Jersey. Because he had access to the huge kilns at Atlantic Terra Cotta Company in Perth Amboy, New Jersey, he was able to make monumental pieces like the twelve one-ton ceramic statues he made for the 1939 New York World's Fair. In the 1940s his popularity declined and he was no longer commissioned to make major pieces, so he made limited-edition figurines, plates, ashtrays, and candlesticks that were sold in department stores like Gumps in San Francisco. At the end of his career in the 1960s, he turned to metal and plastic foam to create more artworks.

Waylande Gregory made commercial pieces that were a bit whimsical and very salable. This 12-inch fish sculpture is a fantasy in pink and purple. Gregory's name and the copyright symbol incised on the bottom show that it was not a unique piece.
(Photo: Rago)

Maija Grotell

Maija Grotell (1899–1973) studied ceramics in her native Finland before coming to the United States in 1927. Her early work in America used innovative glazes, art deco designs, and strong, simple shapes. Some pieces are decorated with art deco skyscrapers and city scenes. She became head of the ceramics department at the

Cranbrook Academy of Art in Bloomfield Hills, Michigan, in 1938 and remained there until she retired in 1966. While at Cranbrook, she developed new layered and high-fire glazes, and her work became increasingly abstract. Many pieces were decorated with cuts and gashes that she filled with slip or glaze. She also decorated her pieces using the pâte-sur-pâte technique, building up layers of slip to contrast with the glazes.

This 1940s glazed stoneware vase is typical of just one of the many glazes, art deco designs, and shapes Maija Grotell developed in her more than forty years as a potter. (Photo: Wright)

Glen Lukens

Glen Lukens (1887–1967) studied ceramics at the Art Institute of Chicago in 1913, then developed a pottery program to rehabilitate wounded soldiers returning from World War I. He was fascinated by the bright blue glaze on an Egyptian figure he had seen in a museum, and in 1924 he went to California to try to re-create the glaze. Using clays and minerals he dug up in Death Valley, he developed a close copy of the Egyptian blue. Lukens continued to develop rich, dense glazes—in turquoise, yellow, orange, and crimson—that had an important influence on other California ceramics. Lukens used molds to form his pieces, employing a potter's wheel only to trim and shape the pots. In the early 1930s, Lukens began a thirty-year career teaching at the University of Southern California, where his students included Beatrice Wood, Vivika Heino, and F. Carlton Ball, who all became important potters. He left USC in 1945 to help establish a folk pottery industry in Haiti. In the early 1950s he stopped working in ceramics and concentrated on working in glass.

The thick walls on this flat dish are covered with dripping pink, green, and ivory crystalline glaze. Glen Lukens, who was fascinated with new glazes, made this dish but left it unmarked. (Photo: Rago)

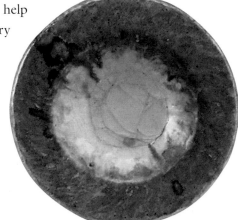

The Natzlers—Gertrud Amon and Otto

Gertrud Amon (1908–1971) and Otto Natzler (1908–present) were born in Vienna, met in 1933, and established a studio in 1935. Gertrud threw thin-walled, simple, classical shapes on the wheel, while Otto developed the glazes. A few months after Hitler's regime occupied Austria in 1938, they married and fled from Vienna to the United States. The Natzlers set up a workshop in Los Angeles and were soon winning awards at national ceramics exhibitions. Gertrud continued to produce graceful, delicate pieces until the 1950s and 1960s, when her pieces became larger and more complicated. During this time Otto's famous glazes became more varied. Best known were his Pompeian and Crater glazes, which displayed pockmarks and blisters, and his multilayered, rough-textured Lava glazes. After Gertrud's death in 1971, Otto continued working, creating heavy, masculine pieces that he decorated with his distinctive glazes.

Otto and Gertrud Natzler had the ideal partnership. They met, worked together, married, and continued to work together for another thirty-three years. Otto developed the glazes; Gertrud threw the pots. This 6¼-inch-high vase with crystalline glaze was made in 1961. (Photo: Wright)

The Pillins—Polia and William

The pottery decorated with pictures of elongated figures of women is easy to identify as the work of Polia (1909–1992) and William Pillin (1910–1985). Once seen, it is always remembered. Polia Sukonic, a Polish immigrant, and William Pillin, a Ukrainian immigrant, came to the United States as children, met in Chicago, and married in 1929. Polia planned to be an artist, William a poet. In the early 1940s, Polia studied ceramics and then taught pottery techniques to William. The Pillins moved to Los Angeles in 1948 and set up a pottery. William shaped, glazed, and fired the clay. Polia painted the pieces, often with pictures of women, children, flowers, birds, fish, and other animals. William experimented with glazes and produced some bowls and vases without decorations. Pillin pieces are marked with a stylized *Pillin* signature.

Polia and William Pillin worked together in their California studio. William formed and fired the clay. Polia added the colorful, often exaggerated decorations of women and natural subjects. This 7½-inch-high vase has a typical decoration of two women. (Photo: Treadway)

Mary and Edwin Scheier made this vase decorated with a band of strange figures,
probably inspired by Mexican or Indian drawings. The interior has a glossy dark blue glaze.
The 7½-inch-high vase is marked with an incised Scheier 95.

The Scheiers—Mary Goldsmith and Edwin

Although both had some training in the arts, Mary (1908–present) and Edwin Scheier (1910–present) didn't work in ceramics until after they married in 1937. They discovered a red clay in Glade Spring, Virginia, and set up a pottery there. Their early wares were utilitarian—tableware and jugs—and reflected a southern folk tradition. Mary threw the pots, and Edwin decorated them. Many of his designs were primitive human "stick figures" in high relief or sgraffito. They moved to Durham, New Hampshire, in 1940 to teach ceramics at the University of New Hampshire. They created new green, blue, pink, and purple glazes. Edwin decorated flat bowls and plates with bold sgraffito designs illustrating biblical and fertility themes. Following World War II, the Scheiers spent a year helping establish a ceramics industry in Puerto Rico, where Edwin developed an interest in Latin American Indian art. The animal and human figures in his designs during the late 1940s and 1950s reflect this interest. The Scheiers moved to Oaxaca, Mexico, and then to Green Valley, Arizona, where they operated potteries. In their later years, they also made heavier pieces, large vases and chargers, with dark glazes and surfaces that had a scarred appearance.

Peter Voulkos

Peter Voulkos (1924–2002) introduced revolutionary ceramics techniques and shapes. From 1949 to 1952 he studied ceramics and worked at Montana State University in Bozeman and the California College of Arts and Crafts in Oakland. He was resident potter at the Archie Bray Foundation in Helena, Montana, from 1952 to 1954. Voulkos's early work was conventional. Many of his pieces were decorated with bold abstract designs using the wax resist technique. After he moved to California in 1954, his work became increasingly experimental and controversial. Pieces were not made in ordinary shapes. Voulkos introduced a rocking pot, a tall form pierced by ceramic pieces similar to the struts of a rocking chair. He used nails, pipes, and bottles to

This huge stoneware charger is 90 inches in diameter. It was made by Peter Voulkos in 1990. The ripped rim, slashed surface, and irregular hole are typical of his later work. (Photo: Rago)

decorate his pieces. His glazes were splashed on and worked into slashes on the surfaces. His most important works after 1972 were large plates decorated with punctured holes, slashes, and imbedded porcelain pellets.

Carl Walters

Carl Walters (1883–1955) was a painter until he was thirty-nine years old, when he made his first ceramics at his studio in Woodstock, New York. Beginning in 1922, he produced ashtrays, candlesticks, bowls, vases, and plates, many with decorations inspired by Near Eastern designs. He is best known for his colorful ceramic sculptures of animals, especially tigers, lions, hippopotamuses, horses, and cows. Walters preferred surface decorations in abstract patterns and bright colors. He was also known for his glazes. Toward the end of his career, Walters established the ceramics department at the Norton School of Art in West Palm Beach, Florida.

Carl Walters liked bright glazes like the one used on this 10-inch-diameter bowl. The black engobe decoration is a design of diamonds and flowers. Walters' name is incised on the bottom.

Thelma Frazier Winter

(See page 292 in the Silver and Other Metals chapter.)

Beatrice Wood

Beatrice Wood (1893–1998) was born in San Francisco, studied art in Paris, then returned to the United States in 1914 and became part of a group of avant-garde artists in New York. Wood became interested in ceramics after she returned to California and took her first pottery class in 1933. Later she studied with Glen Lukens, Gertrud and Otto Natzler, and Otto and Vivika Heino. She opened her studio in Ojai, California, in 1948. Wood is famous for her unusual luster glazes in green, gold, pink, and blue and her whimsical figures. In her nineties she produced some of her finest work, tall chalices in golds, greens, pinks, and bronzes. Known for her rebel nature, her zest for living, and her fondness for chocolate, Wood worked until she died at the age of 105.

Beatrice Wood was not only probably the longest-lived twentieth-century American potter (105), but also one of the most famous. This footed vase is covered in gold and amber luster glaze. It is signed Beato. (Photo: Rago)

Studio Potters

Alice in Wonderland figure by Edris Eckhardt. (Photo: Rago)

Pottery and Location	Birth and Death Dates	Mark
Laura Andreson Los Angeles, California	(1902–1999)	
Alexander Archipenko New York, New York	(1887–1964)	Archipenko
Arthur E. Baggs Columbus, Ohio	(1886–1947)	AEB 1938 / MP / AEB
F. Carlton Ball Oakland, California	(1911–present)	F.C. Ball
Charles Fergus Binns New York, New York	(1857–1934)	CFB 1916
Paul Bogatay Columbus, Ohio	(1905–1972)	BOGATAY 60 / Paul Bogatay
Cornelius Brauckman Los Angeles, California	(1864–1952)	BRAUCKMAN ART POTTERY
Rose Cabat Tucson, Arizona	(1914–present)	CABAT
Paul E. Cox New Orleans, Louisiana	(1879–1968)	THE PAUL E. COX POTTERY NEW ORLEANS
Hunt Diederich New York, New York	(1884–1953)	
Edris Eckhardt Cleveland, Ohio	(c.1906–1998)	Edris Eckhardt
Marion Lawrence Fosdick New York, New York	(1888–1973)	FOSDICK
Bernard Frazier Lawrence, Kansas	(1906–1976)	Pottery inscribed with signature
Waylande Gregory Bound Brook, New Jersey	(1905–1971)	WAYLANDE GREGORY
Maija Grotell New York, New York	(1899–1973)	MG
Thomas Samuel Haile Ann Arbor, Michigan	(1908–1948)	Pottery inscribed with signature

Pottery and Location	Birth and Death Dates	Mark
Otto Heino Los Angeles and Ojai, California	(1915–present)	
Vivika Heino Los Angeles and Ojai, California	(1909–1995)	
Clara Maude Cobb Hilton Marion, North Carolina	(1885–1969)	Hilton
Edgar Littlefield Columbus, Ohio	(1905–?)	19 39
Glen Lukens Los Angeles, California	(1887–1967)	GLEN LUKENS
Marie Martinez New Mexico	(1881–1980)	Marie + Julian
Karl Martz Nashville, Indiana	(1912–1997)	
Leza McVey Cleveland, Ohio	(1907–1984)	Pottery inscribed with signature
Reuben Nakian New York, New York	(1897–1986)	
Gertrud Natzler Los Angeles, California	(1908–1971)	G + O NATZLER
Otto Natzler Los Angeles, California	(1908–?)	G + O NATZLER
Dorothea Warren O'Hara Darien, Connecticut	(1875–1963)	Pottery inscribed with signature
Polia Pillin Los Angeles, California	(1909–1992)	W + P Pillin
William Pillin Los Angeles, California	(1910–1985)	W + P Pillin
Henry Varnum Poor New York, New York	(1888–1971)	HP26 Hal 1948
Antonio Prieto Oakland, California	(1912–1967)	A PRIETO

Pottery and Location	Birth and Death Dates	Mark
Ruth Randall Syracuse, New York	(1896–1983)	Pottery inscribed with signature
Louis Benjamin Raynor Alfred, New York	(1917–1999)	*RaymoR*
Hal Riegger New York, New York	(1913–2006)	Pottery inscribed with signature
Adelaide Alsop Robineau Syracuse, New York	(1865–1929)	
Edwin Scheier Durham, New Hampshire, and Green Valley, Arizona	(1910–present)	*scheier*
Mary Scheier Durham, New Hampshire, and Green Valley, Arizona	(1908–present)	*scheier*
Viktor Schreckengost Cleveland, Ohio	(1906–present)	VIKTOR SCHRECKENGOST
Susi Singer Pasadena, California	(1895–1949)	S.S. SUSI SINGER
Toshiko Takaezu Clinton, New Jersey	(1922–present)	
Peter Voulkos Bozeman, Montana	(1924–2002)	VoulKos
Albert Valentien San Diego, California	(1862–1925)	VIP
Carl Walters Woodstock, New York	(1883–1955)	Walters
Marguerite Wildenhain Guerneville, California	(1896–1985)	Pond Farm
Thelma Frazier Winter Cleveland, Ohio	(1908–1977)	THELMA
Beatrice Wood Ojai, California	(1893–1998)	BEATO

SOUTHERN POTTERIES

Southern folk pottery was not appreciated by many collectors until the 1980s. It was considered too crude and primitive. Most southern potters lived in rural areas and made utilitarian vessels—pickle jars, syrup jugs, butter churns, milk pitchers, and baking dishes. Styles and forms rarely changed, and most pieces were undecorated and unsigned. Some southern potteries were operated by the same family for more than a century. Techniques were passed down with few changes from one generation to the next. Potters used local clays and local ingredients for salt and alkaline glazes. They turned forms on a treadle wheel and fired pieces in a groundhog kiln. Decorations on pots were simple; most were incised, but some were painted or sculpted.

Webster Cornelison founded the Cornelison Pottery to make salt-glazed stoneware in Bybee, Kentucky. According to legend, the pottery was established in 1809, although the earliest records date from 1845. The name was officially changed to Bybee Pottery in 1954. It is considered the oldest existing pottery west of the Allegheny mountains. In the 1920s and 1930s, it made art ware. Bybee now makes utilitarian and decorative wares using local clay, grinding it in an antique mill, and throwing and shaping it by hand on a potter's wheel. Today the pottery is run by members of the fifth and sixth generations of the Cornelison family.

Dictionary of Ceramics Terms

Coiling: A method used to make pots that uses long rope-like rolls of clay, coiled to form the desired shape, then smoothed on the inside and outside.

Crystalline glaze: A glaze with clusters of flowerlike crystal designs formed by slow firing of a glaze that contains iron or rutile, large amounts of silica, and small amounts of alumina.

Sgraffito: A decoration made by scratching or cutting a design through slip or glaze before a piece is fired, revealing the ground color underneath.

White sheaves of wheat were carved in sgraffito on this 9¾-inch-high vase made at the North Dakota School of Mines in the 1930s. (Photo: Rago)

Slip: Clay that has been mixed with water to make it the consistency of heavy cream. It can be cast in a plaster mold that absorbs the water and leaves a hardened shell of clay on the walls of the mold. Slip is also often applied to pottery as decoration.

Wax-resist: A decorating technique that brushes designs in wax over clay, slip, or glaze. Later layers of glaze don't stick to the waxed areas, and the finished piece has a two-color design.

Wheel turned: Pottery made by placing a lump of clay on a wheel and shaping it as the wheel spins.

Face jugs like this stoneware devil have been a southern pottery form for centuries. This 10¾-inch jug is marked WA Flowers NC Mtns 1995 AD. (Photo: Brunk)

Toward the end of the twentieth century, southern potters began to use modern forms, glazes, techniques, and marketing methods. In response to increased demand by tourists and collectors, potters began to make more decorative pieces— vases and flowerpots—and fanciful forms, including face jugs, miniatures, and figures of people and animals. Face jugs are dark jugs with distorted faces, crooked teeth, and big eyes. Older face jugs, pieces with alkaline glaze, and jars with cobalt decorations—animals, plants, or people—sell for the highest prices.

Jugtown Pottery

The term *jugtown* was used to mock any community where potters made useful bowls and jugs. In 1918 Jacques (1870–1947) and Juliana (1876–1962) Busbee of Raleigh, North Carolina, opened a teahouse in New York City where they sold pottery from their home state. They opened their own pottery, the Jugtown Pottery, near Seagrove, North Carolina, in 1921. The pottery was marked *Jugtown Ware.* The Busbees hired young local potters who were trained while working. They made plates, pitchers, bowls, milk pots, and preserve jugs. Ben Owen was hired in 1923 to design new shapes for the pots. Collectors have been interested in Jugtown's early art wares inspired by Asian forms and glazes, especially pieces glazed in Jugtown's *Chinese blue.* Jugtown Pottery thrived until 1958. It closed in 1959, then reopened in 1960. In 1983 Vernon Owens, a potter at Jugtown since 1960, bought the pottery. He and his wife, Pam, are the main potters today. The handmade pottery bowls, vases, jugs, candlesticks, and tablewares are made of local red or buff-colored clay.

The Busbees' Jugtown Pottery favored a bright turquoise glaze called Chinese blue. *This Chinese-style vase has the blue glaze with red highlights.* (Photo: Brunk)

Meaders Family Pottery

Members of the Meaders family have been making pottery in Mossy Creek, Georgia, since about 1891. Working alone and with each other, they made pottery using traditional methods and forms and are credited with keeping southern folk pottery traditions alive. They are best known for their face jugs. Cheever Meaders, son of the founder, John Milton Meaders, operated the pottery throughout the first half of the twentieth century. When Cheever died, his wife, Arie Waldrop Meaders, ran the pottery alone for a brief period until their son, Lanier, took over. One of the most famous folk potters in the United States, Lanier is especially well known for his face jugs. When Lanier died in 1998, his nephew David Meaders and David's wife, Anita, carried on the family tradition, making face jugs, pots, and other decorative pieces. Other family members who have worked as potters include Cheever's sons, John Rufus, Edwin "Nub," and Reggie, and Reggie's wife, Flossie; Alva Gusta Meaders; and Cleater James Meaders II and his son, C. J. Meaders III.

Edwin "Nub" Meaders, Lanier's youngest brother, made this stoneware rooster. The mark Edwin Meaders 1-9-1987 is incised on the base of the 15½-inch-high figurine. (Photo: Brunk)

Owen and Owens Family Potters

Benjamin Franklin Owen (1848–1917) of Seagrove, North Carolina, had two sons, James H. and Rufus. James (or his son Melvin—authorities disagree as to which) changed the family name to Owens, so there are two lines of potters in the same family, one named Owen and one named Owens, which creates some confusion.

Benjamin Wade Owen, Rufus Owen's son, worked at Jugtown Pottery from 1923 until it closed briefly for a year in 1959. He then opened Old Plank Road Pottery in Seagrove, which

Ben Owen III made this Asian-style vase with brown and turquoise glaze in 1988. The 9-inch-high vase is decorated with incised rings around its shoulder.

operated until 1972. He was especially well known for his Asian-influenced shapes and Chinese blue glaze. Benjamin Wade's son Ben Jr. had worked with his father at the Old Plank Road Pottery and reopened the pottery in 1981. His son Ben Owen III inherited the family talent and the business, now called Ben Owen Pottery. His work is influenced by his grandfather's style, and he uses some of Ben Sr.'s traditional shapes and colors.

Rufus Owen's brother James H. Owens, from the branch of the family with an *s* at the end of the name, began working as a potter in 1883, when he was seventeen. He started his pottery in Seagrove in 1910. He made pots for Jugtown Pottery as well as his own shop, so some of his work has the Jugtown mark. In the late 1930s, his son Melvin opened his pottery, now called M. L. Owens Pottery. Melvin's early pottery was traditional and functional, but later he also created art pottery, face jugs, and Rebecca pitchers. Seven of Melvin's eight children became potters. Boyd Owens operates Original Owens Pottery near Seagrove. Vernon owns Jugtown Pottery.

Other Important Southern Potteries and Potters

Other well-known southern potteries include Brown's Pottery (c.1924–present), Cole Pottery (1922–1997), Pisgah Forest Pottery (1926–present), and Seagrove Pottery (1953–1991), all in North Carolina, and Hewell's Pottery (1890–present) in Georgia. Important potters include Burlon Bart Craig (1914–2002), Charles Boyd Craven (1909–1991), and James Goodwin Teague (1906–1988), all from North Carolina.

TWENTIETH-CENTURY CALIFORNIA POTTERIES

In the early twentieth century, California potteries were making useful dinnerware and kitchen pieces, glazed tiles, garden ware, and terra-cotta building tiles. Decorations were inspired by Mexican designs, the Arts and Crafts movement, Spanish-Moorish influences, and the art deco style. Tiles marked with the name *California* were being made by 1911. Colorful, inexpensive, solid-color California dinnerware, like Franciscan and Bauer, was popular in the 1930s, and by 1950 about six hundred potteries used the word *California* as part of the company mark. There was even an organized group in the late 1940s that promoted California pottery at giftware shows. Many firms made inexpensive, colorful dinnerware, vases, and figurines that were unlike the traditional pottery and porcelain made in England, Asia, Ohio, or along the East Coast of the United States. California wares were inspired by Mexican and Asian ideas, art deco and modern designs, plus some of the unusual "looks" that were pure West Coast. Easily recognized California items include round-faced, costumed figurines often decorated in pink, blue, and other pastels, and solid-color dinnerware in bright colors.

California potteries and tile factories of interest today include: Bauer (1909–1962), Catalina (1927–1937), Gladding, McBean (1875–1984), Malibu Potteries (1926–1932), Metlox (1927–1989), and Pacific Clay Products Company (1881–1940s). Other, smaller companies include Caliente (trade name for Haldeman Pottery, 1933–1953), Cemar Clay Products (1945–1957), De Lee Art (c.1936–1958), Padre (1930s–1940s), Poxon China Company (1916–1928), and Tudor (late 1920s–1930s).

De Lee Art was active in the 1940s and '50s. It made pottery vases and figurines that were usually in the shapes of children like these, labeled Danny *and* Dimples.

J. A. Bauer Pottery

John A. Bauer moved his stoneware business from Paducah, Kentucky, to Los Angeles in 1909. It made flowerpots and useful stoneware items. About 1914 the company developed an art pottery line of glazed vases, bowls, and jardinières. The art pottery with matte green glazes on a redware body was made until the mid-1920s. Bauer introduced a line called California Art Pottery, or Cal Art Pottery, in 1938. The Cal-Art line included vases, flowerpots, jardinières, candleholders, and Madonna figures. Its glazes were in

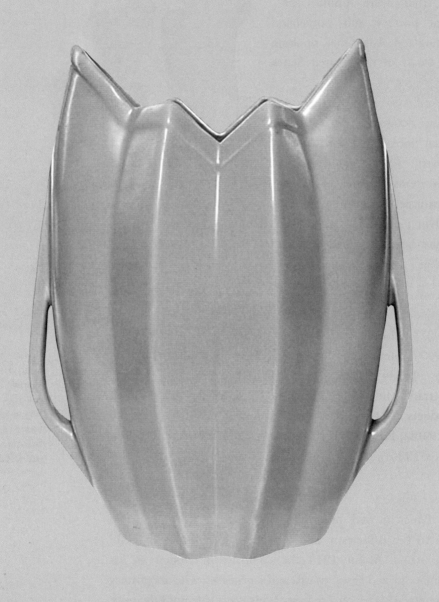

The pink color of this 10-inch-high Bauer vase suggests it was made in the 1940s or '50s. It is marked Bauer USA. (Photo: Treadway)

six new matte colors—yellow, green, blue, white, pink, and cream—as well as regular turquoise and burgundy gloss. In the 1940s and 1950s, pastel glazes were used. Tableware was introduced in 1930 and became the company's mainstay. (See pages 72–74 for more on Bauer dinnerware.) J. A. Bauer closed in 1962.

Catalina Pottery

William Wrigley of chewing-gum fame and fortune bought the island of Catalina in California in 1919. Wrigley and David Renton started a tile factory to provide clay building materials for a resort they were developing on the island. By 1927 the company, known as Catalina Pottery, was also making decorative pottery, which was outselling tiles by the 1930s. The company was by then called Catalina Clay Products Company. It made thrown vases (most in solid colors or blended-color glazes), large plates decorated like the tiles, vases with flower frogs, salt and peppers, candlesticks, bowls, clocks, flowerpots, cups, pitchers, carafes, lamp bases, bookends, belt buckles, buttons, and wall pockets. Catalina pieces were decorated and glazed in vivid colors—red orange, blue, green, yellow, and black—Mexican-inspired colors popular for California pottery. Solid color dinnerware was produced from 1929 to 1934. Until 1932 Catalina's dishes were usually made from brown clay; from 1932 to 1937, mainly white clay; and from 1937 to 1941, white clay exclusively. The company had money problems and was taken over by Gladding, McBean and Company in 1937. Production moved to the Gladding, McBean pottery on the mainland. No more tile was made, but Catalina dinnerware continued to be produced.

Florence Ceramics Company

Florence Ward (c.1898–1991) started making ceramics in Pasadena, California, in 1939. By 1942 she was making figurines, busts, wall plaques, smoking sets, lamps, boxes, candleholders, and other gift-shop items in a kiln next to her garage. The "garage"

Catalina Pottery was known for its tiles, but by the 1930s, plates like this one made with a tile-inspired three-color design were popular. It is 11 inches wide and is marked Catalina Island. (Photo: Treadway)

CATALINA MARKS

Early Catalina pieces were marked with an ink stamp. Later an incised mark *Catalina, Catalina Island, Catalina Isle,* or *Catalina Island Pottery* was used. A silver and black paper label is found on some pieces. Catalina Pottery pieces made by Gladding, McBean are marked *Catalina Pottery* and often also have *Made in USA* as part of the ink stamp. Similar wares were made by other California potteries. In 1947 the trademark reverted to the Santa Catalina Island Company.

Florence ceramics, especially the figurines, are wanted by collectors. This 7½-inch-high porcelain lady in a pink tiered dress and bonnet is named Melanie.

period ended in 1944, when Florence Ceramics moved to a plant that eventually employed fifty-four people. The company expanded again in 1948, moving to a larger facility with modern equipment. The business continued to grow until 1965, when it was sold to Scripto Corporation and the product line changed. Scripto made advertising ware under the Florence name until 1977.

Florence Ward designed most of the original pieces. The best-known figurines picture men and women in nineteenth-century clothing. Many were inspired by *Godey's Lady's Book* or by paintings by Old Masters. A bird line was designed by Don Winton (who owned Twin Winton Studios), and a contemporary animal line was done in the mid-1950s. Pieces are marked with an ink stamp that includes the words *Florence Ceramics*.

Hedi Schoop Art Creations

Hedi Schoop fled Germany for Hollywood, California, in the early 1930s. Her slipcast ceramic figurines were popular before she started Hedi Schoop Art Creations in 1942. She also made figural planters and vases. Her company closed in 1958, but Schoop then did freelance work for other potteries.

Animal figurines by Howard Pierce were usually slim and sleek with little extra detail, but this 10-inch-high modern cat with no mouth or tail is still a recognizable cat.

Howard Pierce

Howard Pierce started his studio in Claremont, California, in 1941 after leaving Manker Ceramics. He made bird, animal, and human figurines for the giftware trade. He also made jasperware with backgrounds of brown, green, or blue, and a line of vases and lamps. Pierce moved his studio to Joshua Tree and semiretired in 1968. He continued to produce some pieces until his death in 1994.

Although Hedi Schoop was well known for her figurines, she also made tableware like this footed compote with flower decoration.

Pink and blue were favored colors, animals had grins, and all Kay Finch figurines were humorous like this flower-decorated pig. It is 6½ by 8 inches, but Kay Finch also made larger pigs.

Sascha Brastoff decorations present a world of fantasy and glamour. The handle of this egg-shaped covered bowl is a gold-leafed ball. (Photo: Treadway)

This pottery girl must have looked very different when a small plant was tucked into the hole. The planter, by Weil, is in the popular pink tones used in the 1940s.

Kay Finch Ceramics

Kay Finch Ceramics were made in Corona Del Mar, California, from 1939 to 1963. Kay Finch started making ceramics in a kiln at home. Her whimsical animal figures were sold to shops, and the firm expanded. When World War II began, imported ceramics from Germany and Japan were no longer available, and business again increased. Kay Finch made figurines of all sorts of animals, Chinese maidens, Godey figurines, and Santa Claus, as well as vases, ashtrays, and luncheon sets. Pieces were hand modeled and hand painted in pastel colors. The pieces were expensive. By the end of the 1940s, the company was exporting ceramics to nineteen countries. Kay Finch was also a well-known dog-show judge, and her canine figurines reflect her understanding of dogs. Many of her other animals—cats, pigs, elephants, and monkeys—have very human expressions. After Braden Finch, Kay's husband and partner, died in 1962, she closed the company. Some of the molds were sold to Freeman-McFarlin, and she continued to design for that firm until 1979. Early Kay Finch pieces are marked with an incised name. Later pieces have an ink stamp or an impressed mark that includes the words *Kay Finch*. The ink mark can wash off.

Sascha Brastoff

Costume designer Sascha Brastoff (1918–1993) opened a ceramics plant in Los Angeles in 1947 and made hand-painted vases, bowls, ashtrays, and figurines. In 1953 he managed a production staff of eighty workers. Overglaze gold trim and flamboyant decoration were his hallmarks. He introduced fine china dinnerware in 1954. The company's ceramic products also included earthenware dinnerware as well as sculptures and enameled metal pieces. Brastoff retired in 1963. The pottery continued for another ten years. Brastoff signed his work *Sascha Brastoff*. Work done by his staff was signed *Sascha B.*

Weil of California

The California Figurine Company, founded in the late 1930s, became Weil of California in the early 1940s. The Los Angeles company made dinnerware, kitchenware, figurines, and art ware. Max Weil, the owner, died in 1954, and the company closed in 1955.

METLOX POPPETS

Metlox poppets are whimsical earthenware figures partially decorated with glazes. Each poppet had a tag with a name and comical description of the character, which ranged from a cigar-store Indian to Dominique, the nun, and Babe, the baseball player. Some had attached bowls that could hold pencils, keys, or small flower arrangements. Eighty-eight figures were made from the mid-1960s to the mid-1970s. The Metlox Potteries made dinnerware, figurines, vases, and cookie jars in its Manhattan Beach, California, plant from 1927 to 1989.

Metlox poppets look handmade, but they are commercial figures. This woman with a baby, like all poppets, was made of red clay that was partially glazed.

California Potteries

Pottery and Location	Dates	Mark
American Pottery Los Angeles, California	1940–1946	
Architectural Pottery Los Angeles, California	1950–1971	
Batchelder Ceramics Pasadena, California	1936–1951	BATCHELDER LOS ANGELES
J. A. Bauer Pottery Los Angeles, California	1909–1962	
Marc Bellaire Culver City, California	early 1950s–1994	
Brayton Laguna Laguna Beach, California	1927–1968	
California Faience Berkeley, California (Stopped making art ware c.1930.)	1924–early 1950s	
Catalina Pottery Catalina Clay Products Company Santa Catalina Island, California (Gladding, McBean bought the plant and made Catalina lines until 1947.)	1927–1930 1930–1937	
Cleminson Clay The California Cleminsons El Monte, California	1941–1943 1943–1963	
De Lee Art Los Angeles, California	c.1936–1958	
Desert Sands Barstow, California	1960s–1970s	
Doranne of California Los Angeles, California	1950s–1980s	

Pottery and Location	Dates	Mark
Florence Ceramics Company Pasadena, California	1942–1977	*Florence Ceramics*
Freeman-McFarlin Potteries El Monte and San Marcos, California	1951–1986	F - McF USA 319
Garden City Pottery San Jose, California	1902–1987	
Gladding, McBean and Company Los Angeles, California	1875–1984	
Hagen-Renaker Monrovia and San Dimas, California	1946–present	
Halcyon Art Pottery Halcyon, California	1910–1913 1931–1940	
Haldeman Pottery Burbank and Calabasas, California	1933–1953	*Caliente*
Hedi Schoop Art Creations North Hollywood, California	1942–1958	*Hedi Schoop* S
Heath Ceramics Sausalito, California	1945–present	HEATH
Howard Pierce Claremont and Joshua Tree, California	1941–1994	HOWARD PIERCE
Josef Originals Monrovia, California	1946–1985	
Kay Finch Ceramics Corona Del Mar, California	1939–1963	
Kaye of Hollywood North Hollywood, California	early 1940s	*Kaye*
Brad Keeler Glendale and Los Angeles, California	1939–1952	*Brad Keeler*

Pottery and Location	Dates	Mark
Maddux of California Los Angeles, California	1938–1976	
Malibu Potteries Malibu, California	1926–1932	MALIBU
Metlox Potteries Manhattan Beach, California	1927–1989	
Betty Lou Nichols La Habra, California	c.1949–1962	
Pacific Clay Products Company Los Angeles, California	1881–1940s	PACIFIC
Poxon China Company Vernon, California	1916–1928	
Roselane Pasadena, Baldwin Park, and Long Beach, California	1938–1977	Roselane
Sascha Brastoff Los Angeles, California	1947–1973	
Vernon Potteries/Vernon Kilns Vernon, California	1931–1958	
Walrich Pottery Berkeley, California	1922–1930	
Weil of California/California Figurines Los Angeles, California	c.1941–1955	
Barbara Willis Pottery Los Angeles, California	1943–c.2000	
Winfield Pottery Pasadena, California	1929–1962	Winfield

CERAMICS: ODDS AND ENDS AND MORE

American ceramic companies in the Northeast and Midwest were also making expensive, high-quality everyday pottery. These companies primarily made figurines, informal dinnerware, and vases. The design and quality of some of these pieces have made them of interest to collectors and museums.

Glidden Pottery

Glidden Parker established Glidden Pottery in Alfred, New York, in 1940. The pottery made stoneware dinnerware and art objects, including bowls, vases, teapots, platters, and ashtrays. The pieces were often the newest mid-century modern shapes and colors. They were individually glazed and hand painted. By 1946 the pottery was producing six thousand pieces a week. Glidden stopped production at the end of 1957.

Right: This Glidden stoneware vase has holes to hold the branches. The mid-century shape and muted stripes are typical of Glidden's pottery. The vase is 16½ inches high.
(Photo: Rago)

Below left: This 15½-inch vase has a matte black glaze partially covered with a multicolor drip. The vase is marked Royal Haeger. The glaze combination was called peacock glaze by the company.

Haeger Potteries

Haeger Potteries, established in Dundee, Illinois, in 1871, started making art pottery in 1914. The business prospered, and Haeger added another pottery in Macomb, Illinois, in 1939. In addition to art ware, Haeger made dinnerware, lamps, and florist ware. The most popular line, *Royal Haeger*, was introduced in 1938. It was designed by Royal Hickman, who worked at the pottery from 1938 to 1944 and again from the 1950s to 1969. Today Haeger is managed by Alexandra Haeger Estes, the great-granddaughter of the founder, and continues to produce art ware and other ceramics.

Hull Pottery

The A. E. Hull Pottery Company, established in 1905 in Crooksville, Ohio, made art pottery and commercial wares. It is Hull's three-dimensional Little Red Riding Hood accessories like cookie jars and sugars and creamers, made from 1943 to 1957, that excite collectors. Other favorites are the matte vases and art wares of the 1940s, and the high gloss art wares of the late 1940s and 1950s. Popular dinnerware patterns include *Mirror Brown* (1960–1985) and *Wildflower* (1946). A flood and fire in June 1950 destroyed the factory, but it was reorganized as the Hull Pottery Company and reopened in 1952. The firm closed in 1986.

Commercial and florist wares by Hull were sold in quantity in the 1940s. Raised flower decorations were popular. The 8-inch-high vase is in the Poppy *pattern, and the 12½-inch vase is in the* Magnolia *pattern.*
(Photo: Treadway)

Watt Pottery Company

William J. Watt and his three sons started Watt Pottery Company in Crooksville, Ohio, in 1922. It made jars, jugs, tableware, and mixing bowls. In 1935 Watt began making pieces with bold, hand-painted underglaze decorations that are popular with collectors. *Apple, Starflower, Rooster, Tulip,* and *Autumn Foliage* are the best-known patterns. *Apple,* the most popular pattern, can be dated from the leaves. Originally the apples had three leaves; after 1958 two leaves were used. Many bowls were made as "giveaways" in big stores. Some pieces had imprinted ads on them with the name of a company and phrases like "To A Good Cook." The company closed in 1965 after the plant was destroyed by fire.

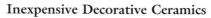

Watt kitchenwares with large, informal, hand-painted designs were practical, inexpensive, and decorative. This casserole in the Teardrop *pattern could be heated in the oven.*

Inexpensive Decorative Ceramics

There has always been a market for inexpensive giftware, dime-store pottery, grocery-store premiums, kitchen sets, florist ware, and other inexpensive decorative pieces. During the twentieth century, some were made in the United States, some in other countries. Many of the more collectible pieces today—especially figural vases, bottles, and containers—were designed by importers

in the United States and made abroad where manufacturing was less expensive. By the 1950s, cheaper imports from Japan and Germany had taken the market away from California and Midwestern potteries. Popular ceramics sold in large quantities included lady head vases used by florists; sets of dishes for chips and dip, condiments, and relishes; salad bowls; mixing bowls; kitchen sets that contained egg timers, calendar holders, spoon holders, and salt and pepper shakers; and even bottles for water to sprinkle clothes before ironing. Many of these pottery pieces have the look of the fifties and sixties, with slick, simple lines and pleasant, smiling faces on people or animals. By the 1980s, most were considered kitsch and ignored by all but a few collectors. But by the 1990s, salt and pepper shakers, head vases, and imports marked *Lefton* or *Holt Howard* were so popular there were special clubs, shows, and books for collectors.

Lady Head Vases

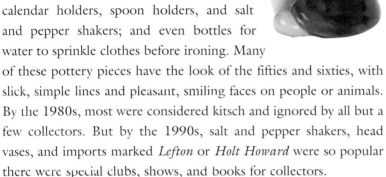

Lady head vases, or head vases, are just what the name implies, vases shaped like a woman's head. Most vases are the head of an attractive young woman, sometimes with added hands, a pearl necklace, or even a parasol. Others are heads of babies, clowns, animals, or religious figures. A few are heads of men. A hole in the top of the head or hat was filled with flowers and made an attractive small bouquet.

Most of the heads sold to florists for use as vases were made from the 1950s to the 1970s. A few head vases were made in the 1930s by American companies like Royal Hickman, but after World

In the 1950s, inexpensive knickknacks sold at tourist shops and dime stores were usually imports from Japan or Germany. This bud vase, marked Kreiss, came in at least three different colors. It was made in Japan for Murray Kreiss and Company.

A vase shaped like the head of a woman with or without a hat could hold flowers. The idea was popular in the 1960s, when this blond wearing pearl earrings and a necklace was made. The vase is marked Inarco.

War II ended in 1945, some small Japanese potteries started making these vases for American importers. The vases, if marked, have an ink stamp or paper label with the name of the importer, not the maker. Importers' marks found on lady head vases include *Brinn's China-Glassware Company, Enesco Corporation, Enterprise (ESD), Fitz and Floyd, Holt Howard, INARCO* (International Artware Corporation), *George Zoltan Lefton Company, Lego, Lipper & Mann, Napco, Norcrest China Company, Relpo* (Reliable Glassware & Pottery Company), *Rubens Originals, Samson Import Company, Shafford Company,* and *UCAGCO* (United China & Glass Company).

Head vases were made in the United States by Betty Lou Nichols Ceramics, Ceramic Arts Studio, Florence Ceramics, Haegar Potteries (Royal Haegar), Hull Pottery, Nelson McCoy Pottery, Pennsylvania Dutch Potteries, Shawnee Pottery Company, Spaulding China Company (Royal Copley, Royal Windsor), Stanford Pottery, Van Briggle Pottery, and Weil of California.

Lady head vases were so popular with florists that from the mid-1950s through the 1960s planters shaped like a whole person were produced. These planters and vases were used by florists and sold in five-and-dime stores. Some were made for holidays like Halloween, Christmas, Valentine's Day, and Thanksgiving. Most are figurines of women similar to those by Royal Doulton or cute children in bonnets and full-skirted dresses that hid the flower vase. They were imported by many of the same companies that imported lady head vases, including Enesco, Inarco, Lefton, and Relpo.

Holt Howard

Holt Howard was a New York City importing company started in 1949 by John and Robert Howard and Grant Holt, who met as college students. Holt Howard's first products were Christmas items made and sold in the United States. The Santa Claus mugs were so popular the company designed other mugs. By the 1950s, Holt Howard started importing giftware

Collectors like Holt Howard products because they are unusual, amusing, and almost always marked with the date. This 1958 Cozy Kitten *string holder is part of a set that included salt and pepper, memo minder, instant coffee bowl, and more.*

from Japan and other countries. Pixieware, amusing condiment holders with lids that have a knob shaped like a whimsical head, was introduced in 1958. It is probably the most popular Holt Howard item collected today. More than sixty different pieces were made. New related pieces are sold today by Curt Blanchard, a former Holt Howard designer.

Other collectible Holt Howard lines include Coq Rouge (red rooster), Cozy Kitten, Jeeves, Merry Mouse, and Santa Claus. Holt Howard also produced some unusual pieces like bobbing figures made with springs and small figures called candle climbers that were made to cling to wax candles. Collectors like the Holt Howard marks because they include the year the piece was made. Paper stickers were also used. The company was bought by General Housewares Corporation in 1968, and after several changes in ownership, it was sold to Kay Dee Designs in 1990.

Cookie Jars

The 1930s and after saw manufacturers producing modeled, colorful cookie jars. Nelson McCoy Pottery made the best-known jars, including covered wagons, log cabins, antique autos, locomotives, clowns, and animals. Two-faced cookie jars, many picturing Disney characters, were made by the Leeds China Company of Chicago. Cookie jars made by Shawnee Pottery included a sitting elephant, a Dutch boy, Puss-in-Boots, Mr. and Mrs. Pig, and a sailor boy. Roseville Pottery made cookie jars in several flower patterns, including water lily, magnolia, freesia, and clematis. Hull Pottery produced several styles, including a bean pot, a baby duck, and an apple. Red Wing made the Dutch girl and a French chef, as well as many jars to match its dishware.

ANDY WARHOL'S COOKIE JARS

Pop artist Andy Warhol was an avid collector of cookie jars—and just about everything else. A 1987 auction of more than 125 of his ceramic cookie jars brought $250,000! After a brief spike in cookie jar prices as a result of this sale, collectors were disappointed that interest in and prices for most jars soon settled down to more reasonable levels, $50 to $300 each.

Cookie jars were made by many American companies and also imported from Japan and Germany. This American Shawnee Winnie cookie jar is a collectors' favorite. It was made in many colors and with different "dresses" on the pig.

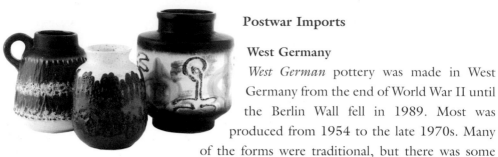

Postwar Imports

West Germany

West German pottery was made in West Germany from the end of World War II until the Berlin Wall fell in 1989. Most was produced from 1954 to the late 1970s. Many of the forms were traditional, but there was some experimentation with asymmetry and exaggeration. West German potters made jugs and vases. They also made wall plaques that were often decorated with oriental designs or stylized animals. Early decorations tended to be in soft colors on white backgrounds. By the mid-1960s, strong, bold colors—red, orange, yellow, blue, and black—were more common. About 1965, potteries began to use lava or volcanic glazes—thick drip glazes and pumice glazes with fine cratering. Most of this pottery was marked only *West Germany*. The best-known companies were Bay, Ruscha, ES Keramik, Lindner, Scheurich, Rosenthal, Sgrafo, and Dumler & Breiden.

These vases have the "look" of the pottery marked just West Germany. *Few pieces had factory names. Pottery with lava glazes, bold colors, and modern shapes were exported to the United States and Europe.*

Occupied Japan

During the American occupation of Japan after World War II, from 1945 to 1952, the *Occupied Japan* label was required on pottery, porcelain, toys, and other goods made in Japan to be sold in the United States. At first most of these goods were inexpensive and often of poor quality, but the quality gradually improved. Copies of Hummel figures, early Meissen, dinnerware patterns, and other popular designs were made. Don't be surprised at shows to see plates and vases upside down so the mark can be seen. A true Occupied Japan collector thinks the mark is more important than the object.

Almost any type of ceramic object was made in Occupied Japan to be sent to the United States. This child's tea set has luster decoration.

AMERICAN PORCELAIN

Porcelain was first made in America about 1738. During the next decades, more potters made porcelain, but none of the businesses lasted more than about ten years. So by the middle of the nineteenth century, Jersey Porcelain and Earthenware Company, Tucker and Hemphill, Smith Fife and Company, and Charles Cartlidge had all closed. Late in the century, porcelain was again being produced. Knowles, Taylor and Knowles of East Liverpool, Ohio, made mostly pottery and dinnerware, but it also produced a porcelain called *Lotus ware* from about 1891 to 1896. Onondaga Pottery of Syracuse, New York, was making Imperial Geddo porcelain by 1891, and it continued manufacturing porcelain and other ceramics during the 1900s under several names. It is now Syracuse China Corporation.

Trenton, New Jersey, was home to several important porcelain manufacturers. Ceramic Art Company, founded in 1889, became Lenox, Inc., in 1906 and is still making quality porcelains. Ott and Brewer, Cook Pottery Company, Greenwood Pottery Company, and Willets Manufacturing Company were other Trenton porcelain makers. These early porcelain firms made expensive pieces that often had hand-painted or hand-applied decorations. Their best work was as good or better than most of the Japanese, English, and German porcelains of the time.

U.S. firms continued making porcelains, especially dinnerware, during the twentieth century. By the 1970s international competition led to the closing of many small companies, particularly in Ohio and New Jersey. By 2000 most dinnerware sold in America was made in England or Japan, or in Hong Kong, Thailand, Sri Lanka, Bangladesh, and other countries with low labor costs.

Union Porcelain Works made some fantasy pieces like this "gamblers" pitcher. King Gambrinus, the god of beer, is shown on this side of the pitcher. The other side shows a gambler. The spout and handle are imaginary animals.

Edward Marshall Boehm, Inc.

The animal and bird figures made by Edward Marshall Boehm, Inc., are known throughout the world and are found in many museums and private collections.

Edward Marshall Boehm (1913–1969) was from Baltimore, Maryland. He studied animal husbandry, managed a farm, then joined the U.S. Army, married, and in 1945 returned to Great Neck, Long Island, where he worked for a veterinarian. Boehm made models of animals and birds as a hobby. He developed a hard-paste porcelain and, in 1949, started making sculptures at a Trenton, New Jersey, studio. He established the Osso China Company in 1950. His wife, Helen, joined the company and marketed his pieces. Two of his first sculptures were purchased by the Metropolitan Museum of Art in 1951. Even though it was an artistic success, the firm had financial problems. The company was reorganized in 1953 as Edward Marshall Boehm, Inc. Edward died in 1969. Helen traveled to England in the early 1970s and established Boehm of Malvern England Limited. The English firm produced wares based on Boehm's old designs and also made bone china figures. Hard-paste porcelain figurines and plates are still made by the New Jersey and the English firms. Some of his designs can be found on limited-edition plates by Lenox.

Cybis had a distinctive style, and the girls pictured as figurines are calm, thoughtful, and have simple clothes and surroundings. This is Alice Seated, *a limited edition issued in 1978 at $350.* (Photo: Limited Edition Collectibles)

Cybis

Cybis Porcelains was founded by Boleslaw Cybis, a Polish painter and sculptor who was born in 1895 in Lithuania, lived in Poland, and moved to the United States in 1939. He started Cybis Art Productions on Long Island, New York, in 1940, and made plaster of Paris figurines and art ware. In 1942 Cybis was a founder of Cordey China Company in Trenton, New Jersey. The firm made porcelain gift-shop items. He started Cybis Porcelains about 1950. Cybis died in 1957, but the company is still in business. It makes porcelain sculptures of animals, birds, flowers, American Indians, children, women, and other figures in limited and unlimited editions.

Bird figurines by Edward Marshall Boehm are world famous. This realistic Towhee on a stump was issued in 1963. It is 7½ inches high. (Photo: Rago)

Lenox

Walter Scott Lenox (1859–1920) and Jonathan Coxon (1837–after 1896) founded the Ceramic Art Company in Trenton, New Jersey, in 1889. In 1906 the name of the firm was changed to Lenox, Inc. Designs used by the company always changed with prevailing styles. Early pieces were similar to Irish Belleek. They were often thin, with a nacreous glaze and the creamy color that is still used. Art nouveau patterns were introduced during the 1900 to 1910 period. Many of the pieces were made with sterling silver overlay. Elaborately painted fish and game sets were produced. The art deco look was in style by the 1920s, and Lenox made appropriate deco figurines and dishes. The firm started making pastel-colored wares in light pink, blue, green, gray, or yellow about 1940. Lenox created White House dinnerware sets during the Roosevelt, Truman, and Reagan administrations. Lenox has continued to make both old and new designs for the giftware and dinnerware markets.

This pre-1932 vase by Lenox is decorated with hand-painted red and pink roses. The 18¾-inch vase is white with gold trim at the rim.
(Photo: Rago)

Pickard China

Wilder Pickard (1857–1939) established Pickard China in 1893 in Edgerton, Wisconsin, where artists decorated fine white china purchased from other firms. The company moved to Chicago in 1897. There the Pickard China Studio specialized in hand painting art pieces, vases, and dessert and tea sets. In 1911 Pickard developed a process to cover much or all of a piece with gold, and the all-over-gold *Rose and Daisy* pattern continues to be popular. Pickard pieces were hand painted until the mid-1920s, when the company gradually introduced decal decorations. By 1930 Wilder Pickard's son Austin joined the firm, and they decided to manufacture porcelain as well as decorate it. A manufacturing plant that made pottery, earthenware, and porcelain dinnerware was built in Antioch, Illinois, in 1937. Pickard China is now run by the fourth generation of the family. It still makes fine dinnerware, decorative accessories, and collectibles.

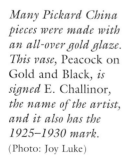

Many Pickard China pieces were made with an all-over gold glaze. This vase, Peacock on Gold and Black, *is signed E. Challinor, the name of the artist, and it also has the 1925–1930 mark.*
(Photo: Joy Luke)

No one knows why Warwick China is marked IOGA. *This 11½-inch-tall vase dates from before 1920. It has a shaded overall matte finish decorated with pinecones.* (Photo: Antiques At Time Was)

Adelaide Alsop Robineau

Adelaide Alsop Robineau (1865–1929) began her career as a china painter and had her own studio in Syracuse, New York. She became interested in making her own earthenware and porcelain in 1899. She and her husband began publishing *Keramic Studio*, an influential ceramics journal in 1900.

Adelaide Robineau made and marked this 4-inch-high vase and kept it in her family. The handles are decorated with carved irises. The glaze is celadon and oxblood. The mark is AR/1920/48. (Photo: Rago)

Robineau began to experiment with porcelains and developed a fine grand feu (high-fired) ware. She also developed matte and crystalline glazes in colors ranging from light brown to blue, green, and yellow. Her later glazes included dark blue, dark green, red, white, and black. Some porcelain vases were carved and pierced with intricate designs. Between 1905 and 1910, she also made glazed porcelain doorknobs.

Robineau studied the work of French Sèvres ceramicist Taxile Doat, who was known for his high-fired porcelains and pâte-sur-pâte decoration. Doat came to America to work at University City Pottery (see page 13) near St. Louis in 1909. In 1910 Robineau joined him at the pottery, where she perfected her technique of carving porcelain and developed a semiopaque translucent glaze. In 1911 she returned to Syracuse and started the Four Winds Summer School. She was on the staff at Syracuse University from 1920 until she retired in 1928.

Willets pieces were often Victorian in appearance, with odd-shaped handles and bunches of flowers as decoration. This large, early vase with hand-painted wild roses and gold dragon handles has the belleek mark.

Warwick China Company

Warwick China Company was founded in Wheeling, West Virginia, in 1887. It made vitrified chinaware, which was an unusual product for an American company. Its most desirable nineteenth-century pieces were decorated with portraits of monks or Indians. Other pieces featured floral decorations, birds, animals, and fraternal emblems. Until about 1914, some pieces were made with a brown tone finish that resembled the glaze used by the more expensive Weller and Rookwood art pottery. Warwick made many types of useful dishes, including tableware, hotel ware, and fine china. Most of the decorations were applied decals. The factory closed in 1951.

Willets Manufacturing Company

Three brothers, Joseph, Daniel, and Edmund R. Willets, founded the Willets Manufacturing Company in Trenton, New Jersey, in 1879. The company made belleek, often hand painted, in the late 1880s and 1890s in shapes similar to those used by the Irish Belleek factory. (See page 136.) Willets also made white graniteware, majolica, semiporcelain, and porcelain toilet sets, dishes, doorknobs, and novelties, but it is best known for its belleek. The company stopped working about 1909.

Early Twentieth-Century American Porcelain Companies

Some of the firms making porcelain in the United States from 1900 to 1917 are listed here.
Porcelain pieces from most of these companies are rare.

Porcelain Company & Location	Dates	Mark
American China Company Toronto, Ohio	1894–1910	
Edward Marshall Boehm, Inc. Trenton, New Jersey Malvern, England	1950–2003 1971–1992	
Ceramic Art Company Trenton, New Jersey	1889–1906	
Cook Pottery Company Trenton, New Jersey	1894–c.1930	
Cybis Porcelains Trenton, New Jersey	1950–present	
French China Company Sebring, Ohio	c.1898–1929	
Greenwood Pottery Company Trenton, New Jersey	1868–1933	
Homer Laughlin China Company East Liverpool, Ohio Newell, West Virginia	1896–1929 1929–present	
Lenox, Inc. Trenton, New Jersey	1906–present	
Onondaga Pottery Company **Syracuse China** Syracuse, New York	1871–1966 1966–present	
Pickard China Edgerton, Wisconsin Chicago and Antioch, Illinois	1893–1897 1897–present	

Porcelain Company and Location	Dates	Mark
Pope-Gosser China Company Cochocton, Ohio	1903–1958	
Sèvres China Company East Liverpool, Ohio	1900–1908	
Syracuse China (See Onondaga Pottery Company)		
Trenton Potteries Company Trenton, New Jersey	1892–1969	
Union Porcelain Works Greenpoint, Brooklyn, New York	1886–1928	
University City Pottery University City, Missouri	1909–1915	
Warwick China Company Wheeling, West Virginia	1887–1951	
Wheeling Pottery Company Wheeling, West Virginia	1879–c.1910	
Willets Manufacturing Company Trenton, New Jersey	1879–c.1909	

Chapter 2

TABLEWARE

© THE TWENTIETH CENTURY saw astounding changes in the American home and American food. The nineteenth-century housewife killed the chicken, plucked its feathers, and cleaned, cut, seasoned, and cooked it on an open flame. By 1990 she went to a grocery store and bought either a heat-and-serve prepared meal or a cut-up and cleaned chicken ready to cook quickly in the oven. In the early 1900s, refrigerated railroad cars made just a few out-of-season fruits and vegetables available. By the 1950s, frozen food technology made vegetables and fruit from the United States and other countries available year round. These changes required new dishes for different ways of cooking and serving. At the beginning of the century, luxuries like fresh asparagus were served with tongs on special oblong dishes, and grapes were served in special baskets with grape scissors. To evaluate and date twentieth-century tableware, it is necessary to consider not only the different styles of design, but also the changes in food preparation, household help, lifestyle, fads, and the worldwide economics of manufacturing dinnerware.

The middle-class American family in 1900 had servants and many children. They lived in a large house, often without electricity. Formal family sit-down dinners were the rule,

Dot is the name of the pattern on this Hall China cook-and-serve casserole that kept food hot for the dinner or buffet table. It is part of the Gold Label line made in the mid-1950s.

with many courses and correct special dishes and serving pieces for each course. The dishes used for important holiday or party entertaining might have been made in England, France, Germany, Japan, or the United States. The most popular "best" dishes were French Haviland. Everyday dishes were probably ironstone from England, Germany, the United States, or Asia, some plain white, some decorated with transfer designs or decal decorations.

World War I (1914–1918) cut off the supply of dishes from Germany and Japan. Americans bought everyday sets made in Ohio, West Virginia, or New Jersey. After the war, families wanted to buy new furniture and dishes for new homes. New ways to entertain came into fashion and influenced the market for tableware. In the 1920s, bridge parties were popular, and card players were served on bridge-table sets of dishes: four place settings often decorated with cards. The snack plate, a large plate with a space to hold a matching cup, was a new form. Dinner dishes were sold in smaller sets, eight instead of twelve place settings, because dining rooms and dining tables were smaller. The cocktail party was another fashionable way to entertain, even in the days of Prohibition (1920–1933). Cocktail shakers, martini pitchers, and all sorts of bar paraphernalia were created.

In the 1930s, spaghetti sets were introduced. The set included a large covered serving bowl, six small bowls and a separate dish for grated cheese. Corn-on-the-cob sets became popular; a set of long narrow bowls, often decorated to look like ears of corn, was sold with a large serving bowl. Deviled-egg plates with sections shaped for egg halves were introduced. Dishes designed specifically for a holiday like Thanksgiving or Christmas were marketed. In 1938 the English firm Spode made the first dinnerware set decorated with a Christmas tree. Other companies soon followed. A large turkey platter decorated with Thanksgiving scenes was available from many companies, even those in countries that did not celebrate Thanksgiving.

The 1940s and '50s saw the family eating together in the dining room at a table set with tablecloth and napkins, matching dishes, and silverware. But entertaining became less formal. Groups gathered to talk, play games like bridge, canasta, and Scrabble, and munch snacks, perhaps from the new chip 'n' dip set. Friends and neighbors held progressive dinners, going from house to house, each hostess serving a course in special dishes. After the end of World War II in 1945, the returning servicemen and their families needed new houses and furnishings. Acres of tract homes like Levittown on Long Island offered one-story, affordable houses with one living-dining area, not two separate rooms, and very simple woodwork and walls. This new type of home and the lack of household help led to entertaining with buffet dinners. Ceramic and metal casseroles were made to both cook and serve food. Modern shapes were created for dishes. Rimless plates that could be stacked on a buffet table and easy-to-hold cups became popular. Mix-and-match colors made it easier to buy dishes a few at a time. *American Modern* dinnerware by Russel Wright or Homer Laughlin's solid-color *Harlequin* dishes were the first choice of most newlyweds. Stores promoted the idea of breakfast sets, luncheon sets, and dinner sets of dishes. Casual designs were preferred. Grilling outdoors led to many new serving pieces, like sets of forks and tongs for the grill. Cocktail parties continued to be favored, and new mixed drinks were invented, including the Moscow Mule served in the proper copper mug and South Seas fruit drinks served in Tiki-shaped pottery glasses. In 1954 Swanson introduced the first TV dinner in a foil tray, and dinner and dinner dishes have never been the same since.

In the 1960s, dishes and glassware were still sold in sets of eight to keep prices low, but open stock made it possible to add to the set

Ever sit with a plate filled with food in one hand and a cup of coffee in the other while trying to eat in a crowded room at a friend's party? In 1944 this Blue Ridge Fruit Fantasy snack set was designed to solve the problem, a popular idea even today.

The ad says it all— china for the carefree way of life. Rimless plates had the newest look but made eating a bit more difficult. The peas slid across the plate and, with no rim as a barrier, fell on the table.

later. Chip 'n' dip sets were still popular. All of the special dishes of the 1930s, such as deviled-egg plates and corn-on-the-cob sets, were back. So were cocktail parties, cookouts, and progressive dinners. Television changed the eating habits of the nation, and many families ate while watching a favorite show. But the most unexpected change was that interest in gourmet cooking returned with Julia Child's popular television show, *The French Chef*, which encouraged sophisticated cooking, wine tasting, and proper dishes for cooking and eating. Contemporary pottery seemed suitable for this type of dinner. Very expensive, artistic dinnerware like that by the German company Rosenthal was made and sold to the wealthy, and formal dinner parties returned. There was little emphasis on ethnic or healthier foods at this time.

The automatic dishwasher (invented in 1946) and microwave oven (invented in 1955) became standard kitchen appliances by the 1970s. Dishes had to be made with no gold trim because it sparked in the microwave. Sturdy edges on plates avoided chipping in the dishwasher.

The 1980s and '90s saw quick dinners, often with prepared foods or restaurant-prepared fast-food. Ethnic foods, quick meals, health food, and gourmet cooking all became popular subjects for television shows and helped expand the eating tastes of Americans. Family meals on weekdays became harder to schedule because children had more and more after-school activities. Weekends and holidays were the time for family dinners and fancy table settings. Heirloom dishes and unmatched groups of dishes were favored to create "an individual look."

AMERICAN DINNERWARE FROM 1930 TO 1970

From about 1930 to the 1970s, American potteries made dinnerware sets that were sold in department stores and other sets of inexpensive everyday dinnerware that were given as premiums in grocery stores and sold in dime stores and department stores. During the 1970s, many people who had never thought about collecting became interested in buying and using older dinnerware like

No sugar bowl made before 1950 ever looked like this. The covered bowl looks a little like an egg topped by a knob. The sugar spoon handle could fit in the notch. This pattern of Red Wing dinnerware, Bob White, was made from 1956 to 1967.

Dinnerware Shapes and Sizes

Collectors need to understand the table settings of the past. The dinner sets of the early twentieth century had pieces that may be unfamiliar today.

After-dinner cup: demitasse, smaller than regular cup

Baker: uncovered, oval vegetable bowl

Berry bowl: part of set, serving bowl, 6–8 inches in diameter; individual bowls, 3–4 inches in diameter

Butter dish: covered, round or rectangular; a "quarter pound dish" is a rectangular dish that holds a ¼-pound stick of butter

Casserole: covered, round vegetable bowl, usually heatproof

Celery dish: oval platter or shallow dish, usually 11–12 inches long

Compote: dish with stem and foot

Console: low oval bowl, usually 12 inches long, meant to be used on a long table with matching candlesticks

Coupe soup: shallow pottery bowl, usually 7–8 inches in diameter

Cream soup: 2-handled bowl, about 4½ inches in diameter, sometimes covered, usually with underplate

Cup and saucer: conventional size for tea or coffee

Demitasse: after-dinner coffee cup, smaller than regular cup

Drip-o-later or dripper: an additional piece put between cover and coffeepot. Coffee is put in the top or spreader, hot water is poured in and drips through to the pot to make coffee.

Fast stand: see gravy boat

Fluted or French baker: uncovered, oval, pottery vegetable bowl, straight sides, small and large versions

Gravy boat or sauce boat: oval dish with 1 or 2 spouts, sometimes with handle, usually with underplate. An attached underplate is called a fast stand.

Nappy: square or round, flat-bottom dish with sloped sides, for ice cream, vegetables, fruit, or other saucy foods, usually 6 inches across

Onion or lug soup: pottery bowl with tabs instead of open handles

Pickle dish: small oval platter or shallow dish, usually 9 inches long

Plate: square or round, for serving or individual

dessert	6 inch
bread	7 inch
salad	7½ inch
luncheon	8–9 inch
breakfast	9 inch
dinner	10 inch
grill	10½ inch, divided into three sections
sandwich	11–13 inch serving, usually with 2 handles
chop	13-inch serving

Hall refrigerator pitcher

Reamer: a dish and pointed-top cone used to extract juice from lemons, oranges, and grapefruits

Refrigerator or leftover sets: pottery or glass dishes and pitchers used for storage, originally sold with refrigerators

Sandwich server: large plate, usually with center upright handle

Sauce boat: see gravy boat

Tidbit: serving dish, sometimes 2 or 3 layers with upright handle

Viktor Schreckengost

Viktor Schreckengost (1906–present) is a man of extraordinary creative powers, a genius. He has designed printing presses, oscillating fans, steam buses, comfortable metal chairs, lawn mowers, cab-forward trucks, bicycles, and pedal cars, and he even helped develop radar for pilots during World War II. But he is best known for his work in ceramics. The Cowan pottery Jazz Bowl he designed has become one of the most famous examples of American art deco ceramic design. The blue and black bowl decorated with abstract signs, streetlights, and skyscrapers was ordered by Eleanor Roosevelt in 1930. Other versions of the bowl were made. Viktor worked for Cowan Pottery from September 1930 until the pottery closed in December 1931, designing many bowls, sculptures, special series of plates, and decorative pieces. At the same time, he was teaching at the Cleveland Institute of Art.

He designed dinnerware for Leigh Potters, Limoges China Company (later American Limoges), Onondaga Pottery (Syracuse China), Salem China Company, and Sebring Pottery. *Manhattan*, a modern shape made in 1935, was one of the first American modern dinnerware designs. Viktor's innovative and popular designs included: *Flower Shop* pattern (1935); a free form shape dinnerware pattern called *Primitive* (1955) with animal pictures that looked like cave drawings; *Christmas Eve* (1950–1999), one of the first seasonal sets picturing a Christmas tree; and ovenproof Jiffy Ware food storage containers (1942).

But Schreckengost was also an artist who made slab form vases; satirical sculptures; huge ceramic female heads representing earth, air, fire, and water for the 1939 World's Fair; monumental wall reliefs like Mammoths and Mastodons (1955 and 1956) on the Pachyderm building of the Cleveland Zoo, and numerous watercolors and paintings, some printed as Christmas cards, calendars, or covers of concert programs.

Viktor Schreckengost's youngest brother, Don (1910–2001), was also a noted ceramics designer. He worked as chief designer at Salem Pottery, Homer Laughlin, and Hall China. His best-known work is the *Tricorne* shape dinnerware set, a classic art deco design he created for Salem China in 1933. A third brother, Paul (1908–1983), was a mold maker at the Gem Clay Forming Company, where in 1938 he created a streamlined teapot that is recognized as an important twentieth-century ceramic design.

Viktor Schreckengost's father was a potter, and Viktor and his brothers must have inherited his artistic talent and understanding of the business of making and selling pottery. Viktor created this Primitive *pattern for Salem China in 1955.*

Don Schreckengost designed the Tricorne *pattern for Salem China in 1933. Bright orange Tricorne dishes are among the most startling modern designs. The set has triangular plates and cups.*

Paul Schreckengost created this rare Gem Company teapot in 1938. (Photo: Los Angeles Modern Auctions)

SCHRECKENGOST'S DESIGN PHILOSOPHY

On one of our visits to his home, Viktor told us his designs were made to be practical, comfortable to use, and economical. One example of this is the *Econo-rim* line of restaurant china he designed for Syracuse China. The plate had a narrow rim that made it possible to serve a full-size meal on a smaller plate. The dishes were designed to nest on top of each other, making it easier to clear the table. This line was used on trains and steamships.

Eva Zeisel

The Hungarian-born designer and ceramicist Eva Zeisel (1906–present) worked in ceramics factories in Budapest, Germany, Russia, Austria, and England before coming to the United States in 1938. She designed ceramics for many different clients and is best known for her dinnerware, including *Stratoware* designed for Sears, Roebuck in 1942 and the elegant, all-white *Museum* dinnerware designed in collaboration with the Museum of Modern Art in New York in 1942 and produced by Castleton China Company. Zeisel's *Town and Country* dinnerware, produced by Red Wing Pottery from 1947 until 1954, was made in a whimsical, bulbous shape,

decorated with matte or glossy glaze and sold in sets of mixed colors. For Hall China Company, Zeisel designed *Tomorrow's Classic* in 1952 and *Century* in 1956. These graceful, solid-white dinnerware shapes were sometimes decorated. Although Zeisel retired from commercial design in the mid-1960s, she continues to create her own work; in the late 1990s, this included designs for Zsolnay and Kispester-Granit in Hungary and KleinReid in the United States.

Eva Zeisel created unique shapes of dinnerware and serving pieces for many companies. Tomorrow's Classic is a pattern designed for Hall China Company. No piece was a traditional shape, no handle or cover like those seen on dishes by others. The lid of this teapot hooks onto the piece near the handle.

Special serving dishes were created in the 1950s. This Town and Country pattern Red Wing covered bowl is called a marmite dish, but did many home dinners include the French soup? Notice the unusual shape of the two handles.

solid-color *Fiesta* ware and decal-decorated dinnerware from Hall and Homer Laughlin. Prices were low—dinner plates were often less than $1—and the dishes could be found at flea markets and garage or house sales. The interest has continued, and prices have gone up for most patterns; rarities can cost hundreds of dollars.

There were two major porcelain dinnerware manufacturers in the United States in the last half of the twentieth century, Lenox and Syracuse China Company. Both made traditional patterns similar to the English designs and also a few typically American patterns, like *Eternal* by Lenox and *Victoria* by Syracuse.

Important twentieth-century designers like Rockwell Kent, Viktor and Don Schreckengost, Ben Seibel, Russel Wright, and Eva Zeisel, who are known for their art pottery, glassware, furniture, or fashionable clothing, designed dinnerware as well.

Bauer

John Andrew Bauer made pottery in Paducah County, Kentucky, and Atlanta, but it is his work in California after 1915 that interests today's collector. He opened a plant in Los Angeles, making redware pots and flower containers, then introduced dinnerware about 1930. Bauer's solid-color line called *Plain Ware*, popular for casual dining, was the first American dinnerware of this type, years before Fiesta ware.

The rings that identify the Bauer Ring pattern can be seen even on this pitcher. The bright colors used for the pattern were a new look for dinner table dishes.

The firm made its famous *Ring* pattern solid-color dinnerware from 1933 until 1962, when the company closed. It is sometimes known as *Beehive* because the cups look like little beehives when turned upside down. Concentric rings cover the entire surface of some pieces, such as pitchers, sugar bowls, and salt and pepper shakers, but only the rims of the plates. Early dishes had faint rings, but from 1936 to 1946 the rings were more distinct. The original colors of the *Ring* pattern were shades of orange red, royal blue, delph blue, yellow, green, ivory, burgundy, and black. Pastels were made during World War II, when the ingredients for the bright glazes were scarce.

Other Bauer patterns included *Al Fresco, La Linda, Monterey, Monterey Moderne,* and the *Brusché* line. Most Bauer pieces were marked in the mold with the incised name *Bauer Pottery, J. A. Bauer,* or, for a 1952 line, *Brusché.*

It is difficult to identify some patterns because companies had names for shapes and names for patterns. This Blue Ridge plate is the Candlewick *shape, but the floral pattern is named* Betty.

Blue Ridge (Southern Potteries, Inc.)

Southern Potteries was founded in 1917 in Erwin, Tennessee. The company made hotel ware and semivitreous dinnerware. Pieces were decorated with decals from 1917 to 1938, then the factory started using hand-painted decoration. Hundreds of different patterns were made. Underglaze hand-painted wares were marked *Blue Ridge.* The company closed in 1957.

If this divided dish looks familiar, it is because Franciscan Desert Rose *is one of the most popular patterns used in America. It was introduced in 1942 and is still being made, although the California company was sold and new dishes are made in England.*

Franciscan

Franciscan is a trademark that appeared on pottery made by Gladding, McBean and Company, a producer of clay products founded in Los Angeles in 1875. Gladding, McBean made its first dinnerware in 1928, and in 1934 it began using the trade name *Franciscan.* China and cream-colored decorated earthenware were also made. The name used in advertisements and marks was changed from Franciscan Pottery to Franciscan Ware in 1936. *Apple, Coronado, Desert Rose,* and *El Patio* were the best-selling patterns. The company was purchased in 1979 by Josiah Wedgwood & Sons, which renamed it Franciscan Ceramics, Inc. All production moved to England.

Frankoma Pottery

John Frank established the ceramics department at the University of Oklahoma in Norman in 1927, then in 1933 he started his own Frank Potteries. Frank changed the name to Frankoma Potteries in 1934, then four years later moved the pottery to Sapulpa and renamed it Frankoma Pottery.

The 1953 Frankoma sugar and creamer in the Lazy Bones *pattern is glazed with a color called* Prairie Green. *Many patterns had irregular shapes and colors based on nature.*

Early Frankoma ware was made of cream-colored clay, but by 1954 the pottery used only local red clay. Frankoma made dinnerware, practical and decorative kitchenware, figurines, flowerpots, and limited edition and commemorative pieces. Its important dinnerware lines include *Lazybones*, *Mayan-Aztec*, *Oklahoma Plainsman*, *Wagon Wheel*, and *Westwind*. In 1965 Frankoma began issuing an annual Christmas plate with a biblical scene in bas-relief. After Frank died in 1973, his daughter Joniece managed the company. It was bought by Richard Bernstein in 1991. The company closed in 2004.

Hall China Company

Hall China Company in East Liverpool, Ohio, was founded by Robert T. Hall in 1903. Over the years, it has made semiporcelain dinnerware, hotel and restaurant ware, cookware, teapots, decal-decorated dinnerware, and kitchen items. Hall continues to make many of these ceramic wares. Its most popular dinnerware lines were the famous *Autumn Leaf*; flower-decorated patterns like *Blue Blossom*, *Crocus*, and *Red Poppy*; and the silhouette-decorated *Taverne*. Collectors are also interested in Hall's solid-color banded

Yellow Rose *is the name of the pattern of this Hall China plate. It was made from the 1930s through the 1950s.*

Autumn Leaf

Hall China Company made the *Autumn Leaf* pattern as a premium for the Jewel Tea Company from 1933 to 1978. Soon *Autumn Leaf* serving pieces were made by other companies, including Crooksville China Company of Crooksville, Ohio; Harker Pottery Company of Chester, West Virginia; and Paden City Pottery of Paden City, West Virginia. The pattern was copied for matching glasses, tablecloths, clocks, and kitchen items, and even *Autumn Leaf* blankets, lampshades, shelf paper, and much more were made.

Jewel Tea Company sold groceries door to door, first from horse-drawn wagons, then after 1926 by truck, then in stores or by mail. Buy enough coffee, tea, spices, or other staples, and you could earn a set of Autumn Leaf *dishes. So, of course, thousands of households used pieces like this* Autumn Leaf *Aladdin-shaped teapot.*

Fiesta, Harlequin, and Riviera Dinnerware

Fiesta ware, a solid-color pattern, was designed by Frederick Hürten Rhead. (See pages 23–25.) It was introduced in 1936, redesigned in 1969, withdrawn in 1973, and reissued in 1986. The plates have a band of concentric circles beginning at the rim.

Cups had full-circle handles until 1969, then partial-circle handles. The original *Fiesta* colors were light green, dark blue, yellow, ivory, and red. Later, turquoise, gray, rose, forest green, medium green, and chartreuse were added. The redesigned *Fiesta Ironstone*, made from 1970 to 1972, was made in mango red, antique gold, and turf green. *Fiesta* was reissued in 1986 using new colors—apricot, black, cobalt blue, rose, and white—but using the original marks and molds. A new color is introduced each year.

Fiesta

Most *Fiesta* is marked with the incised word *Fiesta*. Some pieces were hand stamped before glazing.

Harlequin and *Riviera* were related, less expensive solid-color dinnerware. *Harlequin*, made from 1938 to 1964, was sold without a trademark in F. W. Woolworth five-and-dime stores. *Harlequin* has a concentric ring design, but the rim is plain. Cup handles are almost triangular. *Harlequin* was made in chartreuse, coral, forest green, medium green, spruce green, maroon, mauve blue, gray, rose, red, turquoise, and yellow.

Harlequin

Riviera was made from 1939 to about 1950. It was unmarked and sold exclusively in G. C. Murphy Company variety stores. Plates and cup handles are square. Colors are mauve blue, red, yellow, light green, ivory, and, rarely, dark blue.

Look at the differences in the rings and rims on these three similar plates, Fiesta, Harlequin, *and* Riviera.

Riviera

Saf-Handle teapot and its many other streamlined teapots. Many Hall patterns were made as grocery store premiums, such as *Poppy* made for Great American Tea Company in the 1950s.

Homer Laughlin China Company

The Laughlin brothers, with the unusual literary names Homer and Shakespeare, opened the Laughlin Brothers Pottery in East Liverpool, Ohio, in 1873. Shakespeare later withdrew from the business, and in 1896 the Homer Laughlin China Company was incorporated. In 1897 Homer sold the company to the Aaron and Wells families. A second plant was built in Newell, West Virginia, in 1905. The company is still working in West Virginia, making semiporcelain and vitreous dinnerware, kitchenware, hotel ware, and novelties. *Fiesta, Harlequin,* and *Riviera* are the company's most famous dinnerware lines.

No one seems to know why, but Mexican scenes and images became very popular designs on dinnerware in the 1930s. This Homer Laughlin dish is in the 1938 Mexican-inspired pattern named Hacienda.

Knowles, Taylor and Knowles

East Liverpool, Ohio, was a center of the United States pottery industry. Knowles, Taylor and Knowles was founded there in 1870. It was once the largest pottery in the United States, employing seven hundred people at the beginning of the twentieth century. The pottery specialized in hotel china and also made semiporcelain dinnerware and toilet sets as well as commercial china. Its twentieth-century dinnerware was decorated with decals. At the beginning of the Depression in 1929, Knowles, Taylor and Knowles merged with eight other Ohio potteries to form American Chinaware Corporation, which went out of business two years later. Pieces are marked with emblems and words that include *K.T.&K.*

Knowles, Taylor and Knowles Bluebird pattern was one of the most popular of its era.

Metlox Potteries

Metlox Potteries in Manhattan Beach, California, was founded by Theodore C. Prouty and his son Willis in 1927.

These Metlox raisin-colored salt and pepper shakers are almost lovable. The shape has become famous, perhaps because it was used for popular characters called Shmoos *in the 1948 Li'l Abner comic strip.*

The company made ceramic fittings for neon signs. In 1931 it started manufacturing dinnerware; by the mid-1940s, some dishes were hand painted. Ownership changed when Evan K.

Shaw bought the firm in 1946. Metlox bought molds and the rights to the trademark *Vernonware* from Vernon Kilns in 1958. Metlox had two divisions, each with its own mark: Poppytrail (1946–1989) and Vernonware (1958–1980). In addition to dinnerware, Metlox made pottery planters, vases, cookie jars, and figurines, including Disney characters (c.1946–1956). The company closed in 1989.

Pfaltzgraff Company

Pfaltzgraff is the oldest pottery in America. Since its founding in York, Pennsylvania, in 1811 by the German immigrant George Pfaltzgraff, it has

The most popular pattern made by Pfaltzgraff is Yorktowne, *made since 1967. The shapes of the teapot and other pieces were inspired by dishes made in Colonial times.*

been operated by five generations of the Pfaltzgraff family. The name *Pfaltzgraff Pottery Company* was first used in 1896. The company originally made salt-glazed stoneware crocks and jugs, then added red clay flowerpots in 1913. Art pottery was produced from 1931 to 1937. The pottery began making kitchenware in the 1930s and added giftware and dinnerware in the 1940s and '50s. The firm's name changed to *Pfaltzgraff Company* in 1964.

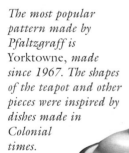

American Modern
Dinnerware—Russel Wright

Modern designs came into fashion in America in the 1930s. Hall China Company's *Airflow* teapot, *Raymor* dinnerware by Roseville Pottery, and the *American Modern* dinnerware pattern designed by Russel Wright (1905–1976) were important examples of the modern look.

American Modern was made by Steubenville Pottery Company of Steubenville, Ohio, from 1939 to 1959. During the 1950s, *American Modern* outsold all other dinnerware patterns marketed in the United States. *American Modern* was made in colors that were then unfamiliar for dinner sets—muted tones called Seafoam Blue, Cedar Green, and Chutney. The dish shapes were different, too. The dinner plate has no rim; the celery dish is a curved free-form cross between a bowl and a plate; the cups turn in at the rim. Eventually, other patterns of dishes designed by Wright were made by Iroquois China Company, Harker Pottery Company, Paden City Pottery (distributed by Justin Tharaud & Son), Sterling China, Edwin M. Knowles China Company, and J. A. Bauer Pottery Company.

Later in his career, Russel Wright designed plastic dinnerware, including the *Meladur*, *Residential*, *Home Decorators*, and *Flair* lines. Wright also designed furniture, glassware, metalware, and woodenware. (For more on Russel Wright, see pages 197, 219, 222, and 291.)

American Modern was the best-selling dinnerware pattern in the United States from 1939 to 1959. The solid-color mix-and-match sets were made by Steubenville Pottery Company.

Harmony House

Harmony House wasn't a company; it was a mark used on dinnerware sold by Sears, Roebuck & Company. Harmony House dishes were made by Hall, Harker, Homer Laughlin, Laurel Pottery, Salem China, Universal, and other factories from 1940 until the early 1970s. During the last years of production, the dishes were made in Japan.

Sears made sure its Harmony House dinnerware patterns were up-to-date and as attractive as more expensive wares. This Rosebud plate has rosebuds and scattered leaves on a rimless modern dish. It was made in Japan in about 1959. (Photo: Replacements)

Pfaltzgraff now makes casual dinnerware patterns of earthenware or porcelain, kitchenware, and novelties. Popular Pfaltzgraff dinnerware patterns are *America, Heirloom, Heritage, Village,* and *Yorktowne.*

Shawnee Pottery

The Shawnee Pottery Company was founded in Zanesville, Ohio, in 1937. The company made dinnerware, art pottery, vases, flowerpots, florist wares, lamps, cookie jars, and novelty ware. *Corn King* and *Corn Queen* were its most popular dinnerware lines. These yellow and green pieces were molded and colored to resemble three-dimensional ears of corn, with kernels of corn and leaves. They range from dinner plates to teapots to salt and pepper sets. *Corn King* was sold from 1946 to 1954. *Corn Queen,* which has lighter yellow kernels and lighter green leaves, was made from 1954 until the pottery closed in 1961. Many Shawnee dinnerware patterns were sold through S. S. Kresge Company, F. W.

This is a Shawnee Corn King covered butter dish that was part of a set that included dinner dishes, mixing bowls, teapots, cookie jars, and even relish trays.

Woolworth Company, and Sears, Roebuck and Company. Shawnee made over two hundred different cookie jars.

Vernon Kilns

Vernon Kilns opened in 1931 in Vernon, California. It made dinnerware and figurines until it went out of business in 1958. The molds were bought by Metlox Potteries, which continued to make some Vernon patterns. Collectors look for Vernon's plaid patterns and solid-color dinnerware and the special plates and figurines designed by Rockwell Kent and Don Blanding. Figurines licensed by Walt Disney Enterprises (1940–1942), especially *Fantasia* characters, are favorites.

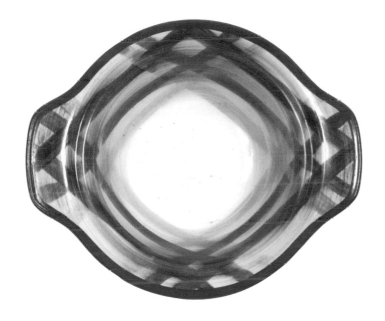

IS IT POTTERY OR PORCELAIN?

Pottery is opaque. You can't see through it. *Porcelain* is translucent. When a porcelain dish is held in front of a strong light, it is possible to see the light through the dish. If a piece of pottery is held in one hand and porcelain in the other, the piece of porcelain will be colder to the touch. If a dish is broken, a porcelain dish will chip with small shell-like breaks, while pottery cracks on a line. Pottery is softer and easier to break, and it will stain more easily because it is more porous. Porcelain is thinner, lighter, more durable,

Vernon Kilns made six plaid patterns, each a different color combination. This bowl is Tam o'Shanter, the rust, chartreuse, and dark green plaid.

EUROPEAN DINNERWARE USED IN THE UNITED STATES

Dinnerware in the average American home in the early 1900s was usually china from Limoges, France, especially Haviland, for "good" dishes and English ironstone or American whiteware for every day. Stylish Haviland dishes were delicate-looking, with

Clues to Dating American Dinnerware
by Color, Pattern, and Shape

Dishes are often designed in the newest styles to go with other new household furnishings. After a little study, it is possible to determine the approximate age of a dish by its shape, colors, and pattern. Decorations like Mexican scenes, abstract designs, the type of border, the flowers pictured, or even the lack of a pattern (just an overall color) all give clues to when a piece was designed. Throughout the twentieth century, classic patterns remained popular for "good" dishes, and the traditional eighteenth- and nineteenth-century designs by Haviland, Royal Copenhagen, Royal Doulton, Royal Worcester, Spode, and Wedgwood were copied by their original manufacturers and others.

Date		Colors	Patterns	Shapes and Materials
1900–1920		Pastels, violet, white background	Violets (flowers), calendar plates	Traditional shapes, plates with rims and shaped edge Arcadia *by Syracuse China, 1900–1920*
1920–1940		Pastels, cream white or ivory, often with elaborate gilding; bright, saturated colors (California pottery; Homer Laughlin's *Fiesta*)	Floral borders; abstract Czech and German patterns available but not popular in America; solid-color ware, often mix-and-match	Round edge/rim Crocus *by Hall China Company, 1920–1940*
1940–1950		Deep red, blue, green; solid colors	Peasant look, hand-painted designs	Modern shapes, rimless, streamlined handles California Contempora *by Metlox*
1950s–1970		Pastels, muted colors like avocado green	Very plain or flowered, Scandinavian look; classic copies, scenes like Colonial Homestead (1950), western; abstract modern; California-style modern; pink and blue fantasy designs; Pop Art look (1960s)	Corning ware (1958); plastic; modern shapes Memory Lane *by Royal China*
1970–1990		Earth and stone colors	Heavy, rough-textured pottery and stoneware; patriotic scenes like Liberty Blue (1977); yellow daisies; simple white, classic formal dishes	Liberty Blue *by Enoch Wedgwood Company*
1990s		Plain white and other solid colors	Geometric, abstract line designs; black and white drawings, sometimes humorous; traditional patterns	Way-out, eccentric shapes; triangular and square plates Corelle *Abundance by Corning*

molded shapes and floral designs in pastel colors, especially violet. During World War I, few dishes were imported, but by the 1920s, potteries in many countries were again making dinnerware for the American market. The new styles called for geometric shapes and bright colors. Manufacturers in Czechoslovakia, England, Germany, Japan, and, of course, France exported tableware to the United States.

For those who were adventurous enough to seek art deco designs, there were dishes from England designed by Clarice Cliff, Susie Cooper, Keith Murray, and Charlotte Rhead. Important English firms, like A. E. Gray, Poole, Royal Doulton, Shelley, and Wedgwood, made dishes with art deco as well as traditional

designs. From the 1920s to the late 1950s, *Chintz* pattern dishes, with an overall design of flowers, by Carlton, Crown Devon, Crown Ducal, Royal Albert, Royal Winton, and Shelley were very popular.

Dating Dinnerware by Design

Themes found in movies, books, and television influenced designs on dinnerware, vases, and figurines throughout much of the twentieth century, and they can give a clue to an item's age. Arts and Crafts ceramics had naturalistic patterns and muted colors. Colonial and rococo scenes and figures dressed in period costume were popular starting in the 1930s because of the great interest at that time in the restoration of Colonial Williamsburg. Mexican and Hawaiian themes were trendy in the late 1930s and 1940s, and hand-painted and decal designs of cactus or hula dancers were common. Disney-inspired designs also appeared by the 1940s. Rustic-looking, California-inspired, mix-and-match pottery was "in" for young marrieds in the 1950s. In the same decade, western designs seemed to follow the popularity of movie cowboys like Tom Mix and Hopalong Cassidy. Stars, planets, and other space-related patterns came in by the late 1950s. A peasant look gained favor in the 1960s. The op-art patterns of the 1960s and 1970s also inspired some ceramics. Wild colors and huge flowers were popular in the 1970s. Fruit and flowers in more natural colors decorated dinnerware in the 1980s and '90s.

Fragonard-style creamer by Cronin China, a 1930s Colonial pattern

Wagon Wheel by Frankoma, a 1950s–1970s Western pattern

Starburst by Franciscan China, a 1950s space-related pattern

A decoration of hand-painted violets, a popular early-1900s pattern, is seen on this dish made in Limoges, France.

Bright colors were used on traditional dishes from Czechoslovakia in the 1920s, even if the pattern was originally made in less startling shades.

The major British potteries, such as Minton, Spode, and Worcester Royal Porcelain Company, made many minimal, almost modern, hand-painted patterns while continuing to produce the traditional porcelain dinnerware that had been used for hundreds of years. There were also earthenware sets with informal designs suited for thicker plates and sturdy shapes.

Clarice Cliff's Bizarre ware is hard to miss. Her designs are bold, bright, and unlike any others that came before her. This milk jug is part of a 1930s breakfast set.

In the 1930s, about one-third of the tableware used in the United States was imported from England, Europe, and Asia. Although British factories were able to supply some dishes during World War II, once the war ended, dishes used in the United States were often made in Germany and Japan in the modern factories that replaced those destroyed by the war. Rosenthal and Hutschenreuther of Germany and Morimura Brothers (Noritake) and Mikasa of Japan exported to the United States during this period.

Although English potteries made dinnerware patterns with embossed rims, such as Wedgwood's *Grapevine*, the dishes were made for Americans, not Europeans. In Europe, mustard and other condiments are put on the rim of the plate during a meal, and a bumpy rim would be hard to wash. In America, mustard and ketchup are not put on the rim, but right on the food.

In the 1950s, foreign potteries tried to make patterns that would be popular in the United States. Simple coupe-shaped plates and plain patterns proved to be the answer. Scandinavian dishes from well-known firms like Arabia AB, Dansk, and Royal

Chintz *pattern dinnerware was made by many factories. This cup and saucer was made by Royal Albert about 1945.*

*Parsley, basil, thyme,
and other herbs
decorate this tea set
marked* Richard
Ginori, Italy.

Copenhagen had a sleek, modern look that appealed to young Americans. Newly designed dishes by the Italian firm Richard Ginori attracted U.S. buyers. Dishes from Austria, Germany, and Italy were sold in the United States by importers that marked pieces with their own names like Ebeling & Reuss (Erphila), George Borgfeldt & Company, Justin Tharaud & Son, or Pasco.

By the 1990s, many potteries in England had merged, and just a few large conglomerates remained. They modernized, updated designs, and continued to export many wares. But still more

changes were to come for the American dinner table because of emerging competition from Asian potteries in Hong Kong, Thailand, and even Sri Lanka; increasing sales of dinnerware sets through chain stores and "big box" stores; and the continuing creation of contemporary dinnerware designs and shapes. Today a bride will probably pick her "good" dishes from open stock patterns by Lenox, Rosenthal, Spode , or Wedgwood. Her everyday dishes probably are sold in a boxed set made in Asia in a design that may be out of production in a few years.

PLASTIC DINNERWARE

Plastic dishes were first made in the United States in the late 1920s. American Cyanamid Corporation developed American Beetleware,

Dansk designs were plain and unadorned but very much at the cutting edge of design in 1950s Denmark. This Flamestone *stoneware coffeepot remains a popular style.*

which was used for dishes given away as premiums with products like Wheaties and Ovaltine. Beetleware dishes were inexpensive to produce, but faded and cracked easily. Another plastic, melamine, was used for dishes beginning in 1937. In 1945 American Cyanamid commissioned designer Russel Wright to create a line of melamine dishes for the average home. Early melamine dishes were solid colors. Then decals and other decoration were added, and by the 1960s plastic dishes came in a variety of patterns.

In the 1950s, melamine dishes, commonly called *Melmac*, were advertised as an "accident-proof" substitute for pottery dinnerware. However, melamine dishes scratched and stained easily, faded, and were not truly unbreakable. By the late 1950s, some plastic dinnerware lines, such as Russel Wright's *Ming Lace* pattern, *Brookpark* by International Molded Products, and Boonton Molding Company's *Candescent* body, were high-quality and competitive with ceramic dinnerware. Sales of plastic stemware and tumblers also grew during the 1950s. Some ceramics and glass manufacturers, including Fostoria Glass Company, Lenox, and Stetson China Company, began to produce their own plastic ware, but these efforts lasted just a

Dating Tableware
by Words Found in Marks

Words found in marks on pottery and porcelain can help tell the date when the ceramics could have been made. Some marks give other important information. Dates given here are the earliest printed examples seen on ceramics or the date the mark was first required because of a new law.

bone china: c.1915
©: first used in 1914
cooking ware: c.1923
copyright: after 1858, usually 20th century
craze proof: c.1960, rarely used after the 1970s
déposé: c.1900 (French word for patented)
designed expressly for: c.1927
detergent proof: c.1944
dishwasher proof: after 1955
fast color: c.1960
for decorative purposes only: 1990s
freezer-oven-table: 1960s

Gesetzlich Geschützt (Ges. Gesch.): 1900 (German words for patented)
handmade: c.1962
hand-painted: c.1935
Incorporated: c.1940
lead free: 1990s
Limited (Ltd.): after 1861
made expressly for, made exclusively for: c.1927
made in: 1887 (usually after 1915)
microwave safe: 1970
NRA: 1933–1936 (National Recovery Administration)
oven proof: 1934
oven tested: c.1935
oven-to-table: 1978

patent applied for: 1902
patent pending: 1940
patented: 1900
®: first used in 1949
refrigerator ware: c.1938, rarely used after 1952
Reg. U.S. Pat. Off.: c.1932
Reg., Rd, Registered, with a number: 1884 (England)
semi-vitreous: 1901
trademark: 1862 (England), 1876 (United States)

22 carat, 22 karat, 22kt., 22k: after 1930s
underglaze: 1903–1945
Union Label, union made: 1930s
USPA approved glaze: 1975 (glaze approved for safety/durability by United States Potters Association)
U.S. patent: after 1900

Brookpark *dinnerware was made in many well-designed patterns. This* Chartreuse *(yellow-green) bowl with matching square plate is from the Arrowhead line.*

few years. Demand for finer plastic ware decreased. By the 1970s, Melmac was no longer popular with consumers or profitable for American makers. Foreign manufacturers from Europe and especially from Asia took over the market.

Plastic dinnerware sold today is made in China and other Asian countries. It is usually colorful and covered with pattern, and looks suitable for picnics or casual summer dining.

Buy a new dinner plate marked *Made in Sri Lanka* and you will see that the sizes of dinnerware have changed. The metric system was adopted by an Act of Congress in 1988. Dishes sold in the United States after that were often in metric sizes. A new dinner plate may be about ¼ inch too large to fit the shelf in a standard 1950s kitchen cabinet. Old patterns made from old molds are in the old sizes.

A clever European design for interlocking cups and dishes in an easy-to-store set was created by Massimo Vignelli for Heller Inc., an American company, in 1964. The melamine plastic dishes came in a range of bright colors.

Chapter 3

TILE

GLAZED CERAMIC TILES have been used to decorate buildings since the days of the ancient Egyptians, but the history of modern tiles starts in sixteenth-century Britain, Spain, and Holland. At that time, overall repetitive designs inspired by Moorish motifs were popular, and so were tiles that featured an object or scene in the center. Most ambitious were scenes formed by joining many tiles. By the nineteenth century, tiles were decorated with transfer prints, hand-applied colors, molded designs, and inlaid (encaustic) patterns. By 1900 some tiles were decorated with photographic images.

The Wheatley tiles used on the top of this wrought iron table were inspired by Moorish designs. Tile-topped tables would not stain from water, food, or alcohol—a practical idea started in the 1920s. (Photo: Perrault Rago Gallery)

Tile designs are influenced by the other decorative arts. At the turn of the twentieth century, art nouveau designs were popular and tiles often pictured intertwined vines and flowers. Plain tiles in muted colors with a rough, hand-tooled look seemed best for the Arts and Crafts home. By the 1920s geometric and abstract art deco patterns were in fashion, and tile surfaces were smooth.

There was a thriving tile industry in the eastern United States by the early 1900s. Massachusetts, New York, New Jersey, and Ohio and other Midwestern states had potteries that made tiles. The Spanish influence on

The first commercially made tile in the United States was produced in 1876 by Samuel Keys at the Pittsburgh Encaustic Tile Company.

architecture in California helped create the demand for tiles there in the 1920s and '30s, and dozens of companies—many still relatively unknown—made tiles for stairways, patios, porch floors, fireplace surrounds, and bathrooms.

By the 1950s tiles were used primarily in bathrooms and kitchens as an easy-to-care-for surface, not as an important part of the decor. Four-inch-square plastic tiles were introduced after World War II; glass, aluminum, and bronze tiles were being used by the 1960s, and iridescent and metallic finishes were popular. Decorated tiles were once again fashionable by the beginning of the twenty-first century. Examples from many countries, with designs ranging from Victorian birds to Picasso drawings, are found in new homes today.

Although art pottery was seriously collected by 1980 and many of the potteries that made vases also made tiles, the only tiles that interested collectors were those made before 1950 by well-known art pottery factories. It was not until 1987 that a national collecting group was organized and tiles designed by important artists or potteries began to sell for high prices. A 14-by-16-inch plaque picturing a scene in Venice designed by Ed Diers for Rookwood Pottery in 1929 sold for $49,500 in 1997. A 12-inch Grueby tile picturing a Viking ship sold for $73,700 at a 2002 auction.

A FEW IMPORTANT AMERICAN TILE MAKERS

American Encaustic Tiling Company

American Encaustic Tiling Company was founded in 1875 in Zanesville, Ohio. The company made inlaid floor tiles with geometric designs, large custom-made relief tiles, imitation mosaic tiles, souvenir tiles, and tiles with raised classical designs. Frederick Rhead, who had worked at the Vance/Avon Faience Pottery, Weller Pottery, Roseville Pottery, Jervis Pottery, University City Pottery, and Arequipa Pottery, was hired as a designer in 1917. The firm continued making tiles and added plaques, plates, figurines, vases, fountains, and other wares. Tiles were an important part of the business by the 1920s.

In 1892 American Encaustic Tiling opened a new plant in Zanesville. Additional plants were established in Perth Amboy, New Jersey (1912), and Los Angeles (1919) and Hermosa Beach, California (1926). Financial difficulties forced the company to close in 1935.

The size of this ten-tile panel, 30 x 12 inches, suggests that it was made to go over a fireplace. American Encaustic Tiling Company made many of these fireplace surrounds, as well as other architectural tiles. (Photo: Cincinnati Art Galleries)

Batchelder Tile Company

Ernest Allen Batchelder started Batchelder Tile Company, an Arts and Crafts–style workshop in Pasadena, California, in 1909. The first tiles he made were for his own home. In 1912 the company was renamed Batchelder and Brown, and in 1920 the renamed Batchelder-Wilson Company moved to Los Angeles. Batchelder made wall and floor tiles, fountains, door frames, fireplace mantels, and special-order architectural items. Early tiles were incised and modeled with vines, flowers, birds, or Mayan Indian designs. Later tiles had flat designs and incised lines. The company closed in 1932, and the plant was sold to Bauer Pottery.

This 12-inch-square Batchelder tile is large and rare. The two molded eagles in the medallion are colored with blue slip (clay). It is stamped Batchelder/Los Angeles. (Photo: Rago)

Beaver Falls Art Tile Company

Francis William Walker started the Beaver Falls Art Tile Company in Beaver Falls, Pennsylvania, in 1886. The company made plain, embossed, and intaglio tiles, plus tiles specially made to decorate stoves. Walker's pale blue, green, purple, and other pastel glazes

The notch at the edge of each of these Beaver Falls tiles is not a flaw but is needed to attach the tile to a metal stove. The tile with the woman in a feathered hat is 3 inches in diameter. The other is just 2 inches.

were unusually free from crazing. Isaac Broome, a noted designer, joined the company in 1890. The firm made tiles with raised designs of people's heads or full figures as well as a series of large panels designed by Broome representing the Muses. Beaver Falls Art Tile merged with the Old Bridge Enameled Brick and Tile Company and the Perth Amboy Tile Works in 1927 to form the Robert Rossman Corporation, which went bankrupt in 1931.

California Art Tile Company

James White Hislop founded the Clay Glow Tile Company in Richmond, California, in 1922, then renamed it California Art Tile Company (Cal Art) the following year. Cal Art tiles in the California Arts and Crafts style have a matte finish with muted colors and earth tones. They are decorated with birds, plants, knights, ships, and medieval, Spanish,

Tiles mounted in wooden frames were used as pictures in Arts and Crafts houses. California Art Tile Company (Cal Art) made this 5½-inch-square tile showing a knight on horseback. The matte finish, muted colors, and medieval scene are typical. (Photo: Rago)

Mexican, and western scenes. Cal Art tiles were installed in building lobbies, storefronts, fireplaces, and even floor drains. They were used as bookends and paperweights and were framed to hang on the wall. After being closed for several years during World War II, the company reopened and in 1949 began producing whiteware. Production of tiles declined, and the factory closed about 1956.

California Faience

Chauncey R. Thomas and William V. Bragdon started the art pottery firm of Thomas & Bragdon in Berkeley, California, in 1916 and renamed it The Tile Shop in 1922. The pottery formally became California Faience in 1924, although the mark *California Faience* was used before that. The company cast some art pottery that was covered with a monochrome matte glaze, but its main product was decorative tile, hand-pressed in molds and embellished with polychrome decorations. California Faience made tiles for Hearst Castle in San Simeon, California, in 1927. Designer and metalworker Dirk Van Erp used California Faience tiles in his bookends, trivets, and tables. Business declined during the Depression, and the pottery

This round tile is decorated in cuenca with a white tower and colored landscape. Cuenca is a technique using molded ridges to separate the colors. California Faience made this 5½-inch-diameter tile and stamped it with the name California Faience. (Photo: Rago)

stopped making tiles by 1933. It continued to operate, providing a studio for local artists and producing custom work and its own line of high-quality handmade tiles until Bragdon's death in 1959.

Cambridge Art Tile Works/ Cambridge Tile Manufacturing Company

The Cambridge Art Tile Works was opened in Covington, Kentucky, in 1887 to make enameled and embossed tiles. In 1889 the company merged with Mount Casino Tile Works to form the Cambridge Tile Manufacturing Company. Cambridge made ivory and gold-toned tiles, stove tiles, teapot stands, and colored architectural tiles. In 1927 the Cambridge Tile Manufacturing Company bought the Wheatley Pottery of Cincinnati, renaming it the Wheatley Tile & Pottery Company and operating it as a subsidiary. Wheatley moved to a new plant in Hartwell, Ohio, north of Cincinnati, in 1929 and stopped making art tiles. Cambridge Tile Manufacturing Company continued to manufacture tile until 1985.

Harris Strong's tile pictures were sometimes assembled on flat wooden boards that served as frames. Others were single or groups of framed tiles. All were colorful. The "Queen" is 41 inches tall. (Photo: Rago)

Harris Strong

Harris Strong was born in 1920 in Waukesha, Wisconsin. After working at potteries in New York City, he started his own business, Harris G. Strong, Inc., in the 1950s. It produced decorated lamps, ashtrays, vases, and ceramic tiles. By the early 1960s, he concentrated on contemporary-style tile panels. His hand-decorated tile panels, often groups of six-inch tiles mounted to a frame, were sold through decorators. He moved his company to Trenton, Maine, in 1970 and began working with other decorative arts, including painting and graphics. He stopped making ceramic tiles in the 1970s.

Moravian Pottery and Tile Works

Henry Chapman Mercer founded the Moravian Pottery and Tile Works in Doylestown, Pennsylvania, in 1898. The firm made large decorative tile panels and tiles for fireplaces, walls, ceilings, and

Moravian tiles are unusual, often cut into irregular shapes and decorated with raised designs of pictures and words. Most of the tiles were used architecturally. Notice the red color of the clay showing in the corner where this inkwell is chipped. (Photo: Rago)

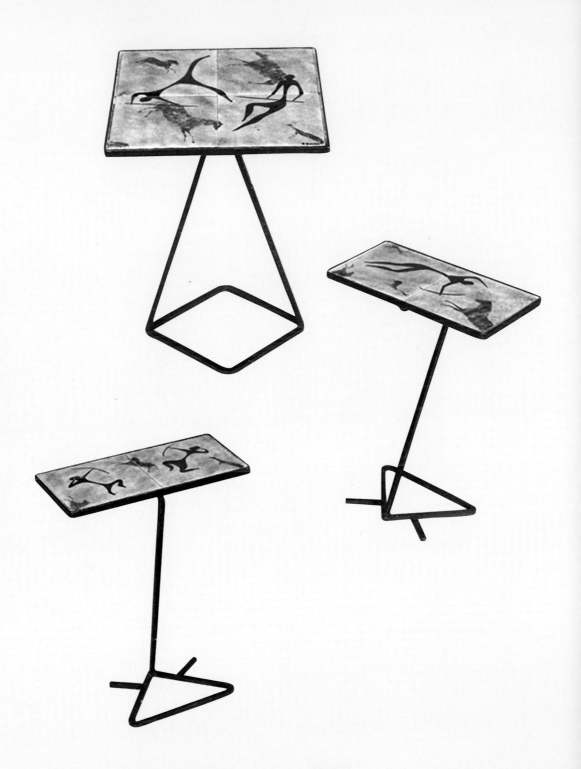

floors. Moravian floor tiles decorate the rotunda and halls of the Pennsylvania State Capitol in Harrisburg, showing about four hundred scenes from the state's history. About 1908 Mercer began making *brocade* tiles, high-relief designs in irregular shapes. Colored clay was cut into small pieces and arranged in concrete to produce the overall effect of a mosaic decoration. The tiles were often cut to the shape of figures in the design. In 1912 Mercer, who feared fire in conventional wooden buildings, completed construction of a huge concrete castle home he called *Fonthill* and a concrete tile works built in the style of a Spanish mission. Tile mosaics decorate the walls of the buildings. He built a third concrete structure, a museum to house his tool collection, in 1916. After Mercer died in 1930, the tile works continued to operate, making standard tiles until 1964. Bucks County purchased the pottery and opened it as a museum in 1969. The Moravian Pottery and Tile Works is a working history museum today, producing reproductions of tiles and mosaics made by Mercer.

J. B. Owens Floor & Wall Tile Company

J. B. Owens opened the J. B. Owens Floor & Wall Tile Company in Zanesville, Ohio, in 1909. It made tiles using the dust-pressed method in which the finely ground raw materials are shaped in molds at high pressure before firing. In 1915 the company built a plant in Metuchen, New Jersey. Owens opened another factory, the Domex Floor & Wall Tile Company, in Greensburg, Pennsylvania, in 1920 that closed in 1927. J. B. Owens became the Empire Floor & Wall Tile Company in 1923. The Zanesville plant burned down in 1928, and the Metuchen plant failed in 1929.

Robertson Art Tile Company

George W. Robertson of the well-known Massachusetts family of potters (Chelsea Keramic Art Works, Low Art Tile Works) moved to Morrisville, Pennsylvania, in 1890 to start his own company, the Chelsea Keramic Art Tile Works. He soon ran out of money, and the fledgling company was reorganized as the Robertson Art Tile Company. George Robertson left the company in 1895. In 1903 Robertson Art Tile merged with two other tile companies to form the National Tile Company of Anderson, Indiana, but the joint

*Opposite Page:
Primitive hunters race
across the tile tops of
these wrought iron
tables. The tiles, by
Robertson Art Tile
Company, are
stamped Robertson.*
(Photo: Rago)

Tiles by J. B. Owens were made by pressing clay dust into molds, then firing. This tile with the raised lines seen on cuenca patterns pictures an art deco design of grapes and vine. (Photo: Rago)

venture ended after three years. Robertson Art Tile continued to work under its own name. The tiles Robertson made during its first twenty years in business were artistic. From 1930 until 1983, the company made standard tiles as the Robertson Manufacturing Company and then as the Robertson American Corporation. The company closed in 1983.

Trent Tile Company

The indentation at the edge of this Trent tile indicates that it was used to decorate a stove. The raised profile of a woman was a popular stove design. (Photo: Cincinnati Art Galleries)

Founded in 1882, Harris Manufacturing Company soon changed its name to Trent Tile Company. Isaac Broome (Ott and Brewer Pottery) was a designer at Trent until he was replaced by the Englishman William Wood Gallimore (Belleek Pottery in Ireland, Ceramic Art Company). Gallimore's designs often portrayed boys and cupids. Trent made dull-finished heavy-relief tiles that were sandblasted after glazing in a patented form called *alto-relievo* (high relief); iridescent, luster tiles; glazed and enameled tiles in all sizes; and large mantel facings. Trent went into receivership in 1939, and the factory was bought by the Wenczel Tile Company of East Trenton in 1940.

American Tile Companies

Rookwood
Pottery Tile
(Photo: Cincinnati
Art Galleries)

Tile Company and Location	Dates	Mark
Alhambra Tile Company Newport, Kentucky	1901–c.1941	
American Encaustic Tiling Company Zanesville, Ohio	1875–1935	
Atlantic Tile and Faience Company Perth Amboy, New Jersey	1908–1912	ATLANTIC
Batchelder Tile Company Pasadena and Los Angeles, California	1909–1932	BATCHELDER LOS ANGELES
Beaver Falls Art Tile Company Beaver Falls, Pennsylvania	1886–1927	
Brayton Laguna Pottery Laguna Beach, California	1927–1968	Brayton Laguna Pottery
Broadmoor Art Pottery and Tile Company Colorado Springs and Denver, Colorado	1933–1939	
California Art Tile Co. Richmond, California	1923–c.1956	CALIF ART TILE CO RICHMOND CALIF.
California Clay Products (CALCO) South Gate, California	1923–1933	CALCO
California Faience Berkeley, California	c.1924–1959	California Faience
Cambridge Art Tile Works/ Cambridge Tile Manufacturing Company Covington, Kentucky, and Hartwell, Ohio	1887–1985	Cambridge Art Tile Works Covington, Kentucky
Catalina Pottery Avalon, Santa Catalina Island, California	c.1927–1937	Catalina
Claycraft Potteries Los Angeles, California	1921–c.1939	CLAYCRAFT

Tile Company and Location	Dates	Mark
Enfield Pottery and Tile Works Enfield, Pennsylvania	1906–c.1928	ENFIELD
Gladding, McBean & Company Los Angeles, California	1875–1984	GMcB
Grueby Faience Company/ **Grueby Faience and Tile Company** Boston, Massachusetts	1894–1920	GRUEBY FAIENCE CO BOSTON.U.S.A.
Halcyon Art Pottery Halcyon, California	1910–1940	HALCYON CAL.
Handicraft Guild of Minneapolis Minneapolis, Minnesota	1904–1919	
Handcraft Tile Milpitas, California	1926–present	HANDCRAFT
Hispano Moresque Tile Company Los Angeles, California	1927–1932	HISPANO MORESQUE TILE CO. LOS ANGELES
Kraftile Company Niles, California	1926–1997	Kraftile
Los Angeles Pressed Brick Company Los Angeles, Santa Monica, Richmond, and Alberhill, California	1887–1926	COMPLIMENTS OF L.A. PRESSED BRICK CO.
Malibu Potteries Malibu, California	1926–1932	MALIBU
Moravian Pottery and Tile Works Doylestown, Pennsylvania	1898–present	MORAVIAN
Mosaic Tile Company Zanesville, Ohio	1894–1967	
Mueller Mosaic Tile Company Trenton, New Jersey	1909–1941	FAIENCE MMC
Muresque Tiles/Muresque Tile Oakland, California Denver, Colorado	1925–1934 1936–1942	MURESQUE TILES INC 1001 23rd Ave, Oakland, Cal.

Tile Company and Location	Dates	Mark
National Tile Company/ National Tile and Manufacturing Company Anderson, Indiana	1903–1966	NATIONAL PAT. APL
New York Architectural Terra-Cotta Company Long Island, New York	1886–1932	NORTHWESTERN TERRA COTTA CHICAGO
Olean Tile Company Olean, New York	1913–1958	
J. B. Owens Floor & Wall Tile Company/ Empire Floor and Wall Tile Company Zanesville, Ohio Metuchen, New Jersey	1909–1923 1923–1929	OWENS ART
Pacific Clay Products Los Angeles, California	1881–c.1940	PACIFIC
Perth Amboy Tile Works Perth Amboy, New Jersey	1915–1930	Mark unknown
Pomona Tile Manufacturing Company Pomona, California	1923–1966	POMONA MADE IN U.S.A.
Providential Tile Works Trenton, New Jersey	1886–1913	PROVIDENTIAL T T N.J. TRENTON
Robertson Art Tile Company Morrisville, Pennsylvania	1890–1930	HAR
Rookwood Pottery Cincinnati, Ohio	1880–1967	
Rushmore Pottery Keystone, South Dakota	1933–1942	RUSHMORE POTTERY BLACK HILLS
San Jose Pottery San Antonio, Texas	1940–1953	
Santa Monica Brick Company Santa Monica, California	1923–1940	

Tile Company and Location	Dates	Mark
Shawsheen Pottery Billerica, Massachusetts Mason City, Iowa	1906–1911	∫P
Star Encaustic Tile Company Pittsburgh, Pennsylvania	1882–1914	**S.E.T. CO.**
J. H. Strobl Pottery/ Strobl Tile Company Cincinnati, Ohio	1901–1922	S
Harris G. Strong Bronx, New York Trenton, Maine	1952–1969 1970–1999	*Harris G. Strong*
Trent Tile Company Trenton, New Jersey	1882–1939	TRENT TILE TRENTON N.J. U.S.A
Tropico Potteries Tropico, California	1920–1923	TRoPICO
Universal Potteries, Inc. Cambridge, Ohio	1956–1960	
WACO Tile Clayton, Washington	1920s–1930s	WACO
Walrich Pottery Berkeley, California	1922–1930	W
West Coast Tile Company Vernon, California	1912–1919	
Wheatley Tile and Pottery Company Cincinnati and Hartwell, Ohio	1927–1936	WP · W
Wheeling Tile Company Wheeling, West Virginia	1913–1960	WHEELING
Zanesville Tile Company Zanesville, Ohio	1905–1907	ZB ZANEWARE MADE IN USA

Chapter 4

British Art Pottery

THE ART POTTERY movement started in Great Britain in the 1860s and continued into the twentieth century. Potters were influenced by the designer and craftsman William Morris, who encouraged artists to create objects by hand. Although most art pottery was made in small shops and sold locally, it was also produced by large commercial firms like Doulton and Company, which made salt-glazed vases and figurines with overall incised, carved, and colored decorations and vases with applied three-dimensional snakes or strange animals. Other famous early art pottery pieces were weird birdlike creatures by the eccentric Martin Brothers and terra-cotta vases and figures by Watcombe Terra-Cotta Company. Minton's Art Pottery Studio and many small studios that made vases and dishes considered the painted surface design more important than the shape of the object. Oriental and medieval influences were apparent in their work, which often pictured storks, bamboo, peacocks, sunflowers, fish, birds, and full-faced women and children. By 1900 small country potters like C. H. Brannam rethought traditional pottery forms to create art pottery, including redware with sgraffito decoration and figures of outlandish animals, especially cats.

This odd little open-mouthed man is a smoker *ashtray marked* C.H. Brannam/Barum. *The cigarette was placed in the mouth, and smoke went out the holes in the head.*

Collectible Goss China

Collecting small crested china souvenirs made by Goss and other companies was a craze in England at the turn of the twentieth century. Travelers wanted inexpensive souvenirs of the resorts, historic spots, famous people, places, and buildings they visited. William Henry Goss and his son had a pottery that made

small, white porcelain souvenir items decorated with coats of arms or local scenes. By 1910 ninety percent of the homes in England supposedly had at least one Goss china piece. The hobby peaked about 1914 and slowly declined until production stopped in 1940. Collectors rediscovered it in the 1970s. The souvenirs were hand made and hand painted, usually by young children. Small teapots, busts of famous people, animals, birds, cars, cottages, shoes, pitchers, and urns were made, many only a few inches high. The company also produced large busts, figurines, dinnerware, and other marketable ceramics.

Goss souvenirs were very popular and usually very small. This bust of a man, perhaps Caesar, is 5¼ inches high, which is large for a souvenir but small for a decorative bust. It is made of undecorated bisque.

This 9¾-inch bottle-shaped vase with an inlaid Moorish design was made at the Lambeth factory. It is stamped Doulton/Lambeth. (Photo: Rago)

Before World War I (1914–1918), most inexpensive pottery was decorated with German lithographic transfers. After the war, buyers did not want German goods, and British makers of tableware hired young girls at very low wages to again hand-paint dishes and vases but with "modern" abstract decorations.

By the 1920s the British economy was suffering, tastes were changing, and many art potteries went out of business. Then new ones appeared to create pieces in the studio pottery tradition. Influenced by the ideas and work of Bernard Leach, these new potters designed wares to be sold to buyers interested in avant-garde design. But the wares were not meant to be mass produced. (For more on Bernard Leach, see page 120.)

DOULTON AND COMPANY

John Doulton started a small pottery in Lambeth in 1812. By 1882 it had become a large pottery named Doulton and Company that made many types of tableware, vases, and figurines, as well as kitchen ware and flowerpots. Doulton was making art pottery by the 1870s, and well-known artists, including Hannah Barlow and George Tinsworth, were working at the pottery. Many pieces were one-of-a-kind. Wilton Rix patented *Marqueterie*, an unusual ware produced from about 1887 to 1900, made from slices of clay of different colors put together to appear marbleized. *Lambeth* ware with incised designs of animals and birds was made by Hannah Barlow. *Persian* ware white tiles, produced between 1884 and 1900 and again between 1919 and 1922, were influenced by the art pottery of William De Morgan. They were decorated with Near Eastern designs in turquoise blue, green, and orange. Doulton's art pottery included stoneware, silicon ware, Carrara ware, and majolica.

Royal Doulton

In 1902 the *Royal Doulton* era began. The word *Royal* was added to the trademark used by Doulton and Company when King Edward VII granted the company this special right. Art ware and tableware continued to be made, but tastes were changing. Dull-colored salt-glazed ware was out of style. Shelves filled with vases, and figurines popular in Victorian times were no longer fashionable.

Rouge flambé ware, with its impossible-to-miss red glaze, was first shown in 1904. Vases with this red transmutation glaze that changed to blues and blacks in random patterns were one-of-a-kind pieces. Later, animal figures were covered with the flambé glaze. Rouge flambé pieces are still made. Sung flambé ware was made from 1920 to the early 1940s, with just a few made later. Chang ware (1925–early 1940s) was covered with a thick, dripping transmutation glaze. The final flambé colors of both were determined by the heat of the kiln. From 1924 to 1930, a series of jugs, ash pots, and tobacco jars reminiscent of old Toby jugs were made. Other art wares developed before 1950 include pieces with crystalline glazes from the early 1900s until 1918, Titanian ware, and Kingsware. *Titanian* ware, made from about 1915 until the early 1930s, was a thin porcelain in pastel colors—greenish grays, smoky blues, and mellow greens—with mottled and clouded effects. It pictured landscapes, flowers, birds, and animals.

Each piece of Royal Doulton with flambé glaze is unique because the heat of the kiln determines the coloration. This 5-inch-high vase is marked Sung, flambé, Noke *(the name of the art director), and* F. Allen *(the name of the artist).*

Royal Doulton's line of Kingsware was produced between about 1898 and 1939. Kingsware was not thrown on a wheel, but made from slip poured into plaster molds. The body of the piece was a dark brown slip, and low-relief designs were made from colored slip. The piece was finished with a transparent ivory glaze. Kingsware came in a variety of shapes ranging from jugs and mugs to coffeepots and candlesticks, but the most collectible are the whiskey flagons.

Series Ware

Series ware, introduced in 1906, is decorated with underglaze pictures based on many subjects, including Shakespeare's plays, Dickens's novels, Old Coaching Scenes, the poem "Jackdaw of Rheims," and Castles and Churches. In the 1970s the term *limited edition* became popular to describe plates and other pieces made in limited numbers, often in a series. Before that, in the 1930s, Doulton had made special commemorative jugs and presentation pieces that were limited to about five hundred. These have raised decorations picturing people and places. Some limited editions commemorated royal events. But to most buyers, it is the limited-edition plates, tankards, and plaques first made in 1972 that are wanted. Limited-edition series like Royal Doulton's annual Christmas plates or the four plates in the Commedia Dell'Arte series, designed by Leroy Neiman and issued from 1974 to 1978, were once popular but now are of little interest to collectors.

Figurines and Character Jugs

To many of today's collectors, Royal Doulton means figurines, character jugs, or expensive sets of dishes. A few figurines were made at the end of the nineteenth century. Between 1909 and 1914 some small figurines were produced; they gained in popularity, and Royal Doulton figurines have been made every year since. At first they were realistic models of people, like the *Old Balloon Seller* or *Top o' the Hill*. By 1978 Royal Doulton artists were working in a more contemporary manner and produced figurines like the *Images* line of streamlined white figures with little detail.

Opposite Page:
Each Royal Doulton figurine is marked with an HN number. The lower the number, the older the figure. Pierette *was designed by Leslie Harradine and is numbered HN664, dating its introduction to 1924.*
(Photo: Sotheby's)

In 1934 Royal Doulton started making character jugs, pitchers shaped like the bust of a person with just the head and shoulders shown. At first the jugs portrayed famous English characters of history, literature, and song, but by the 1980s well-known movie, television, and political figures from other countries were included. The jugs had appropriate handles: Long John Silver's handle was a figural parrot, Clark Gable's was a movie camera. Character jugs come in four sizes, ranging from large, 5¼ to 7 inches high, to tiny, just 1¼ inches or less. Rarities like the *Granny* with no teeth (the common version has one tooth) or the red-headed *Clown* have sold for thousands of dollars each.

Toby jugs, drinking mugs shaped like a full figure of a seated person, have been made by Doulton since 1939. Rarities include actor Charlie Chaplin and music-hall star George Robey, tobies that have sold for over $7,000 each.

Tableware

Royal Doulton is well known for its tableware. In 1907 the company built a new china-works, and since then it has made both bone china and fine earthenware sets. Dishes range from expensive sets with raised gold decorations and hand painting made for royalty and millionaires to lower-priced sets decorated with copper-plate engravings and hand-painted, lithographed, or silk-screened designs. Popular patterns in traditional shapes include *Tonkin* (oriental flower decoration), *Sarabande* (platinum trim), *Old Leeds Spray* (bunches of flowers and no trim), and *Grantham* (wide speckled rim and floral center). Other modern patterns include *Tapestry* (band or rectangles enclosing pieces of fruit) and *Morning Star* (bone china pattern on a contemporary shape with rimless plates and cylindrical coffee pot). In the 1970s and 1980s, Royal Doulton made sets of stoneware in informal patterns. *Marbella* (brown and beige overall decoration), *Fieldflower* (red poppy-like flowers), *Tangier* (white plate with a design of blue and yellow stylized flower heads and yellow center), and the all-white embossed *Ting* pattern were made in modern shapes with mugs, casserole dishes, and plates with flat rims. Contemporary patterns include *Touch* (streamlined, irregular and elongated shapes) and *Symmetry* (full, round shapes).

MOORCROFT

William Moorcroft worked as a designer for James Macintyre and Company of Burslem, England, from 1898 to 1913, then started his own firm. His most familiar wares are decorated with floral and fruit designs on dark blue backgrounds. Huge numbers of these pieces were in hardware stores, drugstores, and gift shops in Canadian towns in the 1940s.

Moorcroft pottery was made in many different designs. From 1910 to 1918 Moorcroft made *Florian* ware, which featured cornflower or brown chrysanthemum designs on red, mottled green, or yellow and purple. It also made *Pansy* and *Pomegranate* in more muted shades of yellow and green. Another popular pattern featured light purple wisteria that looks more like grapes. *Pansy* was decorated in the colors of real pansies. Other wares pictured toadstools, daffodils, and landscapes. Some luster-decorated lines and flambé lines were made in the 1920s. In the 1930s, exotic flowers like waratah, poppies, protea, orchids, and freesia were featured. By the late 1930s, the colors were more subdued, often beige or light blue, and designs included fish, peacock feathers, or wheat. Most of these designs were made for many years, and today the company still makes many types of pottery using old and new designs.

Moorcroft has always made decorative tableware as well as mugs, candlesticks, beads, boxes, ashtrays, ink-wells, and small plaques for jewelry. Moorcroft's miniature pieces, less than four inches high, are popular with collectors. The company was sold by the Moorcroft family in 1984 and today continues in business using the old name and marks.

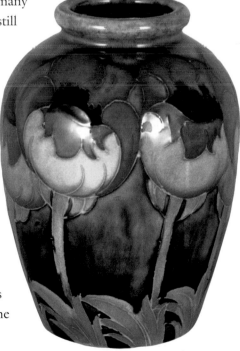

Most Moorcroft pottery was decorated with flowers. This Poppy *vase was made in the early 1920s. It is almost 7 inches high.*
(Photo: Waddington's)

There are bluebirds and flowers on this 1930s vase by Poole subsidiary Carter, Stabler & Adams. The 9½-inch vase has impressed, incised, and painted marks identifying the designer, shape, and company. (Photo: Waddington's)

RUSKIN

The Ruskin Pottery was started near Birmingham at the end of the nineteenth century by the art potter Edward Richard Taylor (1838–1912) and his son William Howson Taylor (1876–1935). Edward retired in 1904. Chinese ceramics from the Sung and Ming Dynasties, especially glazes, were an important influence on William Taylor's work. The pottery was noted for its exceptional mottled, luster, and flambé glazes. Ruskin Pottery made a variety of products, including tiles, vases, bowls, tableware, and even buttons and hatpins. The pottery stopped making new pieces in 1933, but continued to glaze and sell the remaining wares until 1935.

The word *Taylor* or initials *WHT* appear in early marks from 1898 on. In 1909 the *Ruskin Pottery* trademark was registered, and *Ruskin* was then found in marks.

Ruskin art pottery had unusual, colorful glazes. This 9-inch vase has a dripping crystalline glaze. There are three handles, one out of sight. (Photo: Treadway)

POOLE POTTERY

Poole Pottery was founded in England in 1873 and worked under several names, becoming Poole Pottery Ltd. in 1962. The company was originally owned by Jesse Carter, and his name appeared in the mark until 1952.

At the beginning of the twentieth century, the company was known for tiles and architectural and garden ceramics. Poole's luster glaze in red, green, and shades of gray and blue used on some tiles

Poole introduced oven ware in 1961. Dinnerware was an important part of the Poole pottery ware made from the 1970s to 1990s.

MERGING COMPANIES

Sales and mergers have reduced the number of firms in the English pottery industry from hundreds of makers to a group of just a few large companies. Minton, Royal Crown Derby, Royal Doulton, Royal Worcester, Shelley, and Spode are all part of Royal Worcester Spode. The Waterford-Wedgwood group includes Cauldon, Coalport, Johnson Brothers, Rosenthal, Royal Doulton, and others.

In the early twentieth century, Poole made tiles based on actual photographs. A transparent glaze filled in the recessed parts of a white tile to create a dark and light finished tile that looked like a photograph.

won several awards. Artists Harold and Phoebe Stabler, who worked at Poole starting in 1911, designed an unusual series of pottery figures, bookends, candelabra, and dinnerware with colored glazes that were produced into the 1930s. The series featured peasants, children, animals, and birds. Stoneware vases, teapots, bowls, candlesticks, and other useful wares with hand-painted colored geometric or floral designs were the main product from 1915 to the early 1920s.

In the 1920s the company created modern, bold designs using thick stripes as well as a ware made of unglazed terra-cotta decorated with geometric designs that recalled American Indian pottery. Other plates, bowls, and vases were made of red earthenware partially covered with decorations that included stylized grapes and leaves, animals, birds, or flowers to create an informal peasant look. This type of design, but covering more of the surface of the object, was continued into the 1940s. Sylvan ware, introduced in 1934, featured bowls and vases made in simple free-form shapes decorated with solid colors, stripes, or abstract patterns. Wares of the 1950s had the look of the time: stylized fruit and vegetable motifs, undecorated one- or two-color dinnerware, and modern shapes. The fifties line most popular with today's collectors is the white earthenware giftware in modern shapes with contemporary patterns of stripes and swirls in muted colors. By the 1970s, the shapes were still modern, but some designs featured roosters and more peasantlike patterns.

Poole made studio-type wares as early as 1921, when a decorative arts subsidiary, Carter, Stabler & Adams (CSA), was created to make art pottery. By the 1930s the firm was a pioneer in art deco and modern designs, and in the 1960s the Poole Pottery Studio was established. During the 1960s and '70s, it produced pottery with bold abstract designs in intense colors, a variety of unusual textured surfaces, and some unusual shapes. The Poole Studio was reestablished in 1995 with well-known artists creating contemporary designs. It was sold in 2004 and is working under new owners.

Shelley China came in many different styles. This pottery vase is marked with the British Registry mark for 1918. The carnation design was probably airbrushed.
(Photo: Antiques At Time Was)

The Bride's Choice

After World War II, a middle-class bride went to a department store or gift shop bridal registry and listed the dishes and other gifts she hoped to get as wedding presents. The dinnerware patterns were almost all traditional, the type of dishes her mother used. In the 1960s and 1970s, usually a less formal type of dinnerware was selected, and heavy pottery or pewter was the choice of some brides. By the 1990s, traditional, formal patterns were again in fashion. English companies like Minton, Spode, Wedgwood, Royal Worcester, and Royal Doulton made dinner sets in patterns from the eighteenth, nineteenth, and twentieth centuries as well as contemporary, often startling, designs. The English firms competed with each other and with makers from France, Germany, the United States, Japan, and Denmark.

This 1960s bone china gravy boat with underplate is in the Old Country Roses *pattern. Royal Albert, the maker, joined Royal Doulton in 1971, and this popular pattern is now sold by Royal Doulton. Since 2002 the dishes have been made in Indonesia.*

SHELLEY

Shelley china is so distinctive it is easy to spot at a show. Its modern angular shapes, flower-garden designs, chintz patterns, and unusual shapes and colors have become familiar. The company began in 1860 as the Foley China Works owned by Henry Wileman. By 1872 Wileman had a partner, Joseph Shelley, and the company became Wileman & Company. Shelley's son Percy joined the business in 1881. When Percy took over the company in 1896, he hired Frederick Rhead (a famous designer who later made *Fiesta* ware in the United States) as art director, and the pottery's designs got a new look.

Shelley china, the name used to describe all pieces made from the late nineteenth century to the present, consists of many types of ceramics. *Dainty White* shape with fluted panels and scalloped edges was made from 1896 until 1966. Sets were plain white or decorated with touches of color or painted flowers. Finished pieces were given many different pattern names depending on the decorations. From 1910 to 1940 the pottery made porcelain tea ware, coffeepots, teapots, sugar bowls, creamers, cups and saucers, and plates in many shapes. Octagonal plates, triangular plates, almost-square plates, ring handles, triangle handles, solid handles, and paneled cups were all new shapes. For the collector, the most distinctive features are the decorations showing flower gardens or severe geometric designs. By the 1950s Shelley, like most potteries, made dinner sets and vases in modern streamlined shapes. It also made earthenware vases and dishes. Shelley produced nursery wares—baby plates and mugs decorated with nursery-rhyme figures or with the typical drawings of children by Mabel Lucie Attwell.

About 1910 the company began using the trade name and marks *Shelley China* (from 1910) and *Shelley* (from 1912), and in 1925, the name was officially changed to Shelley. Most pieces have a pattern number painted on the bottom. Allied English Potteries acquired the company in 1966. It is now part of Royal Doulton Tablewares Group.

STUDIO POTTERS

The studio pottery movement in England started in the 1920s. Individual potters and designers created pots and figures in new and sometimes eccentric styles. The ideal of a small pottery where pieces are handmade continued through the century. New techniques, unusual glazes, and even the use of materials other than clay were tried. Some designers also worked for the large ceramics companies creating unusual shapes and decorations for vases and dinnerware.

Clarice Cliff

Clarice Cliff (1899–1972) was a decorator and designer who began work at A. J. Wilkinson's Royal Staffordshire Pottery in Burslem, England, in 1916. She is known for her original, bold, geometric art deco designs. By 1927 she

Chintz

Collectors rediscovered chintz pattern dishes in the 1990s. Chintz ceramics were first made at several English factories in the late 1800s. They went out of style by the 1960s because newlyweds wanted simpler dinner sets, not plates with flower decoration from edge to edge.

Early hand-painted chintz patterns from the nineteenth century were inspired by the printed cotton fabric called *chintz*. By 1900 designs were color lithographed onto the china. Some patterns were used by more than one manufacturer. Often colors were changed and the pattern was renamed. English patterns were often copied by Japanese and Czechoslovakian makers and exported to the United States. At first chintz was used for vases and trinket boxes, but by 1920 chintz dinnerware patterns were popular, especially in America. The patterns were considered exotic but still "homey," suitable for a bungalow.

Royal Winton, manufactured by Grimwades Ltd., was a leading brand of chintz ceramics from 1928 to 1963. *Summertime*, a 1932 pattern, is the most sought after. Other makers of chintz were A. G. Richardson & Co., Arthur J. Wilkinson & Co., Arthur Wood & Sons, Crown Ducal, Elijah Cotton (trade name *Lord Nelson*), James Kent, and Shelley.

Chintz pattern dishes with decoration both inside and out bring the highest prices. Unusual forms are also in demand.

Chintz patterns were so popular in England in the 1930s that dozens of patterns were made. This stacking teapot and sugar bowl set in the Black Beauty *pattern is marked* Lord Nelson Pottery, *the trade name used by Elijah Cotton Ltd., a Staffordshire pottery. (Photo: Antiques At Time Was)*

had her own studio at Newport Pottery in Burslem, where she designed *Bizarre* ware, a hand-painted line of dishes and vases with vivid geometric patterns. The unique patterns Cliff created from 1928 to 1936 were very popular. She was named art director at Newport, and the pottery decided to make only her designs. She created other art deco designs, including *Fantasque*, *Chintz*, and *Crocus*, which remained in production for over thirty years. Cliff's work inspired similar designs by other makers. Her name was used on new pottery until 1964. She retired in 1963.

Susie Cooper

In the 1940s, breakfast in an American middle-class home was often served on dishes by the English designer Susie Cooper (1902–1995). Cooper's modern shapes and abstract designs sold well in England, but more conservative American buyers preferred her less unusual dishes made with rings in shades of beige and brown.

Cooper started as a designer for A. E. Gray & Company in 1922, and her work was so popular that by the next year it was marked with a backstamp saying *designed by Susie Cooper*. She continued designing for A. E. Gray until 1929, had her own business designing pottery from 1929 until the 1960s, then worked for Wedgwood starting in 1966. The Susie Cooper Wedgwood lines were made only until 1979, but Cooper kept working until 1986. Her designs reflected the tastes of her times, going first from modern to traditional to sell to Americans, then to subdued modern shapes with muglike cups and cylindrical teapots in the 1950s, and to op-art patterns in the late 1960s. Her dishes were always stylish, functional, and affordable. She used bright colors, geometric banded patterns, stylized flowers, incised designs, spiral motifs, and polka dots. Today collectors can easily find examples of the 1950s banded sets and other conservative patterns. The art deco patterns of the 1920s are more expensive and more difficult to find.

Keith Murray and Wedgwood

Josiah Wedgwood started making pottery in the eighteenth century, and some of his designs and products, like jasperware, continue to be popular today. In the twentieth century, Josiah Wedgwood & Company began to think about marketing its ceramics in the United States. It opened a New York office in 1906 and aggressively promoted Wedgwood products throughout the United States. By 1930 the company realized a new look was needed, and Keith Murray (1892–1981) was hired to design vases and tableware. He created simple streamlined shapes, often with concentric ridges and a solid-color glaze as the only decoration. The glazes were muted, matte colors ranging from *moonstone* and *straw* to celadon and *turquoise*. Murray also designed stoneware decorated with dark glazes. Wedgwood made many of his designs into the 1950s. Murray's pieces were marked with his full signature until 1940, then with his initials and the Wedgwood mark. Clare Leighton and Eric Ravilious also were important Wedgwood designers.

Keith Murray changed the look of Wedgwood in the 1930s. This white vase with a ringed neck is typical of his geometric vases. The design of this 11-inch vase has been copied by many other potteries.

Wedgwood patterns made for many years, like *Napoleon Ivy* and *Chinese Teal*, and those that are more contemporary in appearance, like *Minimal* and *Quadrants*, are still best sellers in the United States.

Bernard Leach

Bernard Leach (1887–1979) is considered the father of contemporary studio pottery in England. He was born in Hong Kong and studied pottery in Japan and Korea. In 1920 he moved to England and started his own pottery in St. Ives, Cornwall, using local clay. At first he made slipware, later stoneware. Many of his simple, Asian-inspired stoneware vases have brushwork decorations of carp or abstract lines. He used Asian techniques and Asian designs, but his tableware and jugs, bowls, and vases are familiar British forms made by throwing the shapes on a wheel. Glazes were usually brown, beige, or black. By the 1930s his workshop was making useful wares for reasonable prices, not the unique forms favored by many young artists. He is said to have made more than one hundred thousand pieces.

The talent of the master potter Bernard Leach is shown in this bowl. It has his typical tan spatter glaze. The Japanese influence is obvious. The bowl, made in about 1950, has the impressed mark of St. Ives Pottery.

Lucie Rie

Trained by Josef Hoffmann, Michael Powolny, and other important artists in Vienna, Lucie Rie (1902–1995) was a well-known potter in Europe before she fled to England in 1938 to escape the Nazis. At the end of the war, she had a studio in London and made red earthenware; after 1948 she also made stoneware and porcelain. Rie made tableware in the 1950s and 1960s, then started to make one-of-a-kind bottles, vases, and bowls. Her pieces are simple and elegant. Many were made with thick, pitted white glaze. Others have speckled glazes or vivid green, yellow, magenta, peacock blue, and gold textured glazes. Many of her vases have long, slim necks with flared tops.

This 12-inch stoneware vase was made by Lucie Rie in about 1980. It has a pitted glaze that was typical of her work and is stamped with the artist's monogram. (Photo: Sotheby's)

British Art Potteries, Designers, and Studio Potters

This table lists art pottery makers and designers with dates and marks. Parentheses enclose the birth and death dates of the artist. Other dates given are approximate working dates of the pottery or artist.

Pottery and Location	Dates	Mark
Ashby Potters Guild Woodville, Derbyshire	1909–1922	
Ault and Tunnicliffe **Ault Potteries Ltd.** Swadlincote	1923–1937 1937–1975	
Baron Pottery Rolle Quay, Barnstaple	1895–1939	
C. H. Brannam Barnstaple	(1855–1937) 1879–present	
Burmantofts Pottery Leeds	1880–1904	
Carter, Stabler, and Adams (Subsidiary of Poole Pottery) Dorset	1921–1963	
Clarice Cliff Staffordshire	(1899–1972) 1927–1964	
Susie Cooper Staffordshire	(1902–1995) 1922–1986	
Walter Crane London	(1845–1915) 1867–1915	
Della Robbia Pottery Birkenhead, Cheshire	1894–1905	
William De Morgan Chelsea, London Merton Abbey Fulham, London	(1839–1917) 1860s–1907	
Doulton and Company **Royal Doulton** Lambeth (1853–1956) and Burslem (1882–present)	1854–1902 1902–present	
Elton Sunflower Pottery (Sir Edmund Elton) Clevedon, Somerset	1884–1922 (1846–1920)	
Grimwade Brothers **Grimwades Ltd.** Stoke-on-Trent	1885–1900 1900–present	

Pottery and Location	Dates	Mark
Bernard Leach St. Ives, Cornwall	(1887–1979) 1920–1972	
Macintyre & Co. Burslem	1860s–1913	
Martin Brothers Fullham, London Southall, Middlesex	1873–1930s	
William Moorcroft Burslem, Staffordshire	(1872–1945) 1897–1945	
Bernard Moore Stoke-on-Trent, Staffordshire	(1850–1935) 1870–1915	
Keith Murray London	(1892–1981) 1930s–1948	
Pilkington Tile and Pottery Co. (Pilkington Royal Lancastrian) Manchester	1892–1938 1948–1957	
Poole Pottery Dorset	1873–present	
Lucie Rie London	(1902–1995) 1940s–1990s	
Royal Aller Vale & Watcombe Art Potteries Torquay, Devon	1901–1962	
Ruskin Pottery Smethwick, Birmingham	1898–1935	
Torquay Terracotta Co. Hele Cross, Torquay	1875–c.1905	
Josiah Wedgwood and Sons, Ltd. Burslem, Etruria, Barlaston, Staffordshire	1759–present	

Chapter 5

Pottery and Porcelain from Europe and Japan

AT THE TURN of the twentieth century, the United States had thriving ceramic industries in New Jersey and the Ohio–West Virginia area, but economic conditions following World War I brought changes. Less-expensive dishes were being made in Europe and Asia, and some American potteries closed. The Depression caused more economic hardships, and many more factories closed. Beginning in the 1930s, fine dinnerware from England, Germany, and Japan squeezed out all but a few American factories. At the same time, clever, colorful art deco designs from Czechoslovakia, Austria, and England attracted young buyers who wanted something modern, while inexpensive restaurant wares and serving bowls were imported from Asia. The industry slowly moved overseas.

AUSTRIA

The Wiener Werkstätte designers in Vienna, Austria, not only created their own style but also trained artists who brought the style to other countries. Many famous potters worked in Vienna from 1905 to 1931, including Valerie (Vally) Wieselthier, who influenced

Opposite Page: Art deco pottery sold well in the United States. This hanging double-mask of a woman in the popular colors of orange and black was made by Goldscheider of Austria. (Photo: Rago)

the work of Viktor Schreckengost (see page 71). Other potters inspired by the Wiener Werkstätte were the Cowan potters and Cleveland School artists; Lucie Rie, who became a famous potter in England (see page 120); and Gertrud and Otto Natzler, American studio potters (see page 29). Wiener Werkstätte artists created one-of-a-kind handmade figures from 1917 to 1920, then designed production ceramics that were manufactured until 1931.

Wiener Werkstätte ceramics had the finger marks and rough quality of hand-worked clay. Figures of women were elongated, and faces were angular with straight noses. Round-faced cherubic children with garlands of flowers were also popular. Animal figures often displayed a humorous, childish look. All of the work used strong colors like bright yellow, orange, red, and blue. Tablewares were often decorated with strong geometric designs in black and white or a single color.

CZECHOSLOVAKIA

Quality pottery and porcelain have been made in the area historically known as Bohemia since the late eighteenth century. At the end of World War I in 1918, Bohemia, previously part of Austria-Hungary, joined Moravia and Slovakia to form Czechoslovakia. Quantities of tableware and pottery marked *Czechoslovakia* were made in the new country and exported to the rest of Europe, North and South America, and Australia during the 1920s and '30s. Important Czechoslovakian factories included Royal Dux maker of porcelain and faience figurines; Peasant Art Industries, producer of colorful pottery decorated in the folk art tradition for export to the United States; and the Amphora factories, which made vases, pitchers, planters, and figurines in Egyptian and art deco styles. Amphora pieces made before 1918 were marked *Austria*. After 1918 they were marked Czechoslovakia. The ceramics industry prospered until Hitler

PEASANT ART

Czech immigrant Joseph Mrazek (1889–1959) came to the United States in his teens. In 1917 he began decorating pottery with Czech folk art designs in New York City. He soon rented a ceramics factory in Letovice, Czechoslovakia, and in 1925 he built his own pottery there. Mrazek's Peasant Art Industries made lamps, plates, bowls, vases, pitchers, cups and saucers, clocks, and other items. The pottery was decorated with birds, fruit, flowers, and art deco designs in brilliant colors, predominantly orange. Wares were exported to the United States and sold in department stores. The factory closed in 1933.

Amphora, one of the most famous Czechoslovakian potteries, made this three-handled vase. The organic form and iridescent glaze were often used. (Photo: Treadway)

Importers—Erphila and
Other Hard-to-Identify Marks

Some of the most eye-catching ceramics used in the United States were brought over from Europe by companies that specialized in importing, not manufacturing, giftware. These companies often put their own marks on goods they imported. Some European china and glass with an importer's mark was shipped to the United States by Ebeling & Reuss, a Philadelphia company established in 1886. After 1935 it used the mark *ERPHILA: ER* for the company name, *PHILA* for Philadelphia. At first the company imported antique-looking mustache cups and smoking sets; by the 1930s it was selling dinnerware and humorous pottery and porcelain, including animal-shaped pitchers from Czechoslovakia. Ebeling & Reuss also imported giftware made in England, France, Belgium, Denmark, Italy, Finland, and Sweden. During World War II, it found new supplies in South America, Mexico, and China. In the 1950s it distributed copies of the popular English chintzware patterns. The company is now located in Allentown, Pennsylvania, and is owned by Strathmore Corporation. It is still distributing giftware and dinnerware.

Other importing companies of note that marked wares with their own names were Enesco Corporation (Chicago, 1958–present), Fitz and Floyd (Dallas, 1960–present), George Borgfeldt Corporation (New York, 1881–1970s), Holt-Howard (New York, 1949–1990), Justin Tharaud & Son (New York, 1950–1980), Otto Goetz (New York, 1920s–1930s), and Raymor (New York, 1942–1980s).

Erphila is the mark of an importer that ordered from many factories and countries. The maker's name is not used. This poodle teapot, probably from the 1950s when poodles were popular, has Bobby embossed on the collar. It is 9 inches tall.

Picasso Designed Ceramics, Too

Pablo Picasso became interested in ceramics in 1946 when he visited the Madoura Pottery in the south of France. The next year he returned and began designing, making, and decorating tiles, dishes, pots, vases, and other ceramic objects. Between 1947 and 1971, Picasso created 633 different designs at the Madoura workshop—plates with designs reminiscent of his paintings, flower holders shaped like ducks, pitchers that look like birds, and jugs that look like people. Some were limited editions. His prototype pieces with original designs were copied by hand by one of the Madoura potters. Collectors and museums today are interested in any of the Picasso ceramics.

Picasso designed this limited edition Madoura Pottery tile. (Photo: Treadway)

occupied the country in 1938. Most factories closed during World War II, then were reopened and nationalized in 1948. The ceramics industry recovered slowly. Dishes and giftware are still exported to the United States from Slovakia and the Czech Republic, the two countries formed in 1993 after the fall of the Soviet Union.

FRANCE

One of the most important events in the history of design in the twentieth century was the birth of art deco at the 1925 Paris World's Fair (see page 217). Artists from all over the world displayed their most imaginative work to gain recognition and to share with others. A French exhibit labeled *Limoges, The Porcelain Capital of the World* showed work by Arhenfeldt, Bernardaud, GDA (Gerard, Dufraisseix, and Abbot), Charles Field Haviland, Theodore Haviland, Lanternier, Serpaut et Tharaud, and others. These factories made not only figures and vases but also dinner sets that looked different from any made before. Buyers could select a new pattern that had dotted rims, or abstract tree and vine patterns, or geometric borders. A palette of gray, black, and gold was popular; so were black, gold, and bright colors. Whimsical bird-shaped pitchers by Edouard Marcel Sandoz for Theodore Haviland, as well as simple shapes given the deco look with the help of strong decoration and colors, were available. But the startling, sleek art deco look of these stylized figures and objects was not accepted worldwide for about ten years. Art deco furniture, metalwork, textiles, and jewelry were eventually made in many countries, but even today the most sought-after art deco pieces were created in France.

In the early 1900s, before the Paris exposition, potters had been making vases decorated with curving vines, long-haired sensuous women, and other typical art nouveau designs.

Humorous ceramics are an old tradition. This Theodore Haviland, Limoges set by Edouard Marcel Sandoz was made in 1916. The duck coffee pot, pelican cream pitcher, and pigeon sugar bowl had to get a smile at breakfast.
(Photo: Neal)

Felix Bracquemond, Ernest Chaplet, Taxile Doat, Emile Gallé (see page 159), and Edmond Lachenal are among the better-known French potters of this era.

The pottery industry in Europe survived the 1930s Depression and World War II. Old factories like Haviland, Longwy, Quimper, and Sèvres continued to be important during this time, and they are still working. In the 1950s Georges Jouve (1910–1964) made solid-color minimalist vases and sculptures that led the way for other French designs. Other innovative groups, like the Madoura workshop that offered designs by Picasso, created unique ceramics. The city of Vallauris, home to Madoura, became filled with studio potters experimenting with techniques and designs. Some ceramics reflected the art movement of the time and used cubist, abstract, and even op-art designs.

From the 1970s to the 1990s, many unique dinnerware shapes were made in France. Plates that were square, oval, rimless, and even sectioned were featured. Most dishes were white and decorated with line drawings in dark colors. Want a demitasse set that serves a really small cup of coffee? One set by Raynaud had plates, cups, and a teapot that looked as if they had literally been cut in half.

In the last years of the twentieth century, the "artist ceramics" potters were making pots with irregular shapes and lavalike glazes; sculptures with undulating, often abstract, shapes; and vases or sculptures with cartoonlike characters, birds, and animals.

GERMAN POTTERY AND PORCELAIN

Important pottery and porcelain has been made in Germany for centuries. Goebel (Hummel), Meissen, Rosenthal, Royal Bayreuth, and Villeroy & Boch are the most familiar names. Other German factories of note include Goldscheider, Hutschenreuther, KPM (Koniglichen Porzellan-Manufaktur) of Berlin, and Nymphenburg.

Goebel-Hummel

The F. W. Goebel factory was founded by Franz and William Goebel in Oeslau, Germany, in 1871. The company made many types of dishes and figurines. Then in 1935 Goebel put the first *M. I. Hummel* figurine on the market, and a new era began. The famous Hummel figurines were made in collaboration with Berta Hummel (then sister Maria Innocentia) and the convent she had entered. Even today, her drawings of children at work and play are the basis of all Hummel figurines. The figurines were popular with tourists and became even more popular when the American military was stationed in Germany after World War II. Soldiers sent Hummels home as gifts and started a collecting craze. Older Hummels were wanted and could be dated by their marks. While old figurines went up in price, new ones that cost more to make also became expensive. The company encouraged the craze with clubs, bulletins, special edition figurines, plates, and more. By the 1990s, however, demand dropped and prices for vintage figurines leveled. New ones are still being made each year, and some are "retired" each year, too. Goebel has also made other popular ceramics, including figurines of red-headed children by Charlotte Byj, gnomes (Co-Boys), a series of pieces shaped like monks, realistic animals and birds, and modern figures of women by Cherry Jeffe Huldah.

Meissen

Meissen is a town in Germany where porcelain has been made since about 1710. The word *Meissen* has come to mean almost any type of ceramic made in the town of Meissen since that time. Twentieth-century Meissen can be reissues of figurines and dishes made in earlier years or modern designs in art nouveau, art deco, fifties, and later styles. The original Meissen factory (now Staatliche Porzellan-Manufaktur) has made porcelains in all of these styles since the early 1900s. It made art nouveau dinnerware, realistic animal figures, and

HUMMEL MARKS

Crown Mark
(Trademark-1)
1934–1950

Full Bee
(Trademark-2)
1940–1959

Stylized Bee
(Trademark-3)
1958–1972

Three Line Mark
(Trademark-4)
1964–1979

Last Bee Mark
(Trademark-5)
1972–1979

Missing Bee Mark
(Trademark-6)
1979–1991

New Mark
(Trademark-7)
1991–1999

Millennium Bee
(Trademark-8)
2000–Present

vases decorated with curved leaves and flowers and covered in crystalline and other variegated glazes. Art deco figurines from the 1920s and early '30s feature men and women with long, slender bodies striking angular poses. The designs of the thirties and forties were what was popular at that time: modern vase and dish shapes with subdued colors. By the 1960s bright colors and bold geometric patterns were in style. At the end of the twentieth century, the factory was making abstract shapes as well as reissues of early traditional pieces.

The woman posed on the couch is typical of Meissen figurines from the 1920s and early '30s. The 29-inch-long figurine was modeled in the 1930s by Paul Scheurich. His name is incised on the bottom near the blue crossed sword and dot mark. (Photo: Sotheby's)

Rosenthal

Walk into a gift shop and look at the vases and dinnerware. The most eye-catching, most colorful, and most innovative are probably part of the Rosenthal Studio line started in 1961. Under the leadership of Philip Rosenthal, son of the founder, the company created new designs beginning in the 1950s. Famous artists like Walter Gropius, Gianni Versace, Tapio Wirkkala, and Bjorn Wiinblad were invited to create new shapes and daring decorations. The idea of innovative, contemporary design has continued at Rosenthal since the 1950s.

The company, founded in 1879 in Selb, Bavaria, made top-quality undecorated table services in the early 1900s. Later, these dishes were decorated with art nouveau-style plants. In 1916 Rosenthal introduced an angular shape, *Maria*, glazed white and decorated with pomegranates in relief. It is still sold today. Art deco figurines of theatrical characters and people in everyday clothes were best sellers in the 1920s and 1930s. Unusual shapes were also popular. In the 1950s a modern rimless plate and straight-

Rosenthal figurines are usually sculptural, not quaint or cute. This 9½-inch figure of a dancer is probably from the 1920s or '30s. (Photo: Treadway)

sided teapot and cup were combined in sets. Decorations were small geometric shapes in muted colors or bold graphics in black or maroon. Pastel-colored vases, made to be useful, had tall necks, cylinder or egg shapes, or unusual abstract shapes with off-center flower holes. One surprising line of accessories was decorated with pictures of Victorian women with big eyes, fluffy hair, and small waists. Additional abstract shapes and designs were featured in the 1970s and '80s. Studio-Line tableware, introduced in 1961, is still being made. Rosenthal even sells very expensive limited-edition sculptures like *Moonhead* by Henry Moore, artist plates by Salvador Dalí (1976), and a tea service by Roy Lichtenstein. Rosenthal continues to make expensive, well-designed porcelain. Dishes range from sets with intricate gold decoration to cocktail plates picturing comic figures. The company also still makes figurines, Christmas plates, giftware, and unusual art wares.

Rosenthal china is always marked with the company name, but the shape of the mark has changed so it is possible to date a piece by the mark.

Royal Bayreuth

The Royal Bayreuth porcelain factory, founded in 1794 in Tettau, Bavaria, is still in business. It made figural and souvenir items from about 1885 to 1915, but its most important products have been tableware and coffee and tea sets. Early twentieth-century lines include *Rose Tapestry*; floral, scenic, and portrait china; and the *Sunbonnet Babies*, *Beach Babies*, and *Snow Babies* series. In the 1970s, Royal Bayreuth introduced an annual series of limited edition *Christmas* plates (1972), *Mother's Day* plates (1973), and *Easter Eggs* (1974). *Sunbonnet Babies* plates and porcelain bells were reissued in 1974, and a new series was issued in 1981. From 1994

Pitchers, sugar bowls, coffeepots, and other dishes made to look like tomatoes, lobsters, fruit, or other natural forms were kitsch but popular in the twentieth century. This Royal Bayreuth set was made in 1902. (Photo: Heritage Galleries)

Colorful art nouveau designs were used on Gouda pottery for many years. Rust and blue-green were used on a lot of pieces, including this 11-inch pitcher. (Photo: Treadway)

to 1996, two sets of Royal Bayreuth porcelain dinnerware used Pablo Picasso's designs. The company continues to make dinnerware and limited edition collectibles.

Royal Bayreuth's marks have changed through the years, and not all pieces are marked. Modern pieces are marked with a stylized crest supported by two lions, the name *Royal Bayreuth*, and the word *Bavaria*.

Villeroy & Boch

Villeroy & Boch was formed by the merger of two ceramics factories in Mettlach, Germany, in 1836. Although most famous for Mettlach steins, the firm was also known for many types of porcelain, Parian (an unglazed porcelain resembling Parian marble), and faience wares in traditional styles. In the 1960s, it began to produce ceramics in contemporary shapes, designs, and colors. Important designers hired in the 1970s included Paloma Picasso and Keith Haring. In the 1980s, the company expanded its products to include tiles and sanitary wares, as well as tableware and crystal.

HOLLAND

Many factories in Holland made art deco and modern pottery. Look for marks that include these names: Amphora (1908–1933, not to be confused with the Czechoslovakian firm described earlier), De Distal (1895–1923), De Porceleyne Fles (1653–present), Haga (1904–1907), or Ram (1921–1945).

Gouda

The area near the city of Gouda in Holland has been a pottery center since the seventeenth century. But today the name *Gouda* refers to art pottery made in and around Gouda from 1898 to about 1964. Plateelfabriek Zuid-Holland (PZH or Plazuid) was a pipe-clay factory that began making art pottery in 1898. Its colorful wares were so popular that by 1914 other factories in the Gouda area began making art pottery, too. Most of the pottery was mass-produced for the middle-class market. Many pieces featured art

Villeroy and Boch suggests beer steins to many collectors, but in recent years, the company has made very modern ceramics. This Spirit of Art box was designed by Keith Haring in 1992.
(Photo: Treadway)

GOUDA MARKS

Plateelbakkerij Zuid-Holland (PZH) Mark used 1926

Zenith Plateelbakkerij en Pijpenfabrieken Mark used c.1920

Plateelfabriek Ivora Mark used c.1925

Plateelfabriek Regina Mark used after c.1938

Firma Eduard Antheunis Mark used c.1920

1891–1926
Black

1926–1946
Black
1946–1955
Green
1955–1965
Green, ® added

1965–1981
Green

1981–c.1984
Gold
c.1984–1992
Brown

1993–1996
Blue

1997–1999
Blue

The decorations on Rozenburg pottery are usually vines and flowers that twist and turn in a unique manner. This six-sided inkwell is 3 inches high. (Photo: Treadway)

Wrythen is the name of this shell-shaped Belleek bowl. It can be dated from the 1955–1965 mark on the bottom.

nouveau or art deco designs and a distinctive matte glaze. Only a few potteries are still working in the area.

Rozenburg

It is easy to recognize earthenware of the early 1900s made by the Rozenburg art pottery (1883–c.1916) in The Hague. The very thin dinnerwares were decorated over the glaze with birds, flowers, and

foliage inspired by Javanese batik-printed textiles. Pale shades of mauve, yellow, orange, and green were favored. The vases and pots had curved shapes and elongated handles and spouts. The name *Rozenburg/den Haag* and a picture of a stork was used as a mark.

IRELAND—Belleek

Belleek Pottery Limited began making Belleek pottery in County Fermanagh, Ireland, in 1863. Since 1929 only this Irish firm may use the word *Belleek* with a capital *B*. The Irish factory made dishes that resemble shells or flowers and used an open-weave basketwork design on many vases. Some pieces are decorated with overglaze gold or pastel colors. The creamy yellow, mother-of-pearl-like glaze used by Belleek Pottery has been copied by other companies, including Knowles, Taylor and Knowles; Lenox; Ott and Brewer; and Willets Manufacturing Company. That is why the word *belleek* is sometimes used generically to refer to the glaze, not the maker.

ITALY

Ceramics made in Italy remained "old-fashioned" until the 1940s. Before then, brightly colored majolica similar to that made for hundreds of years, and classic pieces by the Richard Ginori factory were brought back to the United States by tourists. Italy's amazing furniture, pottery, and glass designs in contemporary styles were not discovered until they were offered for sale in the United States in the 1940s by importers like Raymor. It

was then that rough-textured vases and animal figures with bright turquoise, yellow, or red decorations were added to the modern American living room. Interest in cutting-edge Italian designs has continued.

Marcello Fantoni

Marcello Fantoni (1915–present), who continues to work into his nineties, creates pottery that has mass appeal but is also recognized as art by museums. Fantoni studied ceramics in Rome

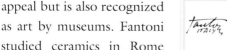

Raymor

Businessman Irving Richards and designer Russel Wright formed Russel Wright Associates about 1936 to promote sales of home accessories designed by Wright. Their most successful product was Wright's *American Modern*

dinnerware, which was introduced in 1939. Richards bought the business, and in 1942 he renamed it *Raymor*. The company continued to sell American Modern but manufactured and distributed products by other designers, including George Nelson, Glidden Parker, Gilbert Rohde, Ben Seibel, and Eva Zeisel. Raymor also introduced pottery made by Italy's contemporary, innovative designers, and many imported pieces were marked *Raymor*.

"Cutting edge" design was available from Raymor, and the company's selections influenced design for years. The 9-inch green vase and the 7-inch turquoise vase have shapes and glazes that continue to be in style. Both vases are marked Raymor, one with a label and one with an overglaze signature.

Some twentieth-century Italian ceramics were made with an old-fashioned look. The Ginori factory made this small covered box in the style of the eighteenth century, but the mark and the words Made in Italy *proclaim its recent production.*

and began working in 1936, when he started the Fantoni Ceramic Studio. He made important marketable and artistic ceramics from the 1950s to the '70s. His work includes both huge pieces for churches and public buildings and small commercial bowls, lamps, and vases. One style that was copied by others was leather-wrapped pottery. Decoration, put on the front of the pottery that was left without the leather covering, was usually a cubist picture of a person painted in dark red, black, and other somber colors. Later, he shaped pots and slab constructions covered with unusual colors of volcanic glaze. Fantoni also made abstract metal sculptures. His works are signed *Fantoni, Italy*, and some that were made for export are marked *Fantoni for Raymor*.

Guido Gambone

Italian potter Guido Gambone (1909–1969) had his own workshop in Naples until 1949, then moved to Florence. He made stoneware pieces, primarily vases, lamp bases, and chunky figures of people and animals. Vase shapes ranged from traditional bottle, rectangle, or flared type to eccentric, unfamiliar modern creations. He liked flat surfaces and sharp edges. His pottery was covered in thick, vividly colored, lavalike glazes. Sometimes a simple, almost comic, line drawing was added. He made many animal figures that were shaped like actual animals but were colored bright turquoise and wore very human grins. Some Gambone pieces are over four feet high, but most were made for use on a table. He signed his name, usually with a drawing of a donkey, on his pottery. His son Bruno Gambone took over the studio in 1969 after his father died. He signs pieces *Gambone* without the donkey drawing.

Lenci

The name *Lenci* means dolls to many Americans. Dolls, usually of felt, have been made at the Lenci factory in Turin, Italy, since 1922. From 1928 to 1964, the factory also made ceramics influenced by Danish, German, and Wiener Werkstätte artists, especially Vally Wieselthier. The pieces are easy to recognize because the style is so unlike that of other firms. Figurines of people and animals in stiff poses emphasized the straight lines and geometric patterns of the art deco style. Bright colors were often used in bold designs, some very childish. Fantasy and playfulness can be seen in some figurines, including one of a nude girl sitting on a large fish. Lenci figurines were made with few protruding parts. Hair was flat and without curls, and clothes clung to the body or draped into a geometric shape. Women figures looked off into the distance and rarely smiled. Figurines of girls, animals, angels, and holy subjects were the most popular. In the 1950s, some Disney characters were made; so were brightly colored vases in abstract shapes and traditional vases with bold flower decorations. Pieces were signed *Lenci, Made in Italy.*

This unsmiling, sophisticated woman with her dogs was made by the Lenci pottery. The figurine is 15¼ inches high and has painted marks on the base. (Photo: Sotheby's)

Ceramic artists also did architectural pieces like this surrealistic fireplace surround made of sculpted and incised glazed terra-cotta tiles. It is a 1957 creation by Salvatore Meli. (Photo: Shapiro)

Salvatore Meli

Although Salvatore Meli (1929–present) was winning prizes at national Italian exhibitions in the 1950s, he earned little fame in the United States until the 1990s. Still some critics say he is the most important of the Italian ceramists of his era. His pottery is known for its large scale and for the wildly free forms he created. Some pieces were painted with underwater or bacchanalian scenes drawn in the cubist style. He used

Piero Fornasetti

Piero Fornasetti (1913–1988) worked in Milan, Italy, from 1935 until his death. Fornasetti (his first name is rarely used today) designed and decorated furniture, fabrics, ceramics, and other types of decorative arts using familiar themes but startling, striking, and unconventional designs. Fornasetti's work ranged from expensive furniture to inexpensive ashtrays, most decorated with pictures of human figures or trompe l'oeil pictures of books, buildings, or other subjects. Most of his designs were crisp line drawings of realistic objects depicted in an unsettling way. His furniture was decorated with unexpected images. The entire surface of a cabinet or screen would be covered with trompe l'oeil pictures of books, cities, buildings, cards, musical instruments, newspapers, or ancient ruins. His ceramics, first made in the late 1940s, used many of the same motifs, but the most widely known are plates decorated with the childlike face of a woman. He did hundreds of variations of his face theme, showing parts of faces, multiple faces, a necklace of faces, a lightbulb face, and many more. He made plates picturing arms, legs, and torsos; a set of twelve could be hung to form a full human body or used to serve hors d'oeuvres. All of these ceramics were made of white porcelain decorated with black outlines, sometimes with added color. He died in 1988, but his designs are still being sold and licensed by Fornasetti of Milan, which is run by his son Barnaba. The demand for vintage Fornasetti has grown. Newer pieces, many made in limited editions, are not always available.

wild colors and exaggerated forms and decorations.

Other Italian Designers

Many other Italian designers who have worked from the 1950s to the present have created pottery of exceptional quality. Ettore Sottsass (see page 231) began designing ceramics in 1956 and has made many ceramic pieces, including huge, colorful columns called *totems*. Fausto Melotti (1901–1986) made terra-cotta sculptures, tiles, and architectural panels, as well as commercial coffee sets, vases, and lamps. His abstract designs, unusual shapes, and unique method of coloring influenced others. In 1997 Achille Castiglioni (1918–2002) designed the *Bavero* porcelain dinner service with plate edges that were folded down.

SCANDINAVIA

Relatively few Scandinavian ceramics were imported to the United States in the twentieth century, but they were an important influence on America designers. From the 1930s to the 1950s, American companies imitated Scandinavian designs that featured banded decorations and flowers or leaves. Between World War I and the 1950s, many designers in Denmark, Sweden, Norway, and Finland were creating decorative wares in a very distinctive, simple style called *Danish Design*. It was inspired by art deco and other emerging ideas and became popular in many countries, including the United States. The Georg Jensen store in New

Yes, this is a vase, but not quite what might be expected. Sottsass designed Euphrates *for Memphis in 1983. It looks like a stack of dishes in three colors.* (Photo: Rago)

Bing & Grøndahl has used underglaze decoration in shades of blue and gray since the 1850s. This vase with a cover was made in 1931. The leafy branches and leaves are both painted and molded. The printed green factory mark that includes the word Danmark is on the bottom.
(Photo: Sotheby's)

York introduced Danish ceramics, furniture, and silver designs of the 1940s and '50s that were sold in the United States.

From the 1950s to the mid '70s, earthenware with the handmade look of Scandinavia's stoneware, including *Flamestone* imported by Dansk Designs, was popular. By the 1970s and '80s, Danish designers were making some objects, especially stoneware pieces, that had a rustic, handmade look even if they were made by machine. Other ceramics had a high-tech, postmodern look. Many small Scandinavian shops were making the smooth, unadorned pottery favored by Scandinavian studio potters. Others liked rough glazes, textured surfaces, and geometric designs. All the work reflected the Scandinavian look also seen in furniture, glass, and silver of the period. Ideas spread very quickly in the twentieth century, and the Scandinavian designs so popular in the United States were soon copied by American firms.

Arabia

The Swedish company Rörstrand founded a subsidiary, Arabia, in Helsinki, Finland, in 1873. Arabia made ceramics in the conservative style of the period. In 1916 Rörstrand sold Arabia to a Finnish company. By the 1940s, it was the largest porcelain maker in Europe. Arabia created dishes based on classic and art deco designs. In the 1930s, the company employed international artists who created unique pieces in a modern manner. Designer Kaj Franck (1911–1989), hired in 1945, made easy-to-use mix-and-match sets and dinnerware with simple shapes and sparse decoration. Arabia became part of the Wartsila company in 1948, and in 1990 the Finnish Hackman Group acquired the company.

Bing & Grøndahl

Frederik Grøndahl, who had worked at the Royal Copenhagen factory as a modeler of figurines, and the brothers M. H. and J. H. Bing started the Bing & Grøndahl Porcelain factory in 1853. In 1889 the company exhibited its first pieces with underglaze decoration. About 1892 the company was making *Seagull* pattern dinnerware, which is still popular. The famous Bing & Grøndahl *Christmas* plates were first made in 1895. The Bings hired designers and ceramists from abroad to make stoneware, first produced in 1914, and porcelain. Figurines of Danish peasants, children, animals, or birds in the company's typical blue and beige coloring were produced after World War II. These figurines were similar to pieces by Royal Copenhagen in both design and muted blue coloring. Unusual blue and white abstract animal figurines were designed by Agnete Jorgensen from 1967 to 1976, and Sten Lykke Madsen from 1962 to 1987 created figures that look like Picasso designs.

In 1987 the company merged with other Danish firms and became part of Royal Copenhagen. Some Bing & Grøndahl dinnerware, figurines, and vases were discontinued; some remained in production, but were marked with the Royal Copenhagen mark. The Bing & Grøndahl name was used only on commemorative and annual pieces and a few overglaze-decorated figurines.

The initials *B & G* and a stylized castle have been a part of the mark since 1898. Many well-known sculptors designed Bing & Grøndahl figurines, and most added a name or initial to the mark.

Dahl-Jensen

Danish designer Jens Peter Dahl-Jensen (1874–1960) was employed at the Bing & Grøndahl works for twenty years. In 1925 he opened his own factory to make porcelain figurines. Before production stopped in 1981, his company produced almost four hundred figurines, about 280 sculpted by Dahl-Jensen. The company closed in 1984. Dahl-Jensen's figurines depicting Danish children and peasants were in the Danish style, but his blues were brighter and he used more colors than other potteries. He also produced a line of animals and exotic figurines of people from Siam (present-day Thailand), Indo-China (present-day Vietnam, Cambodia, and Laos), Spain, and Japan.

The porcelain Great Dane is 11 inches long. It was made by Dahl-Jensen in blue and gray tones even though a real dog would have had black and white fur.
(Photo: Skinner)

Gustavsberg

The twentieth-century ceramics made by the Gustavsberg factory in Sweden were in the art deco style. Best known is the 1930s *Argenta* ware, green or blue glazed stoneware with silver-inlay decorations. The company was founded in 1827 near Stockholm, Sweden. At first it made transfer-printed creamware in the English style and, by the 1860s, majolica. Bone china has been made from the 1860s to the present. Art director Wilhelm Kåge (active 1917–1949) designed many dinnerware patterns in the "functionalist" style. In the 1930s he created *Farsta*, a rust-colored ware that was formed into thick-walled pieces, then glazed in colors that ran over the body and into indentations. In the 1950s, Gustavsberg made heavy textured pottery in unusual modern shapes and also dinnerware and serving pieces decorated with solid glaze or, very often, stripes or leaf-shaped designs. By the 1970s the vases were simple shapes covered in unusual glazes. The company also made plumbing fixtures and pipes and many plastic objects. Bought by Villeroy & Boch AG in 2000, it continues to make sanitary ware, tile, and chinaware.

Gustafsberg

The stylized blue leaves and flowers on this 7-inch vase have been carved, then glazed. It is marked with an anchor and the words Gustavsberg, 1925.

Rörstrand

Rörstrand, Europe's second-oldest ceramics firm, was established in Stockholm in 1726. Rörstrand first manufactured only earthenware, but in 1857 it began producing porcelain. In the early twentieth century, Rörstrand was known for the art nouveau porcelain designed by Alf Wallander, who was artistic director there for

Rörstrand

The mottled brown matte glaze and the scooped bowl shape were used at Rörstrand in about 1955. This dish is 7½ inches long and is marked with the artist's initials, SAH.
(Photo: Treadway)

periods during the years 1895 to 1914. After Rörstrand moved to Gothenburg in 1926, it stopped making porcelain and made only earthenware for the next ten years. Porcelain production resumed in 1936. Gunnar Nylund, artistic director from 1931 to 1958, created streamlined ceramics with an art deco influence in the 1930s. Sleek stoneware in organic shapes was produced in the 1940s and '50s. Dinner services were made from rustic stoneware from 1964 to 1981. Today Rörstrand produces porcelain, earthenware, and stoneware dinnerware. Rörstrand went through several ownership changes before it was acquired by the Finnish Hackman Group in 1990.

Royal Copenhagen

Danish porcelain has been popular since 1775, when the Royal Copenhagen Porcelain Works was founded. The earliest Royal Copenhagen pieces were glazed in cobalt blue. *Blue Flower* (1780), one of the first patterns, is still being made, and like most of the dishes made today by Royal Copenhagen, it is still painted by hand. The company made many figurines and dinnerwares in the nineteenth century. One pattern, *Flora Danica*, introduced in 1790, is still among the more expensive dinnerwares made today. It is decorated with dozens of hand-formed three-dimensional flower blossoms, as well as gilding and painted flowers. In 1885 Arnold Krog became art director of the company, and his underglaze decorations in Japanese- and French-inspired designs were introduced.

Royal Copenhagen made ceramics in many styles. Johannes Hedegaard worked from 1948 to 1966. He designed partially glazed figures made of terra-cotta. This limited-edition girl's head is 13 inches high. It is marked with his signature and the company mark.

By 1900 the Royal Copenhagen factory was producing faience, stoneware, porcelain figures, and many dinner sets and table decorations. Some large fantasy figurines with great detail and elaborate decoration, like *The Princess on the Pea* by Gerhard Henning (1911) and the *National Costume* figures by Carl Martin-Hansen (1906) are still in production. Others, such as *Fairytale* and *Ali and Peribanu*, are available by special order. Figures by Arno Malinowski continued to be made into the 1980s. The 1920s saw stoneware in modern shapes with dark-colored glazes. Most were taken out of production over time, but the stoneware figurines of bears were manufactured until 2005. The 1950s brought a new line of terra-cotta figures.

Royal Copenhagen bought Georg Jensen Silversmiths in 1972, then merged with the Holmegaard Glassworks in 1985 to form Royal Copenhagen A/S. The company then merged with Bing & Grøndahl (1987) and two Swedish glassworks, Orrefors and Kosta Boda (1997), to become Royal Scandinavia. The porcelain is still sold under the name Royal Copenhagen.

JAPANESE POTTERY AND PORCELAIN

Japanese ceramics have been admired for centuries, but in the early 1900s almost all ceramics imported in quantity from Japan were inexpensive, poor-quality pieces made for dime stores and department stores. In the United States before 1950, the name *Japan* on the bottom of a piece came to mean kitsch or poor taste, and

Phoenix, Willow, and Geisha

Three Asian patterns have remained popular for a hundred years or more and have been made in many countries. *Phoenix Bird* or *Flying Phoenix* chinaware shows the blue phoenix on an intricate lacelike background. It was most popular from 1900 to 1945 and was sold in dime stores. *Willow* or *Blue Willow* pattern, made since 1780, pictures a Chinese landscape, pagoda, bridge, weeping willow, and birds. *Geisha Girl*, a colorful porcelain showing geishas in a traditional Japanese setting, was introduced at the end of the nineteenth century.

The Phoenix bird *has been used to decorate Asian porcelains for over one hundred years. (Detail shown)*

Blue Willow *dishes have been made since 1780, but the design has changed slightly. (Detail shown)*

Geisha *girls have been handpainted on porcelains since the 1890s. (Detail shown)*

Googly-eyed dolls were popular, and the googly eyes were used on some inexpensive Japanese dime-store ceramics in the 1930s and '40s. This salt and pepper set looks like a pair of dolls' heads.

Marks on Ceramics from Japan

In 1890 the United States passed a law requiring the country of origin be written on all imports to the United States. *Nippon*, Japanese for *Japan*, was added to pieces beginning in 1891. In 1921 the United States required the English word *Japan;* the words *Made in Japan* were often used.

When World War II ended, the Allied occupying force was in Japan. The words *Occupied Japan* or *Made in Occupied Japan* were required on pottery, porcelain, and other exports. Those words were used between 1945 and 1952. Often the mark was on a removable paper label.

The Occupied Japan *mark was used on many types of porcelain. Most were figurines, planters like this one, salt and pepper shakers, reamers, cookie jars, wall decorations, and other china that was small, easy to ship, and could be sold as a single object, not a dinner set.* (Photo: Mark's Treasure Chest)

good dinnerware and fancy vases were shunned if made in Japan.

But tastes change, and a few types of inexpensive Japanese pottery and porcelain have attracted today's collectors. About 1920, rainbow luster tea sets and other dishes were sold in the United States. Mud figures—partially glazed figurines of people, some holding fishing poles—were made to be used in fish bowls and planters. Children's and doll's tea sets were manufactured in patterns that copied adult-size English and American examples. Blue and white dinnerwares, including those in the traditional *Willow* or *Phoenix Bird* patterns, were also made.

Imports from Japan stopped during World War II. After the war ended in 1945 and Japan was occupied by Allied forces (until 1952), ceramics of poor quality were made in Occupied Japan. Many were inexpensive novelties for dime stores. They copied almost every marketable design. Some pieces were copies of European ceramic favorites. Fake "Hummel" figures and fake "Wedgwood" pottery can be found. Figurines of people or animals, ashtrays, salt and pepper shakers, teacups, toby mugs, teapots, candlesticks, plates, planters, and fish-bowl ornaments were sold by the millions. Speed and cost-cutting kept on affecting the quality of Japanese ceramics after the 1940s. Hand-painting continued, but designs were less complex. Decals were used, many with hand-painted accents. In the 1950s, Japanese factories, constructed when the

Allies helped rebuild the country, gradually began to make better ceramics, especially dinnerware, and the name *Japan* stopped meaning poor quality. By the end of the 1960s, *Made in Japan* was again accepted as a mark of excellence in the United States. Asian countries gradually overtook the American ceramic industry, and today most dinner sets are imported, not made in the USA.

In the 1950s, the craft potters of Japan created many useful pieces in a new innovative style. Unusual glazes, decorations made of slices of clay, angular pots with cut-out appliqués of clay, and burnished, unglazed wares were made. Free-form bowls and unusual flower vases were among the most creative. These ceramics were popular in Japan, but were not exported.

Throughout the twentieth century, two important names in Japanese ceramics have been *Satsuma*, a place, and *Noritake*, a company.

Satsuma

The crackle-glazed, cream-colored pottery with color decoration made in Satsuma, Japan, since the 1600s remained popular into the twentieth century. Over the centuries, the brocadelike, detailed pictures of people and landscapes continued to be used; but the figures became larger and less detailed, the colors were darker, and black became a favored color. From 1918 to 1930, some Satsuma decorators used art nouveau and art deco designs. Irises were a popular art nouveau motif used on buttons, buckles, and vases. Many pieces had raised decorations of thick glaze. During and after

Panels showing landscapes and birds, bands of flowers, brocade designs, and the colors used on this bowl are typical of decorations used on Satsuma pottery. The general rule is the smaller and more detailed the decorations, the older and more valuable the piece. (Photo: Sotheby's)

This Noritake perfume bottle with luster decoration is marked with the light green cherry blossom mark. The art deco look, the colors, and the mark all say it was made in the 1920s.
(Photo: Waiapo)

World War I until about 1928, when German and French blanks were unavailable, blanks from Satsuma were imported into the United States. These undecorated ceramics were hand-painted by women in china-painting clubs, and this pottery is called *American Satsuma*. These pieces have decorations that look more European or American than Asian. Crackled pottery is still being made in the Satsuma style in Japanese potteries near Kyoto and in the area called Satsuma.

Noritake

Today's Noritake Company, originally named Nippon Toki Kaisha Ltd., was started in 1904 by the Morimura Brothers, who in 1876 had founded a company that exported Japanese products. They wanted to make porcelain dinnerware in designs and sizes that would appeal to the American market. Dishes made in Japan at the time were not the standard sizes or shapes used for an American meal because Japanese food required different types of dishes.

The company made porcelain dinnerware and giftware it called *fancyware*. In 1914 the first porcelain dinnerware sets, white dishes with a cream border and a spray of flowers, were exported to the United States. The dishes were marked with a wreath and the letter *M. Nippon* was part of the mark until the law changed in 1921, then *Japan* was used.

The 1920s giftware designs were colorful, bold, art deco patterns. Lusterware with a rainbow iridescence was also made and remained popular until the mid-1930s. But the dinnerware of the 1920s and 1930s had conventional patterns similar to those made in England. By the early 1920s, the company was marketing its china under the name Noritake. From 1922 to the 1930s, a major customer for Noritake dinnerware was the Larkin Soap Company. The dishes were given away with boxes of soap. Noritake made at least eight different dinnerware patterns for Larkin, including *Tree in the Meadow* (1927–1932) and *Azalea* (c.1918–1941), Noritake's most popular pattern.

RAISED DECORATIONS

About 1900 *moriage* became a popular decoration on Japanese ceramics. A white clay mixed to the consistency of toothpaste was trailed on the body of a piece to form a raised decoration. Then other colors could be added. Another form of decoration was coralene beading. Dots of enamel color were added over and over again until a raised bead could be seen. Underglaze and overglaze decoration was also used. Gold was popular.

Collectors call the raised white trim on this vase Moriage. *(Photo: Jackson's)*

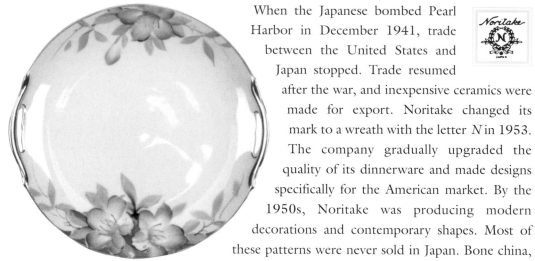

When the Japanese bombed Pearl Harbor in December 1941, trade between the United States and Japan stopped. Trade resumed after the war, and inexpensive ceramics were made for export. Noritake changed its mark to a wreath with the letter *N* in 1953. The company gradually upgraded the quality of its dinnerware and made designs specifically for the American market. By the 1950s, Noritake was producing modern decorations and contemporary shapes. Most of these patterns were never sold in Japan. Bone china, made for a short time in the 1930s, was introduced again in 1967. Stoneware dishes in designs that were popular in the United States were featured in the 1970s. Noritake made quality ceramics at a low price, and by the end of the twentieth century it was one of the world's largest manufacturers of china and had production facilities in many parts of the world.

Collectors pay high prices for the Noritake giftware that was most difficult to make and has the best designs and workmanship. They look for blown-out (relief-molded) pieces from the 1930s and after. Part of the design—perhaps an animal or a child's head—is raised on the molded plate, then hand-decorated. Wall plaques decorated with scenes that look like fine paintings with overglaze gold trim added, and tall decorative vases and urns are among the most sought-after pieces, some selling for thousands of dollars today.

Azalea, the dinnerware decorated with pink azaleas and green leaves, was a popular pattern for twenty-five years. It was a premium made exclusively for the Larkin Soap Company from 1918 to 1941. This cake plate has gold-colored handles.

Place Names in Marks on Ceramics from Europe and Asia

Wars, elections, and laws can change the country name used on dishes. If you have tableware or any item marked with a country name, these are the earliest years or the span of years the name was used on ceramics. Sometimes the mark was written with symbols or letters used by the country that made the tableware, but by 1900 English words were required for dishes imported into the United States. Sometimes the English mark was on a paper label.

China
China: c.1900–present
Republic of China: 1912–1949
People's Republic of China: 1949–present
Hong Kong: 1842–1997 (reverted to People's Republic of China in 1997)

Czechoslovakia
Czechoslovakia: 1918–1993
Republic of Czechoslovakia: 1948–1993
Slovakia and the Czech Republic: 1993–present

Germany
Germany: 1885–1949; after October 3, 1990–present
Four occupied zones (U.S., British, French, Soviet), e.g., U.S. Zone, U.S. Zone Germany: 1945–1949
Federal Republic of Germany (West Germany): 1949–1990
German Democratic Republic (East Germany): 1949–1990

The Friar Tuck pitcher was made by Goebel and has the West Germany mark. (Photo: Antiques At Time Was)

Japan
Nippon: 1891–1921 (the Japanese name for Japan)
Japan or Made in Japan: 1921–1945; 1952–present
Made in Occupied Japan: 1945–1952

Russia
USSR: 1919–1991 (Union of Soviet Socialist Republics, Soviet Union)
Made in the USSR: 1925–1991
Russia, Estonia, Latvia, Lithuania, Belarus, Ukraine, Moldova, and Georgia: after August 25, 1991

Sri Lanka: 1972–present (previously called Ceylon)

Taiwan: 1949–present (separated from China in 1949; also known as Formosa)

Thailand: 1942–present (previously called Siam)

Yugoslavia: 1929–1991
Croatia, Macedonia, and Slovenia: 1991–present
Bosnia and Herzegovina: 1992–present
Federal Republic of Yugoslavia (Serbia and Montenegro): 1992–2003
Serbia-Montenegro: 2003–present

Early twentieth-century French glass is very ornate. This 13¾-inch Daum cameo glass vase is made of layers of mottled colored glass that have been cut away to resemble a grapevine. It even has applied glass snails and grapes. (Photo: James Julia)

Chapter 6

GLASS

⁓ WHILE THE NINETEENTH CENTURY was an age of mechanization in the glass industry, the twentieth century was an age of international influences. Glass tableware and decorative accessories—luxury items in the early 1800s—were common in the American home in the early 1900s. Pressed glass tableware, like tumblers and serving pieces, were usually American-made. More expensive fancy handmade glass vases and stemware were often imported from Europe.

EARLY TWENTIETH-CENTURY GLASS, 1900–1924

Art Glass

Although American glass companies continued to make handmade art glass at the beginning of the twentieth century, public taste shifted from American shaded glassware, like Peachblow or Amberina, to fancier European products like cameo and iridescent glass. New colors, finishes, shapes, and decorations reflected the new styles and subjects favored by artists and designers. Most of the same French and Bohemian companies that produced art nouveau glass in the 1910s went on to art deco designs in the 1920s and early 1930s.

Art glass makers kept up with the popular styles. Many cameo glass companies made art deco–style accessories in the 1920s and '30s. This 8-inch geometric vase was made by Muller Frères in Lunéville, France.
(Photo: James Julia)

Everything Old Is New Again

Early twentieth-century designers and manufacturers revived some ancient Egyptian and Roman glassmaking techniques.

Cameo cutting creates a design on multilayered glass by removing part of the top layer. The process was used by the ancient Egyptians and Romans and by the Chinese in the eighteenth century.

Legras cameo vase (Photo: James Julia)

Cire perdue, literally *lost wax*, is a way to mold glass. A wax model is made in the desired shape and size. It is encased in plaster to form a mold with an opening at the top. The mold is heated so the wax melts and runs out. The mold is filled with molten glass or glass paste to create the finished piece.

Lalique Frise Enfants *(Dancing Children) cire perdue vase* (Photo: Sotheby's)

Iridescence forms on glass when it is buried in soil. Roman glass unearthed by archaeologists inspired nineteenth-century glassmakers to re-create the chemical reaction that gives the iridescent sheen.

Kew-Blas iridescent pitcher (Photo: Skinner)

Chipped ice or **hammered** glass literally has a chipped appearance. The allover finish is created by applying glue to the exterior of a finished piece, then firing it to make the glue crack. As pieces of the hardened glue pop off, divots are left on the surface.

Chipped ice surface (Photo: Myers Fine Art)

Frosted glass imitates the weathering of ancient glass. The matte surface is created by acid treatment or sandblasting. Colorless glass appears gray when frosted.

Enameled designs on glass were used by the twelfth century. Powdered glass mixed with oil was "painted" on the glass, then fired. Art nouveau designs often imitated multicolored, gold-enameled scroll tracery found on Islamic rosewater bottles.

Moser enameled vase (Photo: James Julia)

Pâte-de-verre, literally *glass paste*, was first used by the Egyptians about three-thousand six hundred years ago. Crushed glass is mixed with an adhesive and pressed into a mold.

Daum pâte-de-verre dish (Photo: Skinner)

Tiffany

Louis Comfort Tiffany (1848–1933) trained as a painter in the 1860s and operated his own decorating studio, Louis C. Tiffany & Associated Artists, in the 1880s. In 1885 he established the Tiffany Glass Company, where he made his famous stained glass windows. Tiffany's name has become synonymous with iridescent glassware and leaded glass lampshades and windows.

Tiffany's iridescent glass was made with a special formula developed by Arthur J. Nash that Tiffany later called *Favrile* (from an Old English word meaning *handmade*). In 1892 Louis Tiffany's increased interest in glassmaking led to the founding of Tiffany Glass & Decorating Company, renamed Tiffany Studios in 1902.

Tiffany's glass was made at Tiffany Furnaces in Corona (Queens), New York. Glassworkers shaped the iridescent glass according to Tiffany's specifications into organic forms, often with irregular surfaces, bumps, and swirled tendrils. Many other Tiffany glass styles, such as agate, millefiori, paperweight, and Cypriote, were developed during the following years.

In 1920 Tiffany Furnaces became Louis C. Tiffany Furnaces, but by 1924 he had dissolved his company and sold the factory to Arthur Nash's son, A. Douglas Nash. Nash's company produced similar wares, including *Gold Lustre*, which was usually shaped with ribs or lattice molding. A. Douglas Nash Corporation closed in 1931.

Steuben Glassworks

The Steuben Glassworks was founded in Corning, New York, in 1903 by Frederick Carder (1863–1963) and Thomas Hawkes (1846–1913). The company's glassware included *Cluthra*, *Cintra*,

Tiffany's Favrile *glassware is prized. This 10¼-inch vase is made of iridescent gold glass in the jack-in-the-pulpit shape named for the flower.*
(Photo: James Julia)

Confusing Cameo

Cameo glass often has a signature that is cameo-carved. Some, like *Gallé, Daum*, and *Legras,* clearly indicate the company that made the glass. Other marks are trade names of companies that marketed the glass.

This cameo vase is signed Charder, *a trade name used by glassmaker Charles Schneider. It is a combination of his first* (Char) *and last* (der) *names.* (Photo: Heritage Galleries)

Mark	Company (Country)	Dates used
Charder	Charles Schneider (France)	1926–1933
D'Aurys	Wilhelm Kralik Söhn (Bohemia)	After 1918
D'Argental	Saint-Louis (France)	1919–1925
De Vez	Cristallerie de Pantin (France)	After 1907
Degué	Cristalleries de Compiègne (France)	1926–1939
Kew-Blas	Union Glass Co. (United States)	1890s–1924
Le Verre Français	Charles Schneider (France)	1928–1933
Lunéville	Muller Frères (France)	After 1919
Mont Joye	Legras & Cie. (France)	c.1900–1930s
Richard	Loetz (Bohemia)	After 1918
Soleil	Wilhelm Kralik Söhn (Bohemia)	After 1918
Veles or Velez	Loetz (Bohemia)	1920s

(For more information about these companies, see the chart on pages 164–169.)

Steuben Glassworks decorated layered glass items with acid-etched patterns in the 1920s and '30s. Most of the Asian-inspired designs were used with solid colors, like this jade-green-over-alabaster Matzu *vase.* (Photo: Heritage Galleries)

Verre de Soie, and other styles handmade in a variety of colors. Steuben's *Aurene*, a velvety iridescent glass, remains the most popular of its early products. Aurene was often combined with *Calcite* (white) or *Ivrene* (ivory) opaque glass and hand-tooled to make swirled and feathered designs.

In 1918 Steuben became part of the Corning Glass Works. By 1933 Steuben had reorganized and was producing mostly colorless crystal. Prominent artists and designers, like Sidney Waugh, Donald Pollard, and James Houston, designed decorative glass accessories, figurines, and sculptures. Pollard's floral bowls and vases and many of Houston's animals are still in production. Steuben's crystal is made with light refractive optical glass, giving it extra sparkle.

Daum Frères & Cie.

Jean Daum (1825–1885) founded a glassworks in Nancy, France, in 1878. Early wares were cut and enameled, often with heraldic crests. In 1885 Daum's sons Auguste (1853–1909) and Antonin

(1864–1930) established an art department and introduced Daum's famous art nouveau pâte-de-verre and cameo glass. Vases, bowls, and stemware were decorated with flowers, landscapes, and other natural subjects. In 1900 Daum joined with other important designers of the era, including Émile Gallé and Louis Majorelle, to found the École de Nancy, a cooperative effort of Nancy's arts industries. Daum began making free-form clear glass in the 1950s and reintroduced pâte-de-verre in 1966, using contemporary designs. Daum still makes handmade art glass.

Émile Gallé & Cie.

Designer Émile Gallé (1846–1904) made art nouveau glass, ceramics, and furniture in Nancy, France. He started working with glass in 1867 at his father's company in Lorraine, France, creating enameled designs on clear glass. In 1873 Gallé set up his own studio, where he made art glassware, including lamps, vases, and tableware. He developed his own designs for multilayered glass, many with cameo-cutting and enameling. Gallé also developed a marquetry process that involved embedding pieces of colored glass in the body of a piece to create a design. Designs often featured trees, animals, and insects. A Japanese influence is apparent in his work. The company was managed by Gallé's widow after his death in 1904. The factory closed at the outbreak of World War I (1914–1918) and was reopened by Gallé's son-in-law Paul Perdrizet after the war. It closed in 1931. Pieces made after Gallé's death were marked with a star alongside his name.

Left, above: Daum's cameo glass items often have enameled details. The trees and rain on this 7-inch-wide pillow vase are added enameled details. (Photo: James Julia)

Left: Émile Gallé made this marquetry vase for the 1900 Exposition Universelle. Pieces of pink and green glass were added to a white base while the glass was still molten, and then the vase was blown and tooled into shape. (Photo: Sotheby's)

The Danaides of Greek mythology encircle this 7¼-inch Lalique vase. The design was first produced in 1926 in colorless, opalescent, and patinated (or stained) glass. This version has a blue patina. (Photo: James Julia)

Lalique S. A.

René Lalique (1860–1945) was a designer of jewelry, silver, glass, and other decorative arts in Paris. He opened a glass workshop in Clairefontaine, France, in 1898. Using the cire perdue method (see page 156), he made figurines and vases. About 1907 he started making and designing commercial perfume bottles for Coty and other manufacturers.

Lalique made all types of glassware, including tableware and lamps, most of colorless glass with a frosted finish. His best-known pieces have classical figures as part of the decorations. Other glassworks have copied and even forged his designs, often using his mark, *R. Lalique*. After Lalique's death in 1945, the firm continued to produce his designs but changed the mark from *R Lalique* to *Lalique*.

Ludwig Moser & Söhne, Glasfabrik Johann Loetz-Witwe, and Other Bohemian Glassmakers

Glass by Bohemian makers became popular in the United States beginning in the 1890s. Bohemia spreads across several political boundaries that changed several times from the late nineteenth through the late twentieth century. Today the region spans Germany, Hungary, and the Czech Republic. Moser and Loetz are probably the best-known Bohemian glassmakers.

Ludwig Moser (1833–1916; not to be confused with the designer Koloman Moser) was a glass engraver in Karlsbad, Bohemia (now in the Czech Republic). He founded his own company about 1857. The glassworks made an assortment of cut, engraved, colored, and enameled glass and, like other Bohemian companies, worked with many contemporary artists and designers. The company is still working.

Glassmaker Ludwig Moser was an innovator, creating new techniques and styles. This 8½-inch vase has a padded flower. Two layers, one pink and one green, were applied to the vase and then carefully carved to make a flower. (Photo: James Julia)

Wiener Werkstätte Glass

Several prominent Wiener Werkstätte artists involved with the Austrian Arts and Crafts movement created glass designs for Bohemian companies. The items exhibited the same simple, straightforward designs seen in the movement's pottery, furniture, and textiles.

Wiener Werkstätte artist Otto Prutscher designed this 8¼-inch wine glass for glassmaker Meyr's Neffe about 1907. It was sold in a Vienna shop. (Photo: Sotheby's)

The original Loetz factory was started in Klostermühle, Bohemia (now in the Czech Republic), by Johann Loetz about 1840. After his death in 1848, it was first operated by his widow under the name Glasfabrik Johann Loetz-Witwe (the Widow Johann Loetz Glassworks), which it kept until it closed about 1948. The company changed hands several times before the owner's grandson, Max Ritter von Spaun, took over and the glassworks began making art glass in 1879. Loetz's earliest wares were made of marbled opaque glass that resembled real stones such as agate, aventurine, carnelian, chalcedony, jasper, and onyx. In 1894 the company developed an iridescent gold glass similar to Tiffany's.

Loetz gave evocative names to its designs, such as *Federzeichnung* (Octopus), *Orpheus*, and *Papillon* (Butterfly). The company also made art deco enameled glass in the 1920s and '30s. Its art deco cameo glass was often marked with the name *Richard*. Loetz was one of the largest exporters of glass to the United States in the early 1900s. The company struggled off and on through both world wars, and closed about 1948.

Other Bohemian glassmakers exported their wares extensively to the United States, too. Harrach, J. & L. Lobmeyr, Meyr's Neffe(n), Pallme-Koenig, and Wilhelm Kralik & Söhn among others, made iridescent, cameo, and cut glass.

Loetz glass often mimics nature. The gold iridescent seashells on this 1909 vase look like they're floating on water. The effect is created with a blue oil-spot finish on textured green glass.
(Photo: Jackson's)

Major Makers of Art Glass

This table lists the maker or factory, location, date, and other information about glassmakers of the twentieth century. Parentheses enclose the birth and death dates of the artist. Other dates given are approximate working dates of the factory or artist.

Burgun, Schverer cameo glass vase
(Photo: Heritage Galleries)

Maker, Designer, or Artist and Location	Dates and Related Information
AUSTRIA	
Koloman Moser Vienna	(1868–1918) Designed glass for Loetz, Bakalowits, and Meyr's Neffe.
Dagobert Peche Vienna	(1887–1923) Designed glass for Loetz and Lobmeyr.
Michael Powolny Vienna	(1871–1954) Designed glass for Loetz and J. & L. Lobmeyr 1914–1918.
Otto Prutscher Vienna	(1880–1949) Designed glass for Bakalowits, Meyr's Neffe, Loetz, and J. & L. Lobmeyr, c. 1905.
BELGIUM	
Cristalleries de Val St. Lambert Val St. Lambert	1825–present
BOHEMIA	
E. Bakalowits & Söhne Vienna	1845–present
J. & L. Lobmeyr Vienna	1855–present
Glasfabrik Johann Loetz **Witwe (Loetz)** Klostermühle (now Klášterský Mlýn, Czech Republic)	c.1852–c.1948
J. Meyr's Neffen	1841–1862
Meyr's Neffe Winterberg (now Vimperk, Czech Republic)	1862–1922 Merged with Moser.

Maker, Designer, or Artist and Location	Dates and Related Information
Ludwig Moser & Söhne Karlsbad (now Karlovy Vary, Czech Republic)	c.1857–present
Pallme-Koenig Co. Steinschönau (now Kamenickey Senov, Czech Republic)	1786–1939
Wilhelm Kralik & Söhn Eleonorenhain (now Lenora, Czech Republic)	1877–c.1945
Riedel Polaun (now Desná, Czech Republic); Kufstein, Austria	1856–present

ENGLAND

Gray-Stan Graydon Studios London	c.1926–1936
Liberty & Co. London	1875–present
Nazeing London, Broxbourne	1928–present
Stevens & Williams **Royal Brierley Crystal** **Epsom Glass Industries** Stourbridge	1847–1931 1931–1998 1998–present
Thomas Webb & Sons Stourbridge	1837–1991
Webb Corbett Wordsley	1897–1986 Acquired by Royal Doulton in 1969; name no longer used after 1986.
Whitefriars (James Powell & Sons) Whitefriars, London	1834–1980

FRANCE

Jacques Adnet Paris	(1900–1984) Worked with Almaric Walter, c.1935.

Maker, Designer, or Artist and Location	Dates and Related Information
Appert Frères Clichy	Late 1800s–c.1910
(Joseph-)Gabriel Argy-Rousseau **Les Pâtes de Verre d'Argy-Rousseau** Paris	(1885–1953) 1921–1931, 1952
Cristalleries de Baccarat Baccarat	1764–present
Burgun, Schverer & Cie. **Verreries de Meisenthal** Alsace-Lorraine	1711–1969
Cristalleries de Compiègne Compiègne	1926–1939
Henri Cros Sèvres	(1840–1907) Worked with (Joseph-)Gabriel Argy-Rousseau.
Albert Dammouse Sèvres	(1848–1926) c.1892–1913
Daum Frères & Cie. **Cristallerie Daum** Nancy	1878–present Name change in 1962.
Émile Décorchemont Conches	(1880–1971)
André Delatte Nancy	(1887–1953)
Georges Despret Jeumont	(1862–1952)
Émile Gallé **Émile Gallé & Cie.** (father's company) **Cristallerie d'Émile Gallé** Nancy	(1846–1904) 1867 1873–1931 Glass made by Burgun, Schverer & Cie. until 1894.
Marcel Goupy Paris	(1886–1954) Designed glass for St. Louis.
René Lalique **Lalique S. A.** Paris	(1860–1945) 1898–present Glass made by Legras & Cie. until 1909.

Maker, Designer, or Artist and Location	Dates and Related Information
Legras & Cie. St. Denis	1864–1920 Merged with Pantin.
Jean Luce Paris	(1895–1964) Glass blanks made by Baccarat and St. Louis.
Louis Majorelle Nancy	(1859–1926) Worked with Daum Frères & Cie., c.1905.
Maurice Marinot Troyes	(1882–1960) 1912–1937
Monot (See Cristallerie de Pantin.)	
Muller Frères **Grandes Verreries de Croismares et** **Verreries d'Art Muller Frères Rèunies** Lunéville	1895–1918 1919–1933
Cristallerie de Pantin **Monot & Stumpf** **Monot Père et Fils & Stumpf** La Villette, Pantin	1851–present
Marius-Ernest Sabino Paris	(1878–1961) 1925–1937 1960–present Molds owned by United States firm since 1978.
Compagnie des Cristalleries **de Saint-Louis (St. Louis)** Münzthal	1767–present
Charles Schneider **Schneider Frères et Wolf** **Schneider, S.A. des Verreries** Épinay-sur-Seine, Lorris	(1881–1953) 1913–1937 1946–1981
Verreries de Vallerysthal **Klinglin et Cie.** Vallerysthal	1836–1854 1854–present
Verlys of France (S.A. **Holophane Les Andelys)** Rouen	1925–c.1951 Made by A. H. Heisey & Co., 1955; by Fenton Art Glass, 1966–present.

Maker, Designer, or Artist and Location	Dates and Related Information
Almaric Walter Nancy	(1870–1959) 1895–c.1936 Designed pâte-de-verre for Daum, 1908–1914.
GERMANY	
Theresienthaler Krystallglasfabrik Zweisel	1836–present
WMF (Württembergische Metallwarenfabrik) Stuttgart	1883–1984
SCOTLAND	
John Moncrieff Ltd. **North British Glass Works** Perth	(1834–1899) 1868–1996
SWEDEN	
Kosta Glasbruk Småland	1742–present
Orrefors Glasbruk Småland	1898–present
UNITED STATES	
Frederick Carder Corning, New York	(1863–1963) Steuben Glassworks
Corning Glass Works (See Steuben Glassworks)	
Victor Durand **Durand Art Glass Shop** **Vineland Glass Manufacturing Company** Vineland, New Jersey	(1870–1931) 1924–1932 Bought by Kimble Glass Company.
Fenton Art Glass Company Martins Ferry, Ohio; Williamstown, West Virginia	1905–present

Maker, Designer, or Artist and Location	Dates and Related Information
Fostoria Glass Company Fostoria, Ohio; Moundsville, West Virginia	1887–1986
Handel and Company Meriden, Connecticut New York City	1885–1893 1893–1936
Honesdale Decorating Company Honesdale, Pennsylvania	1901–1932
Imperial Glass Company Bellaire, Ohio	1904–1984
Lustre Art Glass Company Maspeth, Long Island, New York	1920–c.1925
Arthur J. Nash Corona, Queens, New York	(1849–1934) Tiffany Glass & Decorating Company
A. Douglas Nash A. Douglas Nash Associates/Corporation Corona, Queens, New York	(1885–1940) c.1928–1931
Quezal Art Glass & Decorating Company Brooklyn, New York	1901–1925
Steuben Glassworks **Corning Glass Works** Corning, New York	1903–1918 1918–present
Louis C. Tiffany **Tiffany Glass & Decorating Company** Corona, New York	(1848–1933) 1892–1924
Union Glass Co. Somerville, Massachusetts	1854–1924
Vineland Glass Manufacturing Co. **Kimble Glass Company** Vineland, New Jersey	1897–1931 1931–present

United States Glass Company

American glass factories were closing at an alarming rate at the end of the nineteenth century. In 1891 fifteen Ohio, Pennsylvania, and West Virginia glass factories consolidated as the United States Glass Company to improve marketing efforts and, by sharing, to reduce the expense of fuel and glass molds. Three more companies joined U.S. Glass Company in 1892, and by 1894 two new factories had been built by the company.

Each factory was assigned a letter for identification, and orders were handled through a central office in Pittsburgh. Some of the company's best-selling pressed glass patterns were named after states and produced in colored or flashed glass or decorated with ruby or amber stain.

Although many of its factories closed by 1900, U.S. Glass Company continued production until 1963, when its last factory, in Tiffin, Ohio, closed.

The Michigan *pattern was introduced in 1902. This water set is colored with a light pink stain called* Maiden's Blush. *It is decorated with gold enameling.* (Photo: Green Valley)

Opaline Brocade, *also known as* Spanish Lace, *is a blown opalescent pattern that was made from 1899 to 1908. This cranberry opalescent syrup jug was made by National Glass Company. Northwood and Dugan also made the pattern.* (Photo: Green Valley)

Pressed Glass

Because of financial and labor woes in the 1890s, American pressed glass factories suffered hard times. Few new patterns were introduced, and fewer items from existing lines were offered. Elaborate imported glass from Europe influenced tastes, and public interest turned from mass-produced glass tableware to handmade decorative accessories and novelties. American pressed glass manufacturers tried to compete by producing colored pattern glass. Pieces were still made using molds, but they were embellished with gold trim, colored stains, or enameled flowers.

Opalescent Glass

Beginning about 1884, Hobbs, Brockunier, & Company (1863–1888); Northwood Glass Company (1888–1924); Jefferson Glass Company (1900–1930s); and other companies made colored glassware with bluish white patterns and edges. The factories used the

term *opalescent* to describe the glass because of its similarity to the opal gemstone.

There are two molding processes used to make opalescent patterns. The first uses two layers of glass—a colored glass base and an outer layer of glass with an added heat-reactive chemical. The piece is blown into a mold impressed with an allover pattern, then cooled quickly and reheated. The heat-reactive layer ends up as raised areas that become bluish white and stand out against the colored background. The second, less complicated, process uses hinged pressed glass molds. The reactive chemical is added directly to the colored glass. After molding, the pressed glass piece is

Northwood introduced the pressed glass pattern Paneled Holly *around 1905. This is a blue opalescent spooner.* (Photo: Green Valley)

reheated, making the embossed areas change color. Both methods make decorated glassware without extra handwork.

Many pressed glass patterns made in clear and colored glass or with iridescent finishes can also be found with an opalescent finish. Companies also made opalescent pressed glass novelties, like toothpick holders or footed jelly dishes.

Northwood, Jefferson, and Hobbs made opalescent wares until about 1904. From about 1910 to 1920, Fenton Art Glass Company offered some opalescent water sets. In 1939 Fenton introduced its first major opalescent lines, *Swirl*, *Coin Dot*, and *Rib Optic*, in blue, topaz, cranberry, and clear opalescent. Fenton's opalescent *Hobnail* pattern came out in 1940 and is still made today.

Carnival Glass

The popularity of iridescent wares by Tiffany, Steuben, and Loetz were the envy of the pressed glass industry. Fenton Art Glass Company found a way to imitate handmade iridescent glass. Fenton's first line, introduced in 1907, was called *Venetian Art*. Collectors refer to the iridescent pressed glass of this era as *carnival glass*, mainly because the glass was often given away as prizes at carnivals.

Northwood's most popular and abundant carnival glass pattern is Grape and Cable. *When the item is completely covered with the iridescent finish, it is difficult to tell what the base color is. This water set is green.* (Photo: Woody)

Carnival glass is made by adding an iridescent finish to molded glass. After the glass, usually colored, has been pressed in the mold, it is removed. Additional shaping is done by hand with a special tool, then the piece is sprayed with a coating of liquid metallic salts. Many carnival glass patterns were made in full sets to use at the table. Fenton's *Orange Tree* and Northwood's *Grape and Cable* include bowls, plates, and accessories in numerous sizes. Other patterns, like *Basket*, were for novelties made in only one shape. Carnival glass has been reproduced since the 1970s. Information on some companies that reissue and reproduce glass is found on page 185.

Major Carnival Glass Manufacturers

This table lists the maker or factory, location, dates of operation, and marks for manufacturers that made carnival glass. Parentheses enclose the dates the company made carnival glass. Most early carnival glass was unmarked. One later mark, if available, is used for each listing although the makers may have used a variety of marks.

Manufacturer and Location	Dates	Mark
Cambridge Glass Company Cambridge, Ohio	1901–1958 (1910s)	**NEAR CUT**
Dugan Glass Company, **Diamond Glass Company** Indiana, Pennsylvania	1904–1913 1913–1931 (1909–1931)	
Fenton Art Glass Company Williamstown, West Virginia	1905–present (1907–1930s, 1970–present)	
Imperial Glass Company Bellaire, Ohio	1901–present (1910–1930s, 1960s–1985)	
Millersburg Glass Company Millersburg, Ohio	1909–c.1913 (1909–c.1913)	Glass not marked
Northwood Glass Company Wheeling, West Virginia	1888–1924 (1908–1918)	
U.S. Glass Company Pittsburgh, Pennsylvania	1891–1963 (1910–1930s)	
Westmoreland Glass Company Grapeville, Pennsylvania	1889–1985 (1910–1930s)	

AMERICAN DEPRESSION-ERA GLASS, 1925–1944

The name *Depression glass* has become a catchall term that includes the originally inexpensive machine-made glassware produced during the Depression as well as some of the hand-pressed "elegant" patterns of the time and other American glassware made after World War II. Collectors refer to some other types of glass made as late as 1970 as Depression glass.

MACHINE-MADE GLASSWARE

Bottles were first made by machine a year or two after the 1903 invention of the Owens automatic bottle machine. But other glassware continued to be made by hand. The glass was shaped by a group of skilled union workers called a *shop*. One glassmaker gathered the glass from the furnace; another snipped it into the mold; another pressed the mold closed; and yet another lifted it from the mold. The factory also employed nonunion workers for tasks like carrying the molded pieces to the cooling furnace or decorating the surface of the wares. Needless to say, the more workers it took to make glassware, the more it cost to produce and the higher the price.

This Princess *pattern cup is decorated with embossed swags and flowers. Collectors call this* tank-etched *glass because the embossing imitates the acid-etched designs of more expensive wares.*

Tableware and accessories were first made by automatic machinery in the 1920s. Automated equipment controlled the tank of molten glass and moved the mold hinges and plunger that pressed the glass into shape. Conveyor belts carried pieces through the lehr (cooling furnace). The need for fewer workers and the use of poorer-quality glass, called soda or lime glass, reduced costs significantly. Collectors have also referred to the wares of this era as *dime-store* glass.

Decorations on machine-made, or *tank*, glass were usually shaped in the mold. Ribbing and allover patterns imitated the acid-etched and cut designs of handmade glassware and disguised the blurry quality of the soda glass.

Other Depression-Era Glass Manufacturers

This table lists the maker or factory, location, dates of operation, and marks for manufacturers that made Depression glass. One mark, if available, is used for each listing although the makers often used a variety of marks.

Hazel Atlas Chevron creamer in Ritz Blue

Hocking Windsor cup and saucer in pink

Manufacturer and Location	Dates	Mark
Akro Agate Company Akron, Ohio; Clarksburg, West Virginia	1911–1951	
Bartlett-Collins Sapulpa, Oklahoma	1914–present	
Belmont Tumbler Company Bellaire, Ohio	1915–1938	
Central Glass Works Wheeling, West Virginia	1863–1939	
Co-Operative Flint Glass Company Beaver Falls, Pennsylvania	1879–1937	
Dell Glass Company Millville, New Jersey	1930s	
Diamond Glassware Company Indiana, Pennsylvania	1913–1931	
Federal Glass Company Columbus, Ohio	1900–1980	
Hazel Atlas Glass Company/ **Hazel Ware (division of** **Continental Can Company)** Washington, Pennsylvania Zanesville, Ohio Clarksburg, West Virginia Wheeling, West Virginia	1902–1956 1956–1964	
Hocking Glass Company **Anchor Hocking Glass Corporation** **Anchor Hocking Corporation** Lancaster, Ohio	1905–present 1937–1969 1969–present	
Indiana Glass Company Dunkirk, Indiana	1907–2002	
Jeannette Glass Company Jeannette, Pennsylvania	1898–1983	
Jenkins Glass Company Kokomo and Arcadia, Indiana	1900–1932	

Manufacturer and Location	Dates	Mark
Lancaster Glass Company Lancaster, Ohio	1908–1937	
Libbey Glass Company Toledo, Ohio	1892–present Now a division of Owens-Illinois	
Liberty Works Egg Harbor, New Jersey	1903–c.1932	
Louie Glass Company Weston, West Virginia	1926–1995	
Macbeth-Evans Glass Company Indiana (several factories) Toledo, Ohio Charleroi, Pennsylvania Corning, New York	1899–1936 Acquired by Corning	
McKee Glass Company Jeannette, Pennsylvania	1850–1961; Acquired by Jeannette Glass Company	
Seneca Glass Company Fostoria, Ohio Morgantown, West Virginia	1891–1983	
L. E. Smith Glass Company Mt. Pleasant, Pennsylvania	1907–present	
U.S. Glass Company Pennsylvania (several factories) Tiffin, Ohio Gas City, Indiana Wheeling, West Virginia	1891–1963	
Viking Glass Company **Dalzell-Viking Glass Company** New Martinsville, West Virginia	1944–1987 1987–1998 Founded as New Martinsville Glass Company in 1900	
Westmoreland Glass Company Grapeville, Pennsylvania	1889–1985	

"Elegant" Hand-Pressed Glassware

Depression glass collectors use the term *elegant* to refer to American hand-pressed items made from about 1925 to 1955. Even though the glassware was produced in large quantities, the "elegant" factories used higher-quality raw materials and employed skilled glassmakers. Several companies, like Heisey and Fostoria, called their glassware *American crystal*, referring to the lead content in the formula.

Cambridge Glass Company

The Cambridge Glass Company was officially organized in Cambridge, Ohio, in 1901 by the owners of the National Glass Company. By 1907 the firm was bankrupt, but it continued in business after it was purchased by its manager, Arthur J. Bennet.

Cambridge made many types of glass stemware, tableware, and novelties. Early pressed pieces, often marked *Near Cut*, resembled cut glass. Popular Cambridge colors made during the 1920s and '30s, the company's most productive years, include Crown Tuscan (pink opaque), Amberina (shaded red amber), Carmen (ruby), Peach-Blo (pink), Moonlight Blue, Royal Blue, Ebony, and several shades of Emerald Green. Animal figurines, swan bowls,

The bases of these light emerald green Cambridge candlesticks are decorated with entwined flowers. The design is one of many etchings made by the company in the 1920s and '30s.

Akro-Agate

Chances are that you played with glass marbles made by the Akro-Agate Company, founded in 1911 in Akron, Ohio. At first the company distributed marbles made by other companies. In 1914 the firm moved to Clarksburg, West Virginia, where it began manufacturing

glass marbles. Marbles were the factory's only product until 1932, when ashtrays, figurines, bowls, garden pots, and other pieces were added to the line. The glass was an opaque marbleized mixture of two or more colors. After 1942 the factory produced children's toy glass tea sets and glassware. Akro-Agate went out of business in 1951, and its molds, trademark, and other assets were sold to the Master Glass Company of Clarksburg, West Virginia. All of the old molds are thought to have been destroyed.

Akro-Agate's tea sets for children are still popular with collectors. Like most of the sets, this Octagonal set came in a mixed assortment of opaque colored pieces.

RUBA ROMBIC: AMERICAN ART DECO

To collectors, the *Ruba Rombic* pattern, made in 1927 by Consolidated Lamp and Glass Company, is synonymous with art deco. Pieces look like jumbled rectangles joined together. The pattern was difficult to mold, limiting production. Today even a tumbler sells for hundreds of dollars.

Lavender 9½-inch Ruba Rombic *vase* (Photo: Sotheby's)

Duncan's swans were made in a variety of colors. This yellow opalescent swan was made from a Sylvan *fruit dish.* (Photo: Collectors of Crackle Glass)

figural flower holders, and stemware with "nude-lady" stems are among collectors' favorites. Stemware and dinnerware with *Portia*, *Apple Blossom*, and *Rose Point* deep-plate etchings were among the company's biggest sellers.

After changing hands and closing briefly in 1954, Cambridge Glass Company went out of business in 1958. The molds were sold to the Imperial Glass Company and later to other glass factories. Many pieces have been reissued or reproduced.

Consolidated Lamp and Glass Company
Phoenix Glass Company

The *Martele* and *Reuben* glass lines by the Consolidated and Phoenix companies are often mistaken for each other. The Phoenix Glass Company opened in 1880 in Monaca, Pennsylvania. Consolidated Lamp and Glass Company built a plant in nearby Coraopolis in 1895. Both companies made primarily pressed glass and lamp fixtures in their early years. In 1926 Consolidated introduced its *Martele* line—molded vases and accessories with sculptural details similar to Lalique glass.

During the Depression in 1933, Consolidated closed temporarily, and its *Martele* molds were sent to the Phoenix factory. Phoenix produced the line from 1933 to 1936 and sold it under the name *Phoenix Reuben-Line*. There were differences in the quality of glass and the colors used to decorate the finished piece. The molds were returned to the Consolidated factory when it reopened in 1936, but by then Phoenix had created some of its own molds with similar designs. The *Phoenix Reuben-Line* pattern, *Wild Rose*, is often confused with Consolidated's *Dogwood*.

Phoenix stopped making sculptural glass in 1978 and is now part of the Anchor Hocking Company. The factory still operates but no longer makes art glass. Consolidated continued to make art glass in the 1940s and '50s. The factory was destroyed by fire in 1964.

Duncan and Miller Glass

Glassmaking was a family trade for the Duncans. George Duncan bought the Ripley Glass Company in Pittsburgh in 1865. He

The Dancing Girls *vase was made both by Consolidated and by Phoenix. This custard glass version with colored figures is by Consolidated. When Phoenix made the pattern, the background was painted a solid color and the figures were left unpainted.* (Photo: James Julia)

renamed it *George Duncan and Sons* after he deeded equal shares to his sons and his son-in-law, Augustus H. Heisey. The Duncan company joined the U.S. Glass Company in 1891. Augustus Heisey left in 1893 to establish his own businesses, including the A. H. Heisey and Company (see below). In 1894 after a fire, James Duncan relocated the company to nearby Washington, Pennsylvania, and called it George A. Duncan Sons and Company. Manager Ernest Miller joined Duncan as part owner, and the factory incorporated as Duncan and Miller Glass Company in 1900.

All types of pressed, blown, etched, and decorated wares were made. Popular colors in the Duncan lines were blue, chartreuse, and pink and blue opalescent. *First Love*, a floral pattern, is the company's best-known etched pattern. The company closed in 1955, and its equipment and molds were sold to the U.S. Glass Company of Tiffin, Ohio. Several patterns, including *Canterbury*, were later marketed by Tiffin (see page 184).

Several companies made etched patterns called Chintz. *Fostoria offered the largest assortment of items in its pattern. This is a* Chintz *sandwich server—a form that became popular in the 1920s.*

Fostoria Glass Company

Fostoria Glass Company was founded in Fostoria, Ohio, in 1887. This location was chosen because of nearby natural gas reserves. The company was forced to move to Moundsville, West Virginia, in 1891 when the gas was depleted. The company made pressed glass, oil lamps, dinnerware, and extensive lines of stemware. Popular colors are Azure, Rose, Topaz, and several shades of green. Collectors also look for Fostoria floral-etched patterns, like *June Night* and *Versailles*.

In September 1983 the company was purchased by Lancaster Colony Corporation of Columbus, Ohio. The factory closed in 1986.

Heisey Glass

After his partnership with the Duncan family ended, Augustus H. Heisey opened his own factory in Newark, Ohio, in 1896. The company's early pressed patterns imitated cut glass. Heisey introduced the first of its *Colonial* patterns, with simple panels, scallops, and bands, in 1905. Many of these glass lines were made throughout the factory's lifetime. Stemware, mostly blown, was first made in 1914. Much of it had needle-etched or engraved designs.

Edgar Wilson Heisey took over after his father's death in 1922 and introduced the company's trademark colors: Moongleam (green), Flamingo (pink), Marigold (deep yellow), Sahara (light yellow), Hawthorne (light amethyst), Alexandrite (dichroic lavender that changes hue under different lighting), Tangerine (orange), Cobalt (also called Stiegel Blue), and Zircon (a green aqua, later called Limelight). T. Clarence Heisey, Edgar's brother, introduced the company's popular glass animals. He became president in 1942 when Edgar died. The company went out of business in 1957. Its patents, trademarks, molds, and some equipment were sold to Imperial Glass.

Heisey introduced Sahara yellow in 1930 after its first version of yellow, Marigold, proved to be an unstable formula. Empress *is the pattern most seen in the color. This sugar bowl has the pattern's trademark dolphin-shaped feet.* (Photo: Ruby Lane)

Imperial Glass Company

The Imperial Glass Company was founded in Bellaire, Ohio, in 1901 and began making glass in 1904. The company made clear pressed glass and common containers like jelly glasses. In 1910 Imperial added pressed and free-blown iridescent glass to its lines. *Imperial Jewel*, known today as stretch glass because of the way the finish is stretched at the edges, was first made in 1915. The company changed its name to Imperial Glass Corporation at about the same time.

In its later years, Imperial purchased and used molds from several defunct companies, including the Cambridge Glass Company of Cambridge, Ohio; Central Glass Company of Summitville, Indiana; and A. H. Heisey and Company of Newark, Ohio. It became a division of Lenox, Inc., in 1977, and was sold a few more times before it closed in 1984. In an attempt to control production of imitations, Heisey Collectors of America purchased the rights to the Heisey *Diamond-H* trademark and all remaining Heisey molds except the Williamsburg line.

In the 1920s, Imperial made mold-blown art glass called Lead Lustre. The vases are made of opaque white glass and coated with an iridescent finish to resemble the hand-pulled leaves, hearts, and festoons of more expensive makers like Tiffany. (Photo: Heritage Galleries)

Morgantown Glass Works

When the Morgantown Glass Works opened in Morgantown, West Virginia, in 1899, it made clear blownware and pressed tableware. By 1903 blown barware had replaced table items, and the company changed its name to Economy Tumbler Company. Colored glass was introduced in 1910, and the firm gradually expanded its lines to include blown accessories. Economy Tumbler changed its name to Economy Glass Company in 1923 and back to Morgantown Glass Works in 1929. After closing briefly in 1937, the factory reopened in 1939 as Morgantown Glassware Guild. The company was purchased by Fostoria Glass Company in 1965 and closed six years later.

Figural-stemmed cocktail glasses became popular in the 1930s. This green Morgantown Chanticleer *cocktail features another popular bar theme— the rooster.* (Photo: Replacements)

Old Morgantown's most popular stemware, including the *Golf Ball* and *Rooster (Chanticleer)* patterns, was made with clear molded stems topped with blown colored bowls. The company made a variety of colors, ranging from jewel tones, like Stiegel Green, Peacock Blue, and Spanish Red, to earth tones, like Mission Gold, Moss Green, and Nutmeg.

New Martinsville and Viking

The New Martinsville Glass Manufacturing Company opened in 1900 in New Martinsville, West Virginia. In 1937 it became the New Martinsville Glass Company, in 1944 the Viking Glass Company, and in 1987 Dalzell-Viking. The factory closed completely in 1998.

Early wares included clear, solid-colored, and stained pressed glass and some art glass, notably *Muranese,* a handmade shaded glass. After the Depression, the company made its popular *Moondrops* and *Radiance* lines and a selection of glass animals. During the Viking and Dalzell-Viking years, the company reissued many of its own and other companies' older patterns. It also created free-form accessories made of shaded colored glass.

Moondrops *is New Martinsville's most popular pattern. Collectors like pieces in cobalt blue like this tumbler and in ruby.*

Paden City Glass

Paden City Glass Manufacturing Company opened in 1916. The West Virginia company made pressed table and soda-fountain wares. Much of its blank glassware was sold to decorating firms for etching and silver overlay. Paden City opened its own etching and decorating department in 1924. More than twenty different shades of glass were made, ranging from deep colors and black to pastels and white. Its best-known colors are Cheri-Glo (pink) and Ruby. Popular etches are *Black Forest*, picturing deer in a forest scene, and *Peacock* and *Wild Rose*, both floral designs.

American glass companies introduced animal figurines in the 1940s. Paden City Glass made its Pheasant *in Copen Blue, shown here, and in colorless glass. At 12 inches long, this is one of the company's larger figurines.* (Photo: Yester-Years Boutique)

The Paden City Glass Manufacturing Company closed in 1951, and its molds were sold to other factories.

Tiffin

A. J. Beatty & Sons relocated its Steubenville factory to Tiffin, Ohio, in 1888. The company became Factory R of the U.S. Glass Company in 1892. *Tiffin* is the name often used to discuss both the factory and the pressed and blown glass made there. Tiffin specialized in stemware and produced colored glassware, including Twilight (a smoky lavender) and Ebony.

Tiffin employees ran the plant for three years after U.S. Glass Company went bankrupt in 1963. The factory changed hands a few more times, and some Tiffin patterns were made until 1980.

Many companies imitated Lalique's art deco vases. This Tiffin Poppies *vase was also made in black and other colors of satin glass. Sometimes the flowers were decorated with enameled colors and fine beads.*

Reproductions and Reissues

If imitation is the sincerest form of flattery, the glass industry is in love with itself. Much to the chagrin of a beginner, collecting glass is made more difficult by the reuse and imitation of older glass techniques and styles. The glassmakers in the chart have reproduced or reissued older patterns. Many of their items could pass for older glass.

Caprice *salt dishes*

Maker and Location	Dates	Confusing Reissues or Reproductions
Boyds Crystal Art Crystal Art Glass Co. (Elizabeth Degenhart, Harold Bennett) Cambridge, Ohio	1947–present	Carnival glass; Caprice pattern by Cambridge Glass Company
Indiana Glass Co. Dunkirk, Indiana	1904–present	Carnival glass (1971)
Hansen Brothers Mackinaw City, Michigan	1960s	Carnival glass
L. E. Smith Glass Co. Mt. Pleasant, Pennsylvania	1911–present	Carnival glass, Jadite, milk glass
Mosser Cambridge, Ohio	1970s–present	Carnival, Depression, and opalescent glass; Jadite
Wheaton Industries Millville, New Jersey	1888–present	Carnival glass; early American blown and pattern-molded glass
L. G. Wright Glass Co. (distributor) New Martinsville, West Virginia	1937–1999	Carnival, slag, opalescent, and pressed glass made by other companies
Summit Art Glass Company Rosso Wholesale Akron, Ohio	1972–present	Carnival, slag, and milk glass; *Caprice* pattern by Cambridge Glass Company
A. A. Importing (distributor) St. Louis, Missouri	1970s–present	Carnival, slag, milk, pressed, and blown glass made by other companies

Color Names

Here are some of the names used by collectors and manufacturers to describe glassware colors.

Amber
Apricot, Desert Gold, Golden Glow, Mocha, Topaz

Blue-green
Aventurine, Limelight, Teal Blue, Ultramarine, Zircon

Charcoal gray
Dawn, Smoke, Twilight

Clear
Crystal

Deep blue
Cobalt, Dark Blue, Deep Blue, Regal Blue, Ritz Blue, Royal Blue, Stiegel Blue

Green
Avocado, Emerald, Evergreen, Forest Green, Imperial Green, Moongleam, Nu-Green, Olive, Pistachio, Springtime Green, Stiegel Green, Verde

Light blue
Azure, Moonlight Blue, Willow Blue

Medium blue
Capri Blue, Madonna, Ritz Blue

Opalescent
Moonstone

Opaque black
Black, Ebony

Opaque blue
Delphite

Opaque green
Jade, Jade-ite, Jadite

Opaque off-white
Azure-ite, Chinex, Clambroth, Cremax, Ivrene

Opaque pink
Crown Tuscan, Shell Pink, Rose-ite

Opaque white
Anchorwhite, Milk Glass, Milk White, Monax, Platonite

Pink
Azalea, Cheri-Glo, Flamingo, LaRosa, Nu-Rose, Peach-Blo, Rose, Rose Glow, Rose Marie, Rose Pink, Rose Tint, Wild Rose

Purple
Alexandrite, Amethyst, Black Amethyst, Burgundy, Hawthorne, Heatherbloom, Moroccan Amethyst, Mulberry, Orchid, Twilight, Wisteria

Red
Carmen, Royal Ruby, Ruby Red

Shaded orange
Amberina, Sunset

Shaded pink
Peachbloom, Peachblow, Peach Blow, Muranese

Yellow
Canary, Chartreuse, Gold Krystol, Marigold, Sahara, Topaz

POST–WORLD WAR II GLASS, 1945–1969

Innovative 1930s designers created a new style with simple curves and little decoration. After World War II, the glass industry in Europe and the United States started up again and continued working in this new, understated style.

Scandinavian Glassware

Glassmakers in Denmark, Finland, Norway, and Sweden—the geographical area known as Scandinavia—have been making art wares since the nineteenth century. In the early years of the twentieth century, the United States was importing more glass from Bohemia and France than from Scandinavia, where glassmakers were making primarily cut or engraved luxury items.

Scandinavian glass designer Erik Höglund created this playful Glasmadamer *(Glass Lady) figural decanter for Boda in the 1950s. It was hand blown and has applied arms and a polished pontil* (Photo: Glasshound)

The style known as *Scandinavian Modern* or *Danish* emerged in the 1930s, although it is often associated with the 1950s. Designers like Alvar Aalto, Kaj Franck, and Tapio Wirkkala introduced a new simple style with fewer surface adornments. Many American and Eastern European makers introduced handmade wares with clean lines and rustic coloring that imitated Scandinavian glassware.

Holmegaard, Kosta, Boda, and Orrefors

After World War II, factories in the United States and Europe had trouble regaining their prewar standing. Swedish and Danish factories were less affected by the war and jumped in to meet demand for blown stemware. In the 1970s, Scandinavian factories set up showrooms in New York City and pooled their manufacturing efforts. The biggest Swedish companies, Kosta and Boda, merged with Åfors in 1964, created the Åfors group in 1971, and were joined by the Danish company Holmegaard in 1985. Orrefors merged with the group in 1990. The companies are still working today as part of the Royal Scandinavia group, which includes porcelain-maker Royal Copenhagen and the Georg Jensen silver company.

The neutral smoke color and simple shape of this cocktail set is characteristic of the designs made by Holmegaard in the 1950s and '60s. (Photo: Hi+Lo Modern)

Swedish mid-twentieth-century glassware was blown by hand or machine. Stemware and tableware usually had plain, undecorated surfaces. Designers in the 1930s through the 1950s made high-quality clear and colored lead crystal glass with gracefully swelled bowls, long drawn necks, and flared stems. Decorated art wares, like vases and sculptures, were irregularly shaped from colored glass with natural streaks and bubbles. Engraving, when used, pictured abstract scenes or geometric designs.

Vicke Lindstrund joined Kosta as head designer in 1950. During his tenure, he created vases like this 7-inch version of Autumn. The internal trees were created by laying colored glass strands and dots between layers of clear glass.

Tapio Wirkkala

Tapio Wirkkala (1915–1985) was a Finnish designer of glassware, silver, ceramics, stoneware, cutlery, wooden ware, furniture, jewelry, textiles, and even banknotes. He was also a sculptor and graphic designer. Wirkkala was chief designer at Iittala glassworks from 1946 until 1985. He also opened his own studio in 1955, worked at Raymond Loewy's New York design studio from 1955 to 1956, and designed for the German firm Rosenthal from 1956 to 1985 and Venini glassworks in Murano from 1959 to 1985. His most famous work includes *Ultima Thule* glasses, the *Coreano* bowl, and *Bolla* bottles by Venini. His simple, flowing, organic shapes were often inspired by nature—leaves, seashells, birds, and fish.

Tapio Wirkkala, an award-winning Iittala designer, created glass accessories that imitated plants and other natural forms. This 10½-inch Kantarelli *vase is shaped like a chanterelle mushroom.* (Photo: Treadway)

Iittala

Iittala and its sister factory, Karhula, have produced glassware in Finland since the 1880s. Iittala made basic household glassware, some decorated by cutting, enameling, or etching. Karhula, which produced mainly bottles and pressed tableware, merged with Iittala in 1917. Iittala still makes glass as part of the Hackman Tabletop group, which includes ceramics firms Arabia and Röstrand-Gustavsberg.

Some of the company's most creative glassware has been the result of design competitions held since the 1930s. The *Flower* set of stacking bowls by husband and wife Alvar and Aino Aalto and his *Savoy* vase have been manufactured continuously since 1937. In 1946 prizewinning designers Kaj Franck and Tapio Wirkkala joined the company, introducing new glass techniques and shapes to the company's lines.

Many modern glass designs have become classics. Alvar Aalto's award-winning Savoy *vase, created for Iittala in 1937, is still made in the original colorless version, in colored glass, and in different heights.* (Photo: Treadway)

Fish Graal *is one of the most popular designs created by Edvard Hald. The seaweed-looking fish design is cased between clear layers of glass. Orrefors developed the* Graal *technique in 1916. Hald designed this 7-inch vase in 1956.*

Mid-Twentieth-Century
Scandinavian and Dutch Glassmakers

This table lists the maker or factory, location, and dates of operation for Scandinavian glassmakers and Dutch designers who worked in the Scandinavian style. Parentheses enclose birth and death dates.

Maker and Location	Dates and Related Information
DENMARK	
Jacob E. Bang Holmegaard Kastrup	(1899–1965) 1927–1941 1951–1965
Holmegaard Naestved	1825–present In 1985 became part of Royal Copenhagen. Joined Royal Scandinavia, Malmö, Sweden, in 1997.
Per Lütken Holmegaard	(1916–1998) Designed for Holmegaard, 1942–1998.
FINLAND	
Aino Aalto Iittala	(1894–1949) Iittala, 1932–1939
Alvar Aalto Iittala	(1898–1976) Iittala, 1932–1939
Kaj Franck Viipuri	(1911–1989) Iittala, 1946–1950; Nuutajärvi (Notsjo), 1950–1976
Iittala Iittala	1881–present Merged with Karhula in 1917. Merged with Riihimäki and Nuutajärvi in 1988. Renamed Iittala–Nuutajärvi Oy. Acquired by Hackman Tabletop in 1990. Renamed Hackman Designor Oy AB in 1994.
Karhula Iittala	1889–present Merged with Iittala in 1917.
Nuutajärvi (Nötsjö) Nuutajärvi	1793–present Merged with Iittala in 1988.
Gunnel Nyman Nuutajärvi	(1909–1948) Nuutajärvi (Notsjo), 1946–1948

Maker and Location	Dates and Related Information
Riihimäki Glassworks Riihimäki	1910–1990 Merged with Iittala in 1988. Absorbed by Hackman Tabletop in 1990.
Timo Sarpaneva Iittala	(1926–present) Iittala, c.1950–1980s
Nanny Still Riihimäki	(1926–present) Riihimäki, 1949–c.1975; Val St. Lambert 1966–1968
Tapio Wirkkala Iittala, Nuutajärvi, Murano	(1915–1985) Iittala, 1946–1985; Rosenthal, 1956–1985; Venini, c.1959–1985
NETHERLANDS	
Andries Dirk Copier Leerdam	(1901–1991) 1914–1971, 1988
Leerdam (N. V. Glasfabriek Leerdam) Leerdam	1878–1891 (Glasfabriek Jeekel, Mijnssen & Co.) 1891–present
Floris Meydam Leerdam	(b.1919) Leerdam, 1935–1984
NORWAY	
Hadeland Glassverk Jevnaker	1762–present
Willy Johansson Jevnaker	(1921–1993) Hadeland, 1947–1988
SWEDEN	
Åfors Eriksmåla	1876–present Merged with Kosta and Boda, 1964. Created Åfors group with Kosta and Boda, 1971. Acquired Johansfors, 1972. See Kosta.
Kjell Blomberg Småland	(1931–?) Gullaskruf, 1955–1977

Maker and Location	Dates and Related Information
Boda Småland	1864–present Created Åfors group with Åfors, Kosta, and Johansfors in 1971. See Kosta.
Gunnar Cyrén Småland	(1931–present) Orrefors, 1959–1970, 1976–present
Ekenäs Ekenässjön	1917–1976
Eva Englund Småland	(1937–1998) Pukeberg, 1964–1973; Orrefors, 1974–1989; Målerås, 1990s
Flygfors Småland	1888–1979
Gullaskruf Glasbruk Småland	1893–1921, 1927–1983, 1990–1995
Edward Hald Småland	(1883–1980) Orrefors, 1917–c.1978
Johansfors Glasbruk Broakulla	1891–present Joined Åfors group in 1971. Absorbed by Kosta Boda; factory closed in 1990. Reopened in 1992 by Norwegian Magnor Glassverk.
Paul Kedelv Småland	(1917–?) Flygfors, 1949–1956; Reijmyre, 1956–1978
Kosta Glasbruk Småland	1742–present Joined Åfors group in 1971. Group bought by Upsala Ekeby in 1975. Adopted name Kosta Boda AB in 1976. Merged with Orrefors in 1990 to form Orrefors Kosta Boda. Joined Royal Scandinavia in 1997.
Nils Landberg Småland	(1907–1991) Orrefors, 1927–1972
Lindshammar Glasbruk Vetlanda	1905–present
Vicke Lindstrand Småland	(1904–1983) Orrefors, 1928–1940; Kosta, 1950–1973

Maker and Location	Dates and Related Information
Tyra Lundgren Småland	(1897–1979) Riihimäki, 1920s; Moser, 1922; Kosta, 1935–1936; Venini, 1935–1948; Reijmyre, c.1960
Ingeborg Lundin Småland	(1921–1992) Orrefors, 1947–1971; Målerås, 1989–1991
Målerås Glasbruk Småland	1924–present
Willem G. de Moor	Flygfors art director, 1939–1949
Gunnar Nylund Värmland	(1904–1997) Strömbergshyttan, 1952–1975; Rörstrand (ceramics), c.1952–1978
Edvin Öhrmstrom Småland	(1906–1994?) Orrefors, 1937–1958
Orrefors Glasbruk Småland	1898–present Merged with Kosta in 1990 to form Orrefors Kosta Boda. Joined Royal Scandinavia in 1997.
Sven Palmqvist Småland	(1906–1984) Orrefors, 1928–1971
Pukeberg Nybro	1871–present
Reijmyre Glasbruk Linköping	1810–present
Royal Scandinavia Malmö	1997–present Industrial group formed by Orrefors Kosta Boda, Boda Nova–Höganäs Kermik, Royal Copenhagen, Georg Jensen, Holmegaard, Venini.
Sven-Erik Skawonius Småland	(1908–1981) Kosta, 1933–1935, 1944–1950
Skrufs Glasbruk Skruv (Småland)	1897–present
Strömbergshyttan Värmland	1933–1979

The sommerso *technique encases, or submerges, one color in another. These playful vases are similar to the designs of Flavio Poli.* (Photo: Hi+Lo Modern)

Venetian Glassware

The islands of Venice have a long, romantic history of glassmaking. In 1291 the presiding Doge of Venice established the island of Murano as a glassmaking area. Venetian glass, itself influenced by Islamic glass designs, influenced Continental tastes. For hundreds of years, the glass produced at Murano has been regarded as among the finest in the world.

Vivid colors, figural shapes, and intricate designs are hallmarks of Venetian style. Many of Murano's artisans worked with techniques used since Roman times, adapting them to create new styles and forms.

Labels Aren't Equal to Marks

Twentieth-century Venetian glass was often sold with a self-adhesive foil label. The labels usually don't identify a maker and are not a guarantee of authenticity. In the 1950s, souvenir shops in Venice sometimes sold Eastern European glass with Murano labels.

Made in Murano or *Murano Glass, Made in Italy* are labels found on glass made since the 1950s. The foil stickers are metallic red or blue, and there are other variations of the wording. *Vetri Murano* and *Vetro Artistico Murano* are trademark labels created in 1981 and 1994 and controlled by Venice's regional industrial association to designate authenticity.

Importers, like Raymor (1942–1980s) and Weil Ceramics and Glass (1950s–present), also added labels to the Italian glass they sold in the United States.

American Mid-Twentieth-Century Glass Tableware

American postwar prosperity did not last long for its glass industry. Luxury glassmakers, like Heisey and Cambridge, could not compete with increased imports from Japan, Taiwan, and Eastern Europe, where new factories were automated. Additionally, American lifestyles were changing. Dinner and cocktail parties were less formal. By the 1960s, brides were not as likely to register for a complete set of fine crystal stemware.

Anchor Hocking, Federal, Fostoria, Libbey, Tiffin, and other American glass companies survived through automation

Major Venetian Glassmakers

Maker	Dates and Related Information (Birth and death dates are in parentheses.)
A.Ve.M (also AVEM, Arte Vetraria Muranese)	1932–present
Alfredo Barbini, Vetreria Alfredo Barbini	(1912–present) 1950–present
Barovier & Toso (Vetreria Artistica Barovier, Ferro Toso Vetrier Artistische Riunite S.A.)	1936–present Acquired Czech firm Bohemia Art Glass in 1998.
Ercole Barovier	(1889–1974) Barovier & Toso lead designer, 1919–1972.
Fulvio Bianconi	(1915–1996) Venini, 1946–1951, c.1965–1968, 1980s; Cenedese, 1954–1962; Seguso Vetri d'Arte, 1978; Vistosi, 1963–1964
Gino Cenedese Cenedese Cenedese & Figlio	(1907–1973) 1946–1973 1973–present
Piero Fornasetti	(1913–1988)
Luciano Gaspari	(1913–present) Salviati & C., 1950–1968, c.1981
Dino Martens	(1894–1970) Salviati, 1932–1935; Vetri Decorativi Ragionere Aureliano Toso, 1939–1959
Carlo Moretti Carlo Moretti SRL	(1934–present) 1958–present
Cristalleria Nason & Moretti	1923–present
Flavio Poli	(1900–1984) Seguso Vetri d'Arte, 1934–1963
Salviati & C.	1859–1988 Acquired by Gardini & Ferruzzi in 1988; name sold to French company in 1995.
Tobia Scarpa	(1935–present) Venini, 1959–1960
Seguso Vetri d'Arte	1933–1992 Sold to Cenedese
Archimede Seguso Vetreria Archimede Seguso	(1909–present) 1946–present Also worked with Vetreria Artistica Barovier & C., 1923; Seguso Vetri d'Arte, 1937–1946.
Vetreria Fratelli Toso	1854–1982, 1987–present
Vetri Decorativi Ragionere Aureliano Toso	1938–present
Paolo Venini Venini & C.	(1895–1959) 1921–present
Vetreria Vistosi	1945–present

Blenko's decanters are well known and gaining in popularity with collectors. This 16-inch amberina decanter was made around 1959. The blown onion-shaped stopper adds to the value. (Photo: Hi+Lo Modern)

or by adapting their pattern lines to include multipurpose stemware in informal designs. Colors and shapes imitated Scandinavian creations. Large assortments of stemware were replaced with whimsical barware.

Blenko and Erickson

Some smaller glassmakers, like Blenko (1923–present) and Erickson Glassworks (1943–1960), held on to their niche by promoting the handmade quality of their wares. Both companies made glass in solid colors with hand-tooled shapes and decorations similar to Italian and Scandinavian designs.

STUDIO GLASS, 1970–2000

From 1900 to the 1950s, most glass was made to be useful, not just decorative. Even Gallé's decorative pieces were intended to be used, perhaps as a vase to hold flowers. Many of Tiffany's iridescent wares were meant to set the table. And Depression glass could be used as an inexpensive second set of colored dinnerware.

In the 1950s, American artists, often trained as potters, became interested in glassmaking. Renewed interest in early twentieth-century glass techniques such as pâte-de-verre led Edris Eckhardt and other artists to experiment with new ways to shape glass. Many early studio glass pieces, like those made by Frances and

Designer Dishes

One of the ways American glass companies tried to compete was to work with well-known designers. Glassware was usually made to complement ceramic dinnerware.

Russel Wright designed several glass lines in the early 1950s: *American Modern* (Morgantown Glass Works); *Twist, Imperial Pinch,* and *Flair* (Imperial Glass Company); *Eclipse, Asterisk,* and *Chess* (Bartlett-Collins); *Theme Informal* (Yamato); and *Snowglass* (Paden City).

American Modern *chartreuse tumblers* (Photo: Hi+Lo Modern)

Eva Zeisel designed *Silhouette* in 1952 (Bryce Brothers); *Town and Country* in 1954 (A. H. Heisey & Co.); and *Prestige* in 1954 (Federal Glass Company).

Prestige *tumblers with* Lo Ball *decal*

See pages 79 and 172 for more information about Russel Wright and Eva Zeisel.

Studio glassmakers often created sculptures. This 12-inch untitled head was made with a casting process created by Edris Eckhardt. Using a method similar to the pâte-de-verre process, the artist shaped crushed glass paste in a mold.

Michael Higgins, were created by fusing, or slumping, layers of flat glass together with heat.

By the 1970s in the United States, studio glassmakers—artists who work independently of a factory—began to use glass in new ways, incorporating such traditional techniques as free-blown shaping and engraving with modern materials like nuts and bolts, metal plates, and plastic. Instead of cups, bowls, and vases, studio glassmakers create figures, sculptures, and even wall hangings.

Edris Eckhardt

Cleveland artist Edris Eckhardt (1907–1998) was famous for her work with ceramics, glass, and enameled metal. After graduating from the Cleveland Institute of Art in 1932, she set up her own studio. As an artist in the Public Works of Art program from 1933 to 1934, Eckhardt produced a number of small ceramic figurines based on characters from children's literature, including *Alice's Adventures in Wonderland* and the Mother Goose stories, for library programs. From 1935 until 1941, she headed the ceramic arts program in Cleveland for the Works Progress Administration (WPA).

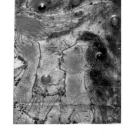

Edris Eckhardt's early works in glass fused colors and metal between sheets of glass. This picture, titled After the Rain, *was created later, in 1975, using the same fusing process.* (Photo: Treadway)

Eckhardt began to work with glass in 1953 and rediscovered an ancient Egyptian technique for making gold glass by fusing gold leaf between sheets of glass. She further developed the technique, using many layers of glass, powdered enamels, foils, and other materials. She also made pâte-de-verre figures and plaques. She signed pieces with her name.

Frances and Michael Higgins

Frances (1912–2004) and Michael Higgins (1908–1999) met at the Chicago Institute of Design, where he was head of visual design. The Higgins Studio, founded in 1948, operated out of the couple's Chicago apartment until 1957, when they started a partnership with the Dearborn Glass Company for the *Higginsware* line of accessories and tableware. Frances first experimented with "bent" glass shapes in 1942. She placed flat pieces of glass on a

mold and baked them in a high-heat kiln. After they married in 1948, they worked together to develop fused glass that trapped powdered colors between layers of clear glass.

In 1966 the Higginses ended their partnership with Dearborn and opened a studio in Riverside, Illinois. They created one-of-a-kind items, many with nontraditional decorations like metal and wood frames or encased objects. The Higgins Studio still operates, directed by longtime associates Louise and Jonathan Wimmer. Pieces are most often marked with the name *Higgins*.

Michael Higgins designed the Rondelay *system as a way to construct colorful walls, windows, or room dividers using 6-inch squares or circles of layered glass fused with connectors. This 48-disk screen was made in about 1960.* (Photo: Treadway)

Harvey K. Littleton

Most glass experts consider Harvey K. Littleton (1922–present) the founder of the American studio glass movement. Littleton grew up with glassmaking because his father was director of research for the Corning Glass Works in Corning, New York. He earned a master's degree in ceramics from Cranbrook Academy of Art in Bloomfield Hills, Michigan. Littleton taught ceramics from 1949 to 1951 at the Toledo Museum of Art, where he met Dominick Labino (see below). Littleton and Labino pioneered new lower-temperature glassmaking techniques and invented new equipment. In 1962, after experimenting with glass for several years, Littleton held two influential glassblowing workshops at the museum and set up the first university-level glassmaking department at the University of Wisconsin in Madison.

Littleton's works are sculptural. His early pieces were made with slabs of glass that were shaped in a kiln or with a blowtorch. Later, he made works using blown or pulled blobs of glass with striations of color. Often the resulting arches were cut into sections and polished.

Dominick Labino

Before collaborating with Harvey Littleton, Dominick Labino (1910–1987), a scientist and engineer, was the director of research

When Harvey Littleton first learned to work with glass, he was determined to create non-utilitarian shapes. This sculpture group from the Folded *series was made from blown tubes of layered glass that the artist stretched and folded in half.* (Photo: Sotheby's)

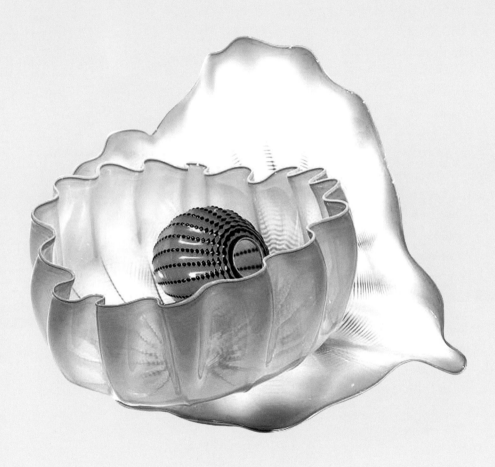

Many of Dale Chihuly's sculptures have organic shapes inspired by nature. This 11-by-22-inch group is from his 1989 Seaform *series.* (Photo: Sotheby's)

at the Johns-Manville Fiber Glass Corporation. While learning how to create his own glass, he gave technical advice to Littleton and other studio glass artists. Labino's recommendations about materials and equipment made new forms and styles possible.

In 1965 Labino retired from his research job and set up a studio in Grand Rapids, Ohio. His works from the late 1960s and the early 1970s were shaped with blown layers of colored glass. Later he experimented with cast glass decorated with molten glass overlays.

Dale Chihuly

Seattle-area artist Dale Chihuly (1941–present) is the best known of the late-twentieth-century studio glassmakers. He graduated from the University of Washington in 1965 with a degree in architecture and later studied with Harvey Littleton at the University of Wisconsin. In 1971 he cofounded the Pilchuck Glass School near Seattle.

Chihuly blew his early pieces himself. After losing an eye and later injuring his shoulder, he had others do the glassblowing while he designed the pieces. While each of his works is unique, he created them in series.

When he first experimented with glass, Dominick Labino used ordinary green soda glass for many of his sculptures. This 1972 arrowhead-shaped piece was made by shaping a glass glob with a blowtorch and tools. (Photo: Skinner)

Glass Tableware Shape Names

Berry set: a set with one 8–9-inch serving bowl and 3–4-inch individual bowls

Bottom's up: a drinking glass made so it cannot be put down because the bottom is rounded, often made with the figure of a woman molded across the sides and bottom

Compote: a footed serving dish with a tall stem

Console or centerpiece: a shallow bowl, often footed, used for floral arrangements. Console sets have matching candlesticks

Goblet: a drinking glass with stem and foot

cordial	1–1½ ounces
wine	2–2½ ounces
cocktail	3–4 ounces
parfait	5 ounces, usually with short stem and tall, narrow bowl
claret	5 ounces
sherbet	5–6 ounces, usually with short stem and broad bowl
champagne	5–6 ounces, usually with tall stem and broad bowl
water	8–10 ounces

Grill plate: a round three-section plate used to serve meat and vegetables in the separate sections, similar to a modern TV dinner tray

Ice lip: specially curved lip of a pitcher to keep the ice cubes from falling out

Ivy ball: a round glass vase, usually with a stem and foot

Plate sizes:

sherbet	6 inches, smaller center, larger rim
bread and butter	6–7 inches, larger center, smaller rim
salad	7–8 inches, some are crescent-shaped
luncheon	8–9 inches
dinner	9–10 inches
chop	13 inches

Reamer: a dish with a pointed-top cone used to extract juice from lemons, oranges, and grapefruits

Sandwich server: a handled tray, usually round, used to serve sandwiches. Some servers have one center handle

Tilt jug: a pitcher with a ball-shaped body and angled neck

Tumble-up: a glass bottle with a small tumbler turned upside down over the neck to serve as a cover and a drinking glass

Tumbler: a drinking glass, usually with a flat base; never has a stem. Some tumblers are footed

whiskey or shot	1½–3 ounces, 2–2½ inches
juice	4–7 ounces, 3¾–4½ inches, often footed
Old Fashioned	8 ounces, 2½ inches
water	9–10 ounces, 4–5½ inches, often footed
iced tea	12–16 ounces, 5½–6 inches, often footed

Other shape names are on page 70.

Chapter 7

FURNITURE

THE WELL-TO-DO home of the 1890s was filled with ornate, carved Victorian furniture, printed wallpaper, patterned rugs, bric-a-brac, and heavy draperies with tassel trim. Pictures covered much of the wall space. This was an era of excess and dark colors. In the early twentieth century, not only were new styles created but some old styles were redesigned slightly and came back into fashion. The very wealthy continued to travel to Europe to buy paintings, decorative arts, and furniture to use back home. At the same time, the middle-class American home was filled with furniture and accessories influenced by famous European designs.

Art nouveau designs from the end of the nineteenth century were never very popular with American furniture designers. Only two important factories were making this style in 1900, the Tobey Furniture Company and S. Karpen and Brothers. The Tobey Furniture Company of Chicago was started in 1875 by Charles and Frank Tobey. The company produced expensive furniture, often made to order. Tobey made art nouveau pieces and furniture in the Mission or Arts and Crafts style. The company closed in 1974. S. Karpen and Brothers, founded in 1880 by Prussian immigrant Solomon Karpen, was another company working in Chicago at the turn of the twentieth century

S. Karpen & Brothers furniture was heavy with dark woods and massive carvings, the American version of art nouveau. This sofa was made about 1900. (Photo: Sotheby's)

making top-quality art nouveau pieces. The firm was bought by Schnadig Corporation in 1952.

Plain, rectangular wooden furniture with straight lines and no nonsense was the first new idea to became popular in the twentieth century. It was called *Mission style* by the makers, but is now referred to as *Arts and Crafts style*. Other twentieth-century furniture styles were the Golden Oak furniture of the late 1800s and early 1900s; art deco designs of the 1920s; "Colonial Revival" pieces, most popular in the 1930s; "Fifties" or Mid-Century Modern styles; Scandinavian styles of the 1950s and 1960s; do-it-yourself furniture kits of the 1970s; "contemporary styles" of the 1980s and 1990s; and unusual designs that were tried for a short time, like the strange vellum-covered chairs and tables by Carlo Bugatti in the early 1900s and the eccentric Italian-made Memphis pieces of the 1980s.

MISSION OR ARTS AND CRAFTS FURNITURE

Ornate Victorian furniture began to lose its popularity in the last few years of the nineteenth century. A new style called *Mission* or *Arts and Crafts* emerged at the beginning of the twentieth century. This simple, functional furniture was usually made of oak. It had very straight lines with little if any decoration. Only the prominent mortise-and-tenon joints relieved the smooth oak surface.

Why was this furniture called Mission? Some sources, including furniture catalogs of the time, claimed the pieces were inspired by the Franciscan missions of California. Some say the name came about because the makers felt the furniture had a mission to be used and appreciated by the public. It was a simple, dignified style without elaboration or ornament. The chairs were made to be comfortable, and the tables were made to be durable.

The best-known maker of the new Mission style furniture was Gustav Stickley. His furniture was inspired by the philosophy and work in England of William Morris. The Mission style of Gustav Stickley became so popular that many other companies made pieces of similar design. The ideas spread to the Sears, Roebuck catalog and finally to the do-it-yourself manuals for school woodworking shops. It was so common by the 1920s that designers turned to a newer look, art deco.

The Stickley Brothers and Their Factories

Gustav Stickley

Gustav Stickley (1858–1942) had four brothers in the furniture business, Charles (1860–c.1928), Albert (1862–1928), John George (1871–1921), and Leopold (1869–1957). Gustav, the originator of Mission furniture, along with Charles and Albert, founded a small chair company called Stickley Brothers Company in Binghamton, New York, in 1884. Gustav left the firm in 1888, and by 1891 that company had closed. In 1888 he became partners with Elgin Simonds. Stickley & Simonds Company had plants in Binghamton and Syracuse, New York. Simonds left the firm in 1898, and Stickley

William Morris

British designer, writer, and artist William Morris (1834–1896) was the leader of the nineteenth-century Arts and Crafts movement in England. He rejected the industrial changes and excessive decoration of Victorian times and advocated a return to the medieval traditions of design and craftsmanship. In 1861 Morris and some associates established Morris, Marshall, Faulkner & Company, a home furnishings firm in London that became Morris and Company and operated from 1874 to 1940. The company designed and manufactured furnishings ranging from textiles and wallpaper to furniture and stained glass. Expert workmanship and traditional methods, like using woodblocks for printing wallpaper and textiles, were hallmarks of Morris and Company. His philosophy inspired the Arts and Crafts movement in the United States.

William Morris designs included not only furniture, but also textiles, embroideries, wallpaper, stained glass, and tiles. His company used distinctive patterns with colorful overall designs of imaginary plants and figures. (Photo: Rago)

Gustav Stickley created the best pieces of American Arts and Crafts furniture. It is heavy rectangular furniture made of oak with metal hardware and no carved embellishments. This sideboard is marked with the red Stickley decal. (Photo: Treadway)

formed the Gustav Stickley Company. The first public exhibition of his *New Furniture* was at a furniture show in Grand Rapids, Michigan, in 1900. Stickley began production of his *Craftsman* furniture in 1901 and changed the name of his company to United Crafts. The company's name changed again in 1904 to Craftsman Workshops. In 1906 *Craftsman* became the registered name for the company.

In 1900 Stickley moved into a building in Syracuse that he later called the Craftsman Building. The building housed his office and showrooms. A year later, he began publishing the *Craftsman* magazine, extolling the philosophies of Ruskin and Morris and the Mission furniture ideas. Stickley had an idealized view of the single workman creating a total piece of furniture in an honest and sincere manner.

The furniture was made of native American fumed oak. Fumed wood was exposed to ammonia fumes, which created a gray, aged look. Stickley used leather, canvas, or simple fabrics for chair seats. The hardware was iron or copper. He decided to promote the name *Craftsman* and marked his pieces with the design of a joiner's compass and the Flemish words *Als ik Kan*, meaning *If I can*. It is sometimes translated as *As best I can*. He added his written signature.

Stickley drew architectural designs for Mission-style houses, then made textiles, rugs, lighting fixtures, copper and brass objects, and furniture to furnish complete rooms.

In 1906 Stickley moved his showrooms and editorial offices to New York City, and by 1910 he had moved his family to Craftsman Farms, his home and model farm in Morris Plains, New Jersey. Stickley experimented with some very different styles of furniture, including the *Chromewald* line, introduced in 1916, that had a color-impregnated finish. However, too many others were imitating his older styles and making Mission furniture at lower prices, and in 1915 he was forced to declare bankruptcy. Stickley retired in 1918 and died in 1942.

Stickley Brothers Company

Albert Stickley and his brother John George moved to Grand Rapids, Michigan, in 1891 and established Stickley Brothers Company. John George moved to New York City about 1898 and left the firm in 1902 to join his brother Leopold. Albert expanded the company's operations to England, opening a warehouse and factory in London in the mid-1890s. In 1902 the firm introduced its *Quaint Furniture* line in the style of English Arts and Crafts, with some decoration, inlay, and simple carving. The furniture was marked *Quaint Furniture/Stickley Bros. Co./Grand Rapids, Mich.* The firm moved away from Mission design with the Stickley Brothers Tudor line in 1909. It then made a range of historical styles. Albert Stickley retired in 1926. The firm stopped working about 1940.

L. & J. G. Stickley Company

Two Stickley brothers, Leopold and John George, established a furniture business in Fayetteville, New York, about 1902. It was incorporated in 1904 as L. & J. G. Stickley Company. It sold Arts and Crafts furniture under the Onondaga Shop label. The furniture followed the designs of Gustav Stickley, but the company used both veneers and laminated woods as well as solid fumed oak. In 1912

Circular dining tables were popular in the early 1900s, when this oak table was made by Stickley Brothers. The curved leg pedestal was their design, different from the straight legs of most Gustav Stickley furniture. (Photo: Treadway)

NAMES FOR MISSION-STYLE FURNITURE

Gustav Stickley called his furniture *Craftsman*. Other manufacturers called their furniture *Arts and Crafts*, *Crafts-Style*, *Hand-Craft*, *Mission*, *Quaint*, and *Roycroft*. To add to the confusion, some of his relatives used the family name, *Stickley*.

L. & J. G. Stickley designed this settle with the popular slat back influenced by the designs of Frank Lloyd Wright. It is 76 inches wide. (Photo: Treadway)

The name Stickley is synonymous with solid, unadorned Mission-style Arts and Crafts furniture. At the same time, it is synonymous with confusion, because the five Stickley brothers worked as partners and competitors in different business ventures. All the Stickley brothers used paper labels, decals, and branded marks on their products.

Craftsman trademark (1902–1904) Red decal Joiner's compass around Dutch words *Als Ik Kan* and the written *Stickley* signature

Stickley Brothers Company (1891–1954) Brass tag or gold decal

L. & J. G. Stickley (1904–1906) Decal

Stickley & Brandt Chair Company (1909–c. 1913) Gold and red decal

This Stickley & Brandt sideboard in the Mission style has original brass oval pulls and a mirrored back. It is 48 inches wide. (Photo: Treadway)

L. & J. G. Stickley introduced a line of furniture influenced by Frank Lloyd Wright's Prairie style. The company began to shift to colonial reproduction furniture in 1916 with its *Cherry Valley* line of American Colonial Revival furniture. A line of Shaker-inspired chairs was offered in 1917. The last of L. & J. G. Stickley's Arts and Crafts furniture was produced in 1922. The company was sold in 1974 to Alfred and Aminy Audi, who continue to operate it as L. & J. G. Stickley, Inc. The company moved to Manlius, New York, in 1985. It has been producing new lines of Mission-style furniture since 1989.

Stickley & Brandt Chair Company

The Stickley & Brandt Chair Company was formed in Binghamton, New York, and run by Charles Stickley and members of the Brandt family from 1891 to 1918. The company made elaborately carved chairs and rockers and did not do much work in the Mission style until 1909, when it began marketing its *Modern Craft* line of furniture.

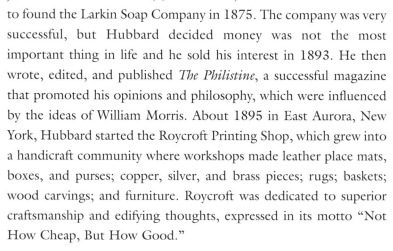

Elbert Hubbard and the Roycroft Community

Elbert Hubbard (1856–1915) was born in Bloomington, Illinois. He joined his brother-in-law, John Larkin, to found the Larkin Soap Company in 1875. The company was very successful, but Hubbard decided money was not the most important thing in life and he sold his interest in 1893. He then wrote, edited, and published *The Philistine*, a successful magazine that promoted his opinions and philosophy, which were influenced by the ideas of William Morris. About 1895 in East Aurora, New York, Hubbard started the Roycroft Printing Shop, which grew into a handicraft community where workshops made leather place mats, boxes, and purses; copper, silver, and brass pieces; rugs; baskets; wood carvings; and furniture. Roycroft was dedicated to superior craftsmanship and edifying thoughts, expressed in its motto "Not How Cheap, But How Good."

Mission furniture was first mentioned in the Roycroft community's 1901 catalog. Heavy oak or mahogany chairs and tables were made with a Roycroft mark. The community made many types of furniture—chairs of all sorts, slant-top desks, lamps, library tables, picture frames, chests of drawers, serving tables, and bedroom sets. The hardware was often copper or brass that was handmade in the shops. An adaptation of the trademark has been used since 1977 on pieces made by the Roycrofters-at-Large Association, an organization working to keep alive the history and philosophy of the Roycroft community.

This Mission chair made by the Roycroft community had a hand-tooled and embossed covering, but the seat cover has been replaced with plain leather. The chair once belonged to Elbert Hubbard. (Photo: Rago)

Elbert Hubbard and his second wife, Alice, died on the British ocean liner *Lusitania* when it was sunk by a German submarine in 1915 (during World War I). The Roycroft shops were managed by Elbert Hubbard II until they closed in 1938.

Other Important Mission Furniture Makers and Designers

William H. Bradley

Will Bradley (1868–1962) was a graphic designer, not a furniture manufacturer. But any study of Mission-period furniture must include the Bradley room designs that were made for the *Ladies' Home Journal* from November 1901 to August 1902. The designs incorporated the best of the English and American ideas of Mission, plus the additional skills of Bradley.

Harvey Ellis

Harvey Ellis (1852–1904) was a designer for Gustav Stickley's United Crafts. The furniture he designed had inlaid patterns of copper and pewter, or other details that were unlike the usual Stickley oak furniture. His designs continued to be made for a short time after his death.

Charles and Henry Greene

The Greene brothers, Charles (1868–1957) and Henry (1870–1954), were architects in Pasadena, California, beginning in 1893. Their firm, Greene and Greene, is best known for the buildings and furnishings it designed from 1903 to 1909, although it worked until 1922. After their partnership dissolved in 1922, the brothers continued to work independently. When Greene and Greene designed a house, the firm also designed its grounds and furnishings, all uniquely suited to the house. The furniture was made from a variety of woods, including Honduras mahogany, teak, ash, maple, and oak, and it was often trimmed with inlaid fruitwood, ebony, metal, or abalone shell. The Gamble House in Pasadena, designed by Greene and Greene in 1908, is an outstanding example of Arts and Crafts–style architecture in America and is still open to the public as a museum.

Charles P. Limbert made many plain Mission pieces. This table has interesting cutouts in the sides and an oval top, plus a lower shelf that might hold a vase. It is 30 inches high. (Photo: Treadway)

Charles P. Limbert

Charles P. Limbert (1854–1923) established his furniture company in Grand Rapids, Michigan, in 1894. In 1905 he moved its manufacturing operations to Holland, Michigan, and kept the showroom in Grand Rapids. Charles P. Limbert Company is best known for its lines of Mission furniture called *Limbert's Holland Dutch Arts and Crafts*, produced from 1902 until about 1917, but it made other styles until 1944. Most pieces were made of white oak in many finishes, including Fumed Oak and Early English. Copper hardware and Morocco leather cushions were standard, and some pieces were inlaid with ebony designs. It was marked with the Limbert trademark, a craftsman at his bench, branded into the wood.

Charles Rohlfs

Charles Rohlfs (1853–1936) was a designer, furniture maker, and successful stage actor. He worked in Buffalo, New York, designing furniture in many styles, including Mission. By the 1890s he was making plain oak pieces similar to those popularized by Gustav Stickley. His later pieces had fewer straight lines than those by other makers of Mission. The parts were curved and often notched

Greene & Greene furniture is rare because it was designed for a specific house. This ash bench was made in about 1904 for a Long Beach, California, home. The handles for the drawers and the seat rails are the same cloud lift *design.* (Photo: Treadway)

together, and they were decorated with carvings. His furniture is easy for a collector to recognize from the shape of the base of a table or the arm of a chair. Some pieces by Rohlfs were branded with the letter *R* and the date.

Rose Valley Association

The Rose Valley Association, a utopian Arts and Crafts colony, was founded in 1901 by Philadelphia architect William Price. The workers made furniture in the Mission manner and marked their pieces *Rose Valley Shops* with a rose and the letter *V* in a buckled belt. The pieces were medieval in design and more ornate than the Stickley Mission designs. The furniture shop closed in 1906, and the community went bankrupt in 1909.

Frank Lloyd Wright

The famous architect Frank Lloyd Wright (1867–1959) designed Arts and Crafts furniture for his home in Oak Park, Illinois, as early as 1893. He also created some Mission-style furniture for use in his studio and several homes he designed during the first two decades of the twentieth century. The early pieces were made by custom shops under his direction. Later he became interested in the possibilities of machine production of his furniture. He believed the machine enhanced his designs. Wright produced furniture in many other styles, including art deco, international, and modern, and he designed furniture for commercial buildings as well as homes.

Wright designed all the furniture for the Johnson Wax Building in Racine, Wisconsin, including three-legged secretary chairs that tipped over if one did not sit in them correctly.

Although most Wright furniture was custom-designed for his houses or other buildings, in 1955 he developed the *Four Square* line of furniture for the Heritage-Henredon Furniture Company.

FROM ART DECO AND BAUHAUS TO THE FIFTIES

There were two main types of new design after World War I. The German Bauhaus designers used good design for production of machine-made goods, while the French art deco designers created carefully made, handcrafted, luxurious products.

Germany

After World War I, machine-made, mass-produced design was available because of changes in manufacturing, materials, and design. The technically oriented Germans, such as Ludwig Mies van der Rohe (1886–1969) and Marcel Breuer (1902–1981), were designing for the mass market using machine-production techniques and new materials like steel tubes. Handwork was not important; cost-effectiveness was.

France

The French designs introduced about 1910 developed into a new style, now called *art deco*, that was popular from 1920 to 1940. The twining tendrils and the sensuous mood of the art nouveau style was forgotten as many designers

Marcel Breuer

Hungarian-born architect and designer Marcel Breuer (1902–1981) studied furniture design at the Bauhaus in Germany from 1920 to 1924 and then became head of its furniture workshop until 1928. Breuer introduced strong, lightweight tubular steel furniture. He first used tubular steel in 1925 for the *Wassily* chair built of welded ready-made tubes and a webbed seat, back, and armrests. In the 1930s he designed innovative laminated plywood furniture. Breuer moved to America in 1937 and taught architecture at Harvard until 1946. He then opened his own firm in New York City where, until his retirement in 1976, he designed furniture, houses, and public buildings.

Tubular steel was a new material for chair frames when Marcel Breuer designed the Wassily *chair in 1925. The seat, back, and sides are made of leather straps.* (Photo: Rago)

Ludwig Mies van der Rohe

Ludwig Mies van der Rohe (1886–1969), Germany's most important modern architect, was a prominent furniture designer during the late 1920s and the 1930s. His early chairs were made of tubular steel. The *MR20,* a curved tubular steel cantilevered chair with a woven cane seat, was introduced in 1927. The *Barcelona* chair he created in 1929 for the king and queen of Spain has a curved, flat-bar, X-shaped metal base and an upholstered seat attached by leather straps. The *Barcelona* chair is a popular classic and has been made by Knoll since 1947. Mies also designed tables, stools, ottomans, and lounge chairs. He taught at the Bauhaus and was its director from 1930 to 1933. He moved to Chicago in 1938. In America he designed houses, office buildings, and other public buildings, including the Seagram Building in New York, which was completed in 1967.

Barcelona *chair*
(Photo: Treadway)

Gerrit Thomas Rietveld and the Zig-Zag Chair

Gerrit Thomas Rietveld (1888–1964) worked in his father's cabinetry workshop as a teenager in Holland. By 1911 he had his own studio, where he made pieces influenced by Frank Lloyd Wright and other designers and artists who were considered avant-garde. In 1918 he decided to experiment with a different type of design that could be produced using machines. Joints and construction features were intended to be noticeable, and he painted everything in bright colors. Rietveld's best-known pieces are the *Red and Blue* chair (c.1917), made with black laths with yellow or white ends supporting a blue board seat and a red board back, and the *Zig-Zag* chair (1934), made of four square boards forming a zigzag. His designs slowly changed, and by 1927 he had designed molded plywood chairs for commercial use.

These Zig-Zag *chairs look like comic strip drawings. They seem to be made of one bent piece of birch plywood, but there are four pieces. The joints and angles of the bends make the chair strong enough to hold a person.* (Photo: Rago)

began making furniture with straight lines and geometric shapes. By 1920 the new furniture style was called by many different names: *Art Moderne, Moderne,* or *Modernistic.* In 1968 Bevis Hillier, author of the book *Art Deco of the 20s and 30s,* invented the name *art deco.* The term is a shortened form of *Exposition Internationale des Arts Décoratifs et Industriels Modernes,* the title of an exhibit of the new style at the 1925 Paris World's Fair. The French designers exhibiting at the fair made furniture that was luxurious, handcrafted, and expensive—not meant for the common man. The Paris fair concentrated on French designs, and some countries, including the United States and Germany, did not participate.

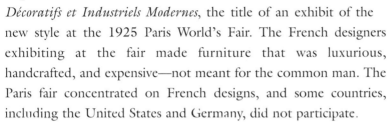

French art deco designers often turned to different styles in their later years. Jean Royere made this mahogany table in the 1940s. Ten years later, he made furniture of perforated metal and Formica in modern styles. (Photo: Treadway)

French art deco style meant low and wide furniture with restrained curves. Heavily upholstered armchairs were popular. Chairs had oval, square, or octagonal backs. Tables often had round or square pedestal bases, and desks were asymmetrical. Mahogany, macassar, ebony, and rosewood were used by major designers. To trim their pieces, designers used expensive and rare materials, such as ivory, lacquer, amboyna wood, sharkskin, mother-of-pearl, tortoiseshell, or bronze. French designers were inspired by many sources. The designs contained suggestions of African, Egyptian, cubism, and earlier French styles in the designs. A few designers made pieces using plastic or metal, and some ultramodern steel and leather pieces, such as Le Corbusier's Basculant armchair, have become famous.

Some French art deco furniture was well made but not as high-style as pieces by top designers. It was made of oak and other less expensive woods and featured carved fruit and flower decoration and marble tops. Dining room sideboards and tables were often made in this style, which became known in the United States in the 1950s as *French Provincial.*

United States

Art deco was not a popular style for home furnishings in America in the 1920s. Average Americans reacted at the end of World War I by turning to several different revival styles of furniture that sparked memories of a romantic, safer past. Almost every old style—from Windsor chairs, Chippendale chests, and wing chairs to bulky, bulbous William and Mary dining room sets and Empire pieces—was slightly changed and marketed to the general public at reasonable prices.

The Depression of the 1930s created a new environment for manufacturers as furniture was redesigned to be even more affordable. Revivals of earlier, comforting styles continued, but art deco and other "modern" styles were introduced. Inexpensive "novelty furniture" like smoking stands, magazine racks, and curio cabinets were introduced.

Art deco

Unlike French art deco furniture, which was handcrafted, expensive, and available only to the well-to-do, American art deco designs were mass-produced products of the industrial age, influenced more by German Bauhaus ideas and men like Emile-Jacques Ruhlmann, Marcel Breuer, and Ludwig Mies van der Rohe. Most of this mass-produced furniture was not made until the 1940s.

Other modern styles

American designers in the 1930s also began to interpret other European styles, and new "streamlined" furniture in light woods by designers like Russel Wright (1904–1976) and Gilbert Rohde (1894–1944) began to appear. The late 1930s saw increased interest in more modern styles for the average home. American designs included ornament-free sofas, streamlined forms, and blond wood. New forms included coffee tables, bridge tables, end tables, cocktail bars, liquor cabinets, bar stools, telephone stands, and glass-topped tables.

By the 1940s, inexpensive copies of art deco and streamlined pieces were being sold, and the least expensive small decorative pieces could be bought in dime stores or from the Sears, Roebuck catalog. Art deco designs could be seen in all sorts of everyday goods: radios, cars, cigarette cases, trays, toys, lamps, pottery, clocks, jukeboxes, cocktail accessories, and kitchen wares. Popular decorative devices were used over and over, and images of flamingos, blacks, Mexicans, naked women, skyscrapers, and streamlined planes and trains abounded.

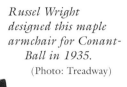

Russel Wright designed this maple armchair for Conant-Ball in 1935.
(Photo: Treadway)

World War II changed the needs of America. After the war, innovations used for the battlefield were put to work at home, creating a very new style of American furniture made from plastics and plywood, Formica and chrome. The industrial look, Mid-Century Modern, had arrived.

MID-CENTURY MODERN

The furniture we call *fifties* today was born in the 1930s. The avant-garde ideas of Europe, especially the machine-made, practical designs of the German Bauhaus group, crept into the work of a few daring designers in America like Donald Deskey, Paul Frankl, and Ludwig Mies van der Rohe. But furniture sales were slow during the years of the Depression and World War II. It was not until the 1950s that there was a strong demand for new furniture to fill the new houses owned by recently married veterans. Some of these young couples turned to the latest designs and modern styles.

The new, smaller living spaces needed smaller furniture. Few homes had servants, and architects and designers tried to create surroundings that required less care. Moldings were not used at the ceiling, floor, or even around the new-style windows that had large single panes. Furniture surfaces were smooth and had little carved decoration or tasseled and tufted upholstery that would require dusting. Built-in units, pieces with storage space, and dual-purpose furniture were popular. Wall-hung bookshelves took the place of bookcases. The new designs were made of materials like Formica,

The Womb *chair got its name because a person could curl up in it easily. The biomorphic* *chair designed by Eero Saarinen is made of chrome-finished steel rods and upholstered* *fiberglass. First made by Knoll in 1948, it is still being manufactured.* (Photo: Rago)

Bakelite, Micarta, foam rubber, aluminum, bent plywood, chrome, and steel.

In the 1950s, kitchen appliances, dishwashers, and stoves were made in the popular colors of the day—pink, gray, lime-green, turquoise, yellow, and chocolate brown. In many mid-twentieth-century homes, the carpet, walls, refrigerator, upholstery, and drapes all featured these colors—no more than three different colors to a room, according to the decorating magazines. Fabrics, paints, and colored surfaces were coordinated by a group of advisors to the home furnishing industry. By the 1960s, Scandinavian Modern or Danish Modern influence inspired decorators to choose blond and other light woods and pale colors, often beige carpet, drapes, walls, and upholstery. The use of color helps to date upholstered furniture and kitchen items from this period.

Odd forms of chairs with descriptive names like *Bubble*, *Diamond*, *Grasshopper*, *S*, and *Womb* appeared in the 1950s. New furniture forms, like the TV stand and the TV tray table, were created to use with new technologies. Another new form was furniture that came in modular units, including desks and drawers, wall-hung shelves, and sectional sofas.

Important United States Furniture Makers and Designers in the 1950s

Important furniture companies during the 1950s included Herman Miller Furniture Company in Zeeland, Michigan; Heywood-Wakefield in Boston; Johnson Handley Johnson in Grand Rapids, Michigan; and Knoll Furniture Company in New York.

Edward Wormley designs for Dunbar Furniture included tables, chairs, and all sorts of furniture. He even designed this globe with a mahogany stand in 1957.
(Photo: Treadway)

Many companies employed important designers. Russel Wright designed pieces for Conant Ball Company in Gardner, Massachusetts, from the 1930s through the 1950s; Samsonite folding chairs and tables and school furniture for Shwayder Brothers in Denver and Detroit in the 1950s; and the Easier Living line of furniture for Statton Furniture Company in Hagerstown, Maryland. Edward J. Wormley (1907–1995) was chief designer and director of design at Dunbar Furniture, Inc., in High Point, North Carolina, from 1931 to 1970. T. H. Robsjohn-Gibbings (1905–1976) designed furniture for the John Widdicomb Company in Grand Rapids from 1943 to 1956.

Charles and Ray Eames

Charles (1907–1978) and Ray (1912–1988) Eames, two of the most important furniture designers of the twentieth century, designed furniture that was in good taste but not expensive. They met at the Cranbrook Academy of Art in Michigan, married, then moved to Los Angeles in 1941. The Eameses experimented with molded plywood and produced leg splints for the U.S. Navy during World War II. They are best known for their designs of simple, attractive, comfortable, and affordable chairs that were machine-made from metal and the molded plywood created originally for the splints. In 1946 an exhibit of Charles Eames furniture at the Museum of Modern Art in New York made him famous. He became a design consultant for the Herman Miller Furniture Company, which has mass-produced Eames chairs from 1948 to the present. Charles was the public face of the company, and he received the awards; however, he said and research shows Ray was equally responsible for the furniture innovations.

Eames LCW plywood chair. (Photo: Treadway)

Important Eames furniture designs include the *LCW* (Lounge Chair Wood) chair of molded and bent birch plywood (1946), the *DAR* (Dining Armchair Rod) molded fiberglass-reinforced plastic chair with thin metal rod legs (1948), *ESU* (Eames Storage Unit) birch and plywood storage unit (1950), wire-mesh chair and wire sofa (1950s), and the Eames rosewood and black-leather lounge chair and ottoman (1956). The furniture was immediately popular with the public. Many Eames chairs have been used in schools and offices, as well as homes. In the 1960s, although the Eameses continued to design some furniture, they turned their attention to making short educational and entertaining films (almost one hundred) and designing exhibits with special lighting and multimedia effects for museums. They created a blockbuster, twenty-two screen multimedia presentation for IBM at the 1964 New York World's Fair. They also designed toys, including the House of Cards, a pack of interlocking cards that could be used by children to build towers and buildings.

Eames ESU *storage unit.* (Photo: Wright)

Herman Miller

Herman Miller Furniture Company made traditional residential furniture when it started in 1923. When Gilbert Rohde became design director of the company in 1932, he realized there was a market for attractive modern furniture, and he completely changed the designs. After Rohde died in 1944, George Nelson became design director. He hired well known designers, including Charles and Ray Eames and Isamu Noguchi. Herman Miller Furniture Company mass-produced the Eameses' classic molded plywood chair from 1949 to 1958. From the 1960s Herman Miller manufactured office furniture systems, meeting the needs of flexible open-office design. The company introduced comfortable ergonomic work seating in the 1970s and '80s and expanded the line, continuing to be a leading manufacturer of office furnishings. During the 1990s, Herman Miller reintroduced some of its classic designs from the 1940 to the '60s.

Fifties manufacturers and advertising agencies liked to give chairs interesting names. The inspiration for George Nelson's Coconut chair is said to have been a curved fragment of coconut. Herman Miller made the chair with a steel shell and vinyl upholstery. (Photo: Treadway)

Italian Furniture Designers

Sometimes Italian designers inspired the designs of the United States.

Carlo Mollino

Carlo Mollino (1905–1973) is famous as an architect and furniture designer, but he was also an inventor, designer of theatrical scenery, stunt flyer, and car racing enthusiast. He was active in Turin from the 1940s until the 1960s, when a building he considered his most important architectural achievement was demolished and he became so depressed he made very few pieces of furniture for the rest of his life. His furniture, designed for a specific client and not mass-produced, tended to be in a streamlined style with organic forms. He designed it, then had it made by some select small workshops. He used natural materials, including multicolored marble and solid wood or plywood with a visible grain. He also used completely artificial materials like steel, glass, Plexiglas, and resins on woven cloth backings called *resinflex*. His important furniture designs include bent and pierced plywood tables with glass tops, the *Ardea* armchair with a wood frame and velvet upholstered seat (1944), the *Gilda* armchair with adjustable wood frame (1954), and the *Cadma* brass and parchment lamp with marble base (1947).

Carlo Mollino's Reale oak table with bevel-edged plate-glass top was designed in 1946. A unique, custom-made version of this table made in 1949 sold in 2005 for more than $3.8 million, a record price for a piece of twentieth-century American furniture.
(Photo: Zanotta)

Mollino is considered one of the most important of the Italian designers. A glass and oak trestle table designed by Mollino in 1948 sold for $3.8 million in 2005, the highest price ever paid for a piece of twentieth-century furniture.

Gio Ponti

Italian architect and designer Gio Ponti (1891–1979) designed everything from art deco ceramics produced by Richard Ginori in the 1920s to printed fabrics in the 1930s, opera and ballet sets and costumes in the 1940s, and the Pirelli office tower in Milan in 1956. His most famous furniture design is the 1951 lightweight

Gio Ponti designed this walnut chair manufactured by Singer and Sons. The walnut frame has curved back legs that keep it from being tipped backward. The backrest, covered in white leather, is suspended in the frame. (Photo: Treadway)

Superleggera side chair made from ash wood with a rush seat, produced by Cassina from 1957. His early furniture combined neoclassical style, luxurious materials, and fine craftsmanship. In the late 1940s and early '50s, his work reflected the streamlined modernism of the time.

Scandinavian Furniture

Designers and cabinetmakers from Scandinavia—Denmark, Sweden, Norway, and Finland—were making furniture with clean lines and classic shapes by the 1920s, but the Scandinavian style was not introduced to stores in America until the beginning of the 1950s. Early Scandinavian designers adapted the best of the old designs. They created chairs that were inspired by an eighteenth-century English chair, a colonial English army chair from India, a Ming dynasty chair from China, or a Japanese director's chair. Scandinavian cabinetmakers strove to make beautiful, comfortable, handmade, innovative, and affordable goods for daily life. The Scandinavian style influenced other Europeans and Americans for the rest of the century. Most top-grade furniture produced in Scandinavia was made by cabinetmakers, not factories, and used teak, oak, and rosewood with fabric or leather upholstery. Designers, when creating a cabinet to store china, would measure the plates, cups, and saucers to be stored in it. Chairs were designed after study of the human body.

*It's easy to see why
Arne Jacobsen called
these* Ant *chairs. They
were made of one piece
of molded plywood on
chromed steel legs by
Fritz Hansen of
Denmark in the
1990s.* (Photo: Treadway)

From 1920 to 1970 Danish designers continued to use new methods of working with wood like the laminated wood *Ant* chair by Arne Jacobsen. Other unusual chairs by Jacobsen are the *Egg* chair and the *Swan* chair, both fabric-covered, foam upholstered molded fiberglass seats with swiveling cast aluminum bases. The most famous Finnish designers were Eliel Saarinen and Alvar Aalto. Saarinen immigrated to the United States in 1923 and, as a founder and president of Cranbrook Academy, influenced American modernism. Aalto developed a technique to make bentwood furniture and in 1935 founded Artek, a furniture design company. Other important Scandinavians who eventually did work for American firms were Hans Wegner, who designed more than two hundred chairs, and Finn Juhl, both from Denmark; and Swede Bruno Mathsson, known for his chairs, sofas, and ottomans made of pressed laminated wood and interwoven webbing.

Scandinavian design came to the attention of Americans in the early 1950s when it was featured at the Georg Jensen store in New York City. Scandinavian furniture, glass, pottery, silver, and wooden wares created a harmonious, soothing environment in the displays. But simple wooden handcrafted furniture with natural unvarnished and unfinished wood, curved corners, neutral colors, and thin wooden parts lost favor by the 1960s, in part because such furniture required well-trained cabinetmakers who knew how to

Finn Juhl

Finn Juhl (1912–1989) is one of the best-known designers of the Danish Modern style that became popular in America in the 1950s. Juhl was born in Copenhagen. He studied architecture, but by the 1940s he focused on furniture and interior design. Juhl is known for the "floating" back and seat that seem to hover on the frame of some of his chairs. His designs were originally handcrafted in Denmark, but by the 1950s they were adapted for mass production in factories in the United States. He designed twenty-four pieces, including chairs, tables, storage units, sideboards, and desks that were mass-produced by Baker Furniture Company in Grand Rapids, Michigan.

Finn Juhl was a popular designer of Danish Modern in the 1950s and after. He liked to use a "floating back" like the one on this Chieftain chair. It is teak with original leather upholstery. (Photo: Treadway)

make pieces by hand. Those with limited budgets could buy less expensive *Danish Modern* pieces with a similar look made by machine in American factories. Danish Modern furniture used blond wood, teak, or walnut; pale colors; and simple fabrics, fiberglass, and wire. Also popular were free-form glass objects, from vases to coffee tables.

THE 1960s

Scandinavian Modern was just one of the furniture styles popular in the United States during the last half of the twentieth century. Pop Art inspired pieces like *Spotty*, a 1963 child's chair by Peter Murdoch of London that was made of laminated sheets of paper decorated with large polka dots. It was sold flat and then assembled at home. The 1970 *Joe* chair, designed and manufactured in Italy, was a huge leather baseball glove complete with label that formed a comfortable and very conspicuous piece of furniture. It was named for baseball great Joe DiMaggio. The *Ball* or *Globe* chair was designed in 1965 by Eero Aarnio of Finland. Many other strange shapes and op-art upholstery materials were used by the daring designers of the 1960s. They used unconventional colors and shapes that were possible because of the availability of inexpensive synthetic materials like polyethylene (plastic) that could be molded into any shape. The Verner Panton stacking chair, the Pierre Paulin ribbon chair, and other designs demonstrated that chairs no longer needed four legs or even upholstery to be comfortable. Thin wire furniture with an op-art look was designed by Warren Platner. Designers liked blond olive burl, sheets of plastic for cabinet fronts, and fat aluminum tubing. Collectors today tend to want the "look," but they pay extra for a name designer.

The huge baseball mitt is not a toy but a famous 1970s chair known as the Joe *chair (for Joe DiMaggio, of course). The chair is 68 inches across and holds two or three people.* (Photo: Treadway)

THE 1970s

In the 1970s, affordable, recyclable furniture was a specialty. Do-it-yourself furniture kits were sold to those with new houses and little money, and the owners assembled and even stained or painted the pieces. Everything was made with flat surfaces, little carving, and few curves. One of the furniture forms introduced in this era is the showcase table with a glass top and a section to display knickknacks inside. Italian designers made furniture unlike any made before; for example, Alessandro Mendini's *Kandissi* sofa with painted wood decoration (1978) and Gaetano Pesce's *Pratt* chairs of molded polyurethane resin (1983).

Designers

Wendell Castle

The furniture by American Wendell Castle (1932–present) shows he is a sculptor as well as a furniture designer. He is interested in "making the whole thing a piece of sculpture." Castle, who works in wood, plastic, and fiberglass, is inspired by both art nouveau and Arts and Crafts style and philosophy. He has used stack laminations of wood to create chairs and tables. Some of his most famous pieces are trompe l'oeil, like the wooden table with a realistic wooden glove as part of the top or a hat rack complete with wooden hat.

Alessandro Mendini

Italian designer Alessandro Mendini (1931–present) was a creator of "radical designs" for Studio Alchimia. He often ignored the simple lines of modern design and instead used new materials to make the elaborate shapes and patterns of the nineteenth century. His best-known work includes the *Proust* armchair that looks like an overstuffed Victorian piece with carved wooden frame and hand-painted upholstery and the *Kandissi*

Top right: Wendell Castle made furniture of wood or fiberglass like this piece known as the Molar settee. It was made in about 1970. Castle is best known for his trompe l'oeil wooden furniture. (Photo: Treadway)

Bottom left: It's a table-chair of lacquered wood with hand-painted decorations. The top folds down; the chair becomes a table. The idea dates back to the eighteenth century; the look is 1984 Mendini. (Photo: Zanotta)

sofa made of colorful fabric and applied painted wood cutout decoration. Both pieces were created for Alchima in 1978. Mendini, who is design director for Alessi (see page 418) and Swatch, the watch company, has designed products for many other manufacturers. Since the late 1980s, Mendini has designed some buildings, including the Paradise Tower in Hiroshima (1989) and a new facility for the Groningen Museum in Holland (1993).

Pesce has designed furniture, floors, buildings, jewelry, clocks, and much more. This 1984 chair is made of colored urethane that blends together to make a unique design. (Photo: Phillips)

Gaetano Pesce

Gaetano Pesce (1939–present), known for his unusual designs and materials, has worked in Italy and the United States. His *UP* series of mass-produced chairs, introduced in 1969, was a set of seven chairs made of molded polyurethane foam. They were compressed in a vacuum chamber until flat and packaged in a plastic envelope, so they were easy to ship and store. When the package was opened, the chairs filled with air and expanded to normal size. His overstuffed *Sit Down* chair, sofa, and ottoman were made of quilted polyester injected with polyurethane foam. Pesce has also designed tables and lamps, jewelry, buildings, and much more.

THE 1980s

Designs of the 1980s are called *postmodern* by many, although the word has been used to describe other designs dating as early as 1950.

Memphis

In 1981 Italian designer Ettore Sottsass Jr. organized an Italian design group with the surprising name *Memphis* to create products in "the new International style." The furniture, lighting fixtures, jewelry, and ceramics designed by this group were very different from the pieces sold in stores. Memphis design was not understood nor accepted and was a financial flop. Memphis products were created by Michael Graves and Peter Shire of the United States and

Colorful furniture with surprising shapes and materials were expected of Memphis designers. George James Sowden of England made this chest in 1981. It is 63 inches high. (Photo: Rago)

Ettore Sottsass Jr.

internationally recognized designers from Italy, Austria, Spain, and Japan. The colorful and outrageous Memphis pieces included Masanori Umeda's wooden boxing-ring bed from the 1981 Memphis collection and Michele de Lucchi's *Continental* table. Trendsetters from the East Coast, Chicago, Los Angeles, and Miami were the major American buyers. The group disbanded in 1988.

Other Designs

Many of the designs considered daring during the years after 1950 were decorative, useful, and inexpensive to produce, so by the 1980s furniture makers in many countries made similar pieces. Ball chairs, molded plastic chairs, tubular metal furniture, blow-up chairs,

Austrian born Ettore Sottsass Jr. (1917–present) studied architecture in Turin, Italy, then set up a studio in Milan in 1945. As a consultant for Olivetti in the 1960s, he designed office equipment, including the bright red plastic body for the *Valentine* typewriter. In the late 1970s, Sottsass joined Studio Alchimia, where he designed plastic-laminate-covered furniture. He left in 1981 to found Memphis, a group of young designers dedicated to creating playful, colorful, unconventional designs for furniture and more. Important Memphis pieces by Sottsass include his 1981 red, black, yellow, and white plastic laminate *Casablanca* sideboard, a tower with arms radiating from it at unexpected angles; his tall 1981 *Carlton* sideboard that can serve as a room divider; and his 1986 *Teodora* chair. In the 1990s, Sottsass focused on architectural and interior design projects, and he also designed glass, ceramics, and, of course, furniture.

The Italian group Memphis was started by Ettore Sottsass, who designed this unusual bookcase. It is over six feet high. This bookcase is often called the icon of 1980s design. Multicolored, patterned laminate was used on many Memphis pieces. (Photo: Treadway)

The ball chair is a design of the 1960s that became even more popular in the 1980s and is still manufactured. The fiberglass and plastic ball is on an aluminum swivel base. The sitter is half hidden inside the chair. (Photo: Treadway)

plastic stacking units for storage, and furniture made of large stiff cushions are just a few of the shapes that were copied and mass-produced. The Mies van der Rohe *Barcelona* chair (1929), the Nelson platform bench (1946), the Noguchi table with a rounded triangular glass top on an abstract base made of two pieces of walnut interlocking at right angles (1947), the Yanagi bent plywood butterfly stool (1956), and even the *Joe* chair can be found today in homes, restaurants, dormitory rooms, and public waiting rooms. Some are copies, some are still being made by the original companies.

NEW DESIGNS OF THE PRE-MILLENNIUM
THE 1990s AND AFTER

There is as yet no universally accepted name for the style of the 1990s. *Modern* and *contemporary* are words that indicate the most recent fashions, and so their meanings change with each era. From 1990 to 2000, the furniture of the trendsetting modern-art lover was sometimes the work of a craftsman-artist-cabinetmaker like George Nakashima, who made studio furniture using slabs of wood in irregular shapes with burls and grains; or Gaetano Pesce, who made humorous pieces like a table with four very different multicolored legs and a free-form top and used odd color combinations. There were also commercial mass-produced pieces like the bent and woven laminated wood *Powerplay* chair designed by Frank Gehry, produced by Knoll.

Ron Arad

One of the highest-priced modern furniture designers is Ron Arad (1951–present), who opened a design studio, One Off Ltd., in London in 1981. He experimented with unusual uses of materials and technology to create famous pieces like the *Rover Chair* made from a salvaged car seat on a tubular steel frame, the vacuum-packed, deflatable *Transformer* bag chair, and the remote-controlled *Aerial* light. He founded Ron Arad Associates in 1989 and expanded his work. His limited-edition, handmade

COMPUTER FURNITURE

Just as the invention of the telephone and television led to new types of furniture like the telephone stand and the TV tray, the personal computer, used in homes since the 1980s, has inspired new types of furniture to accommodate the equipment and the person using it. Workstations for the office and computer desks and chairs for the home are designed for comfort and efficiency. They range from inexpensive chairs, desks, and printer stands available at office supply stores to high-end pieces like the *Navigator* workstation by Italian designers (2000) and the *Freedom* chair by an American industrial designer (2000).

Ron Arad designed chairs to be mass-produced, like this Rover chair with an enameled steel frame and an authentic seat from an automobile. It was manufactured by One Off, Ltd., in 1981. (Photo: Wright)

furniture pieces are often the forerunners of versions made by major manufacturers like Alessi and Vita International. In 2001 Ron Arad's *Little Heavy* steel chair sold for $55,200, yet his plastic stackable chairs are sold for about $300. His steel table *Two Legs and a Table* sold in 2004 for $67,200.

Droog Design

Droog Design is a group of Dutch designers founded in Amsterdam in 1993 by Renny Ramakers and Gijs Bakker. Droog designs furniture, art objects, graphics, interiors, and architectural projects. Its work is eye-catching and witty. The Droog philosophy is a reaction to the extreme ideas of the radical designers. Droog's *Chest of Drawers*, designed by Tejo Remy in 1991, is a pile of assorted drawers tied into a bundle with a strap.

COLONIAL REVIVAL AND OTHER REVIVALS

Perhaps the first Colonial Revival in the United States was in 1876, the year of the U.S. centennial celebration. The "Colonial kitchen" on exhibit at the Philadelphia Centennial Exposition inspired renewed interest in the past and led to a new look at old forms. Furniture from the 1700s, both antiques and reproductions, came back into fashion. Some eccentric designs, like chairs assembled from parts of spinning wheels, were also made. In the 1880s, the Sypher & Company store was selling both antiques and reproductions of antiques. *Colonial Furniture of New England* by Irving Lyon, the first scholarly book that pictured antique American furniture, was published in 1891. For the first time, the public could see real Colonial furniture, and it inspired copies and adaptations.

About 1910 there was another revival of interest in the furniture of our ancestors. A few popular decorators were making copies of

The 1948 catalog from Carl Forslund Furniture Company of Grand Rapids, Michigan, features Colonial Revival furniture. This table mixes Empire and Victorian design ideas. The company suggested you buy a pair for either side of the bed, a twentieth-century decorating idea.

At first this seems like a normal table, but it is made entirely of paraffin and can be used as a candle, although where does the dripping wax go? This is a Droog Design idea from the 1990s. (Photo: Droog Design)

Wallace Nutting

Wallace Nutting (1861–1941) was a clergyman who became famous as a photographer, manufacturer, antiquarian, and author. Nutting is best known for his "prints" that are really hand-colored photographs of landscapes, flowers, Colonial interiors, architectural exteriors, and other scenes. (See page 385.)

The furniture in Nutting's photographs was so well liked he decided it would sell, so in 1917 he started a workshop in Framingham, Massachusetts, to make furniture that copied antique furniture he had bought to furnish the rooms pictured in his photographs. Nutting pieces were handmade in the old manner, although some motor-driven machinery was used. Wallace Nutting marked his furniture with a paper label until 1922. A branded script signature was used from 1922 to 1924, and a branded block signature dates furniture made from 1925 to 1941. Nutting furniture was made primarily from oak and maple often in the style of the seventeenth century. He also made eighteenth-century pine, walnut, and maple cupboards, tables, and Windsor chairs and some mahogany furniture. Over 250 different designs were made.

Nutting's furniture business was never a financial success. He sold many pieces, but it was the prints that made money. The right to use the name *Wallace Nutting* was purchased by the Drexel Furniture Company in the 1950s. It produced several collections of cherry *Wallace Nutting Furniture*.

This Windsor armchair made by Wallace Nutting is a copy of an eighteenth-century chair. Nutting chairs were marked with a paper label or a brand. Another clue is a 400-500 numeral stamped on the bottom, the model number of a Nutting chair. (Photo: Cottone)

authentic sixteenth- and seventeenth-century European furniture to be used by clients who lived in large early-twentieth-century mansions. In 1917 Wallace Nutting, best known for his photographs of Colonial interiors, started to make accurate reproductions of seventeenth- and eighteenth-century furniture. In 1924 the Metropolitan Museum of Art in New York opened the American Decorative Arts wing, giving a new status to "old" furniture.

By the 1910s, many reproductions of earlier styles of furniture were on the market. Authentic copies were made by cabinetmakers like Ernest Hagen of New York City or Nathan Margolis of Hartford, Connecticut. The Margolis shop worked from about 1894 to about 1973. Other makers were inspired by the old, but adapted the styles to create new revival looks that are now collected. "Flemish" high-backed chairs with caned seats, carved oak library tables, and even large, tall bedroom sets were back in style. Carved and curved Victorian furniture became popular again in the 1930s, and dozens of furniture companies made reproductions and adaptations. The 1940s saw a Colonial revival that inspired inexpensive wooden furniture like shoemaker's-bench coffee tables, lamps made to look like wooden candlesticks or churns, and Windsor chairs. Most of these reproductions were made for middle-class families. The well-to-do were decorating with Williamsburg reproductions and other accurate copies of eighteenth-century Chippendale and Sheraton manufactured by quality makers. The 1920s–1930s versions of seventeenth-century Jacobean dining room sets with table, chairs, and cupboards, and carved chairs for the hall and living room came back into style in the 1990s, when those who were buying old homes with large rooms discovered very little modern furniture was made for large, high-ceiling rooms.

Twentieth-Century American Makers of Colonial through Victorian Revival-Style Furniture

Boston, Massachusetts, and Grand Rapids, Michigan, were furniture-making centers in the twentieth century. Important makers of revival-style furniture in Boston were Charak Furniture Company, Irving and Casson, Kaplan Furniture Company, and Old Colony Furniture Company. Grand Rapids companies that made revival-style furniture included Berkey & Gay Furniture Company, John Widdicomb Company, Kindel Furniture Company, Phoenix Furniture Company, and Nelson, Matter & Company.

Other firms that made revival-style furniture were Baker Furniture Factories of Allegan, Michigan; Biggs Furniture Company of Richmond, Virginia; Kittinger Furniture Company of Buffalo, New York; Margolis of Hartford, Connecticut; Potthast Brothers of Baltimore, Maryland; and Meier & Hagen and Sypher & Company, both of New York City.

Lane Company

Lane furniture traces its beginnings back to an abandoned packing-box plant that was purchased for $500 in 1912 and turned into a factory to make cedar chests. Edward Lane, with little manufacturing experience, started the Standard Red Cedar Chest Company in the Altavista, Virginia, plant that his father had purchased. The company, now called Lane Furniture Industries, has continued to make cedar chests, except during World War I when it made ammunition boxes. In 1951 the firm began making small tables and, by 1956, bedroom and dining room furniture. In the 1960s it introduced wall systems, desks, bars, plant stands, and other furniture. Chairs and upholstered furniture were added in the 1960s. Lane made furniture in the popular styles of the day, but best known is the cedar chest. Every one is marked with the name *Lane* stenciled on the bottom. Today Lane makes living room, dining room, bedroom furniture, and, of course, cedar chests.

Cedar chests in many different styles were made by Lane. This 1930s chest has design elements from several early styles.

WESTPORT AND ADIRONDACK CHAIRS

Thomas Lee designed the *Westport* chair about 1900 and patented it in 1905. The children's version was patented in 1922. The plain-line chair, with flat wooden boards and an angled back, was an oddity of style in its day and never became popular. But thousands of similar chairs with slatted seat and back were made from the 1920s and became common by the 1940s. They were usually called *Adirondack* chairs.

Branches from hickory trees were cut and used as slats, arms, and legs of this rustic chair. Sometimes the bark was left on to give the piece an even more rustic look.
(Photo: One of a Kind Antiques)

RUSTIC FURNITURE

The tradition of rustic and twig furniture used in Adirondack lodges beginning about 1875 influenced the informal homes in the western United States in the 1930s. Most rustic 1930s furniture was custom-made for large homes built of stone and logs.

California developed its own rustic furniture influenced by the Arts and Crafts style. Monterey furniture was produced by the Mason Manufacturing Company in Los Angeles from 1929 to 1943. The designs featured the Old West, Mexican motifs, and even cowboys from the movies. The furniture was made of Oregon alder wood, sometimes treated to look dark and old, and had heavy iron hinges, latches, and trim. In the late 1930s, tooled leather and orange-stained wood were used. Over 120 different pieces of furniture were manufactured, along with lamps and other decorative items. Pieces were branded with a horseshoe design or sometimes the word *Monterey*.

Thomas Canada Molesworth (1890–1977) moved to Cody, Wyoming, in 1931 and opened the Shoshone Furniture Company, where he made rustic-style furniture. His pieces featured carved western motifs on cabinets and animal figures on beds. He used twigs to make end tables and huge pole frames for chairs and sofas. Chairs were often upholstered in leather. Many ranches and hotels in the area were furnished with Molesworth designs. Molesworth's shop closed in 1958.

Jack Kranenberg also made western rustic furniture. Working in Jackson, Wyoming, in the 1940s, he used burled pine, buffalo and bear cutouts, and loose cushions on his pieces.

Molesworth created a room filled with his unique furniture inspired by Indian and cowboy motifs. This chair with the keyhole back, padded seat, and rough, thick legs was designed in about 1935. It was made with different designs on the back. (Photo: Fighting Bear Antiques)

COUNTRY FURNITURE

The meaning of the term *country furniture* has changed in the past fifty years. When we wrote *American Country Furniture, 1780–1875* in 1965, *country furniture* meant furniture made away from big cities like Boston, New York, Philadelphia, or Baltimore. We wrote: "We feel that the country furniture was the work of an individual with a specific need in mind, and the crudely shaped log often served as well as the more stylized chair or table." Country furniture was primarily a less sophisticated interpretation of city furniture. It could include furniture from the 1700s to the 1900s. Painted chairs like those by Hitchcock, ladder-back chairs, simple curly maple chests, and other pieces—many in museums—were included.

Many pieces in our book would not be called *country* today. Mary Emmerling's book *American Country*, published in 1980, changed the meaning of the word. Although Emmerling's book pictured many authentic old and rare rural pieces, decorators, shop owners, and collectors began to think that the "country" look included not only old, simple pieces and primitive, painted furniture, but also newer commercial pieces that might deliberately have peeling paint or a very distressed finish. Because true antique country furniture was in short supply, decorators began to look for substitutes, and the term *country* came to include newer commercial pieces.

Today collectors use the term to refer to a style that includes both old and new furniture and accessories, so *country* also includes rag rugs, quilts, and shelves of fabrics with old-fashioned patterns. Experts who once narrowly defined the term *country* now avoid it, using *primitive*, *rustic*, or *unsophisticated* instead.

Shaker Furniture

Shaker furniture became a worldwide icon of furniture design when it was featured at Expo 67, the 1967 world's fair in Montreal, Canada. The very modern look of the designs that originated with the Shakers, a religious sect that arrived in America from England in 1774, was a surprise to many. The Shaker religion preached the importance of honesty, integrity, goodness, trust, hard work,

Hopalong Cassidy, Tom Mix, and other movie cowboys were stars in the 1930s and '40s and inspired pseudo-western furniture and accessories for children's rooms. Most of this "cowboy" furniture was mass-produced and available at Sears or inexpensive furniture stores.

equality, and celibacy. The self-contained sect made its own nails; wove strips of fabric for chair seats; invented the flat broom, circular saw, and clothespin; and even helped Mr. Borden create evaporated milk. Shakers believed their dedication to work and perfection were a reflection of their dedication to God, and the products they sold to outsiders were known for reliability and quality. Over six thousand followers lived in nineteen settlements about 1850, but by the 1940s most of the communities were empty and in 2006 only four Shakers remained. Although a few people collected Shaker furniture in the 1890s, it wasn't until the 1950s that most collectors, museums, and researchers discovered the virtues of the Shakers and their architecture, furniture, inventions, and products.

The best Shaker furniture found today was made by the Shakers for their own use. Sewing tables, desks, chests, boxes, and even cabinets that had once been built into the wall are seen in restored Shaker settlements, museums, and private collections. All have the same Shaker characteristics: simple straight lines, no added carving or adornment, parts shaped in special ways to be useful, and painted or stained wood chosen for its structural advantages as well as the graining. Recent research has found that the walls and floors of the rooms and some built-in furniture were painted or stained bright yellow, blue, or brown, although the old colors that remain now are faded.

The only furniture Shakers made to sell to outsiders were chairs. Each community made slightly different chairs, but all had the same simple turned posts topped by rounded finials; slat backs; tape or rush seats; and straight, although sometimes angled, legs. Each chair was lightweight and strong. Sizes ranged from 0 for children to 7 for large adults. The chairs were made one at a time by a single craftsman. Tape seats were colorful and practical, of no interest to bugs, and easy to clean. A few atypical chairs using bentwood parts or other "worldly" changes were made by the Shakers in the early twentieth century.

The Shakers made furniture like this table with slim legs, no added carving, useful parts like the drop leaves, and attractive wood. The cherry and birch table was made and used in about 1830 at a Maine settlement. (Photo: Skinner)

Waterfall Furniture

The Depression of the 1930s forced furniture manufacturers to create inexpensive furniture for the middle class. A new method was invented to kiln-dry red gum tree wood, which had always cracked when dried. Waterfall furniture was made with red gum tree lumber core plywood, which was strong and cheap. The drawer fronts on chests were veneered with a striped wood, the edges of the tops were rounded, and the finished pieces were a style known as *waterfall*. Sometimes instead of real wood veneer, a picture of the veneer was printed on paper, then glued to the wood.

Waterfall style was popular for bedroom sets and dining rooms, but it was also adapted to other furnishings like the 1934 Stewart-Warner tombstone *model table radio. Notice the striped wood veneer and rounded edges. (Photo: Mike Schultz)*

The painted furniture decorated by Peter Hunt started a nationwide craze. His patterns and books were used by amateurs, like the owner of this bench, who decorated their own pieces of wooden furniture. (Photo: Eldred's)

The Shakers produced furniture from about 1790 to 1940. However, Shaker furniture with its clean lines was a major influence on modern designs, especially the work of Scandinavian furniture designers. Since the 1950s, accurate as well as poor reproductions and adaptations of Shaker furniture—including tables, chests, and chairs—have been made.

Hunt for Hunt

Peter Hunt, a Cape Cod designer, began painting pseudo-Pennsylvania German designs on plain wooden furniture in the 1940s. His patterns were also available for do-it-yourself projects. Today collectors buy both expensive pieces painted by Peter Hunt himself and less expensive homemade versions of Hunt Patterns painted by talented housewives. Hunt signed most of his work.

FURNITURE NOT MADE OF WOOD

Wicker and Rattan

Rattan, the stem of a climbing palm found in Asia, has been used by European furniture makers since the sixteenth century. It was called *Oriental cane*. By

Heywood-Wakefield

the middle of the nineteenth century, it was being used for many pieces of Victorian wicker furniture in the United States. Wicker was light and durable, so ideally suited for porch and garden furniture. Although wicker was out of fashion by the late 1800s, it again gained favor in 1921, when the Coconut Grove nightclub opened in Los Angeles and the tropical look was "in." Thick round strands of rattan were used to make furniture that was both art deco and Polynesian in style. Movie stars in California furnished their dens, bars, and porches with rattan furniture, and it was soon fashionable in all parts of the country. The decor often featured fake palm trees and Hawaiian flower-printed upholstery as well. Some named the look *Tropical Modern* or *Tropical Deco*.

At the beginning of the twentieth century, Heywood Brothers and Wakefield Company was the world's largest manufacturer of chairs and its largest importer of rattan. In 1921 the company purchased the Lloyd Manufacturing Company of Menominee, Michigan, maker of synthetic machine-woven wicker called *Lloyd Loom*. That same year, Heywood Brothers and Wakefield, headquartered in Gardner, Massachusetts, simplified its name to the Heywood-Wakefield Company. It made blond, streamlined wooden furniture from the 1930s through the 1960s. The company went bankrupt in 1981 and has had several owners since. For a time in the 1980s and 1990s, it once again made wicker furniture. South Beach Furniture bought remnants of Heywood-Wakefield in 1992 and began reproducing original designs. It is still making blond Heywood-Wakefield Modern furniture.

Heywood-Wakefield furniture made from light wood was popular starting in the 1930s. This Heywood-Wakefield china cabinet with sliding glass doors has a champagne finish. (Photo: Rago)

Reed, a grassy plant similar to straw, was used for early American wicker. The term *reed* is sometimes used as another name for the core of the rattan vine. Ypsilanti Reed Furniture Company of Ionia, Michigan, and Heywood-Wakefield made rattan reed furniture. Austrian designer Paul Frankl, who moved to the United States in 1914, studied techniques for making furniture of wicker and other cane fibers in Japan and the Philippines. In 1929 he designed reed furniture for Ficks Reed Furniture Company, which is still making wicker and rattan furniture in Cincinnati, Ohio.

Metal Furniture

Wrought-iron garden furniture was popular in the 1800s. Toward the end of the century, lightweight chairs, tables, settees, and plant stands made of twisted steel wire were used in gardens, indoor greenhouses, and garden rooms. At the beginning of the twentieth century, cast iron was grain-painted to resemble wood. Then chrome and aluminum, much lighter-weight metals, were used with their original silvery finish. By the 1930s, parts for metal furniture were machine-made.

Tubular Steel

Marcel Breuer made the first metal furniture from tubular steel in 1924, when he was studying at the Bauhaus. Four years later he designed the cantilevered chair *Model No. B-32*, made of a single

Le Corbusier, who worked in Paris, made chromed steel chairs as early as the 1920s. He designed this chaise longue in the 1960s. It has a chrome-plated tubular steel frame with cowhide upholstery and a black lacquered steel base.
(Photo: Treadway)

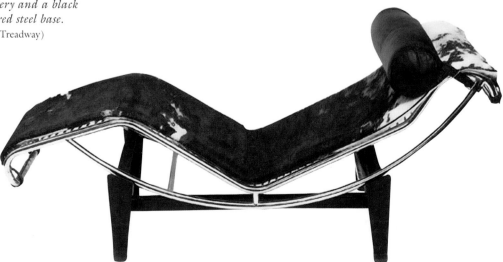

length of tubing, wood, and cane—a design that is still popular. In 1927 examples of metal furniture by other designers were displayed at an important German exhibition. Thonet, the company known for its bentwood furniture in the nineteenth century, began to mass-produce tubular steel chairs in 1928. Designers made tubular steel chairs with glass, canvas, or even leather seats. D.I.M. (Décoration Intérieure Moderne) of France and PEL (Practical Equipment Limited) of England were making the metal chairs, tables, and desks by the 1930s. PEL's most famous chair is the *Model RP6*, a stacking chair made of tubular metal and canvas.

Warren McArthur made what is now the best-known tubular furniture made in the United States. His company, Warren McArthur Corporation, operated in Rome, New York, from 1933 to 1948. Other important American designers of metal furniture were Donald Deskey, Walter Kantack, and Gilbert Rohde, all working in New York, and Kem Weber in Los Angeles. American companies that have manufactured metal furniture include Herman Miller, Inc., of Zeeland, Michigan; Howell Company of Geneva, Illinois; Troy Sunshade Company of Troy, Ohio; and Widdicomb Furniture Company of Grand Rapids, Michigan.

Brass Beds

Brass beds became popular in America in the middle of the nineteenth century. Early brass beds had canopies and elaborate decorations, but gradually the canopy disappeared and, by the early 1900s, decorations became more open and symmetrical. Some of the best beds were made totally of brass, with no supporting iron core. They were plain, made with only straight lines. There were few design changes until the 1920s, when typically art deco designs

This anodized aluminum chair designed by Warren McArthur in the 1930s is unusual because it has blue and yellow anodized couplings and red vinyl upholstery.
(Photo: Wright)

Brown plastic was molded to form this side chair designed by Vernor Panton for Herman Miller. It is surprisingly comfortable because the plastic shape was formed to fit the curves of the body. (Photo: Rago)

were produced. The demand for brass beds ended in 1930, and it was not until the 1960s that they again gained favor. Reproductions and new versions of brass beds are still being manufactured.

Plastic Furniture

Although the first plastics were invented in the mid-nineteenth century, plastic was not in general use for household items until the 1920s and 1930s. It was used as an alternative to rubber and for radios cases or kitchen-tool handles. By 1927 plastics like vinyl and nylon were developed. Research during World War II led to even more types of plastics, and by the 1950s designers were experimenting and creating lightweight, colorful, inexpensive plastic furniture.

New materials made new styles of furniture possible. In the 1940s, "organic" designs were created. One of the first popular mass-produced plastic chairs was probably the *DAR* chair designed by Charles and Ray Eames in 1948 and produced by Zenith Plastics for Herman Miller Furniture Company. The *Womb* chair (1947) and the single-pedestal *Tulip* armchair (1955), designed by Eero Saarinen and manufactured by Knoll, were designed to be made of fiberglass-reinforced plastic. In the 1950s, designers wanted affordable good design for the masses, and molded plastics made this possible. Great colors were introduced without using fabric upholstery. A chair no longer had to have three or four legs and a seat; a curved piece of strong plastic would do. The Italian-made *Universale* stacking chair designed by Joe Colombo in 1965 and manufactured by Kartell was the first chair made in one piece by injection molding. Verner Panton's 1968 stacking chair was the first cantilevered chair made from a single piece of plastic. Many other designers and manufacturers had technical problems with plastic well into the 1960s. Legs would break, seats would crack, and heat would soften the plastic.

It may look like a cactus, but this limited-edition molded green foam plant is actually a coat rack designed in Italy in 1972. (Photo: Wright)

In the 1900s, furniture was made from many types of plastic, including Bakelite (c.1909), Formica (invented in 1913 as a substitute "for mica" in electrical insulation, used for furniture starting in the 1920s), Lucite (1930s), acrylics (1930s), fiberglass (1930s), and ABS (acrylonitrile butadiene styrene, 1950s). Soft plastics like vinyl and polyurethane foam were used to make inflatable furniture, first designed by the Italian firm of De Pas, D'Urbino and Lomazzi in 1967. Many mass-produced yet one-of-a-kind pieces were designed by Gaetano Pesce from multicolored resin dripped into molds or over other forms to create random patterns in color and shape.

Plastic furniture is still popular. Medium-priced chairs and tables, both copies of earlier designs and new styles, are available. Garden furniture made of molded plastic to resemble wicker, iron, or stone sells for very low prices. Stylish contemporary designs, like the injection-molded one-piece clear and colored plastic *Louis Ghost* chairs designed by Philippe Starck in 2002 and the *Briton* garden bench designed by Paolo Rizzatto in 2003, sell for higher prices.

CLOCKS

Lux Clock Company in Waterbury, Connecticut, made many novelty clocks that kept time, moved, and sometimes made noise. This 1928 cat clock wags its tail (the pendulum) and moves its eyes. The clock case is made of pressed sawdust and resin.

At the beginning of the twentieth century, the *tambour* or *Napoleon hat* clock, a simple round-faced clock in an elongated, curved, dark wood or marble case, was found on many mantels. Rectangular Arts and Crafts-style oak clocks were also popular. Some of the most sought-after clocks made from 1900 to 1950 were animated clocks in the shape of dogs, cats, flowers, or clowns sold by Lux Clock Company, August Keebler, Westclox, and others. These clocks operated with a key-wind and pendulum mechanism that could wag a puppy's tail or a clown's necktie. *Mystery* clocks made by Cartier and a few others were popular between 1913 and 1930. The hands of these glass-faced, often jeweled clocks seemed suspended in the center of the clockface; no works could be seen. Mystery clocks continue to be made.

Windup Clocks

Windup clocks made of marble, onyx, and metal were made in sophisticated art deco styles in the 1920s. Chrome, brass, copper, Bakelite, Formica, celluloid, and glass were used for clock cases for living room and bedroom clocks in the 1930s. Eight-day windups were made in modern designs. Other clever clocks shaped like airplanes or statues with an added clockface, cartoon characters, even a series of clocks with neon trim were fashionable. An alarm clock with a drawing of a cartoon character like Mickey Mouse or Popeye was in the children's bedroom; the character's moving arms pointed to the time. Other animated alarm clocks showed a man sawing wood, a car racing around a road, and other moving scenes.

The sophisticated appearance of this Lux mantel clock with griffins and a gold dial hides the fact that this is just a windup clock. (Photo: Deco Days)

Battery Operated Clocks

The battery-powered clock was common in the late nineteenth century, but its batteries were large and often leaked. In 1902 Herbert Scott patented a battery-operated clock that was made by Every-Ready Electric Specialties Company. The case was made with two brass pillars that held the batteries. A popular battery-operated clock was the *Bulle* clock patented in England in 1922. But the average household in the United States did not use a battery-operated clock until the 1930s. Alarm clocks, figural clocks, mantel clocks, and many other types were made with slight variations in design to hold the new power source. Inexpensive plastic wall clocks were popular in the 1930s kitchen. The red and white color scheme of the rest of the kitchen dictated the color. Some designers created amusing kitchen clocks shaped like chefs or apples or teapots in the typical forties styles.

Nelson clocks were often designed with spokes radiating from the center. Many had no numerals; the position of the hands told the time. This Ball *clock with painted wooden balls and brass rods has remained a favorite since the 1950s.* (Photo: Treadway)

Electric Clocks

In the 1920s, art deco clocks that plugged into the electric wall socket were designed with geometric shapes and simple lines. The deco marble, bronze, and art glass clocks were copied in cheap bronzed pot metal, chrome, glass, and wood. More expensive clocks were also popular. Green metal figural clocks by Frankart, silver and gold clocks set with precious jewels by Cartier or Tiffany, and glass clock cases by Daum, Lalique, and Sabino were found in upper-class homes.

Bar customers couldn't miss this electric wall clock first made in 1936. The clock face is black. The other colors are created by green and red neon. The clock was named Aztec *because the design was inspired by Mexican pyramids.*

The electric digital clock design created in 1933 by Kem Weber for Lawson Time, Inc., took clock design in a new direction. The traditional dial was gone, and the numbers, not the hands, moved. A hum replaced the tick-tock, and the bell chime became a buzz. Thousand of copies soon followed.

Other important twentieth-century designers also created more familiar electric clocks. In 1933 Gilbert Rohde designed a clock with a chrome base and a face with the hours marked by chrome balls on a round blue mirror. Russel Wright created inexpensive, plastic-cased kitchen clocks for General Electric in the 1940s. George Nelson designed the *Ball* clock in 1949; twelve sticks with balls on the end radiated from the center of the clockface to mark the hours. Many versions of this design were made. The round,

The Kem Weber electric digital clock was a totally different-looking clock. The numerals moved, there were no hands, and the clock didn't tick. This streamlined clock with a copper and brass finish, the Zephyr, *inspired many digital clocks that followed.* (Photo: Mike Schultz)

Henry Dreyfuss
Industrial Designer

Henry Dreyfuss (1904–1972) designed the famous *Princess* and *Trimline* phones, the round Honeywell thermostat, and the *Big Ben* alarm clock often found at flea markets. Dreyfuss apprenticed with well-known industrial designer Norman Bel Geddes in 1923, and in 1929 he opened his own design office in New York City.

Known for his unfussy decorations and simple, functional shapes, Dreyfuss created many items that were so well designed they needed no instruction book. In 1930 Dreyfuss designed the black cradle phone with a dial for Bell Telephone Company. He kept improving the phones, making them easier to clean and repair, and harder to damage. The *Model 500* phone (1949), made of less expensive plastic, was lighter and more durable and comfortable to use. The *Princess* phone with a lighted dial (1959) and the *Trimline* phone (1965) with a push button dial on the handset, not the base, were also his designs. He created alarm clocks for Westclox, redesigning the 1909 Big Ben alarm clock in 1931, then again in a streamlined style in 1939.

The 1931 Sears, Roebuck Toperator washing machine that combined all controls into one area on the top, a 1932 electric toaster, the 1934 G.E. monitor-top refrigerator that got rid of the hard-to-clean round top, the 1935 Hoover vacuum cleaner, insulated carafes for American Thermos Bottle Company (1936), RCA television sets from 1946, and the Honeywell round-dial easy-to-read wall thermostat (1953) were all designed by Dreyfuss. But he is probably best known for his 1938 design for the famous *Twentieth Century Limited*, called the most glamorous American train ever. The train was decorated with pastels, not the usual green and brown. He designed the train inside and out, including dinnerware by Buffalo China Company and menus.

glass Nelson *Steering Wheel* clock from the 1950s was framed by a metal band with brass strips indicating the hours and metal hands tipped with an oval and an arrow. Nelson designed hundreds of clocks based on the idea of the rays of a "sun" marking the hours for the moving hands. Usually numerals were not used. By the 1950s, there was the clock radio, and Peter Max added colorful decoration to clock radios made by General Electric in the 1960s. The 1980s saw the clock radio cased with a tiny television set.

Designers continued to make clocks in styles that would blend with the most contemporary styles. Some clockmakers created unusual, even eccentric clocks unlike any ever seen before. Clocks from the 1990s include confusing Italian-designed clocks by Gaetano Pesce that are made of irregular flat slabs of multicolored resin, clocks made by studio artists that resemble a grouping of colorful unrelated metal pieces that move with each tick or tock, and a French clock that looks like a large crystal snail. Many abstract nineties clocks were made of brushed aluminum and neon and ran on a quartz battery.

Chapter 8

Lamps and Lighting

LIGHTING CHANGED DRAMATICALLY with the invention of the lightbulb in 1879. The shape of the electric bulb and the nature of a light source with no flame made it possible for the first time to design a lamp with the light focused down or at an angle. Electric lamps could be made with shades that would screen or direct the light.

The invention of the electric lightbulb made it possible to design a lamp that lit a tabletop. The colored slag glass in this lamp by Edward Miller & Company gave an added glow. (Photo: Fontaine's)

EARLY TWENTIETH-CENTURY LAMP MAKERS

The best-known names in early twentieth-century American electric lamps are Tiffany, Handel, and Pairpoint. All three companies made elaborate art glass lampshades in art nouveau and art deco styles using striking shapes and colors, usually mounted on bronze bases. Table lamps by the "big three" sell for the highest prices, but there are similar, signed lamps by less famous but respected makers (see box on page 259) and also lamps that are well made but unmarked and unattributed. Lighting fixtures in the Arts and Crafts style were made by Gustav Stickley's Craftsman Workshops, Elbert Hubbard's Roycroft community, and a few other shops. Emeralite and Aladdin lamps are also popular today.

RECORD PRICES FOR TIFFANY LAMPS

In 1998 a Tiffany *Peacock* centerpiece lamp sold for $1,875,500 and a Tiffany *Magnolia* leaded glass and gilt-bronze floor lamp sold for $1,762,500.

A record $321,100 was paid for this Tiffany Studios Poinsettia floor lamp. The shade is decorated with pink, red, and amethyst poinsettia blossoms and green and amber leaves. (Photo: Doyle New York)

Tiffany

Tiffany Studios made lamps from about 1891 to 1928. It was owned by glassmaker and artist Louis Comfort Tiffany, the son of Charles Lewis Tiffany, founder of the New York store Tiffany & Company. (See page 268 in the Silver and Other Metals chapter for more on Tiffany.) Tiffany Studios made many types of lamps using electric bulbs, kerosene, or oil. Tiffany was making student lamps, blown-glass oil lamps, and hanging fixtures with leaded glass globes by 1898. Bronze table and floor lamp bases were introduced in 1899, when three of the most famous lamp designs were made: the *Dragon Fly*, the *Nautilus*, and the *Tyler Scroll* lamps. His famous lily lamp, first made in 1900, had a series of small shades and bulbs that focused light down to form a circle on the tabletop.

Tiffany Studios made over five hundred different lamp base designs and almost five hundred lampshade designs. Tiffany bases were usually made of bronze; a few had glass accents. Grueby, Teco, and other potteries made pottery bases for Tiffany lamps. The shades were made of pieces of colored glass or iridescent Favrile glass. Bronze, cut-out silver, and blown or molded glass were also used for shades.

The metal base of a Tiffany lamp, or a plate attached to the base, was stamped with a model number after 1902. A model number was also marked on the metal part of the shade. Iridescent glass shades were marked with the engraved word *Favrile*. A client chose both a lamp base and a shade, so many different combinations were possible. The lamp left the Tiffany showroom with a shade and a base with identical numbers. Many "matched" lamps can be found now with different shades. It is claimed that all Tiffany lamps were signed.

Handel

Although Tiffany lamps are the most famous, many other glass-shaded lamps were made in the early twentieth century. Handel lamps made by Philip Handel are considered among the finest.

In 1893 Handel bought out his partner, Adolph Eyden, and in 1903 changed his glass-decorating company's name to The Handel

Tiffany Studios lamps with leaded glass shades are so famous that Tiffany has come to mean both the original, expensive, bronze and glass lamps and the modern glass and plastic copies. The shade of this authentic Tiffany lamp has Favrile glass balls. (Photo: James Julia)

The chipped ice shade, a special type of reverse-painted lamp shade, was developed by Handel. This 18-inch-diameter shade with a parrot design is signed *Handel 6674.* (Photo: James Julia)

RECORD PRICE FOR A HANDEL LAMP

A Handel *Aquarium* lamp with a glass shade painted with an underwater scene of tropical fish sold for $82,500 in 1999.

The Orange Tree *is perhaps the most famous Pairpoint puffy lamp. The 24-inch shade has three-dimensional blown-out oranges and branches. The base is a tree trunk.* (Photo: James Julia)

Company. The firm, located in Meriden, Connecticut, closed in 1936. It made bottles, boxes, vases, and other items of metal, china, and glass. Handel lamps were made for use with oil, gas, or electricity. Desk lamps, table lamps, floor lamps, night-lights, small shades for wall fixtures, and other types of lamps were produced. Most of the pieces were signed *Handel* on a cloth label or impressed, painted, or stamped on the base.

Handel patented his glass lampshades known as *chipped ice*, which had a frosted, rough, textured surface on the outside and a painted design on the inside. Other shades were made using a *sand-finishing* technique, scattering glass beads on the surface of the shade and refiring it so the beads would melt and stick to the surface. Handel also manufactured leaded glass, metal-framed glass, and other glass shades. Painted shades are usually signed at the inside edge.

It is estimated that the company made 25,000 lamps a year during the twenty-five years of its peak production. Many of these were ordinary lamps that sold for $6 and up. The highest-priced lamps with leaded glass or reverse-painted glass shades originally sold for $150.

Pairpoint

Pairpoint lamps were made from 1890 to 1929 in New Bedford, Massachusetts. The company manufactured glass and silver-plated wares as well as lamps. It made pressed, cut, and decorated glass shades. There are three basic types of Pairpoint shades. Some shades were made with vertical ribs, and occasionally these featured floral designs. The second type were glass shades decorated with scenic designs. The most expensive style is what collectors refer to as a *blown-out* or *Puffy*, a glass shade made with three-dimensional designs, such as an owl, roses, or an orange tree. All of the shades were frosted, then decorated. Shades can range in size from 3½ inches to 22 inches in diameter. Bases were often made to match the shade; for example, a tree-trunk base was fitted with an orange-tree shade. Bases were usually made of metal with a brass, bronze, copper, or silver finish. Glass also was used for bases, and a few wooden bases are known. The shades were not always signed, which makes identification difficult. A few pieces are stamped *The Pairpoint Corporation*. Others say *Patented July 9, 1907*.

Arts and Crafts

In the early years of the twentieth century, lamps in the Arts and Crafts style were made with hammered copper, bronzed metal, or oak bases and mica, colored glass, or woven willow lampshades. The uncomplicated metalwork designs, straight lines, and geometric shapes of the Arts and Crafts style contrasted with the organic, curved, floral art nouveau designs also popular at this time. Tiffany Studios and Handel produced lamps in both styles. Gustav Stickley made lamps of heavy oak and metal and did not favor the colorful leaded or painted glass used by other makers. Other important Arts and Crafts lamp manufacturers were Heintz Art Metal Shop, Jefferson Company, Moe-Bridges Company, the Roycroft community, and Dirk Van Erp Studio.

The Dirk Van Erp hammered-copper lamp with an orange mica shade in the shape of a Chinese hat is among the most famous Arts and Crafts lamps. (Photo: Craftsman Auctions)

Emeralite

Office desks in the 1920s usually had a lamp with a green glass shade thought to reduce glare and eyestrain. *Emeralite* lamps were made from 1909 to the 1940s by H. G. McFaddin & Company of New York City. The lamps had a brass or bronze base and a green glass shade lined with white opal glass. The company's slogan was "Be kind to your eyes." Similar green-shaded lamps were produced by other firms. The William E. Gray

FRANKART

Frankart, Inc., of New York City mass-produced nude dancing-lady lamps, ashtrays, and other decorative art deco items in the 1920s and 1930s. They were made of a white lead composition and spray-painted. *Frankart Inc.*, the patent number, and the year were stamped on the base.

Art-deco lamps by Frankart often featured women as part of the green or gray painted base. They were frequently copied. (Photo: David Negley's)

Company of Utica, New York, made the *Rex-O-Lux* lamp in the 1920s. The New York City firm of S. Robert Schwartz made *Greenalite* lamps.

Aladdin Lamps

Kerosene lamps became popular after the start of the modern petroleum industry in the middle of the nineteenth century. The lamps of the 1890s used round wicks with air supplied to the flame through a central tube. In 1905 a German kerosene lamp was made with a mantle that fit over the burner to give a better light. Victor Johnson of Kansas City, Missouri, saw the German lamp and started a company in Chicago to make and sell this type of lamp. He called his company the Mantle Lamp Company of America and then named his product the *Aladdin Lamp.* An instant success, it gave more light and used less fuel than earlier kerosene lamps. Improvements continued, and the company made many types of Aladdin lamps, including table, hanging, bracket, and floor lamps. Kerosene lamps for home use were manufactured at the Aladdin factory in Nashville, Tennessee, until 1968. The company also made electric lamps and still makes lamps in other countries.

The Aladdin lamps most popular with today's collectors are the glass models made in the 1930s. A variety of styles were made in amber, peach, white, moonstone, cobalt blue, red, and many other colors. The glass finials used with these lamps are hard to find today and can sell for over $100.

Early Twentieth-Century Lamp Manufacturers

Manufacturer and Location	Dates	Mark
Bradley & Hubbard Meriden, Connecticut	1852–1940	
Craftsman, Gustav Stickley Syracuse, New York	1901–1915	
Classique Milwaukee, Wisconsin	c.1920	CLASSIQUE
Dirk Van Erp Studio San Francisco, California	1909–1977	
Duffner & Kimberly New York, New York	c.1906–1926	DUFFNER & KIMBERLY
Handel Company Meriden, Connecticut	1885–1936	
Heintz Art Metal Shop Buffalo, New York	1906–1935	
Jefferson Glass House/ Jefferson Lamp Company Follansbee, West Virginia	1907–early 1930s	
Edward Miller & Company Meriden, Connecticut	c.1881–1920	
Moe-Bridges Company Milwaukee, Wisconsin	c.1920–1930	MOE BRIDGES
Pairpoint Corporation New Bedford and Sagamore, Massachusetts	1880–present	
Riviere Studios New York, New York	c.1910	Lamps rarely marked
Roycroft East Aurora, New York	c.1895–1938	
Tiffany Studios Corona, New York	1878–1933	TIFFANY STVDIOS NEW YORK

Italian glass of the 1950s was daring. Barovier & Toso made this glass, brass, and enameled metal chandelier that inspired many copies. (Photo: Wright)

Top Right: These were the ultimate dressing table lamps in the 1930s, an art deco design made of aluminum, Bakelite, and glass. (Photo: Wright)

Bottom Left: This 1950s pole lamp, made by the Italian firm Arredoluce, was adjustable. (Photo: Wright)

THE MID-1920s TO THE 1960s

From about 1925 through much of the 1930s, art deco designers created lamps that softened the light cast by electric bulbs. They replaced colored-glass shades with frosted, opaque, and smoked glass and designed uplights, indirect lighting with bulbs that shone upward. Stained glass went out of favor, and bronze, painted metal, alabaster, marble, lacquer, chrome, aluminum, and mirrored glass came into style.

The best art deco lamp designs originated in France. Some well-known designers are Edgar Brandt, famous for his serpent lights; Damon and La Maison Desny, known for their sleek modern pieces in chromed or nickel-plated metal; D.I.M. (Décoration Intérieure Moderne), whose lamps include the *Saturn* hanging light with a white glass globe circled by nickel-plated rings; and Italian-born Marius Ernest Sabino, who created lights ranging from small lamps to large chandeliers and also architectural lighting for hotels and restaurants. Edmond Etling & Company, a retailer that commissioned pieces, was known for small crystal and chromed metal lamps. Robj was a dealer who sold eclectic lamps, such as a Japanese geisha figure holding a parasol for a shade.

Lamps changed dramatically after World War II. There were daring lamps with asymmetrical shades and amoebalike pottery bases, pole lamps, and floor lamps with thin, swiveling, and cantilevered arms. French and Italian designers led the way for high-style lamps. In the United States, Isamu Noguchi made a lamp of a paper cylinder held on three rodlike legs. George Nelson's table lamps resembled suspended hot air bubbles. Copies were made in every price range.

No one would guess this colorful French art deco pate-de-verre sculpture by G. Argy Rousseau is really a lamp meant to sit on a radio. It is 9¼ inches wide. (Photo: James Julia)

Lamps made in the United States in the 1950s often had a pottery vase as the base and a stiff, drumlike shade like this one made of mica, not linen or plastic. The Fulper lamp is 25 inches high.
(Photo: Treadway)

Potteries, including Fulper, Nelson McCoy Pottery, and Red Wing, made popular lamps that used a vase or figurine as the base. Chrome-plated domes hung from geometric stands. Pivoting lamps on industrial-looking stands were fashionable. Plastic was often used for lamp bases and shades.

The very, very popular pole lamp from the 1950s had a pole with suction cups at the floor and ceiling and swiveling, cone-shaped, colored lampshades. There were novelty lamps like the animated-action or "motion" lamps that had cylindrical shades decorated with pictures of merry-go-rounds, airplanes, forest fires, tropical fish, and more. The heat of the lightbulb in the base caused the shade to revolve, making it look like the picture was moving. Unusual lighting from the fifties includes Moss lamps with Plexiglas bodies, spun-glass shades, and spinning figurines. High-gloss ceramic TV lamps shaped like animals, people, boats, cars, flowers, vases, or planters had almost-hidden small bulbs that gave a dim light thought to relieve eyestrain caused by watching television. Also popular were oversize lamps with huge shades and heavy metal or plaster figural bases featuring calypso dancers, cowboys, cartoon characters, and people in exotic dress, as well as an endless variety of lamps with free-form shades and bases. The hit of the 1960s was the lava lamp, an ever-moving glob of goo; the lamp was used for amusement, not for light.

This Econolite Corporation motion lamp from 1955 has a shade that turns to create the illusion of water rushing over the top of Niagara Falls.

CONTEMPORARY LAMP DESIGN— THE 1970s TO 2000

Lighting designers in the 1970s experimented with new materials—plastics and other synthetics—and new sources of illumination, including halogen bulbs, fluorescent and neon tubes, and LEDs (light-emitting diodes). The neon *Asteroide* floor light (1968) and the *Alogena* series of halogen lamps (1970) are examples of these innovative

Plastic lamps in extreme styles by less well-known makers are still inexpensive and startling. This Casati Ponzio lamp from the Lamperti Design Studios is 13 inches high.

New Lighting Technologies

Thomas Edison produced his first **incandescent** lightbulbs in 1879.

George Claude invented the first practical **neon** lamp in 1911. Neon was used primarily for signs.

Frosted lightbulbs were developed in 1925.

Fluorescent lighting was patented by Edmund Germer in 1927, but its use in businesses wasn't widespread until the 1970s.

Halogen lamps were used in the motion-picture industry in the early 1960s. By the 1980s Halogen torchère or pole lamps were found in many homes.

Track lighting was introduced in the 1960s.

The first visible-spectrum **light-emitting diode (LED)** was developed in 1962 for a General Electric laboratory. Though initially expensive, LED lights are extremely energy-efficient and last longer than incandescent lighting.

Digital dimmers were introduced in the 1980s.

DROOG DESIGN

Droog Design, a collaborative founded in Amsterdam in 1993, has created innovative, playful designs for modern lighting. Droog lamps include the *milk bottle lamp*, a frosted-glass milk bottle with a bulb inside hanging from a chrome top; the *milk bottle chandelier* made of a group of twelve hanging frosted-glass milk bottles; and the *85 Bulbs* chandelier, a cluster of light bulbs hanging from black cords gathered in a bundle at the ceiling. (See page 234 for more on Droog Design.)

This lamp, shaped like a volcano topped by an umbrella, is the creation of the radical design group U.F.O., started in Florence, Italy, in 1967. It was assembled from found objects, including a real umbrella. (Photo: Private Collection, Miami)

designs. The oil crisis of the 1970s led to energy-efficient designs, such as the *Tizio* task light (1972), which became popular in the 1980s, and the *Sintesi* task light (1975), both examples of 1970s high-tech design.

The late 1970s and the 1980s saw the introduction of bold postmodern designs from Studio Alchimia and the Memphis studio (see pages 230–231). Examples of designs from this period include the decorative *Sinerpica* table and floor lamps that use a small bulb that casts little light (1978) and the cactuslike *Atomaria* floor light (1981–1984), both for Studio Alchimia. New technologies resulted in increased energy efficiency and improved lighting in the 1990s. Lighting that adjusts color and intensity like natural sunlight was developed by Artemide with its *Metamorfosi* collection (1996).

Twentieth-Century Lamp Manufacturers

Manufacturer and Location	Dates	Mark
Arredoluce Monza, Italy	c.1945–1970s	MADE IN ITALY ARREDOLUCE MONZA
Arteluce Milan, Italy	1936–1974 (purchased by Flos in 1974)	ARTELUCE MADE IN ITALY
Artemide Pregnana Milanese, Italy	1959–present	Artemide Made in Italy
Frankart, Inc. New York, New York	1920s–1930s	FRANKART, INC.
Fulper Flemington, New Jersey	1858–1935 (Vasecraft Lamps c.1910–1917)	FULPER
H. G. McFaddin & Co. **The Emeralite Company** **Tilaram** New York, New York	1909–1939 1939–1960 1960–1962	EMERALITE DESK LAMP No 8734
Lightolier New York, New York Fall River, Massachusetts	1904–present	LIGHTOLIER
Mantle Lamp Company Chicago, Illinois **Aladdin Industries** Nashville, Tennessee **Aladdin Mantle Lamp Company** Clarksville, Tennessee	1908–1949 1949–1999 1999–present	MANTLE LAMP CO 21c Aladdin

Manufacturer and Location	Dates	Mark
Moss Manufacturing Company San Francisco, California	1937–1968	
Muller Frères Lunéville, France	c.1905–1936	
Nessen Lighting (Associated with Walter von Nessen) New York, New York Mamaroneck, New York	1927–present	
O-luce Milan, Italy	1945–present	
Phoenix Glass Company Monaca, Pennsylvania	1880–present (Became division of Anchor Hocking in 1970)	
Pittsburgh Lamp, Brass and Glass Co. Pittsburgh, Pennsylvania (After bankruptcy, reorganized as Kopp Glass Inc., which is still in business)	1904–1926	
Stiffel Lamp Company Chicago, Illinois	1932–present (Brand purchased by Salton c.2001)	

Chapter 9

SILVER AND
OTHER METALS

ALTHOUGH HUNDREDS OF SILVER manufacturers were creating their own silver patterns in the United States during the twentieth century, two names are the most familiar: *Tiffany* and *Gorham*. These and other sterling silver manufacturers, including International Silver (the result of many small companies merging in 1898), Towle Silversmiths, and Reed & Barton, are still making both traditional and contemporary silverware in "open stock" patterns. That means that often an old set can be completed or filled in at any time. Many of these and other companies also made silver-plated hollow ware and flatware that was less expensive than sterling silver. Until the 1970s, a "best" set of silverware was sterling. Then stainless steel became the choice of some important designers, both for looks and for price.

Silverware for the table, like all other household items, is made with a "look" that is in the style of the day so it will sell. Twentieth-century silver designs ranged from art nouveau to Mission, art deco, streamlined, mid century modern, postmodern, and the very unusual contemporary designs. Silver manufacturers and designers worked in more than one style.

This puzzling art deco box held cigarettes. It was made in the 1930s by Cartier of Paris from silver with onyx, coral, and black enameled trim.
(Photo: Sotheby's)

Tiffany & Company

The famous store Tiffany & Company traces its origins back to Tiffany & Young, a stationery and fancy goods store started in New York by Charles Lewis Tiffany and James B. Young in 1837. Sixteen years later, when Charles Tiffany took control of the business, it was renamed Tiffany & Company. Among its customers were the rich and famous of the nineteenth century, including Abraham Lincoln, Mark Twain, the Vanderbilts, William Randolph Hearst, and Tom Thumb.

By 1848 the store was selling its own silver and jewelry as well as jewelry, silver, and decorative pieces manufactured by others. Louis Comfort Tiffany, Charles's son, a successful interior decorator and artist, designed jewelry for the company after 1902. His studio also made pottery, lamps, and silver that were sold at Tiffany & Company. But most of the jewelry and silver sold at Tiffany & Company in the twentieth century was furnished by other manufacturers. The important pieces still made by Tiffany were usually special-order trophies or monumental silver or gold pieces exhibited at expositions. A limited number of art nouveau pieces were made from 1908 to 1919. The 1920s art deco designs from Europe led to a new look for the silver sold at Tiffany & Company. Tea sets and silver tablewares with angular shapes, square plates, aerodynamic styling, and new materials like Bakelite were created. This style, called *Retro Modern*, lasted into the 1940s.

Tiffany & Company made this four-piece tea and coffee set and tray with inlaid wood surface and silver rim. It is in Colonial Revival style.
(Photo: Sotheby's)

Walter Hoving became the owner of Tiffany & Company in 1955, and once again its silver designs changed. He hired designers who created pieces inspired by nature—seedpods, leaves, and fish scales. In 1985 Tiffany's acquired 1918 Frank Lloyd Wright designs for glass and silver that had never been made and, using new technology, produced the pieces until 2000. Designers important in other fields, like Michael Graves, created teapots and cups. Elsa Peretti, best known for her jewelry, designed hollow ware in 1978 and 1979. Her designs featured asymmetrical handles on irregularly

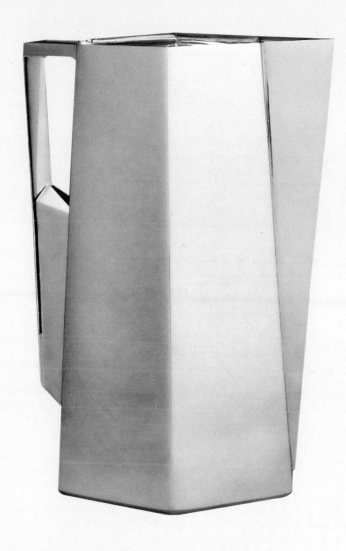

Frank Lloyd Wright designed houses, then designed their furniture and some of their accessories. This silver water pitcher was designed in 1918 but was not made until about 1985.
(Photo: Sotheby's)

curved bowls with plain, undecorated surfaces. She is still designing important silver tableware and jewelry.

Gorham Company

The history of the well-known Gorham Company goes back to Jabez Gorham, who formed his own company in 1818. The name became Gorham & Company, then Gorham Manufacturing Company, then Gorham Company. The company was making coin silver spoons by 1831, and by the mid-nineteenth century Gorham was making silver-plated serving pieces, hollow ware, napkin rings, and much more. It was also known for flatware and souvenir spoons in both silver and silver plate. Soon after the Civil War (1861–1865), the company was selling silver in all parts of the United States. Most large silver tureens, punch bowls, coffeepots, and serving pieces were made in the Japanese and art nouveau styles from the 1880s to about 1910. Some of these were made of mixed metals—copper, brass, and silver.

By the early 1900s, much silver, especially pieces by Arts and Crafts designers, was made with hammered surfaces, suggesting that the piece was handmade. This technique was used by many silver manufacturers through the 1930s; even today, some patterns have pseudo-hammer marks. Like Tiffany & Company, Gorham also made huge silver presentation pieces.

At the beginning of the 1900s, most Gorham patterns were in the Colonial Revival style. Some patterns, like *Medallion*, are out of production but wanted by collectors. Some traditional patterns, like *Louis XV* and *Chantilly*, are still popular and available today. For a short time, from 1897 to 1912, Gorham produced *Martelé*, a line of silver that was made from silver of a higher quality than sterling. (Sterling quality is 925 parts of silver out of 1000; *Martelé* was 950 parts silver.) *Martelé* was handmade in the art nouveau style. It was expensive then and is now bought by collectors and museums for even higher prices. In 1901 Gorham produced a line called *Athenic* that was made with silver, copper, glass, and ivory. It, too, was in the art nouveau style. When art deco became popular, it was not ignored by Gorham. In 1925 the company hired Erik Magnussen, a well-known Danish designer. Magnussen created pieces with advanced designs like his cubist-inspired coffee set made of triangular pieces of sterling silver with panels of silver gilt and black oxidized silver. Magnussen's *Manhattan* serving pieces have handles that resemble skyscrapers.

Gorham had to change when World War II prohibited the use of copper and permitted only limited use of silver. The company turned to war production, making cartridge cases and other small metal parts, then returned to its prewar production in 1946. Gorham's 1950s and '60s best sellers were heavily embossed floral flatware patterns and some modern designs. The company was bought by Textron in 1982 and diversified into china, glass, pewter, stainless steel, and even collectible plates. Informal dining, the preference among people about fifty and younger, called for heavy pottery dishes with pewter or stainless steel flatware. Some of Gorham's stainless pieces were based on old silver designs, but most were simple and modern. Gorham was purchased in 1989 by Dansk International Designs, which was acquired in 1991 by Brown-Forman. It continues to make both popular old patterns and new contemporary styles.

Important American and European Silver Makers

This table lists silver makers with location and marks. Dates given are approximate working dates. Birth and death dates for individuals are in parentheses.

Silver Maker and Location	Dates	Mark
Buccellati Milan, Italy	1919–present	
Cartier Paris, London, New York City	1847–present	
Cellini, Inc. Warwick, Rhode Island	1961–present	
Christofle Paris, France	1830–present	
Gorham Company Providence, Rhode Island	1818–present	
Harald Nielsen Copenhagen, Denmark	(1892–1977)	
Omar Ramsden London, England	(1873–1939)	
Reed & Barton Taunton, Massachusetts	1824–present	
Eliel Saarinen Helsinki, Finland; Bloomfield Hills, Michigan	(1873–1950)	Items marked with name
Gerard Sandoz Paris, France	active c.1925–1931	Items marked with name
Shreve, Crump & Low, Inc. Boston, Massachusetts	1796–present	
Harold Stabler Keswick, England	(1872–1945)	
Tiffany & Company New York, New York	1837–present	
Towle Silversmiths Newburyport, Massachusetts	1882–present	
Tuttle Silversmiths Boston, Massachusetts	1890–1955	
Wallace Wallingford, Connecticut	1871–present	

STUDIO SILVERSMITHS

About 1900, when the Arts and Crafts movement was introduced as a way of life, homes needed not only craftsman-style furniture, textiles, and pottery, but also tablewares. A few independent silversmiths opened studio shops and made sets of silver by hand in very limited quantities.

From the 1920s to the 1950s, independent silversmiths in many cities continued to make unique silver. Since the 1950s, many silversmiths have made silver in modern abstract designs. Some work for established retail stores, while others sell at high-end craft shows and exhibitions. Important jewelry makers often designed impressive crosses or chalice cups for churches. Others made tea sets, silverware, or even silver sculptures. Award-winning silversmiths in the United States during the years 1970 to 2000 include Sue L. Amendolara, Michael J. Banner, Richard Mawdsley, Robyn Nichols, and Linda Weiss.

STAINLESS STEEL AND ALUMINUM FLATWARE

Stainless steel was invented in 1913, and soon companies were making inexpensive, thin stainless steel flatware. Expensive, heavy stainless sets of knives, forks, and spoons became popular in the 1970s. Anodized aluminum flatware was created by David Tisdale Design in 1986.

Studio silversmiths developed very individual designs. This 10-inch-wide handmade sterling silver bowl is by the Rundahl Shop in Illinois. It has a stylized fruit design that was often seen on the company's silver.
(Photo: Treadway)

Allan Adler

Allan Adler (1916–2002) learned silversmithing from his father-in-law, Porter Blanchard, then started his own business in Los Angeles in 1939. His silver, entirely handmade, was very simple and geometric with clean lines. During World War II, he worked for the government making silver tubes for radar systems, and he was able to buy rationed silver to use in his workshop. After the war ended, he sold his silver pieces from four of his own shops in California as

Studio silver shops like the Kalo Shop made what sold best: flatware, bowls, vases, and jewelry. Candelabra like this were not made in quantity. It is 6½ inches high and is made from hand-wrought sterling silver. (Photo: Treadway)

well as in important stores like Marshall Field's, Gump's, and Neiman Marcus. He continued to make silver hollow ware and jewelry into the twenty-first century.

Allan Adler specialized in plain, geometric, handmade silver for the table and for jewelry. This flatware pattern was made in the 1950s.
(Photo: Sotheby's)

Kalo Shop

The Kalo Shop was started in Chicago by Clara Barck Welles (1868–1965) in 1900. Kalo silversmiths made hand-hammered flatware, hollow ware, and jewelry in the Arts and Crafts style. Kalo pieces often were made to order with an applied cutout monogram. The silver was sold at the Kalo Shop in Chicago and from 1914 to 1918 also at a branch store in New York City. Welles retired to California about 1940 and gave the shop to some of her employees, who ran it until 1970.

Marshall Field & Company Craft Shop

Marshall Field's department store in Chicago added a craft shop and metal foundry to its jewelry workroom in 1904. Craftsmen made silver flatware and hollow ware. Much of the silverware had hammer marks and imitated Colonial silver patterns or were made with bands of raised flowers and leaves. The shop also made brass, gold, and platinum items to sell in the store. The shop closed in 1950.

The butterfly woman dish in the art nouveau style is 7¾ inches wide. It was made of sterling silver by Marshall Field's craft shop in the early 1900s.
(Photo: Sotheby's)

Horace Potter

Horace Potter (1873–1948) opened the Potter Shop in Cleveland in 1899 to sell his decorative metalwork and jewelry. It later became the Potter Studio, then Potter Bentley Studios in 1928, and Potter and Mellen, Inc., in 1933. The company made and sold jewelry, silver, and brass hollow ware and also sold china, giftwares, and enameled bowls, trays, and boxes by many artists. Horace Potter hired other artists who made silver and pottery. Potter Studio was well known for its bookends, desk sets, and covered cigarette boxes

Potter Studio made many objects with antique stones and carvings as decoration or handles. This desk set is made of hammered copper with carved ivory insets. Similar boxes were made of silver. (Photo: Treadway)

of silver or brass, often with an antique ivory, jade, or glass finial. In the 1950s Potter and Mellen's best-known gift for a bride was an antique Chinese bowl or an art pottery bowl by Cowan, Pewabic, or Rookwood that had a handmade metal cover with an appropriate antique finial. Potter Mellen still sells jewelry of its own design.

Arthur J. Stone

Arthur J. Stone (1847–1938) came to the United States from England and established his workshop in Gardner, Massachusetts, in 1901. He made traditional presentation silver and ecclesiastical silver as well as other pieces that copied great historic metal masterpieces, including "Paul Revere" bowls and teapots. His tablewares were inspired by seventeenth- and eighteenth-century American and English metalwork. Many pieces were marked with the company name, the outline of a hammer, and the initial of the silversmith who worked on them. Stone used delicate chased designs that often included the initial of the client. In 1937 he sold the business, and it was renamed Stone Associates.

Arthur Stone designs often included chased lines and the initials of the owner of the silver. This bowl is 5 inches in diameter. (Photo: Skinner)

Studio Silversmiths

This table lists studio silversmiths with their locations and marks. Dates given are approximate working dates. Birth and death dates for individuals are in parentheses.

Silversmith and Location	Dates	Mark
Allan Adler Los Angeles, California	(1916–2002)	ALLAN ADLER HANDMADE STERLING
Porter Blanchard Los Angeles, California	(1886–1973)	STERLING / PORTER BLANCHARD
William Waldo Dodge Asheville, North Carolina	(1895–1971) 1920s–1930s	ASHEVILLE SILVERCRAFT HAND WROUGHT STERLING
Clemens Friedell Los Angeles and Pasadena, California	(1872–1963)	CLEMENS FRIEDELL PASADENA STERLING HAND WROUGHT
Gebelein Silversmiths, Inc. Boston, Massachusetts	1897–1986	GEBELEIN
Handicraft Shop Boston, Massachusetts	1901–1940	STERLING H 7S 1906
Robert Riddle Jarvie Chicago, Illinois	(1865–1941) The Jarvie Shop 1905–1920	JARVIE STERLING
Kalo Shop Chicago, Illinois	1900–1970	KALO M 3 2 3 S
Lebolt & Company Chicago, Illinois	1899–after 1985	LEBOLT & COMPANY HAND BEATEN STERLING
Erik Magnussen Copenhagen, Denmark; Chicago, Illinois; Los Angeles, California	(1884–1961)	ERIK MAGNUSSEN
Marshall Field & Company Craft Shop Chicago, Illinois	1904–1950	MADE IN OUR CRAFT SHOP MARSHALL FIELD & CO
Peter Müller-Munk Berlin, Germany; New York, New York; Pittsburgh, Pennsylvania	(1904–1967)	Items marked with *P* in circle or name
Falick Novick Chicago, Illinois	(1878–1957) 1909–1957	STERLING HANDWROUGHT BY F. NOVICK CHICAGO

Silversmith and Location	Dates	Mark
Old Newbury Crafters Amesbury, Massachusetts	1915–present	ONC STERLING HAND FLUTED
Carl Poul Petersen Copenhagen, Denmark; Montreal, Quebec, Canada	(1895–1977)	PP PETERSEN HAND MADE STERLING
Philip Paval Los Angeles, California	(1899–1971)	Items marked with name and initials
Horace Potter	(1873—1948)	H.E. POTTER STERLING
Potter Studio	c.1899—1928	
Potter Bentley Studios	1928—1933	POTTER BENTLEY STUDIOS
Potter and Mellen, Inc. Cleveland, Ohio	1933—present	POTTER MELLEN STERLING
Katharine Pratt Boston, Massachusetts	(1891–1978)	PRATT STERLING
Julius Randahl New York, New York; Chicago, Illinois Randahl Shop in Park Ridge, Illinois	(1880–1972) 1911–1965	JJOR STERLING HAND WROUGHT
Peer Smed New York, New York	(1878–1943)	PEER SMED
Arthur J. Stone Gardner and Boston, Massachusetts	(1847–1938)	Stone STERLING T
Unger Bros. Newark, New Jersey	1872–1919	STERLING 925 FINE
Mildred Watkins Cleveland, Ohio	(1882–1968)	MILDRED WATKINS
Kem Weber Hollywood and Santa Barbara, California	(1889–1963) 1927–1950s	Items designed by Weber, marked with manufacturer's name
Marie Zimmermann New York, New York	(1879–1972)	MARIE MAKER ZIMMERMANN

POPULAR SILVER FROM OTHER COUNTRIES

Georg Jensen and Scandinavian Design

The most famous Scandinavian silver firm is Georg Jensen Silversmithy, founded in 1904. The jewelry, silverware, and hollow ware made by Georg Jensen and his designers created a look that was unlike other pieces made in the early 1900s. His designs influenced the silver made in the United States, England, and other countries for many years.

The earliest pieces by Jensen were primarily art nouveau, with flowing lines and natural forms like leaves or acorns as part of the decoration. An Arts and Crafts influence was evident in the obvious hammer marks and the solid, handmade look of many pieces. Jensen simplified designs so that large undecorated surfaces showed the beauty of the silver, while small details, usually fruit or leaves, were added as handles, finials, or feet. The silver had a gray matte sheen, not a bright polish. Some of these early designs, like *Acorn* pattern flatware, are so popular they are still being made.

Jensen's Acorn *pattern was designed in 1915. The tip of each knife, fork, and spoon is a stylized acorn shape. Other companies have made similar patterns. The serving fork and spoon are each 8 inches long.* (Photo: Treadway)

By the 1920s, Georg Jensen designs had become even simpler. The matte finish was less popular, and the influence of art deco design was obvious. In the 1930s, Sigvard Bernadotte created minimalist designs that were geometric, simple, and formal. His famous flatware pattern, *Bernadotte*, was designed in 1939. It has handles that are a series of raised vertical ridges. Geometric forms influenced the designs of the 1950s and '60s. By the 1970s, the abstract forms popular in jewelry were also being adapted to flatware and dinnerware.

The Georg Jensen store opened in New York City in 1924 to encourage the sale of Danish-made silver, ceramics, and other giftware. When World War II cut off the supply of Danish-made silver, the New York store arranged for some American companies to make Jensen look-alikes. These were all marked *Georg Jensen, Inc. U.S.A.* After the war, Danish pieces were sold again.

Georg Jensen died in 1935, but his company still prospers with worldwide sales. Between 1985 and 1987, Georg Jensen Silversmiths merged with several Danish firms to become part of the Royal Copenhagen Group, and after more ownership changes, it is now part of Royal Scandinavia. The firm continues to make and sell both its oldest and newest designs.

English Silver

The English have been known for fine silver and silver plate for centuries. The traditional designs introduced in the eighteenth century and later have remained popular and are still being made. Fortunately the English have had very strict laws about silver guilds, makers, quality of silver, and markings. All silver of sterling quality made in England must be stamped with a mark that indicates the maker, date, location, and quality of silver. These marks are registered with the U.K. Patent Office, and most are easily found in reference books or on the Internet.

Liberty & Company

Liberty & Company is one of the most famous stores in London. The original store was established in 1875. The owner, Arthur Lasenby, had art nouveau fabrics made for the store. Egyptian and Moorish furniture was imported; later, Arts and Crafts pieces were sold. By the early 1900s, the store was selling art pottery by C. H. Brannam, the Aller Vale Pottery, and Moorcroft, all marked *Made for Liberty & Co.*

Archibald Knox designed this clock for Liberty & Company. The blue enamel and raised decoration are typical of both the silver and the pewter made in the early 1900s. This clock is stamped English Pewter, Made by Liberty & Co.
(Photo: Sotheby's)

Silver was an important part of the store's sales from the beginning. In 1894 the first silver mark, *L Y and Co.,* was registered, probably to use on imported pieces of Japanese and other silver. The *Cymric* line, introduced in 1899, was a success, and soon a new company was formed with W. H. Haseler to make much of Liberty's silver. These pieces were marked *L and Co.* The partnership in silver manufacturing ended in 1926, but a few designs were made into the 1930s. Liberty & Company's silver style was a blend of Arts and Crafts, art nouveau, and the original ideas of Liberty designers, especially Archibald Knox, who worked for Liberty from 1899 until 1911. The smooth surface of a silver clock, box, or picture frame was decorated with applied or chased strapwork that curled into the recognizable Liberty look. Often enamel, especially blue enamel, enhanced the design. Colored stones were added as ornaments on larger pieces, such as the tops of boxes or sides of tankards. The *Cymric* line included bowls, tea sets, mirrors, serving spoons and forks, napkin rings, clocks, boxes, and serving pieces. *Cymric* was discontinued in 1927. *Tudric,* a similar line made of pewter, was in production from 1901 until 1939, when the iron molds were donated to the wartime scrap drive.

While Liberty remains an important store and fashion influence, it has not continued to create new silver designs. It sells silver pieces made by others. Liberty still creates trend-setting fabrics and furniture and sells the newest designs from other countries, including Japan, China, and Russia.

METALCRAFT ARTISTS

Silver was not the only important metal used by craftsmen making decorative arts for the home. Iron, brass, steel, and copper were also used in many ways. Gates, fences, fireplace equipment, small pieces of furniture, vases, lamps, and architectural trim were made from these metals.

Samuel Yellin

At the beginning of the twentieth century, hand-forged ironwork was used as decorative elements both inside and outside buildings. Sam Yellin (1885–1940), one of the top ironsmiths in the United

MEXICAN SILVERSMITHS

Mexican silversmiths made bowls, pitchers, ashtrays, cigarette boxes, desk sets, and silverware as well as jewelry. (See pages 313–314.) The most famous jewelers, Spratling and Los Castillo, were the best-known makers of silver tableware, and both companies are still working.

These odd silver and wood candlesticks were made by William Spratling in about 1967. (Photo: Sotheby's)

States, was born in Poland, where he learned the blacksmithing trade. He worked in Germany, Belgium, and England before moving to Philadelphia in 1906. In 1909 he opened his own shop, later called Samuel Yellin Metalworkers. Soon his ironwork was used on buildings by famous architects, and his gates, fences, railings, screens, lighting fixtures, fire screens, and even lamps, boxes, and lanterns were in demand. Yellin's designs often incorporated vines and leaves, grotesque animal heads, chased lines, twisted parts, and hammer marks. Pieces were usually marked *Samuel Yellin* until 1985, when the mark became *Yellin*. He trained hundreds of workers, many of whom continued his ideas at their own forges and made ironwork that was often similar to pieces by Yellin.

Yellin is best known for his large architectural ironwork, but he also made small pieces like this wrought-iron candlestick. It is stamped Yellin *on a leg.* (Photo: Freeman's)

Marie Zimmermann

Marie Zimmermann (1879–1972) may have been the most important metalcraft artist working in the United States in the twentieth century. Zimmermann created Arts and Crafts jewelry of gold set with precious stones and enamels. She also made metalwork of all kinds—silver hollow ware and flatware, jeweled boxes, flower containers, vases, iron gates, furniture, wood carvings, and even tombstones. She worked with wood, silver, precious and semiprecious stones, steel, copper, bronze, iron, and gold. Her ironwork included many fences, gates, and fountains for large estates. Zimmermann is praised today for the quality of her metalwork as well as her designs.

Many of her vases and bowls were based on early Chinese shapes—best known were the Chinese "poly-lobed" shapes. Her low petal bowls were made of bronze with a finish she created from paint and chemicals that left a patina of dark brown, blue-black, orange-red, or green. Other lobed vases of silver, black, blue, and green were finished with gold plating and lacquer. Her copper vases in antique Chinese shapes were finished with gold plate, or gold plate and lacquer, or pigmented wax and paint. Many pieces were spun on a lathe, not raised by hand as might be expected, then chased with subtle designs.

The Chinese influence can be seen in the shape of this two-piece centerpiece made by Marie Zimmermann. The vase and its wirework base are made of hammered gold-plated copper. (Photo: Rago)

Fire screens originally kept the heat away from those sitting nearby. This 20-inch art deco square screen by Edgar Brandt was purely decorative. (Photo: Sotheby's)

Zimmermann was interested in flowers, gardening, and nature, and she used many flowers, leaves, and vines as decoration. Her flower holders and vases were not only beautiful but also popular with serious flower arrangers because of the way they held flowers standing in water. She even made serving pieces with rhodium-plated silver to help eliminate the need for polishing.

Zimmermann's metalwork was usually marked *M Zimmermann, maker* or with an *M* over a *Z* in a circle.

Other Ironsmiths

Frenchman Edgar Brandt (1880–1960) was a major ironsmith. His first important work in the United States was the ironwork on the Cheney Building in New York City. The building's iron doors were made with stylized palm fronds and fountains, designs later copied by many working in the art deco style.

Other important ironwork names in art circles are Chicago architect Louis Sullivan (1856–1924), who designed iron gates and hardware for buildings like the Chicago Stock Exchange, and Rose Iron Works of Cleveland (1904–present), which has made screens and furniture, as well as smaller household items.

Copper Craftsmen

Craftsmen made Arts and Crafts–style decorative pieces using copper, a metal that had generally been ignored except for utilitarian pieces. Silver was used with copper, gilt, brass, or stones to make hollow ware in a style called *Japonisme*. The style reflected a romantic view of Japanese art popular in Europe and the United States at the beginning of the twentieth century. Teapots were made of copper decorated with silver birds or flowers. Or a teapot could be of silver decorated with other metals. Arts and Crafts designers of the early 1900s liked the subtle shading of

In 2005 a carved and painted wooden box with ivory and jewel trim and cast bronze handles and hinges that was made and owned by Zimmermann sold for $117,500. (Photo: Rago)

Heintz metal pieces often have a factory-applied patina that when damaged or cleaned improperly cannot be restored. This well-cared-for bronze vase with applied sterling silver daffodils has the original green patina in great condition. (Photo: Treadway)

copper against dark oak furniture and preferred hardware of darkened copper. Hammered copper gave a handcrafted look.

Some of the best copper bowls of the period, as well as lamps, were made by Dirk Van Erp (1859–1933), who opened his Oakland, California, studio in 1908. His most famous lamps had a hammered copper base with a cone-shaped copper or copper-and-mica shade. (See page 257.) The Heintz Art Metal Shop made small objects like ashtrays, bookends, desk sets, vases, and smoking sets with a bronze or copper patina and silver overlay. Metalsmiths at the Roycroft community made copper accessories and lamps they sold to the public. Other Arts and Crafts shops making copper accessories included the Benedict Manufacturing Company of East Syracuse, New York; Carence Crafters of Chicago; Cellini Shop of Chicago; Harry Dixon of San Francisco; the Handicraft Shop of Boston; Robert Riddle Jarvie of Chicago; Karl Kipp of East Aurora, New York; Old Mission Kopper Kraft of San Jose and San Francisco; and the Onondaga Metal Shops of East Syracuse, New York.

Roycroft metalwork rarely had raised or applied designs. This copper piece has no added decoration, just flat copper cut and shaped into a tobacco jar and pipe holder. It is marked with the Roycroft stamped orb & cross mark. (Photo: Freeman's)

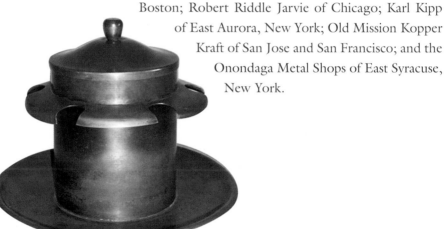

Arts and Crafts Coppersmiths

This table lists coppersmiths with their locations and marks. Dates given are approximate working dates. Birth and death dates for individuals are in parentheses.

Coppersmith and Location	Dates	Mark
Benedict Manufacturing Company East Syracuse, New York	c.1900–1930s	
Carence Crafters Chicago, Illinois	1908–c.1918	
Cellini Shop Chicago, Illinois	1914–1969	
Harry Dixon San Francisco, California	(1890–1967) c.1908–1967	
Handicraft Shop Boston, Massachusetts	1901–1940	
Heintz Art Metal Shop Buffalo, New York	1906–1930	
Robert Riddle Jarvie Chicago, Illinois	(1865–1941) c.1900–1920	
Karl Kipp East Aurora, New York	(1882–1954) 1908–c.1931	
Old Mission Kopper Kraft San Jose and San Francisco, California	1922–1925	
Onondaga Metal Shops East Syracuse, New York	1901–1904	
Roycroft East Aurora, New York	1895–1938	
Gustav Stickley (Craftsman Workshops) Syracuse, New York	1898–1915	
Stickley Brothers Grand Rapids, Michigan	1891–c.1940	Items marked with catalog number
Dirk Van Erp Oakland and San Francisco, California	(1859–1933)	

Chase Brass & Copper Company

It is a long way from plain copper nails and rivets to internationally famous art deco chrome, copper, and brass giftwares by name designers, but that is how Chase Brass & Copper Company of Waterbury, Connecticut, progressed. It also made buttons and industrial products like copper pipe before it realized, in the 1930s, that money was to be made in well-designed metalware. The chrome ice bowl with a curved handle and tongs designed by Russel Wright, the copper-plated copper-alloy cat bookend by Walter von Nessen, the food warmer by Lurelle Guild, and many other low-cost yet high-style pieces of copper, brass, and chrome were sold by Chase from 1930 to 1942, when the Specialty Sales Division closed. Vintage serving pieces, lamps, and cocktail ware are coveted by collectors and used by party givers for a retro look.

Bright chrome and black Bakelite handles make this "Continental Coffee Making Service" eye catching. Walter Von Nessen designed the pot, creamer, and sugar for Chase. (Photo: Rago)

New types of copper accessories became popular in the 1930s. Ashtrays, cigarette boxes, match holders, vases, and desk accessories were handmade in the art deco style by many of the same metalworkers who made silver.

HAMMERED ALUMINUM

Aluminum was first used as tableware in 1850, when, because it was expensive to extract the metal from the ore, it was more valuable than gold. But it was not until 1900, when a cheaper method of producing aluminum was discovered, that everyday household items were made of the metal. At first, some thought aluminum was poisonous and would contaminate food, but by 1910 those fears were over and companies were selling aluminum cooking pots. From the 1920s to the 1960s, decorative hand-hammered aluminum was a favorite wedding gift. Repoussé (raised) designs were made by hammering the aluminum on a steel die. Sometimes designs were incised or carved. Handles were often made of twisted rods or leaf-shaped pieces. Hammer marks were always evident. Look for aluminum trays and bowls by Arthur Armour of Grove City, Pennsylvania (1933–1982); Farberware of Brooklyn, New York (1930–present); Rodney Kent Silver Company of Brooklyn, New York (c.1950s); and Wendell August Forge of Grove City, Pennsylvania (1923–present). Using designs by industrial designer Lurelle Guild, Kensington, Inc. (a subsidiary of

The hammer marks are part of the decoration of this napkin holder marked Rodney Kent. *Sometimes the aluminum was not really hammered; pseudo-hammer marks were molded into the metal.*

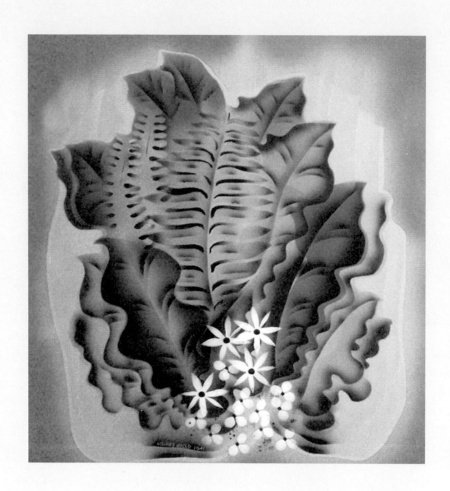

Edward Winter made this 32-by-29-inch enamel-on-steel panel called Untitled Mural *in 1941. It was part of a set of panels that was used on the wall of a restaurant in Cleveland, Ohio.*

Alcoa—Aluminum Company of America—in New Kensington, Pennsylvania) produced Kensington ware from 1934 until about 1965. It was plain anodized aluminum ware with brass or wooden trim. Hammered aluminum serving pieces were out of style by the seventies, but collector interest brought the style back in the 1990s, and some pieces are being made today.

SPUN ALUMINUM

Another popular metal used for household goods in the 1940s was spun aluminum. Several housewares companies made bowls, mugs, beer trays, and other pieces, but the most famous and most expensive today are the aluminum serving dishes by Russel Wright, including an ice bucket, relish tray, pitcher, cheese and cracker set, canapé ball tray, and other pieces. Many had handles or cutting boards made of walnut.

ENAMEL

A well-to-do bride of the late 1940s and '50s in some parts of the country could expect to get a gift of at least one enameled ashtray, bowl, or box designed and made by an artist. Enameling is not a new art. It has been used since ancient times, and the basic techniques used

Lurelle Guild— Industrial Designer

People sometimes are confused when reading the name *Lurelle Guild* and think it is a group of designers. But *Lurelle* is the designer's first name and *Guild* (rhymes with *child*) is his last. Lurelle Guild (1898–1985) started as a magazine illustrator of interiors in the 1920s. He noticed that many ideas and designs he included in the drawings were being adopted by manufacturers, so in 1927 he became an industrial designer. During his career, Guild designed as many as a thousand products a year. Claiming "Beauty alone does not sell," Guild created designs for the popular taste—practical and up-to-date, never ahead or behind the times. His best-known designs for today's collectors are the sleek aluminum pieces created for Alcoa's Kensington division after 1934 and the 1937 Electrolux vacuum cleaner with sleigh feet. Other important Guild designs were cooking utensils for Wear-Ever Aluminum Company (1932), small home accessories like lamps and candlesticks for Chase Brass and Copper, silverware for International Silver, air-conditioning units for Carrier Engineering Corporation, and a refrigerator for Norge.

The smooth finish and modern look of this Kensington tray is what sets it apart from many hammered aluminum pieces. The tray in the Mulolo Pineapple *design is 13¾ inches long.*

Russel Wright made spun aluminum serving pieces. The metal has a brushed, velvety look, not the bright shiny surface of chrome. This five-piece spaghetti service has wrapped willow trim. (Photo: Rago)

Gertrude Twichell of Boston made this set of nesting bowls about 1916. The largest, covered bowl is copper with an enameled knob. The two smaller bowls that nest inside have turquoise enameled interiors.

today were developed by the sixteenth century. Many attractive nineteenth- and twentieth-century enameled bowls and brooches were made in Limoges, France. Early in the twentieth century, Arts and Crafts artists used enamel, but sparingly. Pieces could be copper trays with a few enamel leaves or copper-covered bowls with an enameled circle set in a bezel on the top. In the 1920s and '30s, a few Boston artists, like Elizabeth Copeland, Katharine Pratt, and Gertrude Twichell, started using enameling for clockfaces and commercial jewelry. By the 1950s, the new mid-century style of enamel work became an important art and design medium. Professional artists made and signed one-of-a-kind enamel-on-steel murals for inside or outside buildings, as well as bowls, ashtrays, boxes, vases, and jewelry. Amateur enamelists, using precut copper pieces, made innumerable round bowls and rectangular plaques, often unsigned, that can be found at almost any flea market today.

One of Cleveland's best-known pioneer enamelists was Edward Winter. Ferro Enamel Corporation, maker of porcelain-type enamel for stoves and appliances, let Winter use the company's steel blanks and huge furnace to experiment with enamels. Winter made large murals at the plant but also created dishes made from saucepan lids and other precut metal pieces. Soon he was selling enameled bowls, ashtrays, and plates in department stores and gift stores in all parts of the country. His design techniques evolved from realism to abstraction and influenced other craftsmen. Thelma Frazier Winter, who worked at Cleveland's Cowan Pottery, joined her husband, Edward, and made enamels in her unique style, picturing large-eyed mice, owls, angels, or children.

There is an owl in the tree on this footed enameled 11½-inch bowl by Karl Drerup. The entire interior surface is covered with small pictures of birds and plants.

Another Cleveland enamelist, Kenneth Bates, used stylized geometrics and floral designs as well as distorted views of people or places. His work was too detailed to be made in great quantities, but he is significant because he not only taught many enamel artists and made some important enamels, but in 1951 he also wrote one of the first books on how to make modern enamels.

Karl Drerup, a painter living in New Hampshire, started teaching and making enamels in 1946. His detailed, realistic designs are one-of-a-kind. Oppi Untracht of New York City enameled clocks, jewelry, bowls, and vases, and he wrote several books on enameling. Enamels by all these men are in museum exhibits today. Mildred Watkins worked in silver but also did enamels of exceptional quality. Other enamelists to look for are Jean and Arthur Ames, Sascha Brastoff, Fern Cole, Annemarie Davidson, Edris Eckhardt, Gerte Hacker, Doris Hall, Charles Bartley Jeffery, Mitchell Kamen, Kalman Kubinyi, Serge Nekrassoff, John Puskas, Edward Star, Harold Tishler, Ellamarie and Jackson Woolley, and Claire Wyman. Other very commercial enamelists are listed in many Christmas catalogs, from Gump's to Georg Jensen.

Enameling became a do-it-yourself art project, and by 1954 kits were sold in crafts stores. At the same time, commercial enameled jewelry was made by several firms. Best known is the American company Renoir, which in 1952 began marking its enameled jewelry *Matisse*. Modern enamelists now exhibit at craft and art shows in all parts of the country, and many are doing exceptionally skillful and innovative enamel dishes and jewelry.

There have also been some twentieth-century European enamelists of note. Most often seen in the United States is the work of David-Andersen of Norway, Henning Koppel of Denmark, and Phoebe and Harold Stabler of London. Italian enamelist Paolo De Poli created colorful enamels with embossed, hammered surfaces.

Chapter 10

JEWELRY

꙰ JEWELRY MADE AT the beginning of the twentieth century was created using the art nouveau, Arts and Crafts, and Edwardian designs first seen in the late nineteenth century. Some Victorian designs were used until about 1914. Many of the old styles came back into fashion in the 1980s and are still being copied.

EARLY TWENTIETH-CENTURY JEWELRY STYLES

Art Nouveau

Art nouveau jewelry that was made from the late nineteenth century until the start of World War I in 1914 had curving, asymmetric lines, sensuous women with flowing hair, dragonflies, snakes, butterflies, vines, irises, poppies, and other flowers. Designers incorporated both French and Japanese design ideas in their pieces. Opals, moonstones, pearls, peridots, and other colored stones were popular. The art nouveau jewelry by René Lalique is the most important—and the most expensive. Many pieces were enameled, some with a transparent enamel called *plique-à-jour*. A few American firms, like Tiffany & Company and Marcus & Company, made important art nouveau pieces of gold,

This necklace has a posturing woman, enameling, and plique-à-jour embellishments, all popular art nouveau ideas. The necklace is made of 18 karat gold and has diamonds and pearls among the vines and flower petals. (Photo: Skinner)

precious and semiprecious stones, and enamel. Silver and even brass jewelry set with glass or inexpensive stones was made by Wm. B. Kerr & Company, Unger Brothers, and others. Most pieces were made with die-stamped designs. Art nouveau jewelry was out of style by 1914, only to reappear in the 1990s.

Arts and Crafts

Arts and Crafts designs were popular from about 1890 to 1920. The jewelry, like the metalwork and some furniture, was made by artists who believed in the importance of handmade work of a single craftsman. The pieces had hammer marks and even rough edges or uneven lines to show they were handmade. Designs were simple, using straight lines and geometric shapes as well as a few curves inspired by earlier art nouveau pieces. Long thin chains, rings, and pins were popular. Inexpensive materials like silver, pewter, copper, brass, and cabochon stones, even glass, were used. Turquoise stones and turquoise blue enamel were popular. A new form of brooch was introduced, made from brass sheets cut in rectangular, circular, and other uncomplicated shapes, then acid-etched or hammered and sometimes set with stones, glass, or ceramics that looked like cabochon stones. Similar pieces have been made ever since by amateurs, often at summer camp.

Expensive Arts and Crafts jewelry was made by single artists or groups in Boston (Edward Everett Oakes), Chicago (The Kalo Shop), Cleveland (Potter Studio), and New York State (Gustav Stickley's Craftsman Workshops in Syracuse and the Roycroft community in East Aurora). In England, companies like Liberty & Company and Charles Horner made silver and gold jewelry, sometimes with enamel and a few precious or semiprecious stones. Theodor Fahrner of Germany and the Wiener Werkstätte in Vienna made jewelry in the Arts and Crafts style. Many pieces, even some by talented craftsmen, are un-marked. Judge a piece by its design and the quality of the workmanship as well as by

Theodor Fahrner manufactured inexpensive costume jewelry in Germany. He used silver or low-karat gold and semi-precious stones, but he hired talented art deco designers. This silver pendant decorated with coral and black enamel is stamped TF.
(Photo: Skinner)

The Kalo Shop in Chicago made this gold and amethyst brooch. It has the solid, sturdy look of Arts and Crafts, not the delicate look of earlier jewelry. (Photo: Skinner)

Delicate platinum necklaces with dangling chains set with diamonds and pearls like this one were popular in Edwardian times. Negligee *is the proper name for this necklace with two uneven suspended drops.* (Photo: Skinner)

Geometric shapes were part of art deco design. This platinum and diamond brooch is set with 115 diamonds. Many deco pieces also used colored stones. (Photo: Skinner)

the fame of the maker, although signed pieces tend to be of more interest to serious collectors and museums.

Edwardian

Edwardian-style jewelry also was popular from about 1890 to 1920. Delicate pendants and bar pins of platinum filigree set with diamonds and pearls were the rage. Colored stones—amethysts, sapphires, green garnets, rubies, and turquoise—were used along with diamonds cut into new shapes, including emerald, marquise, and baguette cuts. Necklaces, large brooches, tiaras, and earrings were created with garlands of bows, flowers, and tassels. Briolette cut stones—drop-shaped diamonds or other transparent gems with a pointed top and rounded bottom—were suspended on brooches, necklaces, and earrings. The sautoir, a long, sometimes waist-length necklace that ends in a tassel, was another new form.

ART DECO

During the war years 1914 to 1918, very little jewelry was made, but after World War I women were eager to buy something new. The fashionable flapper dresses went well with bracelets, brooches, necklaces, and rings in the new art deco style. For the first time, costume jewelry was considered fashionable, and designers like Chanel used ropes of huge pearls or pins with stones too large to be anything but faux jewelry meant to make a statement. Art deco was in style from about 1925 to the late 1930s. Both expensive "real" jewelry and costume jewelry followed the same design guidelines. Pendant earrings, dress clips, charm bracelets, ropes of beads with tassels, circle pins, and octagonal rings were popular. Pearls, rubies, sapphires, emeralds, diamonds, coral, jade, and onyx were used for the colorful jewelry. The Asscher cut, named for Dutch diamond cutter Joseph Asscher, featured multiple facets that gave more sparkle to a square-shaped diamond. Stones were often cut in geometric shapes—triangles, trapezoids, and hexagons—then set in bezels and used to make bracelets, necklaces, and pins. Flexible bracelets made from a solid band of colored stones set in a stylized design were a new idea called *fruit salad* by some experts. Pins made from a mass of multicolored stones, some carved in special shapes, were also identified as *fruit salad* pieces. The pin with a flower-filled basket was another innovation. Short flexible necklaces were introduced in 1934. Expensive gold and diamond pins shaped like amusing animals or people were the unusual result of fine jewelry imitating costume pieces.

THE DUCHESS OF WINDSOR'S CHARMS

The Duchess of Windsor's charm bracelet designed about 1935 by Cartier sold in 1987 for £235,000 (about $376,000), a record price. Hanging from the diamond bracelet were nine crosses set with diamonds, amethysts, emeralds, and sapphires and inscribed with references to special occasions, including the duchess's 1944 appendectomy.

Collectors have nicknamed jewelry like this fruit salad. *This rhodium-plated metal pin is made of stamped glass stones that imitate precious gems.* (Photo: Doyle New York)

RETRO MODERN

From about 1935 to 1945, retro modern (now usually called *retro*) jewelry was in style. Colored stones and gold came into fashion as the earlier white look of diamonds and platinum faded. Streamlined shapes and three-dimensional designs were popular. Realistic flowers, animals, and birds were part of some designs. Pink gold, green gold, and gold-colored gold were often used in a single piece of jewelry. Large link bracelets and flexible strap bracelets were in fashion. Symmetrical pairs of clips made in geometric shapes remained in style.

Cartier still makes jewelry shaped like panthers or leopards. This onyx and diamond panther brooch was made around 1960. It is articulated—made so the head can turn. (Photo: Sotheby's)

During the first half of the 1940s, distinctly feminine jewelry was fashionable. Sprays of flowers, birds, and butterflies were in style. But the most popular design was the two-tone gold pin shaped like a bow with the "knot" made of rubies or sapphires—often synthetic stones, not natural ones. Large rectangular colored stones, especially aquamarines, were used in rings and retro pins. Small earrings that hugged the earlobe were stylish. Important American jewelers of the day included Cartier, Seaman Schepps, Tiffany & Co., and Van Cleef & Arpels.

FINE JEWELRY—1945 TO 2000

Mid-Century—1945 to the 1960s

After World War II ended, impressive, expensive-looking jewelry came back in style. A ring set with a marquise or a pear-shaped diamond was the engagement ring of choice for many brides-to-be. Dome-shaped rings set with clusters of gemstones were also in style. Diamond jewelry set in platinum was best; yellow gold was used for colored stones. Matching sets of bracelet, necklace, earrings, and a brooch were popular. The starburst pin was stylish, as was the circle pin. So were pins shaped like cartoon animals and people. Cartier of Paris designed the articulated leopard pin as part of *Big Cat* jewels in 1947. Once again fine jewelry makers copied humorous costume jewelry. The conservative socialite, however, preferred the circle pin of plain gold or gold set with pearls or other understated stones.

If the pin is shaped like a three-dimensional bow and has yellow gold and rubies as part of the bow, it is a retro piece of jewelry. (Photo: Skinner)

Fashions in jewelry change as quickly as fashions in dresses, so old jewelry is continually broken up—the stones removed and reset in a more fashionable style. Each precious stone has a value, and the diamond from an out-of-style engagement ring could be used to create an affordable starburst pin with the addition of some small diamonds and an artistic setting.

Queen Victoria wore a gold bracelet with charms holding family pictures. Silver heart charm bracelets were popular about 1900, diamond and gold deco charms in the 1920s, and gold story-telling charms in the 1950s. This gold bracelet is from the 1960s. (Photo: Skinner)

Wristwatches

Although the first wristwatch may have been invented in 1868 by Patek Phillipe, pocket watches were the usual portable timepiece until the twentieth century. Early watches were hand-wound. Then in the early 1950s miniature batteries were invented and the first electric wristwatches were sold in 1957. Miniaturization made the first quartz watches possible in the late 1960s.

Rolex watches, gold- or steel-cased, are the best-selling vintage watches today. This stainless steel, chronograph wristwatch with registers, tachometer, and telemeter was made in 1955. (Photo: Skinner)

Collectible watches range from expensive Cartier lady's watches set with diamonds and Rolexes that tell the time, day, date, month, and moon phase to inexpensive novelty and fashion watches, like Mickey Mouse watches introduced in 1933 and Swatches, first marketed in 1983.

Mickey Mouse wasn't the only Disney character to be featured on a watch. Donald Duck is on the face and strap of this 1936 watch. Donald's arms move to indicate the hour and minute. Mickey Mouse moves on the seconds indicator. (Photo: Hake's)

Jean Schlumberger designed this 18 karat gold, platinum, and diamond brooch for Tiffany & Company. The antelope head has exaggerated horns curved to form a circle pin. It is only 1½ inches in diameter. (Photo: Skinner)

Charm bracelets were the rage once more. The 1952–1961 television show *This Is Your Life* ended each program with the presentation of a charm bracelet made especially for the guest of honor. The charms for the show were made by Walter Lampl's company, which had been making charms since 1921.

In the 1960s, Tiffany & Company introduced the work of designer Jean Schlumberger. He used diamonds and colored gems, enamel, and gold to make pieces shaped like animals, fish, insects, flowers, and other designs from nature.

Americans also bought the work of Italian firms—very large, flashy pieces set with Roman coins or huge gems from Bulgari; and, from Buccellati, elegant, classic designs larger than the originals to create a more showy look. Ethnic themes, op art, Pop Art, and abstract and organic forms inspired designs during these years. Precious stones were used with gold in traditional settings, but many designers also liked to use hunks of raw crystals of emeralds, quartz, amethyst, topaz, or crystallized agate in settings of twisted wire, sticklike pieces of gold, and abstract forms. Pyrite, rock crystal, rose quartz, tourmaline, and other semiprecious stones were used by some of the more creative designers. Rings were large, with high domes or three-dimensional boxes decorated with precious stones.

1960s to 2000

In 1961 the first International Exhibition of Modern Jewelry was held in London. Experienced jewelers and many artists who usually worked as painters or sculptors made jewelry for the exhibition. They used abstract designs and unusual materials like bone, glass, or beach pebbles; metals like iron, bronze, brass, and, of course, silver and gold; as well as gold granulation, acrylics, resins, rubber, anodized aluminum, and carved gemstones. All these ideas inspired the jewelry that followed the exhibition, and more new ideas soon emerged photo etchings, rainbow hued titanium, intricate cloisonné enamels, pearls suspended by nearly invisible nylon thread, woven wire "cloth," and lights operated by tiny batteries were just a few. Even the gems changed shape. Special fantasy-cut transparent stones in irregular shapes were created by Bernd Munsteiner, the German gem cutter.

Artist-jewelers created unique pieces. One piece resembled a small gold ribcage, another was more like a gold piece of crumbled paper. Tangles of wire and rough stones; realistic hands, ears, or faces; pendants shaped like lipstick tubes; and strange combinations of geometric shapes were all part of the look of jewelry at the end of the twentieth century. *Organic, geometric, asymmetric, story-telling, huge, pornographic, humorous,* and *almost*

Buccellati still makes large, hard-to-miss pieces of expensive jewelry. This gold cuff bracelet is set with sapphires and cabochon emeralds. (Photo: Skinner)

Half & Half *is the name of this necklace made by Art Smith in Greenwich Village, New York. The brass necklace and its unusual design is one of many pieces made by this artist-jeweler, who died in 1982.* (Photo: Skinner)

unwearable are adjectives that could be used to describe the jewelry. Artists making this type of jewelry include John Paul Miller, a Clevelander who rediscovered the ancient technique of gold granulation, and Margaret Craver of Boston, who used a sixteenth-century form of enameling. Rings were made with square, not round, shanks; large stones were used; pendants hung from stiff metal necklaces or black cords; pins had geometric shapes; and large fabric and bead fantasies were worn as necklaces. Jewelry was more sculpture than ornament.

Large commercial jewelry stores sold more-traditional jewelry-animal pins, pieces with large precious stones, gold "chandelier" earrings, thin chains studded with diamonds, heavy ropelike gold or silver chains, pins featuring one semiprecious arch-shaped stone, delicate chains with a tiny charm, and groups of suspended chains holding single stones. Color-enhanced stones like blue topaz and yellow diamonds were available. Much precious-stone and enameled jewelry in old designs was made in Turkey, India, and Spain. Some pieces, especially *plique-à-jour* (transparent enamel) pins, were made to pass as antique pieces. Asprey, Aaron Basha, Buccellati, Bulgari, Cartier, Cellini, Chanel, Oscar Heyman, Fred Leighton, Mikimoto (pearls), Seaman Schepps, H. Stern, Tiffany & Company, Van Cleef & Arpels, and Harry Winston are some of the most famous companies making jewelry seen in stores in the United States. Important jewelry designers include John Hardy, Yuri Ichihashi, Elsa Peretti, Paloma Picasso, Nicholas Varney, and David Yurman. (See the chart on pages 421–435 for information on jewelry makers.)

COSTUME JEWELRY—1920 TO 2000

Art Deco 1925 to c.1939

Costume jewelry before 1925 closely resembled pieces made from real gold and gemstones, and this tradition continued in the art deco era. Rhinestones, glass (colored, cut, or molded), fake pearls, plastic, and marcasite, set in gold-colored or rhodium-plated metal or

Attractive pieces of jewelry in the designs most popular at the moment were sold in large department or jewelry stores. Poodles have been popular since the 1950s. This 3½-inch poodle pin made of gold and precious gems is signed Robert Altman. (Photo: Skinner)

This 1½-inch pin showing a duck emerging from an egg has a Lucite jelly belly body and a red glass eye. Made in 1943, it is marked Trifari. (Photo: Doyle New York)

silver, were substitutes for diamonds and precious stones set in platinum or gold. In better pieces of costume jewelry, stones were set in bezels or prongs, not glued. Many costume pieces were original in design. Glass beads from Czechoslovakia in different sizes and shapes were used for necklaces or parts of pins. Necklaces made in China of natural rock crystal are sometimes overlooked by collectors because they look like less-valuable glass beads. Some pieces looked Egyptian in design, with sphinxes and obelisks. Some were revivals of the Victorian look, often with black glass or molded cameos. And some, inspired by the architecture of the time, were as dramatic, geometric, and stylized as skyscrapers. Avant-garde designs inspired by cubism, surrealism, and other painting styles were made by Elsa Schiaparelli, a dress designer. Today the most collectible costume jewelry was by famous name designers or companies like Hattie Carnegie, Chanel, Ciner, Coro, Eisenberg, Miriam Haskell, Hobé, Kenneth Lane, Napier, Schiaparelli, and Trifari.

1935 to 1950

The Depression and then World War II changed the look of costume jewelry. Price was important, and many costume pieces were inexpensive. When the war started, metals needed for the war, crystal from Europe, and fake pearls from Japan were unavailable. Lucite and other plastics were substituted. Most costume jewelry imitated real jewelry, and rhinestone clips, floral pins, and colored stone and gold-colored metal pieces were made. Some designers created pseudo-Victorian pieces. The *jelly belly* (clear Lucite cut in cabochon shape) animal pins by Trifari, Coro, and others do not resemble any precious jewelry. Humorous wooden pins were popular in the 1940s. Patriotic war jewelry featuring flags, eagles, V for Victory, and military insignia was introduced at this time. Some of these designs were revived after the September 11 attacks in 2001.

1950 to 1975

Modern jewelry designs by a few individual artists and craftsmen were quickly copied in costume jewelry during the 1950s. There was something for everyone: unusual jewelry of copper; traditional pieces made to look like real gold; imitations of ivory, precious stones, pearls, and almost every other material used in precious jewelry. Enameled copper jewelry was created by Renoir and marked *Matisse*. Several companies made unmarked enameled pendants with abstract designs. Frank Rebajes of New York made both artistic copper jewelry and some less-extreme designs for the conservative buyer. Cute animal pins that looked as if they had been made from real gold and gems were available. Asian figures with cream-colored plastic faces that resembled ivory were made by Nettie Rosenstein, HAR, Selro, and others. Multicolored glass stones cut to look like gems were used to make sets of jewelry—

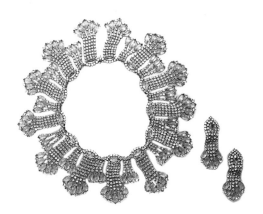

Dating Costume Jewelry By Color

Color can help date costume jewelry. It was made to go with the fashions of the day. Pale purple glass, amethyst, and opals were popular about 1910. Crystal, black, silver, and bright colors like red, yellow, blue, and green were used in the 1920s. Bright stones and rhinestones were in vogue in the 1930s. Red, white, and blue were popular in the war years of the 1940s. Turquoise, chartreuse, coral, red, royal blue, and other strong colors were used into the 1950s and '60s. Yellow was popular in the late 1960s and early '70s. Gray-green and rust were in style in the 1970s. In the 1980s, mauve and teal were the "in" colors. Sage green, pumpkin, and wheat came into style in the early 1990s, and by the end of the decade they were replaced by red violets, magentas, and plum. Turquoise, coral, and chartreuse came back early in the twenty-first century.

1910

1930s

1940s

1950s and '60s

Costume jewelry became fashionable in the 1930s, when top dress designers like Coco Chanel created costume jewelry that did not look like precious jewelry. Chanel's long ropes of large faux pearls or "diamonds" were meant to be an eye-catching fashion accessory.

No one could ignore the necklace and 3-inch pendant ear clips by Kenneth Lane. The 1960s jewelry used prong-set clear and aqua rhinestones. The large necklace was not meant to look like a piece with precious stones. (Photo: Doyle New York)

Enameled copper jewelry was popular in the 1950s, when both amateurs and large companies made unusual designs. Renoir of California marked this red pendant Freeform, *with the word* Matisse *in script.* (Photo: Jitterbug Jewelry)

a matching necklace, pin, earrings, and ring. Fruit-shaped pins and earrings, especially strawberries, were made with pieces of colored glass placed close together so no metal showed in what is called a *pavé* setting. Faux pearls and cut crystal were used for multistrand necklaces. Crown-shaped pins, fleur-de-lis, butterflies, and flowers were in fashion. The charm bracelet, still a favorite, held larger and larger charms until, by the 1960s, heavy link bracelets held hefty 1½-inch disc charms.

And Then—

Traditional styles continued, but in the United States by the 1980s, many pieces of costume jewelry were made by individual craftsmen from found objects assembled to form pins or necklaces. Bottle caps, photos, screws and bolts, buttons, shells, unusual beads, and other small objects were used. Some pieces even featured flashing lights activated by tiny batteries. Costume jewelry in the 1990s also copied fine jewelry of the day, including the silver rope styles of David Yurman, the lopsided heart by Elsa Peretti at Tiffany, and Mikimoto diamond studded pearls.

An unusual new type of jewelry, often made of silver or brass, was created in the United States beginning in the 1940s. It was unlike any earlier gold or silver jewelry. Pins looked as if they had been made of spirals of beaten wire; stiff wire necklaces curved to hold on the neck without a clasp; silver rings were set with rutilated quartz, fused glass, or a variety of unrelated cabochons.

Pioneering craftspeople in New York City (especially in Greenwich Village), Chicago, San Francisco, and Provincetown, Massachusetts, created avant-garde designs that were very different from commercial jewelry. It is no longer a shock to see jewelry made of bits of wire, moving pieces, and irregular chunks of metal with

A craft show artist made this pin with dangling charms in the 1980s. It is made of thin plastic, buttons, movie film, and plastic bubble-gum charms.

wood, stone, plastic, ivory, or glass insets, but in the 1950s modernist jewelry was unfamiliar. It became popular with young, educated, middle-class women who wanted something "different." Its low price, often under $50, added to the attraction.

Some of the craftspeople were recognized artists like Alexander Calder and Harry Bertoia. Most were individuals, men and women, who wanted to do it *their* way. Perhaps the best known today are Betty Cooke, Margaret De Patta, Claire Falkenstein, Sam Kramer, Ed Levin, Paul Lobel, Peter Macchiarini, Earl Pardon, Frank Rebajes, Art Smith, and Ed Wiener. Others who made work collected today are F. Carlton Ball, best known for his pottery (see page 26); Frances Higgins, best known for her glass; and Henry Steig, writer, painter, and jazz musician. Other still-unknown craftspeople made similar asymmetrical silver pieces. The modernist style was soon made with less handwork and more duplication so it could be sold in shops across the country. Fortunately, most pieces are marked with the maker's name or initials.

Mood Rings

Mood rings were a fad in the 1970s and again in the 1990s. The glass stone in the ring changed colors to indicate the wearer's mood—dark blue when the person was happy, black when tense or stressed. The stone contained or was on top of liquid crystals that changed color with the wearer's body temperature, thus supposedly reflecting the person's emotions.

Swarovski

The Austrian firm Swarovski was founded in 1895 to manufacture cut crystals. In addition to optical products and grinding tools, it produced decorative stones from crystal for jewelry and fashion accessories made by others. In the 1970s, Swarovski introduced a series of crystal animal figurines that continue to be popular. At the end of the twentieth century, it created chandeliers and other large decorative pieces. Swarovski still makes crystal beads used in jewelry and on dresses, shoes, and handbags.

Swarovski crystals have added to the glitter of costume jewelry since 1895. This 1970s necklace was made in France using red and green Swarovski flower-shaped stones called Margaritas. *(Photo: Doyle New York)*

Peter Macchiarini (1909–1991), an important creator of Modernist jewelry, started working in California in 1936. He made this pin of silver and polished wood. (Photo: Private Collection, Miami)

CONTEMPORARY JEWELRY

By the 1970s, handcrafted jewelry had incorporated previously unused shapes and materials. Carved stone, metal printed with photographs, oxidized steel, aluminum, fur, feathers, leather, rubber, acrylic, and glass were used with silver, gold, and semiprecious stones. Most pieces were made in unusual geometric shapes with overlapping parts. One 3-inch pin looked like an open can of sardines; another was a pendant made from computer circuit cards.

ETHNIC AND EUROPEAN JEWELRY

The unusual, modernist fifties jewelry was not the only choice available for someone who wanted silver jewelry. A very different look was available in jewelry made by American Indians, Mexicans, or Danes.

American Indian Jewelry

American Indian jewelry has attracted collectors for years. Each tribe has its own distinctive designs and techniques. Early jewelry was made for use in ceremonies and as portable wealth. Later jewelry was made for tourists. In 1935 Congress created the Indian Arts and Crafts Board to promote development in Indian communities through arts and crafts. Many new silversmiths were trained, guilds and cooperatives were formed, and Indian jewelry became more artistic and more expensive. After World War II, a new generation of Indian artists created distinctive pieces with a modern look using traditional materials. Some of the jewelry made by these artists from the 1930s to the present now sells for thousands of dollars. Indian trade jewelry was lighter in weight and more highly polished than older jewelry, and it was often decorated

Top Right: A 1970s French jeweler made this plastic bead necklace of tubular and shaped beads. The pink color was very popular at the time.
(Photo: Skinner)

Engraved and reverse-painted colored acetate was used with gilt brass to make this necklace by Giorgio Armani in 1995.
(Photo: Doyle New York)

with arrows, suns, thunderbirds, and other designs chosen for their "authentic" look. Some of it was mass-produced, and many copies have been made in Mexico and Taiwan.

Most authentic Indian silver and turquoise jewelry collected today was made by the Navajo, Hopi, Zuni, and Indians from the Rio Grande Pueblos of the Southwest. From about 1868 to 1900, the Navajo made jewelry from melted-down coins, wire, and other metal objects. In 1890 a law made it illegal to deface U.S. coins, but jewelry continued to be made from Mexican coins until about 1930. Sterling silver jewelry was made after 1900 from thinner sheet silver and machine-drawn wire. Many hand hammered designs found on early southwestern Indian jewelry are similar to those found on Mexican and Spanish silver and leatherwork or to designs used by the Plains Indians.

The Zuni learned silversmithing from the Navajo in the 1870s and began making turquoise jewelry in the late 1800s. They taught the Hopi and tribes from the Rio Grande Pueblos how to work silver in the 1890s. The Hopi are known for their overlay work made since the late 1930s. The Pueblo tribes are known for their work with beads, shells, and mosaics.

Mexican Silver Jewelry

In 1929 William Spratling moved from New Orleans to Taxco, Mexico. He started designing jewelry made from the silver, amethyst, and obsidian available nearby. A local master silversmith and about eighteen apprentices made the pieces he designed. Ten years later, his shop had grown and he had three hundred Mexican craftsmen making silver jewelry and tableware. Taxco became a destination for tourists who wanted to buy silver, and hundreds of silversmiths began working in shops in or near the city. The best and

Zuni silver jewelry designs became distinctive in about 1915. The colored stones—often turquoise, coral, jet, and shell—were set in patterns. Indian symbols like the Knifewing man on this mid-twentieth-century bracelet were used.

Ed Wiener made castings for some of his jewelry. When he died in 1991, his daughter inherited 1,700 molds. She sells his jewelry today but marks the new pieces *EW*. The old ones are marked *Ed Wiener*.

The Navajo started making silver jewelry in about 1860. It was portable money and gave status. In about 1900 they added turquoise stones and Indian symbols to attract the tourist trade. This bracelet was made in the 1950s. (Photo: Skinner)

most expensive jewelry was made by a few now-famous shops like those of Hector Aguilar, Antonio Pineda Gomez, and the four Los Castillo brothers, who were among the original apprentices in the Spratling workshop. Other well-known silversmiths, including Margot van Voorhies Carr (known as Margot de Taxco) and Sigfrido Pineda (Sigi), were not in the original group but trained in the Taxco shops.

Another important maker was Frederick Davis, who is credited with founding the Mexican silver jewelry industry. Davis started working in Mexico City in the 1920s and made pieces with a primitive look based on early Mexican designs. His jewelry was very different from the work of Spratling and his apprentices. Designs were simple, often abstract and modern, but a Mexican influence was always apparent in the jewelry.

Other important Mexican silversmiths include Bernice Goodspeed, Hubert Harmon, Enrique Ledesma, Isidro Garcia Piña, Matilde de Poulat, and Salvador Vaca Teran.

In the 1940s and '50s, Mexican jewelry artists preferred blue, green, and black semiprecious stones. Inlaid stones and abalone shell, tortoiseshell, copper, brass, ebony, and other natural materials were selected and arranged for color and pattern. Colored enamel was used by a few, most successfully by Margot de Taxco, who, in spite of her name, worked in Mexico City. Most silversmiths also made bowls, vases, silver flatware and serving pieces, and other small silver objects like letter openers, salt dishes, ashtrays, and desk accessories.

Scandinavian Silver Jewelry

Scandinavian design for jewelry, as well as furniture and other decorative arts, was quite different from the designs seen in other countries. Before 1900, artists in Denmark, Norway, Sweden, and

Margot de Taxco, the former wife of Antonio Los Castillo, opened her own shop in 1948. Her enameled silver is best known. This snake necklace and bracelet are from the 1950s, but newer versions have been made.

Finland based their design on motifs from the Viking Age, the eighth through the eleventh centuries. The Scandinavians also produced regional folk jewelry that was not very popular in other countries. Arts and Crafts designs were seen in jewelry made in Denmark beginning in the early 1900s. The work was a reaction against poor-quality manufactured goods. Silver jewelry was made using semiprecious stones, often cabochons, usually opaque like moonstones, carnelian, opals, malachite, or lapis; amber; mother of pearl; and porcelain plaques. Georg Jensen and others founded workshops and created jewelry inspired by Japanese, French, English, and other traditions. Plantlike leaves and buds were often part of the design. Silver was made with a hammered, not a polished, surface. But the "hammer" marks often were made by machine, not by handheld hammers.

Georg Jensen jewelry, first made in 1904, is still popular. This 1¾-inch silver and lapis brooch, made in about 1915, has the flower and leaf designs used in many Jensen pieces. The number 193 and the Jensen mark are on the back. (Photo: Skinner)

Denmark's Georg Jensen is the most important of the Scandinavian jewelers. He trained as a goldsmith and a sculptor before he started working as a journeyman in a metalworks in 1901. He opened his own workshop in 1904 in Copenhagen, and it grew into the large company that is still working. (For more information on Georg Jensen, see pages 279–280.) Jensen's work was immediately in demand, and by 1910 he was selling pieces in several countries and had won a gold medal at the 1910 world exposition in Brussels. His shop made hollow ware as well as jewelry, and he hired many of the famous Danish designers, including Sigvard Bernadotte, Henning Koppel, and Harald Nielsen. In 1924 Danish gallery owner Frederik Lunning opened a store in New York City and sold Jensen silver and other Scandinavian pieces. This was the beginning of the acceptance of Scandinavian design in the United States. Jensen's shop used a series of changing marks, and pieces can be dated from the marks. Designers' initials are also found on some pieces. The shop used 826 silver until 1914, then 830 or 925 silver until 1932, then sterling (925) after that. The shop also made gold jewelry and, of course, porcelains and silver hollow ware. In the 1950s, Danish designs changed, and Georg Jensen began to make modernist jewelry. The pieces by designers Henning Koppel and Nanna and

Jorgen Ditzel were among the best. The firm continues to make cutting-edge designs in the latest styles.

The other Scandinavian countries also made silver jewelry. Norwegian designer David-Andersen made enameled pieces that are popular today, as well as very modern pieces. Other designers worked in the modernist styles. Finland also had silver jewelry shops and designers making modern pieces. Costume jewelry in similar designs was made from other metals, including iron, nickel, brass or steel, wood, colored stones, porcelain, and glass.

The simple lines of this silver pendant with an inset turquoise stone help identify this necklace by David-Andersen of Norway. David-Andersen also made many enameled pieces. (Photo: Treadway)

Czechoslovakian Glass Jewelry

Glass has been made since the thirteenth century in the area of central Europe known as Bohemia. The region became a province in the Republic of Czechoslovakia in 1918 and is now part of the Czech Republic. In the nineteenth century, Josef Riedel had started an industry there making straight glass rods for beads and rhinestones. By 1918 many Czechoslovakian glassmakers working in their homes were making glass beads, faceted glass stones, and rhinestones for jewelry. The glass beads were made in and near the city of Gablonz. From there, they were exported and sold in retail stores all over the world. From 1918 to 1938, the export business was booming. Plain beads were sold to Africa, multicolored beads to South America, and finished jewelry to the United States and Europe. Designs followed the fashions from art deco to Egyptian revival to modern. Pieces are usually marked on the spring ring clasp with some form of the name *Czechoslovakia.* Glass bead production stopped during World War II, and after the war many jewelers moved to West

Long necklaces of glass beads were popular in the 1920s, and most of the beads came from Czechoslovakia. This 50-inch-long necklace has cube- and wafer-shaped beads of ruby or clear glass. (Photo: About Mimi's Gems)

Memphis-designed jewelry is easy to recognize. It is abstract in design, colorful, and unlike any other. This 3-inch pin can be worn with any side as the top. The mark Zanini for Acme/Los Angeles is molded on the back.

Germany. In 1948 all private jewelry companies in Czechoslovakia were closed, and from then on, jewelry exports were handled by a government-run company. Although Czechoslovakian glass has remained popular worldwide, little jewelry is made for export today.

Memphis Jewelry

Memphis, an Italian design group started in 1981 by Ettore Sottsass (see page 231), created startling designs that ignored many of the "rules." A table could have a free-form top and four very different looking legs, each finished in a different color. Memphis jewelry was also unique. It was made from white metal, then partially enameled in bright colors. Surface design was important, and so were strange, free-form shapes. One earring of a pair did not match the other earring, although they were obviously related. Pins and earrings often had dangling parts. One pin resembled a black-and-white checkered table and another an orange overstuffed chair. They sold as a pair. A silver-colored abstract-looking pin made for a museum was actually the "footprint" of its new building. Necklaces were usually colored enamel pieces in odd shapes that overlapped to form a curved "collar" hung on the neck from a black cord. One designer made pieces that looked like African masks or animals. Another mimicked Greek columns. The colors, black and white trim, and shapes all echo the designs used for Memphis furniture. Acme Studio in Los Angeles made over one hundred Memphis jewelry designs by fourteen designers starting in 1985. The name *Acme* or *Acme Studios* appears on the back of the jewelry. Acme is still making some pieces of Memphis-designed jewelry, although Memphis disbanded in 1988.

PLASTIC COSTUME JEWELRY

Celluloid was the first plastic used for jewelry. It was invented in 1868 to make billiard balls. By the early 1900s, manufacturers had a process for setting stones or metal into celluloid, and it became a versatile material for costume jewelry. Popular celluloid pieces included bangle bracelets studded with rhinestones; figural pins;

Celluloid was used for many different types of costume jewelry. This painted celluloid and rhinestone brooch was made in the 1930s "for a woman of good taste." (Photo: Jitterbug Jewelry)

Could this be anything but a "fun" piece of jewelry? Colored Bakelite was used to make this dog's head with movable eyes. The polka dots and other details are painted. (Photo: Skinner)

dress clips and chain necklaces with small pendants; and pins, buckles, or earrings looking like realistic flowers and petals.

Cellulose acetate, sometimes incorrectly called "celluloid," was, unlike celluloid, nonflammable, and by the late 1920s it, too, was used for jewelry. It was also used in the 1960s and after by Lea Stein, who made animal pins from sheets of the colored plastic.

The most sought-after plastic costume jewelry is made of Bakelite (thermosetting phenol formaldehyde resin), which was invented in 1907. The costume jewelry of the 1930s was cheerful, colorful, and upbeat so it would improve the mood of the women living through the trauma of the Depression. Almost every type of jewelry was made from Bakelite—whimsical pins shaped like animals, fruits, vegetables, or even large red hearts; carved bangle bracelets; charm bracelets; elastic cuff bracelets made of domino-shaped pieces; clips; earrings; and necklaces. Bakelite jewelry could be carved, molded, painted, dyed, or set with metal, stones, or

colored Bakelite. Many pieces were what we now call "fun" jewelry: anthropomorphic animals, cartoonlike characters, unexpected color combinations, or pins with dangling fruit, school supplies, or western objects.

Bakelite was no longer produced after the mid-1960s. In the 1980s, Bakelite and other plastic jewelry became the darling of collectors, and prices skyrocketed. Some modern artists made new pieces from plastic and old Bakelite stock. Polka-dot Bakelite bangle bracelets, carved and painted Lucite pieces, animal pins, and rhinestone-studded pieces, usually signed by the artist, are still being made. Some jewelry made in the 1990s from materials that look like Bakelite has been misrepresented as authentic vintage Bakelite.

Collectors are now also searching for pins that are made of wood or wood and plastic. Clever images, including dogs, cats, cows, horses, African natives, cowboys, even rulers and schoolbooks, were made. Many of these inexpensive wooden pieces of jewelry, now worn by the over-twenty-year-olds, were designed for preteens and teens.

Apple Juice Bakelite

Colorless Bakelite jewelry—bracelets, necklaces, pins, earrings, and even belt buckles—can oxidize over the years turning a light amber color called *apple juice*. (Photo: Skinner)

Record Prices For Bakelite Jewelry

A Bakelite bracelet called the *Philadelphia bracelet* sold in 1998 for a record $17,000. The bracelet had a green hinged body with black, orange, green, red, and yellow laminated fin-shaped teeth on either side of the clasp.

The MacArthur Heart, a red pin with a heart dangling from a horizontal key, is another pricey piece of Bakelite jewelry. Named for General Douglas MacArthur, it is very rare and sells for as much as $2,000.

The MacArthur Heart Bakelite pin was pictured on a 1941 cover of Life Magazine. (Photo: Skinner)

Chapter 11

Toys and Dolls

TOYS HAVE ALWAYS enchanted collectors. Many toys were handmade, hand painted, and hand stenciled as late as 1900. More elaborate, manufactured toys were imported from Germany, France, and England by the end of the nineteenth century. German toy makers produced many types of toys, including boats, fire stations, cars, kitchenware, and toys depicting working people. By 1900 over one-third of all German-made toys were sold to America. The makers just changed the German names on toys to English for the exports. French toys, often quite elaborate and expensive, were not exported in quantity to America until World War I, when German toys were not available.

Manufacturers in the United States were making toys in the early twentieth century, but it was not until after World War I that the industry blossomed. Imaginative toys were made, and many toys inspired by comic strips and celebrities were produced. Manufacturers made toy trains, boats, automobiles, housewares, lunch boxes, familiar animals, and people. British toy makers were also more active after World War I. The best of their toys date from the 1920s and 1930s.

LITHOGRAPHED TIN TOYS

Most lithographed tin toys found today were made between 1870 and 1915, although some were manufactured later. All sorts of wagons, fire engines, stagecoaches, and buses are valuable today; locomotives, trains, and horsecars are better; and old tin boats are

Opposite Page: This comical frog has a tongue that pops out. Wind up the toy, and the frog sways and "walks" across the table chasing a fly that flits about on an attached wire. It is by Georg Kellermann and marked CKO.
(Photo: James Julia)

the rarest. Collectors are especially interested in animated groups of animals or people; toys that make noise with a gong, bell, or whistle; or toys that move. Makers that are of special interest include Lehmann, Marx, Chein, Unique, Wolverine, and Strauss. Their toys bring premium prices.

TOY CARS

The toy auto of the 1920s and 1930s is an important vestige of childhood and a collector's treasure. Collectors distinguish between cars made before 1940 and cars made after World War II. Metal toy cars were not manufactured in the United States from mid-1942 to late 1945 because of the war. Many of the bronze molds that had been used for the earlier cars were melted for wartime scrap metal.

Most toy cars manufactured before 1940 were metal: cast iron, aluminum, stamped steel, or alloys. The most common cars were made of a zinc alloy or of a white metal alloy consisting of lead, tin, and antimony. "Pot" metal was used for very inexpensive cars. It was a mixture of metal scraps that included pewter, lead, tin, Britannia metal, and sometimes metal toothpaste tubes.

Some cars were made of hard rubber. Rubber cars were inexpensive, realistic scale models of old cars or of very streamlined futuristic or imaginative cars. Collectors do not seem as interested in this type of car because rubber hardens, cracks, and ages badly.

Plastic was not used for toys until the late 1930s. Toy makers tried Bakelite first, but it was too fragile and was replaced by Butyrate in the 1940s. However, heat melted Butyrate, so most manufacturers then switched to polystyrene, a tough plastic invented in 1927. Today, car models are made of metal, plastic, or a combination of the two.

Manufacturing Techniques

Miniature metal cars were usually made by stamping, slush-casting, or die-casting. The earliest lightweight metal cars were stamped from sheet steel or tin and had either hand-painted or lithographed decorations. European stamped-tin cars date from the early 1890s.

Die-cast toys like this 4-inch Tootsietoy truck with a Wrigley's Spearmint Gum ad on the side are detailed copies of real trucks. (Photo: Atlanta Antique Gallery)

RULES FOR MOST CAR WHEELS

Wheels can help to date a car. Before World War II, toy cars had open-spoked metal wheels, solid metal disk wheels, solid metal disk wheels with embossed spokes, white rubber tires with metal rims, or solid white rubber tires mounted directly on the axles. The general rule is that white rubber tires were used before World War II and black tires after the war. Black plastic wheels have been used since about 1960.

White rubber tires were used before World War II. This cast-iron Jaeger cement mixer has a nickel-plated mixing tank. The mixer goes around as the tires turn. (Photo: James Julia)

Slush-cast toys were made in molds that pot metal was poured into and right out again, causing a rough interior surface. No mark could be cast on the bottom of a slush-cast toy. Some slush-cast toys are being made today in the old molds.

Die-cast toys were made in a closed mold that came apart into as many as six pieces. This method produced a toy with a smooth interior. Raised lettering could also be part of the casting.

Value

It is important for a toy car to have all original parts. Sometimes the original wheels, headlights, or accessories are missing or have been replaced. Any old toy car, from mint condition to broken, has a resale value. Don't throw anything away before checking with a toy collector. Don't repaint, restore, or even clean an old toy. The original paint helps to identify a toy and shows that it is not a reproduction. An expert can tell whether the paint was applied by dipping, spraying, or brushing and will know the correct color for each make and model. A repainted car is worth less than half as much as a car with the original finish. The general rule has been that any car older than the collector is collectible.

Toy Car Makers

Auburn Rubber Corporation

The Double Fabric Tire Corporation, founded in 1913 in Auburn, Indiana, and reorganized as the Auburn Rubber Corporation in the 1920s, made auto tires for full-size cars. In 1935 the company made a toy soldier of molded rubber and then other toys, including cars, trucks, tractors, and figures of ballplayers. The toy-manufacturing part of the company was purchased by the town of Deming, New Mexico, in 1960, and toys were made there for about ten years.

Buddy L

The Moline Pressed Steel Company, established in 1913 in Moline, Illinois, began making toys under the *Buddy L* name in 1921. It made toy trucks, fire engines, and other vehicles like concrete mixers and road rollers. Most of the toys are from 21 to 24 inches long. They were made from heavy steel, strong enough to hold a child. By the early 1930s, the toys were much lighter in weight. The company has changed owners many times, but it still uses the name *Buddy L* on its toys. Early Buddy L toys were marked *Buddy "L"* with quotation marks. By the mid-1950s, the *'L'* was in single quotes, and later toys were marked *Buddy L* without quotation marks.

The Buddy L toy from the 1920s was large enough and strong enough to hold a small boy. This dump truck is shown with its original box. (Photo: Atlanta Antique Gallery)

Dinky Toy

Meccano Limited, founded in 1901 in Liverpool, England, made toy construction kits using perforated metal parts that had to be bolted together. The company first made clockwork trains, and, after World War I, produced O gauge electric trains. Later on, it made OO gauge. In 1933 Dinky Toy model cars were introduced. Production was curtailed during World War II, but by 1946 new model cars and planes were being produced. The name *Dinky Toy* was stamped on the underside of models after World War II. Faced with competition from Mattel's Hot Wheels, Dinky Speedwheels came out in 1969.

Meccano made a line of French Dinky toys at its factory in Bobigny, France, from 1933 to 1972.

Dinky Toy is a trade name used since 1933. This 1960s Corvair #552's colorful box adds to the value. When a popular book attacked the full-sized Corvair's safety record, sales of the Dinky model dropped, and it went out of production in 1969. (Photo: Atlanta Antique Gallery)

Because pontoons don't slide across the floor easily, the Hubley Company made this cast-iron Friendship trimotor plane with added wheels. The plane is 12¾ inches wide. It has a Hubley decal on the wing. (Photo: James Julia)

The company was sold several times and was out of business by 1980. In 1987 Universal International, owner of Matchbox cars, bought the Dinky name and used it on some models of cars from the 1950s.

Grey Iron Casting Company

The Brady Machine Shop, founded in Mount Joy, Pennsylvania, in 1840, changed its name to *Grey Iron Casting Company* in 1881. The company was making wheeled toys and trains, banks, stoves, and cap pistols by 1903. Best known are its many toy soldiers and its model Fords of the 1920s and after. Grey toys are still being produced by the John Wright division of Donsco in Wrightsville, Pennsylvania.

Hubley

The Hubley Manufacturing Company was incorporated in 1894 in Lancaster, Pennsylvania. It made cast-iron toys, including circus wagons and mechanical banks. Most of the cast-iron cars it made from the 1920s through the 1960s were copies of actual vehicles, and they were advertised with the slogan, "They look just like the real ones." The cars were sometimes marked with the company name cast into the body or with a decal. Many of Hubley's molds were donated to scrap drives during World War II, when the company was making bomb fuses. After the war, Hubley made die-cast white metal and plastic toys. The company was acquired in 1965 by Gabriel Industries, which made toys using the Hubley name for a few years. Gabriel sold its Hubley toy division to CBS in 1978. The Hubley name is still being used.

Kenton

Kenton Lock Manufacturing Company was started in 1890 in Kenton, Ohio. The name changed to Kenton Hardware Manufacturing Company in 1894, and about then Kenton started making toys. Cast-iron toy cars were first made in 1903. Some were stamped *Kenton*. The painted red cars were called *Red Devils.* Many Kenton vehicles had a driver. Kenton was known for its toy commercial vehicles, including buses, tank trucks, dump trucks, and cement mixers. The firm made horse-drawn iron toys until the 1920s and also made iron banks. It stopped making toys in 1952.

Manoil

Manoil, owned by brothers Jack and Maurice Manoil, began making toys in 1934. The company was first located in New York City, but later moved to Waverly, New York. It made slush-cast and die-cast cars noted for their futuristic designs. Tires on early cars were white rubber on red hubs. Postwar models had black rubber tires. The company also made many types of hollowcast soldiers and plastic toys. It closed after owner Jack Manoil's death in 1955.

Tootsietoy

This old Tootsietoy box has colorful graphics that attracted the customer to the toys inside. The set of cars, trucks, and a plane was made in about 1950. (Photo: Randy Inman Auctions)

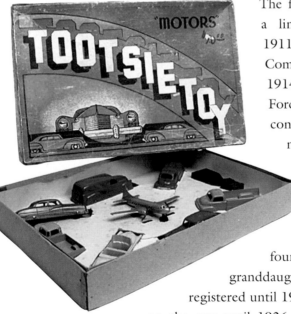

The Dowst Brothers Company of Chicago started as a laundry. It made metal collar buttons, then small metal toys, like miniature irons, stoves, and bicycles. The first Tootsietoy car was a limousine made about 1911 by the Dowst Brothers Company. It was followed in 1914 by a toy Model T Ford. Production was discontinued in 1924 after more than fifty million Tootsietoy Model Ts had been sold.

The *Tootsietoy* name, inspired by founder Charles Dowst's granddaughter, Tootsie, was not registered until 1924 and did not appear on the cars until 1926. In that year Chicago businessman Nathan Shure bought the Dowst firm and merged it with his company, Cosmo Manufacturing, to form Dowst Manufacturing Company. A few models were cast without the Tootsietoy name before 1931, and some of the most valuable have no marking on the bottom. Dowst acquired

Strombeck-Becker Company's toy line in 1961 and changed its name to Strombecker Corporation. Tootsietoy became a division of Strombecker. Tootsietoys are still being made.

The early Tootsietoy cars had open-spoked turning metal wheels. From 1923 to 1933, they were made with solid metal disk turning wheels. Starting in 1927, solid disk wheels with embossed wire spokes were made. White rubber tires on metal rims were introduced in 1933, and by 1937 solid white rubber wheels were mounted on the axles. Solid black rubber wheels were used on post-World War II models, and black plastic wheels were used after 1960.

Most cars were made in the style of the day. In the 1930s Tootsietoys were cast from a zinc alloy, lighter and stronger than the lead alloy used until then. In the 1960s Tootsietoy began to use plastic parts in some of its models. The last all-metal Tootsietoy cars were made in 1969, and since then the cars have had both metal and plastic parts.

Age is not the best indication of value; scarcity is the key. The rarest are the 1925 panel delivery truck marked *Florist*, the 1933 Graham town car series, 1935 LaSalles, and the trucks marked *Hochschild Kohn and Co.* or *J. C. Penney*. The 1932 Funnies series—six comic characters (Andy Gump, Uncle Walt, Smitty, Moon Mullins, Kayo, and Uncle Willie), each in a car—is also high-priced.

Tonka

The first Tonka toys were a steam shovel and a crane made by Mound Metalcraft in 1947 in the basement of a Minnesota schoolhouse. The company made thirty-seven thousand trucks that year. Soon it added semis, wreckers, dump trucks, fire trucks, and forklifts. Pickup trucks were added in 1955, a Jeep in 1962, and a bright yellow Mighty Dump Truck in 1964. In 1955 the company changed its name to Tonka Toys. Hasbro acquired Tonka in 1991 and now produces a line of more than thirty trucks. More than 250 different models of Tonka trucks have been sold.

A line of all the Tonka trucks made in the last fifty years would stretch from Los Angeles to Pawtucket, Rhode Island.

In 1965 Tonka ran a famous TV commercial that showed a full-grown elephant standing on a Mighty dump truck. The strong Tonka toys, like this AAA wrecker truck, have been favorites of boys since the first one was made in 1947. (Photo: Atlanta Antique Gallery)

Matchbox Cars

In 1948 the London firm Lesney Products made its first toys, a diesel road roller, a cement mixer, and a crawler tractor, just 3 to 4 inches long. Lesney designer Jack Odell created the first miniature Matchbox car four years later when he made a brass road roller small enough to fit in a matchbox for his daughter to take to school. Lesney then began a new line of die-cast 1½-inch to 3-inch vehicles packaged in a blue and yellow container that looked like a matchbox. By 1954 Lesney made only matchbox-size models. The early Matchbox I-75 series included construction vehicles, double-decker buses, and models of many cars and trucks. In 1956 the Matchbox Models of Yesteryear series of vintage vehicles made before 1946 was introduced. Boats, airplanes, racing cars, and more models followed. Plastic wheels replaced metal wheels in 1958. Glazed windows were introduced in 1961.

By 1969 annual sales of Matchbox toys reached $286 million. Competition from Mattel's Hot Wheels and financial and labor setbacks in the 1970s led to Lesney's bankruptcy in 1982. Universal Toys bought the company in 1982, Tyco Toys in 1992, and Mattel in 1996. Mattel is still making Matchbox cars.

Hot Wheels

Mattel introduced Hot Wheels in 1968. With special torsion-bar suspension and low-friction wheels, Hot Wheels were the fastest toy cars on the market. They were modeled after popular cars—for example, the Custom Barracuda, Corvette, Mustang, and Volkswagen—and painted in fourteen metallic Spectraflame finishes, ranging from orange, green, yellow, gold, and red to pink, purple, and magenta. Later, Mattel added futuristic cars to the line.

TRAINS

Many early toy trains were made of tin or cast iron with a windup mechanism, but most collectors today are interested in trains with electric motors. An electric-powered train made by Carlisle & Finch in 1896 ran on a metal track, but electric trains became popular only when toy train makers began to use transformers, which made the trains easy to run. Ives Manufacturing Company, founded in

It says VW Golf *on the side of the Matchbox toy box, indicating that the toy car inside is the Golf model Volkswagen. This 1976 toy, just like a real surfer's car, has two surf boards on the top.* (Photo: Toy Car Collector)

A professional restoration adds to the value of a pedal car, just as it adds to the value of a full-size car. This restored Studebaker pedal car is marked with the Murray decal on the rear of the seat. It is 34 inches long. (Photo: James Julia)

Plymouth, Connecticut, in 1868, was already making windup trains when it began making electric trains in the early 1900s. Lionel Manufacturing Company, started in 1900 in New York City, made trains and accessories, and it purchased the Ives Corporation after Ives went bankrupt in 1928. In 1969 Lionel licensed its electric-train manufacturing to General Mills, which produced locomotives, cars, and accessories to promote its cereals. Lionel had several ownership changes in the 1980s and 1990s, and today, as Lionel LLC, it continues to produce traditional model trains, but with the latest wireless technology for its control systems.

Toy trains have been made in Standard Gauge to run on a track with 2⅛ inches between the rails; O Gauge, half as big as Standard Gauge; and HO Gauge, half as big as O Gauge. Also made were OO Gauge, about ¾ inch; and S Gauge, ⅞ inch between the rails.

Other names of interest to the train collector are American Flyer, Dorfan Company, Louis Marx, and Meccano.

PEDAL CARS

When motor-driven automobiles appeared, toy manufacturers added pedal cars to their product lines. Pedal cars were copies of real cars, with side doors, nickel-plated lamps and trim, imitation toolboxes, and rubber tires. One or two children could sit in the car and move it by pushing the foot pedals. Pedal cars from the early 1900s to the 1950s are the most popular with collectors. New cars, copies of recent automobiles, are still being made. Plastic futuristic

This Lionel O Gauge passenger train set has a hard-to-find gunmetal gray locomotive and whistle tender and blue and silver passenger cars.
(Photo: James Julia)

pedal toys were an invention of the 1970s. There are also pedal airplanes and spaceships, but cars are the most popular.

Important pedal car makers include American National, Garton, Gendron, Kirk-Latty, Murray-Ohio (Steelcraft), and Toledo Metal Wheel Company.

BATTERY-OPERATED TOYS

Most of the battery-operated toys sought by collectors were made in Japan from 1946 to 1960. The Japanese faced a shortage of materials at the end of World War II. Makers even searched dumps for tin cans discarded by the occupying United States Army to recycle into toys. Making toys was a cottage industry in Japan. A family would make a single part or do some of the assembly, then pass the toy on to a small factory.

These battery-operated toys included banks, comic characters, animals, people, novelties and games, space toys and robots, and automobiles. The comic characters, animals, and people are the most ingenious. *Charley Weaver*, a TV character, drank a martini while smoke poured from his ears. A reservoir of oil inside the toy was heated with an electric spark, making the smoke. Other unusual battery toys include a teddy bear that draws on a pad, an Indian who beats a drum, a drinking monkey, a smoking Popeye, a pig that flips an egg in a pan, and a man who shaves. A few battery toys of this type are still being made, but they are expensive and often have plastic parts.

CONSTRUCTION TOYS

The second decade of the twentieth century saw not only a building boom in America but also the introduction of three classic construction toys: the Erector Set, Tinkertoys, and Lincoln Logs. Nearly forty years later, Legos came on the scene.

Be sure the battery-operated toy you buy is in working condition. Most of them are difficult, if not almost impossible, to repair. Batteries frequently leaked, damaging the toy.

Charley Weaver was a television character developed by actor Cliff Arquette. This 1962 battery-operated toy has Charley shake his cocktail mixer, pour a drink into a martini glass, and drink. Then his face turns red and smoke comes out of his ears.
(Photo: Hake's)

Erector Set

The Erector Set, invented by A. C. Gilbert in 1913, was a collection of steel strips with evenly spaced holes that could be connected with nuts and bolts. Children built models of Ferris wheels, bridges, skyscrapers, railways, robots, and more. The sets included gears, wheels, pulleys, motors, and other accessories, and in 1924 parts that would build a special model—a locomotive, steam shovel, or zeppelin—were added. Erector sets were popular until the 1960s, when plastic parts were introduced and sales dropped. Meccano Company, an English toy maker that made a similar construction set, was Gilbert's major competitor. Meccano acquired the license to produce Erector Sets in 1990 and still sells them today.

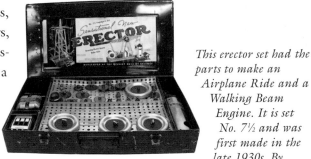

This erector set had the parts to make an Airplane Ride and a Walking Beam Engine. It is set No. 7½ and was first made in the late 1930s. By 1957 the number had been changed.
(Photo: Randy Inman Auctions)

Tinkertoys

Watching his children play with pencils, sticks, and empty spools of thread inspired Charles Pajeau of Evanston, Illinois, to create Tinkertoys in 1914. Pajeau and a partner, Robert Petit, established The Toy Tinkers company and developed several wooden parts, spokes and wheels, that children could assemble into shapes ranging from tall towers and windmills to carousels and rolling vehicles. Playskool, owned by Hasbro, has made Tinkertoy construction sets since it acquired the Tinkertoy line in 1985. In 1992 Playskool introduced colored plastic Tinkertoy sets.

Lincoln Logs

A third classic construction toy, Lincoln Logs, was introduced in 1916. The line of wooden, interlocking logs, green roofs, and red chimneys was invented by John Lloyd Wright, Frank Lloyd Wright's son. Lincoln Logs, which could be assembled into cabins, forts, and bridges, were especially popular in the 1950s because of the popularity of stories and television shows about the frontier, cowboys, and Davy Crockett. Today Lincoln Log sets are manufactured by K'NEX Industries, Inc. of Hatfield, Pennsylvania, and distributed by Hasbro.

Six eight-stud Lego blocks of the same color can be combined in 102,981,500 different ways.

Legos

In 1949 Danish toy maker Ole Christiansen made a set of interlocking red and white plastic blocks using a design by Kiddicraft Company. In the 1950s more colors were added, and by 1958 blocks were made with studs on top that could be locked into the bottom of other blocks to make different shapes. Lego blocks were soon one of the most popular toys in Europe. In the 1960s, wheels, motors, and larger blocks called *Duplo* were added to the Lego product line. Lego sets were introduced in the United States in 1961. Legoland theme park, with models of famous buildings from around the world constructed of millions of Lego blocks, opened in 1968 in Billund, Denmark. The 1970s brought the first Lego people with snap-on heads. By the end of the twentieth century, Lego's products ranged from castles, pirate ships, and Star Wars figures to computer games and programmable robots with microchips.

These Lego sets were made in the 1970s. The boxes picture some of the buildings, vehicles, and even an elephant that can be made with the Legos in the set.

AND STILL MORE TOYS

Comic Strip Toys

All sorts of toys have been made to resemble famous comic characters such as the Yellow Kid, Maggie and Jiggs, or Snoopy. Each toy usually dates from the time of the strip or cartoon, but many revivals occur. During the 1980s there was new interest in Mickey Mouse, Popeye, Orphan Annie, Betty Boop, Flash Gordon, Superman, Spiderman, Batman, and others. Modern comic toys include characters from newspapers, movies, and television, like Peanuts, SpongeBob, and the many Disney characters.

When wound up, Mickey Mouse plays the xylophone and Minnie Mouse rocks in her chair, knits, and flaps her ears. Both tin toys were made by Linemar. (Photo: James Julia)

This robot resembles Robbie from the movie Forbidden Planet. *The 9-inch tin and plastic toy was made in the 1960s by Yoshiya of Japan. When the toy walks, sparks fly.* (Photo: Hake's)

View-Master

View-Master, the twentieth-century version of the Victorian stereoscope, was introduced in 1939 in Portland, Oregon, by William Gruber, whose hobby was stereo photography. Since then more than a billion of the handheld viewers have been sold. During World War II, the U.S. military used the viewers for training. After the war, adults bought them with reels of national parks and other tourist attractions. After View-Master obtained a license to picture Disney characters in 1951, it became a popular children's toy. View-Master reels show historic events like the Apollo moon landing (1969) and movie characters like Indiana Jones, and have been used as teaching tools in medical schools and even as menus in restaurants. View-Master has been owned by several toy companies. It has been owned by Mattel since 1997, and the toys sell under the Fisher-Price name.

Robots

Battery-operated mechanical robot toys became popular after World War II. Most of the robots were made in Japan, Germany, and the United States. Almost all were made of plastic and metal.

One of the first robot toys was the 5-inch tin Atomic Robot Man, made in Occupied Japan in the late 1940s. In the 1950s Masudaya Toys produced a series of five 15-inch-tall robots called *The Gang of Five*: wireless remote *Radicon Robot* with a head that glows, ears that spin, and a chest that glows as the toy rolls forward; *Non-Stop Robot* that moves forward and changes direction when it bumps into an obstacle; *Giant Sonic Robot* with flashing eyes and ears and a piercing train-style whistle; *Target Robot* that has a terrifying roar when the target on its chest is hit by a dart; and *Machine Man*, the rarest of the five.

Other early robots included Ideal's *Robert the Robot* that talked, Louis Marx's 38-inch *Big Loo*, Daiya's 10½-inch *Ranger Robot*, and German-made *Dux Astroman*.

Robots were especially popular in the 1950s. Interest waned with a brief revival in the early

1970s. Then Star Wars figures and other action toys were introduced, and robots and space again fascinated collectors.

Slinky

While trying to develop a device to keep instruments on board ships steady at sea, U.S. Navy engineer Richard James discovered a spring that walked end over end down steps or a sloped board. James recognized the possibilities for turning it into a toy, and two years later, in 1945, he began manufacturing Slinky. Since then, more than 250 million Slinkys have been sold. They are still made in Hollidaysburg, Pennsylvania, on the original eight machines that James used in the 1940s. The Slinky brand was sold in 1998 to Poof Toys.

The original steel wire Slinky is still available. Slinkys have also been made of brass, colored metal, and plastic, and have even been gold-plated. The Slinky Dog was introduced in 1952. Slinkys come in several sizes and can be imprinted with a company's ad.

Pez

Creating a new toy was furthest from his mind when, in 1927, the Austrian food producer Eduard Haas III developed a peppermint breath mint he called *Pez*. Pez mints were popular as a substitute for smoking, so Haas designed a dispenser that resembled a cigarette lighter. The candies were popular in Europe, but when Haas brought them to the United States in 1952, Americans didn't like them. Haas replaced the mints with fruit flavored tablets, placed the head of a cartoon character—Mickey Mouse or Popeye—on the top of the dispenser, and marketed the toy to children. Batman, Tweety, Santa Claus, Spooky Ghost, Elephant, and hundreds of other Pez dispensers have been produced since then. Pez candy has come in chocolate, mint, and many fruit flavors. It is sold in sixty countries. Pez Candy Inc. of Orange, Connecticut, makes the candy, and the dispensers are produced in several countries, including Hungary, China, and Slovenia.

Bullwinkle Moose and Rocky, a flying squirrel, were in cartoons beginning in 1959. There are two versions of this Bullwinkle Pez dispenser. The yellow stem version, made in the 1960s, is the more common. The brown stem is rare. (Photo: Hake's)

Mr. Potato Head

Mr. Potato Head has seen many changes since it was introduced by Hasbro in 1952. Originally the toy was boxed as twenty-eight sharp-pronged

When Mr. Potato Head was introduced, some parents were upset with a toy that wasted food, but kids loved it. This is the original box for the 1952 toy.

PEZ TRIVIA

❀ Feet were added to Pez dispensers in 1987.

❀ A story has circulated that eBay was created by Pierre Omidyar so his wife, an avid Pez collector, could easily buy and sell Pez dispensers for her collection. The story isn't true, but eBay didn't discourage it because it was good for promoting the online marketplace.

❀ *Pez* is a shortened form of the German word *pfefferminz*, which means *peppermint*.

The original Etch A Sketch with a red plastic frame came in this colorful box. It was packaged so that you could try drawing with the unfamiliar toy without opening the box.

plastic face pieces—eyes, ears, noses, mouths—and accessories—a hat and a pipe—that could be stuck into a potato or other vegetable or fruit. Mr. Potato Head was such an instant success that in 1953 Mrs. Potato Head was introduced. Eventually they had a son, Spud, and a daughter, Yam. In 1964 the kit began including a plastic potato. The pipe was eliminated in 1987 in response to anti-smoking campaigns. Today Mr. Potato Head's body and head are one piece, the prongs are less sharp, the face parts are larger, and he sometimes wears a baseball cap and sneakers instead of a derby hat and sensible shoes. Mr. Potato Head was featured in the popular films *Toy Story* (1995) and, with Mrs. Potato Head, *Toy Story 2* (1999).

Hula Hoop

Australian children twirling bamboo hoops around their waists for exercise gave Arthur Melin and Richard Knerr the idea for Hula Hoops. Their company, Wham-O, began to market the colorful plastic hoops in 1958. Hula Hoops became a craze, and people of all ages in many countries were soon swinging the large, lightweight rings around their waists, hips, arms, and legs. More than twenty million were sold the first six months. The fad died out in 1959, but it occasionally reappears. A 1965 version has ball bearings in the tubing so it makes a whooshing noise. Wham-O still makes the "original" Hula Hoop.

Etch A Sketch

The automatic drawing toy that became Etch A Sketch was originally invented in France. Howie Winzeler of the Ohio Art Company saw it at a toy fair in Germany and later bought the rights to produce it at the company's Bryan, Ohio, plant. Etch A Sketch

hasn't changed much since it was introduced in 1960. It is still produced by the same company, but production has moved to China. A variety of Etch A Sketch toys have been made, including a small keychain toggle, a pen, a travel Etch A Sketch, and an Etch A Sketch that makes fifty different sounds. They all work the same way. The reverse side of the screen is coated with aluminum powder and plastic beads. Two knobs control a stylus that scrapes the screen leaving a line. The lines disappear when the box is shaken.

ELECTRONIC GAMES

The 1970s saw the introduction of electronic games. One of the first was Hasbro's Simon, with its pattern of flashing lights and beeps. Magnavox's tennis video game Odyssey, introduced in 1972, was followed by the popular Pong tennis game that Atari brought out for home television in 1974. A big year in the electronic game industry was 1980. Intellivision, the first 16-bit videogame system, was introduced in that year. Pac-Man and the text adventure game Zork also came on the scene in 1980; then Nintendo's Donkey Kong and Super Mario Brothers appeared in 1981. Nintendo released the portable Game Boy in 1989, and Sony's PlayStation came out

Etch A Sketch

A limited-edition Executive Etch A Sketch introduced in 1985 was made of silver with twelve sapphires and a blue topaz on each drawing knob.

Tickle Me Elmo

Elmo is a furry red Muppet character from the PBS children's television program Sesame Street. He giggles when his stomach is poked.

When the $30 Tickle Me Elmo toy appeared on a TV talk show in 1996, the publicity set off a rush to buy the toy. During the Christmas season that year, its price skyrocketed to as much as several thousand dollars, but the price soon fell back to normal.

Electronic and video games were a totally new concept in the 1970s. This is an Atari 2600 computer system in the original box. It came with five games, including Pac-Man.

Can you see that Bild-Lilli was the inspiration for Barbie? This 11½-inch doll had a stand and an unusual hairdo.

in 1994. When Nintendo released the Nintendo 64 console in 1996, the first shipment of 350,000 was sold out in the United States in three days. The games may not be collectibles because the technology is unavailable after a while, but the characters like Mario have been used for figurines, posters, and other collectible items.

TWENTIETH-CENTURY DOLLS

Dolls have been saved for many centuries. A perfectly preserved doll may appear in a box in the attic along with almost-destroyed metal toys or well-worn stuffed animals. Collectors have searched for and purchased nineteenth-century dolls for years. Now prices often reach thousands of dollars for a single rare doll. Twentieth-century dolls are in greater supply, so there are still many opportunities for the astute collector with a smaller budget. Modern dolls that were expensive when new probably are still expensive when compared to dolls that were originally medium- or low-priced big-volume sellers.

The first true-to-life baby doll was the Bye-Lo (1922), the first sad doll was Poor Pitiful Pearl (c.1957), the first physically developed teen girl doll was Barbie (1959), and the first anatomically correct male doll was Baby Brother Tender Love (early 1970s). Some dolls are best known by the maker's name, some for the famous personalities they portray.

Barbie

Barbie, said to have been inspired by the German doll *Bild-Lilli*, was probably the first American teenage doll. She was introduced in 1959 and may be the most successful doll ever made. Mattel, Inc., continues to make the doll, along with a huge wardrobe of clothes and accessories. The 11½-inch fashion doll with small waist and developed bust delighted little girls. Soon there was a Barbie "family." Ken, Barbie's boyfriend, was introduced in 1961. Later came Barbie's sisters Skipper (1964), Tutti (1966), Stacie (1992), Kelly (1995), and Krissy (1999); cousin Francie (1966); and friends Midge (1963), Christie (1968), P.J. (1969), and Steffie (1972).

FAVORITE GAMES

Generations of children and adults have played these popular games. The dates in parentheses indicate the year they were introduced in the United States.

Monopoly (1933)
Scrabble (1948)
Candyland (1949)
Clue (1949)
Wiffle Ball (1953)
Yahtzee (1956)
The Game of Life (1960)
Twister (1966)
Dungeons & Dragons (1973)
Rubik's Cube (1980)
Trivial Pursuit (1982)
Pictionary (1985)

This is an early version of the Monopoly game.

Poor Pitiful Pearl was the first sad doll. Her original clothes were a torn dress, a babushka, black stockings, and boots. She came with "pretty" clothes—a party dress, white socks, and white shoes—so she could be transformed.

This is Barbie #1. She has holes in her feet so she can be placed on a stand with pegs. She has black and white eyes (no color in the iris) and blue eye shadow. Her hair is either blond or almost black. (Photo: Doyle New York)

Then there were Skipper's friends, Barbie's tiny twin brother and sister, and other friends of Barbie and her family. Through the years, Mattel introduced variations and improvements to the family of dolls. Wigs changed, hair grew. Barbie talked and moved at the waist or knee. Barbie has had more than eighty careers, ranging from astronaut (1965, 1986, 1994) and Olympic athlete (1975, 2000) to teacher (1995), dentist (1997), and presidential candidate (1992, 2000).

Over a billion outfits have been produced for Barbie and her friends since 1959. Her accessories have included furniture for every room, a boat, beach bus, camper, dune buggy, plane, bicycle, convertible, hot rod, Corvette, gymnastics set, tennis, golf, skating and skiing equipment, dolls, pets and horses, theater, dress shop, college campus, schoolroom, playhouse, ice cream stand, penthouse, ski cabin, beauty parlor, and even an Olympic ski village.

The first Barbie doll, the most valuable, had holes with copper tubes in the bottom of her feet. Pegs in a base fit into the holes so Barbie could stand up.

Barbie's lingerie set from the 1960s, with tiny pink corset, bra, panties, and slip, is now valued at more than $250.

Other teen dolls were also made, but only a few are bringing premium prices. The most prized are the first Barbie by Mattel; Lilli, made in West Germany; Brenda Starr by Madame Alexander; and G.I. Jane by Hasbro.

Barbie has a huge wardrobe. This Bubble Cut Barbie had a case filled with dresses, sports outfits, boots, shoes, bathing suit, and even a tennis racquet. (Photo: Village Doll & Toy)

Bye-Lo Baby Doll

The Bye-Lo Baby doll, modeled after a real three-day-old baby, was designed by Grace Storey Putnam and made from 1922 until the early 1950s. The doll was manufactured by several factories and distributed in the United States by George Borgfeldt & Company. Bye-Lo Baby, with glass sleep eyes, a wide nose, and chubby cheeks, was America's best-selling doll by 1924. The doll came in sizes ranging from 8 to 23 inches. In the 1920s a tiny all-bisque Bye-Lo Baby in sizes from

4 to 8 inches was made. They had hard or soft bodies and heads of composition, bisque, rubber, or celluloid. Almost all the dolls were marked with the name *Bye-Lo* or *Grace S. Putnam.*

Celebrity Dolls

Many dolls have been made to resemble movie and television stars, celebrities, fictional heroes, heroines, and comic characters. Some of the most famous are Charlie Chaplin (1915), Mickey Mouse (1930), Shirley Temple (1934), the Dionne Quintuplets (1935), Jackie Kennedy (1961), David Cassidy and the Partridge Family (1970s), Elvis Presley (1980s), and Princess Diana (1990s). Famous advertising symbols that have been made into dolls include Aunt Jemima (1905); the Campbell Kids (1910); Rastus, the Cream of Wheat chef (1922); the Kellogg bears (1925); Sprout (Green Giant, 1960s); and Planters Mr. Peanut (1960s). The list is almost endless.

Celluloid

Celluloid toys are overlooked by most collectors, perhaps because they are so fragile. Celluloid is a plastic developed in 1868 by John W. Hyatt. Ivory for billiard balls was expensive, so a $10,000 reward was offered for the discovery of a material to replace ivory. The name *celluloid* is often used to identify any similar plastic, although competitors had trade names like *Pyralin* or *Parkesine.*

Dolls and dolls' heads have been made of lightweight celluloid since the 1880s. By the early 1900s, celluloid dolls with tin windup parts could creep, wave arms and legs, or walk. In the 1930s German and Japanese toy makers began to mass-produce celluloid and celluloid-and-tin toys. The plastic was joined to metal parts, creating a variety of windup toys. When wound, the toys could walk across a table or floor, swing, or rotate balloonlike balls. Celluloid toys are easily crushed.

Flip the Frog was made in the early 1930s. The 6½-inch-tall celluloid figure has movable arms and is marked Made in Japan. (Photo: Hake's)

The Bye-Lo Baby looks like a three-day-old baby. This 1920s doll with a large head and full cheeks was made in Germany. The bisque head is marked Copr. Grace S. Putnam. *Her body is cloth, but her hands are made of celluloid.* (Photo: Skinner)

Shirley Temple was a popular star in the movies, and many dolls were made that looked like her. Years later, television reruns made her a celebrity again, and more dolls were made. These Shirleys are all Ideal dolls. (Photo: James Julia)

These dolls and other celebrity and trademark dolls popular with collectors can be dated easily.

The Ideal Toy Corporation

Toy maker Morris Michtom, famous for the stuffed bears that he began calling teddy bears in 1903 (see page 362), founded the Ideal Novelty and Toy Company that same year. The firm began making dolls in 1906. Its dolls included the first American character doll, The Yellow Kid (1907); sleepy-eye dolls (1914); crying dolls (1920); Shirley Temple dolls (1934); Betsy Wetsy (1934); Magic Skin Baby dolls (1940); Toni, a doll with nylon hair that could be given a home permanent (1949); Saralee, the first mass-produced African-American baby doll (1951); Mary Hartline, a 16-inch doll with a hairstyling set, including curlers; the "life-size," 3-foot-tall, blow-molded vinyl Patti Play Pal (1959); and Crissy, an 18-inch fashion doll (1969). In 1982 Ideal was sold to CBS, which closed the doll division in 1986. Ideal had several owners until 1997, when its owner, Tyco Toys, merged with Mattel. Ideal's early dolls were marked with the name *Ideal* in a diamond. Later, only the name *Ideal* was used. Some were marked with just numbers and the words, *Made in USA*.

Mary Hartline was a radio personality, then a TV star. She led the band on Super Circus, *a children's television program, from 1949 to 1955. Part of her job was to sell Mary Hartline merchandise like this 16-inch doll made by Ideal.* (Photo: McMasters Harris)

Kewpies

Kewpies, plump, nude, elfin creatures designed by Rose O'Neill, were first pictured in the *Ladies' Home Journal* in 1909. Art student Joseph Kallus translated O'Neill's drawings into three-dimensional designs for Kewpie dolls and figurines, which started appearing about 1911. The big-eyed doll with the pug nose, slight smile, tiny blue wings, and topknot was an immediate success with the public. Kallus founded several companies to produce Kewpies, and he owned rights to the production of Kewpies until his death in 1982.

Most old Kewpies are marked with the name *Rose O'Neill* and/or *Kewpie,* either incised or on a paper label.

It is easy to see that this is a Kewpie doll. The name is in the heart on its chest. This 5-inch Kewpie is all bisque. (Photo: Village Doll & Toy)

Felt seems like a strange material to use for a doll, but Lenci dolls were made of felt for almost thirty years. This 1930s, all-felt, 17-inch boy doll has his original clothes and a hand-knit sweater. (Photo: Skinner)

Kewpie and members of the Kewpie family, such as Kewpidoodle Dog, were produced by many companies, including Borgfeldt, Kestner, Gebrüder Voigt, Hermann Voigt, Fulper Pottery, Rex Doll Company, Mutual Doll Company, Cameo Doll Company, and Karl Standfuss. Jesco Imports, Inc., bought the rights to Kewpie products and issued its first Kewpie doll in 1983. In 1995 Jesco stopped making Kewpies and has since licensed Kewpie products to other manufacturers.

Lenci

Lenci dolls were made by a company founded by Enrico and Elena Konig di E. Scavini in Turin, Italy, during World War I. "Lenci" was Elena's nickname. While Enrico was at war, Elena began making dolls. She used felt because Turin was the center of the Italian felt industry. The fabric was steamed and stiffened in a mold that made a three-dimensional seamless face with a firm surface. Details were hand painted. Bodies were usually jointed felt or felt and muslin. Lenci made child, ethnic, lady, personality, and occupational dolls, ranging in size from 4 to 48 inches. One distinguishing characteristic was the doll's hand. The third and fourth fingers were stitched together, while the others were separate.

After World War II, plastic and composition were used to make Lenci dolls. Limited editions of the traditional Lenci dolls were made in the late 1970s.

After Enrico died in 1938, the firm was taken over by the Garella family, who continue to control it. Lenci dolls are still being made.

Lenci dolls are marked in several ways. An ink signature on the foot, ribbon labels, cardboard tags, and metal tags have been used.

Madame Alexander

The Alexander Doll Company was founded in New York City in 1923 by Beatrice Alexander Behrman (1895–1990) and her three sisters. Beatrice trademarked the name *Madame Alexander* for her dolls in 1928—and started using the name for herself.

*The Dionne
Quintuplets were
worldwide celebrities.
These Madame
Alexander dolls show
the quints as toddlers.
The five dolls, each 7½
inches tall, were sold as
a set.* (Photo: Noel
Barrett)

The company's first dolls were rag dolls with pressed features and hand-painted faces. The cloth dolls had pink cotton bodies, mohair wigs, and cotton clothing. Composition heads were introduced about 1935, and by the late 1940s the company was using hard plastic for all doll parts. The dolls were tagged with the name *Madame Alexander.*

Characters from the book *Little Women* were among the company's first dolls (before 1933). Later dolls were based on other book and motion-picture characters, like Scarlett O'Hara from *Gone with the Wind* (1937). The Dionne Quintuplet dolls were among the first dolls to represent living people (five Canadian girls born in 1934). These dolls, sold from 1935 to 1939, were first babies, then toddlers, and were made in sizes varying from 7½ inches to 23 inches. Madame Alexander introduced bride dolls in the mid-1930s. In 1955 the company created 21-inch Cissy, the first full-figured, high-heeled fashion doll, followed in 1957 by a smaller version, the 10-inch Cissette.

Madame Alexander retired in 1988 and sold the Alexander Doll Company. It was acquired by the Kaizen Breakthrough Partnership in 1995, and Madame Alexander dolls are still being made. Madame Alexander died in 1990 at the age of ninety-five.

Raggedy Ann

To amuse his sick daughter Marcella, illustrator and cartoonist Johnny Gruelle made up stories about her favorite rag doll. In 1915 Gruelle patented his design for a rag doll he named Raggedy Ann. She had a simple dress, large apron, scalloped pantaloons, and striped leggings. After Marcella's death in 1916, Gruelle wrote down the stories he had told Marcella and added new ones. From 1918 until his death in 1938, he published twenty-five illustrated books of Raggedy Ann stories. To promote the series, the Gruelle family made cloth Raggedy Ann dolls, which were in such demand by the end of 1918 that Gruelle licensed P. F. Volland Company to manufacture them. The early Raggedy Ann had black shoe-button eyes, red yarn hair, a painted nose and mouth, and striped socks. Soon Raggedy Andy was made to accompany Raggedy Ann. Other friends were the black mammy doll Beloved Belindy, Uncle Clem, and the Camel with the Wrinkled Knees.

Over the years the dolls and accessories—from games and cookie jars to children's clothing and furniture—have been made by many companies, including Applause, Georgene Novelties, Hasbro, Knickerbocker, Molly-'Es, and Playskool.

Ravca

Bernard Ravca (1904–1998) made dolls in Paris from 1924 until 1939, when he came to the United States. His early dolls were made using French bread that was molded and later treated. Each of his dolls had a unique personality. The dolls usually depicted old French peasants. Some of his early dolls were large figures of young people. Among the many dolls made by Bernard Ravca, *American Presidents* dolls, *French Province*

Tin eyes, yarn hair, tags for Georgene Novelties Company, and a heart printed on the cloth body all show that these are old Raggedy Ann and Andy dolls. Each is 19 inches tall. They are wearing traditional clothes, including red striped socks. (Photo: Garth's Auctions)

dolls, historic leaders of World War II, *Portrait* dolls, the lifelike *Real People* dolls, and soldier dolls are most famous. *Ballet* dolls, *Presidents' Wives*, and *Sprites, Pixies and Fairies* are the famous lines designed by his wife, Frances (?–2000).

Ravca dolls came in a range of sizes, from 3 feet tall to less than 1 foot. Ravca dolls were made with silk-stocking faces, spun-wool hair, and painted features. Some of the dolls carry bundles of wood or baskets and wear knit sweaters, stockings, and printed skirts. Frances Ravca used cotton and silk material on padded wires. Ravca dolls are usually labeled with a separate cloth label stitched to the clothing. The Ravcas retired in the early 1980s.

Storybook Dolls

In San Francisco in 1936, doll maker Nancy Ann Abbott started a business that became the Nancy Ann Storybook Doll Company in 1945. Nancy Ann Storybook dolls were made of painted bisque until the mid-1940s, when hard plastic dolls were introduced. The dolls were often issued in series—*Around the World*, *Day of the Month*, *Little Sister*, *Mother Goose Rhymes*, and many more. Popular lines included the *Hush a Bye Baby* dolls, *Nancy Ann Style Show* dolls with elaborate dresses, and *Storybook* dolls like Cinderella and Little Bo Beep. The company went bankrupt in 1965, a year after Abbott's death.

Small Nancy Ann Storybook dolls came in boxes with a see-through cover. They were dressed in frilly clothes, often organdy. These baby dolls, made in the 1940s, have the impressed mark Story Book Doll USA *on the bisque body.* (Photo: Skinner)

These French peasant dolls were made by the Ravcas. The features are stitched and printed on the faces, which are made from a silk stocking. The labels, Burgundy *for the woman and* Auvergne *for the man, tell which region of France they represent.* (Photo: Bertoia)

Vogue Doll Company and Ginny

Jennie Graves founded The Vogue Doll Shoppe in the early 1920s as a cottage industry employing women to sew doll clothes in her home in Somerville, Massachusetts. She designed the clothes, then dressed and sold dolls made by other companies. The business prospered, and in 1945 the company was incorporated as Vogue Dolls, Inc. In 1948 Graves introduced an 8-inch plastic doll that in 1950 was named Ginny, the most popular of the Vogue dolls. At first Ginny had painted blue eyes, then in 1950 she was given strung sleep-eyes. She walked with straight legs as her head turned from side to side in 1954, and in 1957 she was given knee joints and became a bent-knee walker. Vogue sold a selection of outfits for Ginny, from cowgirl costume to Cinderella gown, and also accessories—shoes, purses, belts, and headbands. After Graves retired in 1960, the company was run by family members until it was sold to Tonka Corporation in 1972. Quality declined during several ownership changes. A new Vogue Doll Company purchased rights to Ginny and the Vogue Doll name in 1995, and it is producing a high-quality plastic Ginny dressed in outfits from the 1950s. In 2002 the company reintroduced Just Me, a doll with bisque head and jointed composition body originally sold by Vogue in the 1920s.

Ginny is wearing a pineapple print cotton sundress in the latest style. She has matching underpants, a straw hat, and plastic sunglasses. The box is original. No question about this 1952 doll. She is marked Vogue *on the head, body, and shoes.* (Photo: Skinner)

Some Popular Dolls
Since the 1980s

Strawberry Shortcake—Strawberry Shortcake was introduced in 1979 as a character for American Greetings cards and stationery. She was such a hit Kenner introduced a line of Strawberry Shortcake dolls in 1980. Strawberry Shortcake, Apple Dumplin', Orange Blossom, and the six other original dolls were about 5 inches tall, had jointed arms and legs, and smelled like the fruit flavors they were named for. Later dolls had pets and an imaginary home and came in a variety of sizes. The images were used in books, film, and television. Figurines, jewelry, and "girly" things were made until the popularity waned in the 1990s. Bandai Entertainment revived the line in 2003.

Cabbage Patch Kids—The "must-have" toy of the 1983 Christmas season, more than three million 15-inch, soft-sculptured Cabbage Patch Kids, each with its own birth certificate, were "adopted" that year alone. By 1990, sixty-five million Cabbage Patch Kids had been sold. They are still being made.

American Girl Dolls—The 18-inch American Girl historical dolls, first issued in 1986, represent girls from periods in American history, like Felicity, a 1774 Colonial girl, and Samantha, a 1904 Victorian girl. Nonhistorical American Girl dolls that represent modern girls come in variety of skin, hair, and eye colors, with clothes and accessories, so the doll will look like the girl who owns it. Books, doll furniture, trading cards, and other accessories are made.

Beanie Babies—Ty, Inc., introduced the nine original Beanie Babies in 1993, then added new characters each year until by 2005 more than 1,100 different Beanie Babies had been produced. These inexpensive, understuffed beanbag toys became hot collectibles, especially after 1996, when Ty began retiring some characters. Collectors anxiously bought up all the Beanies they could find, prices went up, the Beanies became scarce, and prices went even higher. Ty stopped production briefly in 1999, and the collectors lost interest. Beanie Babies are still being made for children. The collecting mania has disappeared.

Strawberry Shortcake and her cat Custard were famous American Greetings card characters introduced in 1979. The next year dolls were created by Kenner. The dolls, the first ever sold with a smell, were made with a scent that matched the name.

Some American Doll Makers

Manufacturer and Location	Dates
A & H Doll Manufacturing Company Long Island City, New York	1947–1969
Alexander Doll Company New York, New York	1923–present
Louis Amberg & Son New York, New York	1878–1930
American Character Doll Company New York, New York	1919–1968
American Doll & Toy Manufacturing Company Brooklyn, New York	1892–1909
American Girl Middleton, Wisconsin	1986–present Made by Pleasant Company, which was acquired by Mattel in 1998
Arranbee (R & B) Doll Company New York, New York	1922–1959
Averill Manufacturing Company New York, New York	c.1913–1965
George Borgfeldt & Company New York, New York	1881–1962
Buddy Lee (See D. H. Lee Company, Inc.)	
Cameo Doll Company Port Allegheny, Pennsylvania	1922–1982
Deluxe Reading Toy (Division of Topper) Elizabeth, New Jersey	1955–1972
Eegee's (Goldberger Doll Manufacturing Company, Inc.) Brooklyn, New York	1917–1980s
Effanbee (Fleischaker & Baum) New York, New York	1910–present
Georgene Novelties Company New York, New York	1915–1965
Hasbro Industries, Inc. (Hassenfeld Bros., Inc.) Pawtucket, Rhode Island	1923–present
E. I. Horsman & Aetna Doll & Toy Company Trenton, New Jersey Columbia, South Carolina	1865–1960 1960–1986

Manufacturer & Location	Dates
Horsman, Ltd. Great Neck, Long Island, New York	1999–present
Ideal Novelty and Toy Company **Ideal Toy Corporation** Brooklyn, New York	1903–1938 1938–1982
Kenner Products, Inc. Cincinnati, Ohio	1947–2000
D. H. Lee Company, Inc. (Buddy Lee) Merriam, Kansas	1920–1962
Louis Marx & Company Brooklyn, New York	1919–1980 Sold to Quaker Oats in 1972 and to British firm Dunbee-Combex-Marx in 1975
Mattel, Inc. Hawthorne, California	1945–present
Molly-'Es Philadelphia, Pennsylvania	1929–1970
Nancy Ann Storybook Doll Company San Francisco, California	1945–1965
Remco Industries, Inc. New York, New York	1960s–1974
Terri Lee, Inc. Lincoln, Nebraska Apple Valley, California	1946–1962 2002–present
Ty, Inc. Oakbrook, Illinois	1986–present
Uneeda Doll Company New York, New York	1917–1991
Vogue Doll Shoppe Somerville, Massachusetts	1922–1972 Incorporated as Vogue Dolls, Inc., in 1945. Vogue name sold to Tonka in 1972, Lesney Products in 1977, Meritus Industries in 1984, R. Dakin in 1986. Rights to name sold to new Vogue Doll Company in 1995.
Vogue Doll Company Oakdale, California	1995–present
R. John Wright Dolls, Inc. Bennington, Vermont	1976–present

Female G.I. Joe Dolls

Hasbro introduced the G.I. Joe Nurse Action Doll dressed in a Red Cross uniform in 1967. It didn't sell well and was soon discontinued, so now it is rare and sells for as high as $5,000 in mint condition with the box. No other female G.I. Joe figures were produced until 1997, when Kenner brought out G.I. Jane, a U.S. Army helicopter pilot.

Space Toys

Buck Rogers' 25th Century Rocket Ship and Flash Gordon's Rocket Fighter, produced by Marx in the 1930s and 1940s, are two of the earliest space toys popular with collectors. In the 1950s, the television shows *Space Patrol* and *Tom Corbett, Space Cadet* and the movie *Forbidden Planet* licensed a variety of toys. Television's six *Star Trek* series (1966–2005), the ten *Star Trek* motion pictures (1979–2002), and the six *Star Wars* movies (1977–2005) licensed hundreds of vehicles, dolls, robots, figures, model kits, play sets, and other related space toys.

Star Wars and other recent toys are often packed on blister cards. This 1984 6-by-9-inch card holds a 3¾-inch posable Luke Skywalker figure, a card, and a collector coin. The original packaging adds much to the value of this type of toy. (Photo: Hake's)

ACTION FIGURES AND SUPERHEROES

Hasbro bought the rights to a "doll" designed for boys from its creator Stanley Weston, and in 1964 began producing G.I. Joe, the toy industry's first action figure. Like Barbie, G.I. Joe came with a wide range of accessories—uniforms, weapons, and military gear. By 1965 G.I. Joe was the top-selling toy for children five to twelve years old. Sales dropped as sentiment against the war in Vietnam grew toward the end of the 1960s, so in 1970 Hasbro changed the soldier into an adventurer and introduced the G.I. Joe Adventure Team. G.I. Joe became a hunter, astronaut, paratrooper, deep sea diver, and other action heroes. The original G.I. Joe was 11½ inches tall, but in the 1970s the adventure figures were scaled down to 8 inches, then just 3¾ inches. The original G.I. Joe returned as a 3¾-inch action figure in 1982, as the 12-inch G.I. Joe Duke in 1991, and as the Classic G.I. Joe figure in 1996.

Other action figures came after G.I. Joe. Captain Action figures, first introduced by Ideal in 1966, included Batman, Spiderman, Buck Rogers, and the Green Hornet. Mego produced its line of superheroes from 1972 to 1982. Kenner introduced Star Wars action figures in 1977. Mattel followed in 1981 with its Masters of the Universe series. Then in 1985 Hasbro introduced Transformers, vehicles that with the twist of a few parts changed into menacing

G.I. Joe is deliberately described as an action figure, not a doll, because it was made to appeal to boys. This G.I. Joe Land Adventurer, made by Hasbro in 1974, has flocked hair and beard and is in the original box. (Photo: Village Doll & Toy)

Animal Collectibles

Today thousands of people collect toy bears. Others collect bear novelties that were made as early as 1907, when Steiff made a bear that had a hot-water bottle in its body. Other bear novelties include baby bottle holders, perfume bottles, pillows, handkerchief cases, purses, and muffs.

Perfume in a glass cylinder is hiding inside this 5-inch Schuco teddy bear from the 1950s. The head is removable. The banner on the mohair chest of this souvenir bear says Niagara Falls. *(Photo: Skinner)*

Many other animals have been made into toys. The Steiff Company has always done well with elephants, dogs, and monkeys. All Steiff toys are marked with the famous "button in the ear."

This Steiff mohair tiger has green eyes, an embroidered nose, and painted stripes. Of course, there is a button and tag in the ear. The 10-inch-long tiger was made in the 1950s. (Photo: Skinner)

This Ideal bear has the long arms, embroidered nose, and felt paws often found on early teddy bears. The "well-loved" condition doesn't lessen its value much. (Photo: Antique Bear Shop)

robots. (For more on robots, see pages 340–341.)

TEDDY BEARS

No discussion of toys can omit the teddy bear. *Teddy* was named for Teddy Roosevelt after a hunting trip he took in 1902. The president refused to shoot a defenseless bear, and newspaper cartoonist Clifford Berryman drew a picture of the incident. New Yorker Morris Michtom was inspired by the cartoon to name the stuffed bears his wife made *Teddy's Bears* and to sell them in his shop. The bears were an immediate success, and in 1903 Michtom founded the first teddy bear manufacturing company in the United States, the Ideal Novelty and Toy Company.

A German version of the toy was made about the same time by the Steiff Company. It had been making stuffed animals since 1880. Later many other companies made teddy bears.

Because a "well-loved" teddy bear looks worn and old, it is difficult to decide its age. Vintage teddy bears are usually covered with wool mohair. Artificial silk plush was used about 1930, cotton plush after World War II, then nylon plush and other synthetic fabrics in the 1950s and later. Early bears were stuffed with excelsior, straw, and kapok. Polyester stuffing and nylon or plastic components indicate a modern bear. Boot-button eyes were used before World War I, glass eyes from the 1920s, and plastic eyes and noses from the 1950s. Early noses were usually silk thread embroidery. Vintage bears had felt or cotton paws; later bears had velvet, plush, or leather paws; and by the 1970s paws were ultrasuede. Long arms and a hump back are found on vintage bears. After World War II, bears had shorter arms and flatter faces.

DOLLHOUSES AND DOLLHOUSE FURNITURE

All dollhouses have a value. The older and more complete the furnishings, the more valuable the dollhouse. The earliest dollhouses date from the sixteenth century in Bavaria, but it was not until the eighteenth century that they were a popular plaything for the rich. Furniture and dishes were made to scale by some of the finest craftsmen of the day. By the 1870s, most dollhouses were made on a scale of 1 inch to 1 foot, although ⅛ or ⅖ scales were also used. The furniture was made in the same scales. Many dollhouses of the nineteenth and twentieth centuries were homemade, but commercially made houses are also of interest to collectors. Folding cardboard dollhouses were made by companies like McLoughlin Brothers of New York. Grimm & Leeds of Camden, New Jersey, made cardboard dollhouses that were completely collapsible and sold in a flat package. R. Bliss of Pawtucket, Rhode Island, and other firms used lithographed paper on a wood structure to create dollhouses with interesting detail. Dollhouses and dollhouse furniture were made of paper, cardboard, wood, or metal, and by the late 1940s, plastic.

Barbie's Dream House, produced from 1961 to 1965, came complete with a television and stereo and a framed photo of Ken. Other Barbie houses included Barbie Family House, Barbie Lively Livin' House, Barbie Country Living Home, and Barbie Glamour Home.

Barbie's 1961 cardboard dollhouse room is furnished in the latest style. She even has a television set and stereo in a cabinet and a slat bench that resembles a Harry Bertoia bench from the 1950s.

A dollhouse can be Victorian or modern. The furnishings should represent the life-style of the imaginary family that might have lived there. This Dutch Colonial-style villa made by Moritz Gottschalk about 1910 has original wallpaper and floor paper. (Photo: Noel Barrett)

Schoenhut Dollhouses and More

The Albert Schoenhut Company was established in 1872 in Philadelphia and incorporated in 1897. Schoenhut made toy pianos from its beginning, and today, as Schoenhut Piano Company, it makes toy pianos in St. Augustine, Florida. It stopped making other toys in 1935.

Schoenhut made many types of toys. The Humpty Dumpty Circus, patented in 1903, had a chair, a ladder, and a clown. Pieces were added through the years until there were over forty animals, twenty-nine figures, a tent, wagons, and over forty other pieces of equipment. The earliest animals had glass eyes and woolly cloth manes. Painted eyes and carved manes came later. Before 1910 the circus performers were made with two-part heads: a plaster composition face glued to a wooden base. Figures had bisque heads between 1910 and 1918. One-part wooden molded heads were used later. A reduced-size circus was introduced in 1923 and a miniature set in 1927.

In 1911 Schoenhut patented a wooden doll that fit on a stand and had jointed arms and legs. The company made dolls until 1926. Dollhouses were first offered in 1918. It also made furniture for the dollhouses. Blocks, games (such as pick-up sticks), toy ships, trains, guns, airplanes, and many other toys were produced. Comic character dolls, such as Felix the Cat, Barney Google, and Maggie and Jiggs, were popular toys in the 1920s.

Schoenhut made many different circus performers. Here are Monkey, Ringmaster, and Bare Back Rider. (Photo: Noel Barrett)

A good dollhouse should be furnished to scale with appropriate pieces. The furniture can be from an earlier or later period, just as furniture in a real house is. Furniture can frequently date back several generations.

R. Bliss Manufacturing Company and Dowst Brothers Company of Chicago were important dollhouse makers in the early twentieth century. Bliss, founded in 1832, made its first dollhouse, *The Fairy Doll's House*, in 1889. By 1901 it was selling a series of seven wooden houses with lithographed paper trim and some pierced metal. Most were in the Victorian style with elaborate gingerbread trim, wraparound porches, balconies, and sometimes even turrets. Bliss made wood and cardboard dollhouse furniture that was oversize and heavily decorated, often with lithographed pictures of children or letters of the alphabet—not what would be found in a Victorian home. The company was sold to Mason and Parker in 1914, and dollhouses continued to be made into the 1920s. Dowst made Tootsietoy cardboard dollhouses—a brick colonial and a Spanish mansion—and metal dollhouse furniture from about 1922 to 1937. (For more on Dowst, see page 364.) Other companies that made dollhouses and dollhouse furniture were Arcade Manufacturing Company, Morton E. Converse Company, Rich Toy Company, and Schoenhut Company.

On this Bliss two-room dollhouse, lithographed paper creates a shingled roof, balcony with turned posts, brick chimney, and curtained windows. It is marked R. Bliss.
(Photo: Noel Barrett)

Toy Makers

Manufacturer and Location	Dates	Toys Made and Other Company Information
American Flyer Chicago, Illinois	1910–1966	Trains, airplanes, accessories
American National Company Toledo, Ohio	1894–1941	Pedal cars, pressed steel trucks, bicycles, scooters
Applause Toy Company New York, New York	1979–present	Dolls, plush toys, Simpsons
Asahi Tokyo, Japan	1950–present	Lithographed tin toys, die-cast cars
Arcade Manufacturing Company Freeport, Illinois	1868–1946	Die-cast cars, farm equipment, cast-iron traffic signs, gasoline pumps, banks, dollhouse furniture, kitchen toys. Also made coffee mills, hinges, other household goods.
Arnold Company Nuremberg, Germany	1906–present	Trains, nautical toys
Auburn Rubber Corporation Auburn, Indiana	1913–1968	English Palace Guard toys, military miniatures, animal and wheeled vehicle toys
Bandai Tokyo, Japan	1950–present	Lithographed tin toys, action figures, Power Rangers, Strawberry Shortcake, Tamagotchi, Digimon
Barclay Manufacturing Company West Hoboken, New Jersey	1923–1971	Toy soldiers, slush-cast and die-cast cars
Bassett-Lowke, Ltd. Northampton, England	1899–present	Scale-model railroads
Gebruder Bing Nuremberg, Germany	1866–1933 Post-WWII–1960s	Model steam engines, tin lithograph spring-driven cars, buses, ships, trains. Checker and Yellow taxicabs and Ford Model Ts for the American market.
R. Bliss Manufacturing Company Pawtucket, Rhode Island	1832–1914	Lithographed paper on wood dollhouses, toy firehouses, fire engines, games, tool chests, archery sets
Brimtoy London, England **Wells Brimtoy, Ltd.** Holyhead, Wales	1910–1932 1932–1965	Tin and later die-cast road vehicles, especially post-WWII buses

Manufacturer and Location	Dates	Toys Made and Other Company Information
Karl Bub Nuremberg, Germany	1851–1966	Enameled and lithographed tin cars, trucks, trains (distributed by FAO Schwarz in 1920s and 1930s)
Buddy L East Moline, Illinois	1921–present	Trucks, construction toys, planes, helicopters. Brand bought by Imperial Toys in 2002.
Burnett, Ltd. Birmingham, England	1905–1930s	Lithographed tin vehicles, London buses
George Carette Nuremberg, Germany	1886–1917	Lithographed tin mechanical trains, cars, streetcars, boats, planes
Carlisle & Finch Cincinnati, Ohio	1895–present	Electric trains and other toys (1896–1915). Marine lighting only after 1915.
Carter Tru-Scale Rockford, Illinois	1946–1971	Farm toys
Chad Valley Toys Birmingham, England	1897–present	Stuffed bears and toys, paper construction and tin lithographed toys (1988 trade name sold to English Woolworth's; toys still made in Asia)
J. Chein & Company Harrison, New Jersey New York, New York	1903–1979	Lithographed tin banks, toys, drums, tin boxes, including reproductions of old designs such as the roly-poly tin. Manufacturing of toys ended in 1979. Became Chein Industries in 1970s.
Citroen France	1923–1936	Lithographed tin toy cars
Morton E. Converse Company Winchendon, Massachusetts	1887–1934	Wooden toys, dollhouses, dollhouse furniture, blocks, Noah's arks
Corgi (See Mettoy Company, Ltd., and Mattel)	1956–present	Made by Mettoy beginning 1956; Mattel bought brand in 1993; Corgi Classics bought in July 1999 by Zindart, an American-owned company based in Hong Kong.
Cosmo Manufacturing Company Chicago, Illinois	1888–1926	Trinkets, charms, small novelty toys for Cracker Jack and others

Manufacturer and Location	Dates	Toys Made and Other Company Information
Creative Playthings Framingham, Massachusetts	1951–present	Swing sets, playground equipment, educational toys, usually wooden. Sold to Gabriel Industries, a division of CBS Inc. in 1966; sold to Swing Design in 1986.
Crescent Toys London, England	1921–late 1970s	Toy soldiers, metal toys; later, plastic toys
Dent Hardware Company Fullerton, Pennsylvania	1895–1937	Cast-iron and cast-aluminum banks and vehicles, including Mack trucks, buses, and fire trucks
Dinky Toy (See Meccano)		
Dorfan Company Newark, New Jersey	1924–c.1934	Electric and mechanical trains
Dowst Brothers Company **Dowst Manufacturing Company** Chicago, Illinois	1890s–1926 1926–1961	Tootsietoys, dollhouses Changed name to Strombecker Corporation in 1961.
Ertl Company Dyersville, Iowa	1945–present	Die-cast metal farm and construction toy vehicles
Georg Fischer Nuremberg, Germany	1903–c.1930	Tin toys, many unmarked (such as the Toonerville Trolley)
Fisher-Price Toys East Aurora, New York	1930–present	Toys made of lithographed paper over wood and plastic. Became a wholly owned subsidiary of Mattel, Inc., in 1993.
Gebruder Fleischmann Nuremberg, Germany	1887–present	Tin boats and cars in the 1920s and 1930s, model trains Took over Doll et Cie in 1939.
Garton Toy Company Sheboygan, Wisconsin	1879–1974	Pedal cars, wagons, bicycles, sleds, outdoor toys and furniture
Gendron Wheel Company Toledo and Perrysburg, Ohio	1877–present	Pedal cars, wagons, bicycles, outdoor toys and furniture. Presently makes patient transport equipment and miniature model pedal cars.
A. C. Gilbert Company New Haven, Connecticut	1908–1966	Erector sets, magic sets, cars, scientific toys, trains, tool chests, puzzles Originally called Mysto Manufacturing Company (1908–1916).

Manufacturer and Location	Dates	Toys Made and Other Company Information
Grey Iron Casting Company Mount Joy, Pennsylvania	1881–1968	Cars and related cast toys, toy soldiers
Grimm & Leeds Camden, New Jersey	c.1905	Dollhouses
S. G. Gunthermann Nuremberg, Germany	1877–1965	Horse-drawn vehicles, cars, planes, tin toys, comic character windup toys in early 1960s
Haji (Mansei Toy Company Ltd.) Tokyo, Japan	1951–1960s	Metal vehicles and other toys
Hasbro Pawtucket, Rhode Island	1923–present	Plastic and wood toys, including Mr. Potato Head, G.I. Joe, Play-Doh, My Little Pony
O. & M. Hausser Stuttgart, Germany	1904–1983	Wooden toys, banks. Dolls, toys, soldiers, composition figures under the name Elastolin. Tin toys discontinued by 1957.
J. L. Hess Nuremberg, Germany	1826–c.1941	Tin clockwork and pull-along trains, cars, and toys
Hubley Lancaster, Pennsylvania	1894–1965	Cars and cast-iron toys, horse-drawn wagons, fire engines, circus trains, cap guns
Ideal Novelty and Toy Company **Ideal Toy Corporation** Brooklyn, New York	1903–1938 1938–1982	Stuffed toys and dolls Sold to CBS in 1982. Ideal trade name was still used.
Ives Corporation Bridgeport, Connecticut	1868–1928	Lithographed tin clockwork toys, window displays, horse-drawn vehicles, trains. Lionel produced toys with Ives name until 1933.
JEP (Jouets en Paris) Paris, France	1899–1965	Lithographed tin and clockwork toy cars, motorcycles, airplanes
Kenton Hardware Company Kenton, Ohio	1890–1952	Cast-iron cars, horse-drawn fire trucks, banks, toy stoves, Gene Autry repeating cap pistol
Kilgore Manufacturing Company Westerville, Ohio	1925–1985	Cast-iron cars, including a Stutz roadster, trucks, fire engines, cannons, cap guns
Kingsbury Keene, New Hampshire	1895–1942	Clockwork cars, trucks, buses, aircraft

Manufacturer and Location	Dates	Toys Made and Other Company Information
Kirk-Latty Manufacturing Company Cleveland, Ohio	1894–c.1926	Pedal cars, wagons, bicycles
K'NEX Industries, Inc. Hatfield, Pennsylvania	1992–present	Building sets, Lincoln Logs
Knickerbocker Toy Company New York, New York	1850–1983	Teddy bears, plush toys
Lego Company Billund, Denmark	1932–present	Plastic building bricks and building systems
Ernest Lehmann Brandenburg, Germany trains	1881–present	Clockwork and lithographed tin toys
Lesney Products (See Matchbox)		
Lineol Brandenburg, Germany	1906–1942	Military toys, soldiers, vehicles, composition figures, animals
Lines Brothers Ltd. London, England	1919–1983	Tin clockwork toys and cars
Lionel Manufacturing Company New York, New York	1900–present	Electric trains and accessories Became Lionel LLC in 1993.
Gebruder Maerklin (Marklin) Göppingen, Germany	1859–present	Toy kitchenware, boats, carousels, airplanes, clockwork, steam and electric trains. Plastic train sets in 1950s.
Manoil Manufacturing Company New York, New York	1934–1955	Cars and related cast toys, hollow-cast toy soldiers (dime-store soldiers)
Marklin (See Gebruder Maerklin)		
Fernand Martin Paris, France	1887–1919	Double-action tin mechanical and clockwork toys
Marusan Tokyo, Japan	1947–present	Tin toys, optical toys
Louis Marx & Company New York, New York	1919–1979	Lithographed tin windup toys, electric trains; successfully revived the yo-yo in 1928. Marx Toy Corporation exists today producing reproduction Louis Marx toys and others and is unrelated to the Louis Marx Co. of old.

Manufacturer and Location	Dates	Toys Made and Other Company Information
Matchbox **Lesney Products** England	1948–1982	Die-cast miniature cars and other vehicles
Universal Holding Company Hong Kong	1982–1992	
Tyco Toys Mt. Laurel, New Jersey	1992–1996	
Mattel, Inc. Hawthorne, California	1996–present	
Mattel, Inc. Hawthorne, California	1945–present	Barbie, Hot Wheels, See 'N Say, He-Man, Masters of the Universe, Tickle Me Elmo
McLoughlin Brothers New York, New York	1855–1920	Games, paper dolls, blocks, dollhouses, paint books, board books Acquired by Milton Bradley in 1920.
Meccano Liverpool, England	1901–1979	Dinky Toys, toy car kits, trains, metal construction sets Bought by French corporation and relaunched as Meccano SA, Calais; toys still produced today.
Mettoy Company Ltd. **Mettoy Playcraft Ltd.** London, England Swansea, South Wales	1933–1956 1956–1984	Tin toys, plastic toys after 1945, die-cast Corgi toys from 1956
Milton Bradley Company Springfield, Massachusetts	1861–present	Games, such as the Game of Life, Battleship, Cootie, and Twister; puzzles, blocks Became a division of Hasbro in 1984.
Mound Metalcraft Mound, Minnesota	1947–1955	First Tonka toys Changed name to Tonka Toys in 1955. Acquired by Hasbro in 1991.
MT (Masudaya Toys) Tokyo, Japan	1945–present	Mechanical and battery-operated tin toys
Murray-Ohio Manufacturing Company Cleveland, Ohio Brentwood, Tennessee	1919–1957 1957–present	Pedal cars, wagons, bicycles "Steelcraft" line. Now makes bicycles and lawn mowers.
Ohio Art Company Bryan, Ohio	1908–present	Tin lithographed toys, Etch A Sketch, Disney character toys
Parker Brothers Salem, Mass.	1883–present	Card games, board games, including Monopoly in 1934, Sorry, and Clue Became a division of Hasbro in 1991.

Manufacturer and Location	Dates	Toys Made and Other Company Information
Ernst Plank Nuremberg, Germany	1866–1900	Locomotives, clockwork figures, music boxes, magic lanterns, optical toys, steam engines, streetcars, boats
Playskool Milwaukee, Wisconsin	1928–present	Tinkertoys, peg benches, Weebles Purchased by Milton Bradley in 1968; in 1984 it became part of Hasbro, which closed the plant, but still makes toys under the Playskool name.
Rich Manufacturing Company (Rich Toys) Sterling and Morrison, Illinois; Clinton, Iowa	1915–1953	Wooden toys, dollhouses, pull toys, rocking horses
Rich Industries, Inc. Tupelo, Mississippi	1953–1962	
A. Schoenhut & Company Philadelphia, Pennsylvania	1872–1935	Toy pianos, dolls, comic strip characters, circus animals, dollhouses and furniture
Schuco Nuremberg, Germany	1912–1976	Clockwork toys & cars, mohair-covered mechanical toys After the company went out of business, other companies obtained the right to use the Schuco brand name.
Selchow & Richter Company New York, New York	1867–1986	Games, Parcheesi, Scrabble, Pin the Tail on the Donkey, puzzles Sold to Coleco in 1986, then to Hasbro in 1989.
SH Tokyo, Japan	1959–present	Trademark of Horikawa Toys, Tokyo. Battery-operated robot and astronaut toys
J. & E. Stevens Cromwell, Connecticut	1843–1930s	Cast iron toys, especially banks, garden toys, doll furniture, cap pistols, jacks sets
Strauss New York, New York	1914–1940	Clockwork, windup, and tin toys
Strombecker Corporation Chicago, Illinois	1961–present	Tootsietoys
Sun Rubber Company Barberton, Ohio	1930s–1950s and 1960–1974	Rubber cars, dolls, vinyl toys, floating toys

Manufacturer and Location	Dates	Toys Made and Other Company Information
J. W. Sutcliffe Horsforth, Leeds, England	1885–present	Tin toys, battleships, speedboats with clockwork mechanisms
Tipp and Company Nuremberg, Germany	1912–1971	Tin military toys
Toledo Metal Wheel Company Toledo, Ohio	1887–1930s	Pedal cars, bicycles, playground equipment. Blue Streak line.
Tonka Toys Mound, Minnesota	1955–1991	Steel vehicles Acquired by Hasbro in 1991.
Tootsietoys (See Dowst and Strombecker)		
Toy Tinkers, Inc. Evanston, Illinois	1914–1952	Tinkertoys, bead dolls, pull toys Sold to A. G. Spaulding in 1952.
Tyco Toys Mt. Laurel, New Jersey	1926–present	Games, toys, action figures Became a division of Mattel, Inc., in 1996.
Unique Art Manufacturing Company Newark, New Jersey	1916–1950s	Lithographed tin windup mechanical toys
Universal International Hong Kong	c.1980–2000	Dinky toys, Matchbox cars
Wham-O Manufacturing Company San Gabriel and Emeryville, California	1948–present	Slingshots, Hula Hoops, Frisbee, Super balls, Hacky Sacks
A. C. Williams Company Ravenna, Ohio	1886–present	Cast-iron and nickel-plated cars, rigs, airplanes, tractor toys
Wolverine Supply & Manufacturing Company/ Wolverine Toy Company Pittsburgh, Pennsylvania	1903–1970	Tin toys, Sandy Andy, Corner Grocery, toy kitchen sets, housekeeping toys, wagons, games
Wyandotte Toys **(All Metal Products, Inc.)** Wyandotte, Michigan	1921–1956	Toy guns, rifles, targets, tin and steel windup and lever action airplanes and cars
Y (Yonezawa) Tokyo, Japan	1950s–1970s	Battery-operated and mechanical toys Also known as **Y** or **Yone** or **STS**

Toy Timeline

Teddy bear

Atomic Robot Man

Bye-Lo Baby Doll

Early 1900s
Pedal cars

1903
Teddy bears

1907
Character dolls
(The Yellow Kid)

1922
Bye-Lo Baby dolls

1945
Slinky

1947
Tonka vehicles

1948
Ginny dolls

Scrabble

1949
Candyland

Clue

Legos

late 1940s
Atomic Robot
Man

| 1890 | 1900 | 1910 | 1920 | 1930 | 1940 |

1890s
European
stamped-tin cars

1890s
Electric trains

1911
Kewpie dolls

Tootsietoy

1913
Erector sets

1914
Tinkertoys

1915
Raggedy Ann

1916
Lincoln Logs

1933
Monopoly

1939
View Master

Electric trains

View Master

Barbie

1960
Etch A Sketch

Game of Life

1964
G. I. Joe

1965
Superball

1966
Captain Action
figures

Twister

1968
Hot wheels

1969
Nerf ball

Rubik's Cube

1980
Pac-Man

Rubik's Cube

Strawberry Shortcake

1981
Masters of the
Universe

1982
My Little Pony

Trivial Pursuit

1983
Cabbage Patch Kids

Hacky sacks

Nintendo
Entertainment System

1985
Transformers

Pictionary

1986
American Girl dolls

Super Mario Brothers

1989
Game Boy

Polly Pocket

Tickle Me
Elmo

1950

1952
Matchbox cars

Mr. Potato Head

Pez (came to U.S.)

1953
Wiffle Ball

1956
Yahtzee

1957
Poor Pitiful Pearl

1958
Hula Hoop

1959
Barbie

1960

Hot wheels

1970

Early 1970s
Baby Brother Tender
Love

1972
Odyssey

1973
Dungeon & Dragons

1974
Pong

1977
Star Wars action
figures

1978
Simon

1980

Nintendo

1990

1993
Beanie Babies

1994
PlayStation

1996
Tickle Me Elmo

1990
Betty Spaghetty

Chapter 12

Prints, Photos, and Paper Ephemera

PRINTS, PHOTOGRAPHS, AND all sorts of small paper ephemera, including baseball cards, postcards, and labels, became important to collectors in the twentieth century. Printed pictures, often drawings, were published to illustrate news stories in the nineteenth century. Lithographs, woodblocks, and even etchings were sold at corner stores to illustrate such important events as fires, coronations, sporting events, and celebrities ranging from stage stars to murderers. These were black and white prints that sometimes had added color applied by hand. Chromolithography using as many as twenty-five stones for the colors was developed during the 1830s. In the second half of the nineteenth century, a new type of lithography was used. The stones were stippled rather than engraved with lines, permitting better intermingling of color and finer-quality prints. The finished paper was often lacquered, which gave it a slick, glossy finish. In the twentieth century, benday screens with premade stippled patterns were introduced. By the 1930s, the use of photomechanical halftones replaced stippling with a finer matrix of dots and truer photographic reproduction.

Opposite Page: The New York World's Fair Trylon and Perisphere have become the familiar symbols of the 1939 fair and the changes it heralded. This poster was created by painter Joseph Binder and lithographed by Ginnell Litho. It is 20 by 30 inches. (Photo: Heritage Galleries)

Elysian Fields is a 1920s print by R. Atkinson Fox that was used for a calendar. It is not signed but has been identified from other pictures. The pink and blue coloring is typical of Fox prints. (Photo: Deco Dog's Ephemera)

By the late nineteenth century, groups of artists started making prints that were given away as advertising premiums or sold in frames to be used as home decorations. Many of the artists did original oil paintings or drawings to be reproduced on calendars or magazine covers, or as part of commercial advertisements. The Arts and Crafts artists of the early twentieth century turned to woodblock prints. The inexpensive prints were handmade works by a single artist. Japanese woodblocks changed in character at the same time, and modern designs replaced the traditional images.

A FEW FAMOUS ARTISTS WHO MADE PRINTS

Twentieth-century advertising agencies and magazines used pictures that appealed to the general public. The artists creating these pictures were ignored by art museums but eventually became popular with the general public and collectors. At the end of the twentieth century, some were recognized as artists worthy of respect and display in art museums.

R. Atkinson Fox

R. Atkinson Fox (1860–1935), who produced more than a thousand pictures, was one of the most prolific artists of his time. His subjects ranged from animals (especially cows), landscapes, Indians, and the American West to "enchanted" girls and gardens in the style of Maxfield Parrish. It is difficult to identify Fox's work because he used more than twenty-five pseudonyms and some of his works are unsigned, so many prints are called *Fox-Maybes*. His work is also used on calendars, candy boxes, magazine covers, postcards, and in many other forms. After his death in 1935, interest in his work declined. In the 1970s and 1980s, collectors rediscovered the prints.

Louis Icart

French printmaker, painter, and illustrator Louis Icart (1888–1950) began working in Paris in 1907 as a colorist for a company that sold

Dalila *is a print by Louis Icart made in 1929. The glamorous woman peers out a barred window. The print is 20 by 13 inches.* (Photo: Morphy Auctions)

The dreamy prints by Maxfield Parrish usually included a colorful landscape and attractive people. This is a 1930 calendar sample, Ecstasy. *The picture was at the top, a calendar pad at the bottom.* (Photo: Henry/Peirce)

postcards of attractive women and actresses. He illustrated fashion brochures from about 1910 to 1915 and created a series of etchings of fashionably dressed women. Icart served in World War I, and when he returned he again pictured beautiful women who were increasingly elegant and often risqué. These etchings were popular in the United States as well as France, and Icart made one edition of his prints to be sold in Europe and another for the American market. Collectors are most interested in Icart's work from the 1930s, when his etchings became more colorful and depicted sensuous and sometimes nude women. In the 1940s, Icart concentrated on oil painting, but he continued to create etchings until his death. Reprints of his work are still being made.

Maxfield Frederick Parrish

Maxfield Parrish (1870–1966) is known for his illustrations for magazine covers, books, posters, calendars, and advertisements. Parrish began as a magazine illustrator, creating his first magazine cover in 1895 for *Harper's Bazaar*. Later he drew covers and illustrations for *Scribner's Magazine*, *Collier's*, *Ladies' Home Journal*, and other publications and books. General Electric used Parrish prints on calendars for its Edison Mazda division from 1918 to 1934. Advertisements for Jell-O, Fisk Tires, Ferry's Seeds, and other products featured Parrish illustrations. His illustrations for ads were reproduced

Maxfield Parrish Icons

Maxfield Parrish's first paid commission was a mural of Old King Cole painted for the University of Pennsylvania's Mask and Wig Club in Philadelphia in 1894. This three-panel mural sold at auction in 1996 for $662,500. In 1906 Parrish painted a different Old King Cole mural for the bar in the Hotel Knickerbocker in New York City. This 8-by-30-foot painting now hangs in New York's St. Regis Hotel.

Visit the St. Regis Hotel in New York and have a drink with the famous Maxfield Parrish mural of Old King Cole. (Photo: St. Regis King Cole Bar)

Collectors look for the RCA *Radiotron* and General Electric *Bandy*, two jointed wooden dolls based on designs by Maxfield Parrish that were used to promote the companies' products. GE also used countertop advertising posters that featured Parrish images.

Radiotron man is a 16-inch wooden figure. The design by Parrish was used by RCA in ads. His hat is a radio tube, and his hands had slits made to hold advertising signs. The doll was made by Cameo Doll Company in the 1920s. (Photo: James Julia)

Other Illustrators

Important twentieth-century commercial illustrators include Philip Boileau (1864–1917), George Bellows (1882–1925), William Henry Chandler (1854–1928), Harrison Fisher (1875–1934), Bessie Pease Gutmann (1876–1960), Hy Hintermeister (1897–1972), and Maud Humphrey (1865–1940). Other artists, including Andrew Wyeth (1917–present), Grant Wood (1891–1942), and Salvador Dalí (1904–1989), did prints that were considered more artistic than commercial.

Bessie Pease Gutmann is best known for her prints of children, but she pictured other subjects. Lorelei *is an 18-by-14-inch print of an early bathing beauty.* (Photo: Michael Ivankovich)

Many artists who are known for paintings and sculpture created commercial etchings, lithographs, prints, and even designs for plates that were sometimes sold in limited editions. Pablo Picasso (1881–1973), Marc Chagall (1887–1985), Jasper Johns (1930–present), Robert Rauschenberg (1925–present), Alexander Calder (1898–1976), Andy Warhol (1928–1987), and Roy Lichtenstein (1923–1997) are among the prominent artists whose designs were used for mass-produced plates and other decorative household items.

in prints that were so successful that in the 1930s Parrish was called the most popular American artist of the twentieth century. More than a million copies of *Daybreak*, painted in 1922, were printed. It may be the most widely sold art print of its time. In the 1930s Parrish turned to landscape painting, and he continued to paint until the early 1960s. The Parrish romantic style, colors, stylized figures, and fanciful scenes are easy to recognize.

Norman Rockwell

Norman Rockwell (1894–1978), probably the best-known illustrator of twentieth-century American life, painted illustrations and was art director for *Boy's Life*, the Boy Scouts of America magazine, while still in his teens. From 1916 to 1963, he painted 321 covers for the *Saturday Evening Post*. These covers showed ordinary Americans of all ages at work and play. Among his most famous works were his 1943 *Four Freedoms* paintings and his *Saturday Evening Post* covers from the 1940s and 1950s, like *Rosie the Riveter* (1943), *Homecoming Marine* (1945), *The Gossips* (1948), and *Girl at the Mirror* (1955). In 1963 Rockwell began a ten-year association with *Look* magazine doing magazine illustrations. Rockwell also painted pictures for books, posters, calendars, and advertising. His pictures were put on dishes, medals, trays, postage stamps, Christmas ornaments, puzzles, paint-by-number sets, cereal boxes, and much more. People from his pictures were reproduced as character dolls and figurines. Thousand of prints based on Rockwell's paintings have been produced and sold. Original paintings by Rockwell, although ignored by most art critics, are appreciated by collectors. One titled *The Fumble* sold for $420,500 in 1994, and in 2002 Rockwell's painting of *Rosie the Riveter* was auctioned for $4.96 million. Rockwell plates and figurines were issued in limited editions in the 1980s, but collectors have lost interest in this type of collectible.

WOODBLOCK PRINTS

Woodblock prints by artists from the Arts and Crafts movement in the early twentieth century are popular again after being ignored for the past fifty years. These artists drew their inspiration from the traditional Japanese woodblock prints that were available in America in the second half of the nineteenth century. Japanese woodblock prints were made with readily available tools and materials and demonstrated the skill of the artist. The Arts and Crafts look went well with the uncluttered designs of the Japanese.

Landscapes were popular subjects among the Arts and Crafts woodblock printmakers. Provincetown Printers in Massachusetts, Prairie Printers of the Midwest, and groups in New England, South Carolina, California, and upstate New York created prints that pictured the beauty of their region. The prints were usually of American subjects and could not be confused with work from Japan.

Important American woodblock print artists include Gustave Baumann (1881–1971), Waldo Chase (1895–1988), Pedro de Lemos (1882–1954), Arthur Wesley Dow (1857–1922), Frank Morley Fletcher (1866–1949), Frances Gearhart (1869–1958),

Norman Rockwell's cover for the June 11, 1955, issue of the Saturday Evening Post was copied to make this newsstand advertising poster. The couple is applying for a marriage license.
(Photo: Heritage Galleries)

Gustave Baumann created this woodblock print. It is called Hillside Woods.
The 10½-by-9½-inch print is signed and has its original label. (Photo: Treadway)

Blanche Lazzell (1878–1956), Bror J. O. Nordfeldt (1878–1955), and William S. Rice (1873–1963).

Japanese artists created woodblock prints in the twentieth century that were popular with some Americans. Artists like Kawase Hasui (1883–1957), Ohara Shoson (1877–1945), Hiroshi Yoshida (1876–1950), and Toshi Yoshida (1911–1995) made prints using traditional techniques and subjects but portrayed them in a realistic manner, using Western perspective and Western representation of light and shade.

NUTTING PRINTS

For many years collectors have called the tinted photographs created by Wallace Nutting by the seemingly incorrect name *Nutting prints*. Experts and collectors today refer to them as "prints" or "pictures." The twelve titles that were machine-produced (1938–1942) are sometimes called *process prints*.

Wallace Nutting (1861–1941) was a successful clergyman, furniture maker (see page 236), author, and photographer. In 1904 he opened a photography studio in New York City. He moved to Southbury, Connecticut, the next year, and then in 1912 to Framingham, Massachusetts. Nutting took black-and-white photos that were then colored by hand. His hand-tinted photos feature scenes of America and his vision of Colonial life, including posed domestic scenes in imaginary eighteenth-century rooms. Nutting's catalog offered more than a thousand different views, and he sold more than five million of the hand-colored photos to middle-class families. Each was signed in pencil *Wallace Nutting*, but a staff member, not Nutting, did the signing. From about 1915 to 1925, Nutting employed almost two hundred people.

Machine-produced reprints of only twelve Nutting photographs were made in the 1930s and early 1940s. Thousands

of copies were printed, and these are not as valuable as the originals. You can tell if the picture is one of the four-color *process prints*. The title of the picture is in the lower right where the *Wallace Nutting* signature usually is on an original.

PHOTOGRAPHS

The artistic black and white photograph became important about 1940. Landscape photographer Ansel Adams (1902–1984) helped establish the first photography department at the Museum of Modern Art in New York City in 1940, and in 1946 he started the first academic department to teach professional photography at the California School of Fine Arts in San Francisco.

In the second half of the twentieth century, photography increasingly became recognized as an art form. In the 1970s and 1980s, universities and art schools were offering courses in photography. Art museums that would never have considered buying a photo by Nutting started to collect artistic photographs by the most talented photographers.

The best photographers became as respected and well paid as artists who created oil paintings, and their photographs were marketed through the same galleries and auctions that sold oil paintings and sculpture. Important twentieth-century photographers

Early twentieth-century photographers produced hand-colored "prints" that are now collected. Look for photos by E. G. Barnhill (1894–1959), J. Carleton Bicknell (active c.1910–1930), David Davidson (1881–1967), W. H. Gardiner (1861–1935) and his son H. Marshall Gardiner (1884–1942), William James Harris (1868–1940), Charles R. Higgins (1867–1930), Edmund Homer Royce (1883–1967), Charles Sawyer (1868–1954), Harry Landis Standley (1881–1951), and Fred (Frederick H.) Thompson (1844–1909) and his son Fred (Frederick M.) Thompson (1876–1923).

Ansel Adams took this black-and-white photograph titled Valley View from Wawona Tunnel *in Yosemite National Park in about 1935. It is part of a series of photographs taken at the park.* (Photo: Sotheby's)

DOG-ON-IT

Although best known today for pictures of Colonial interiors and landscapes, Wallace Nutting sometimes made pictures with subtle humor. This signed print of eight puppies on a wooden bench is titled Dog-On-It. *It is a tinted black and white photograph.*
(Photo: Michael Ivanovich)

Record Prices

At a 2005 auction, an Edward Steichen photo, *Heavy Roses, Voulangis, France*, 1914, sold for $108,700; and a Diane Arbus photo, *Child with a Toy Hand Grenade, Central Park, N.Y.C.*, 1962, brought $408,000.

Found Photographs

In the 1990s a few dealers and galleries that sold artistic photographs "discovered" photographs by amateurs. They searched boxes of snapshots, pored over work by news and sports photographers, and looked for other sources of photographs of daily life. The ones they considered the best were matted, framed, and hung in galleries to be sold to collectors as art. These are known as *found photographs,* and indeed many show remarkable artistic talent and photographic skill.

Wedding pictures show the styles and hairdos of the day. This wedding party was photographed in Youngstown, Ohio, in the 1930s.

Bernice Abbott liked to photograph buildings and cityscapes. This is one of a series of pictures she took in Maine in the 1960s. It shows Nadeau's Store with gas pumps, an ice chest, and a man with a string trimmer. (Photo: James Julia)

include Alfred Stieglitz (1864–1946) and Edward Steichen (1879–1973), who promoted photography as an art form in the early years of the century; Ansel Adams, famous for his black-and-white photos of wilderness areas of the American West, especially Yosemite and other national parks; Dorothea Lange (1895–1965) and Walker Evans (1903–1975), who documented rural poverty during the Depression; photojournalists Margaret Bourke-White (1904–1971), Henri Cartier-Bresson (1908–2004), David Douglas Duncan (1916–present), and Alfred Eisenstaedt (1898–1995); Bernice Abbott (1898–1991), famous for her photos of street life in New York City during the 1930s and Maine from the 1960s; Diane Arbus (1923–1971), known for her portraits of people on the fringes

of society; fashion photographer Richard Avedon (1923–2004), who was also recognized for his portraits; and Annie Leibovitz (1949–present), known for portraits of celebrities.

PAPER EPHEMERA

The word *ephemera* is the plural form of the Greek word that means something that lasts through a single day, such as a winged insect. Today the word refers to something minor, usually paper, that was made to be used for a short time and then discarded. Entries in *The Encyclopedia of Ephemera* by Maurice Rickards, published in 2000, include bus ticket, cigarette card, document, lottery ticket, label, fruit wrapper, check, cutout toy, magazine insert, jigsaw puzzle, packaging, price tag, sales tax token, credit card, seed packet, stencil, valentine, and more—from ABC primer to Zoetrope strip. Ephemera can be attractive and is sometimes framed as art. It also can tell much about history and how ordinary people lived. It sheds light on the minor questions most historical and art museums ignore, like "What was used as toilet paper?" Several serious ephemera collections are now in museums, attesting to the importance of the unimportant.

Old cookbooks and recipe pamphlets are collectible today. The covers show the illustration styles and eating habits of the day. The recipes tell what we ate and how food was prepared.

The most famous World War I poster is this one picturing Uncle Sam. The drawing by James Montgomery Flagg was a very successful recruiting poster made in 1917. It was inspired by a 1916 British poster showing Lord Kitchner asking Britons to enlist. (Photo: Heritage Galleries)

Posters

Posters have informed the public about news and entertainment events since ancient times. Twentieth-century movie, travel, circus, sports, and war posters are of special interest to collectors and museums. During World War I, posters were used for propaganda purposes and to recruit soldiers. The most famous example is James Montgomery Flagg's 1917 *I Want You* poster that shows Uncle Sam pointing his finger at *you*.

During the 1920s and 1930s, posters reflected current art styles, including cubism, surrealism, and art deco. Transport posters advertised trains, ships, airplanes, and even the London Underground. Sometimes serious artists, especially European artists like Alphonse Mucha (1860–1939), designed posters. The text of the poster often became part of the design.

Propaganda posters were used during World War II by both the Allies and Hitler. After the war, important artists like Pablo Picasso (Spain), Salvador Dalí (Spain), Henri Matisse (France), and Roy Lichtenstein (United States) made posters that were artistic, with no commercial or advertising purpose. Posters for rock concerts by the Beatles, Rolling Stones, and other popular music groups from the mid-1960s on are of great interest, especially psychedelic posters designed by artists like Peter Max (1937–present). Also important are posters for the Grateful Dead, Jefferson Airplane, and other concerts promoted by Bill Graham or Family Dog at the Avalon Ballroom and other San Francisco venues. Many copies have been made, so collectors should be careful.

Postcards

The earliest picture postcards mailed in the United States were probably the souvenir cards sold at the World's Columbian Exposition in Chicago in 1893. The message was written on the picture side of the penny postcard (not the address side) before March 1907, or it cost two cents to mail. By 1908 postcards had become extremely popular, with nearly seven hundred million mailed annually in the United States alone. Many of these old picture postcards have a value. Historic views, special events, and cards by important postcard artists or publishers are of special interest to collectors.

DATING POSTCARDS

Sometimes you can date a postcard if you know when the postal rates changed. Postcard collectors should keep this table handy.

Year	Rate
1872	1¢
1917	2¢
1919	1¢
1925	2¢
1928	1¢
1952	2¢
1958	3¢
1963	4¢
1968	5¢
1971	6¢
1974	8¢
1975	7¢
1976	9¢
1978	10¢
March 1981	12¢
November 1981	13¢
1985	14¢
1988	15¢
1991	19¢
1995	20¢
2001	21¢
2002	23¢
2006	24¢

Santa is talking to a Victorian child on this mechanical Christmas postcard. Pull the tab and the window opens to show a Christmas scene inside. (Photo: Jackson's)

Photographs or pictures in black and white or sepia were used on cards in the early 1900s. Comic cards became popular during the 1920s. Hand-colored postcards in the 1920–1930 period had a linenlike textured surface. Color film was in use after 1935, and it gave the postcard a modern, professional look. Some of the earliest cards were made in odd shapes—the outline of a beer stein or a bouquet of flowers. Unusual cards called *mechanicals* were also made. Some used a metal spring for the tail of a donkey; others had a double card that squeaked when pressed or a girl who winked when the flaps of the card were moved. Foldout cards, see-through or hold-to-the-light cards, and puzzle cards were also popular. Most cards featured scenic views, greetings, or comics.

Manufacturers and artists became famous for their postcard designs. Names like Raphael Tuck, Ellen Clapsaddle, Bertha Corbett, Howard Chandler Christy, Lance Thackery, Gene Carr, and Frances Brundage add to the value of a card. The most expensive are the pre-1898 cards, woven silk cards, and those from the 1893 World's Columbian Exposition. Also in demand are cards made of unusual materials such as birch bark or aluminum and those that either move or have add-on features like hair. Postcards picturing coins, stamps, early airplanes, fire equipment, advertising, and early autos sell well, and so do special sets of related cards. The ordinary scenic view, glossy photograph, and color-wash cards are the least expensive.

Bathing beauties in revealing suits like this were a little shocking in the 1920s when this apple label was made. M. N. Lettunich, a Watsonville, California, apple wholesaler, opened for business in 1895.

Labels

Labels often speak for themselves. They are small ads promoting a product to either wholesalers or consumers. They picture the hairstyles, fashions, architecture, and transportation of the day. Trademarks, printing styles, colors, bar codes, and even wording—a vegetable name like *telephone peas*—contain clues to the age of a label.

And you ask me sweet blue eyes,
Where the thief went with his prize,
You are the thief, fair disguise.

Some early postcards were romantic, some were humorous, and some featured historic pictures. This colorful postcard pictures an early automobile on a dirt road. Cupid shows that it was a Valentine greeting. (Photo: Hake's)

Lou Gehrig is a player whose fame makes his baseball cards valuable. This Goudey #160 card is from a 1933 set. (Photo: Heritage Galleries)

Old fruit and vegetable crate labels once identified wooden crates of oranges, lemons, apples, pears, asparagus, lettuce, or other foods. There were over two thousand different brand labels for oranges alone by 1930. Spanish señoritas, Indian princesses, birds, horses, Cupids, and Santas were all used on labels. A 1918 study showed it was more important to attract the wholesale jobber than the housewife, and designs became bolder and more masculine. The women on labels were more seductive and wore skimpier clothing.

This Brick's Banquet Hall mincemeat can label tells its own story. The formal dinner party including a waiter, the Federal Prohibition permit, proof alcohol by volume number, and glossy paper indicate a date in the 1920s.

Early labels were produced using a stone lithography process that required a separate stone for each color of ink in the design. The heavy stones were replaced by engraved metal plates in the 1930s. The end of the label era came with World War II, when cardboard cartons were substituted for wooden crates. A two-color stamp on the cardboard was cheaper than paper labels. Most of the unused labels were thrown away or destroyed, but enough of them were stored in warehouses to spark a collecting craze during the 1970s. Today labels sell for $1 to $500. Most expensive are embossed tobacco product labels and labels that feature sports, athletes, or politicians.

Baseball Cards

Baseball cards and other sports cards have been printed since the 1880s, and billions of cards have been produced. The first cards were issued by tobacco companies, but by the 1920s tobacco companies were no longer using the cards as promotions. Candy and gum companies like Cracker Jack (1914–1915), Yuenglings ice cream (1928), and Delong Gum (1933) began issuing cards in the early twentieth century. Topps Chewing Gum Company started inserting baseball cards in gum packages in 1951. Bowman (1948–1955) and Fleer (1959–1963) also made cards, but Topps dominated the field until 1981, when Fleer began making cards again and Donruss and others began making cards. Topps made most of the cards that interest today's collectors. The Topps cards from 1952 are especially valuable. Boys saved baseball cards, flipped them in games, or used them to make noise in bicycle spokes until baseball card collecting became popular with grown men in the 1970s. By the late 1980s prices had skyrocketed. Overproduction and a saturated market caused prices for newer cards to collapse, and several manufacturers stopped making cards in the early 1990s. Today most cards are made by Topps and Upper Deck. Older cards continue to attract high prices. A 1909 card picturing Honus Wagner, the Hall of Fame Pittsburgh Pirate shortstop, sold for $1.265 million in 2000.

Chapter 13

ADVERTISING
AND PACKAGING

RESTAURANTS ARE DECORATED with walls filled with ads; family rooms are cleverly outfitted like country stores with shelves of old bottles and boxes; even museums want store collectibles to use in displays of period rooms or shops. Collectors and researchers search for all of these old, everyday items.

The green Wrigley man is made of tin but has a celluloid suit. He held a tray filled with gum on a store counter.

Before the 1950s, there was some interest in furniture, glass, ceramics, and other decorative arts. The only advertising antiques found in shops and shows were handmade store signs and cigar-store Indians. A few collector-historians searched for early nineteenth-century blown glass whiskey flasks and bitters bottles or for labeled handmade boxes that held Shaker herbs. Twentieth-century advertising was available only in thrift stores and garage sales.

During the 1950s, a few collectors started hunting for old advertising. Ivory soap packing crates and Diamond Dye cabinets could be found on the curb, ready to be picked up as city trash. Old bottles, boxes, labels, and

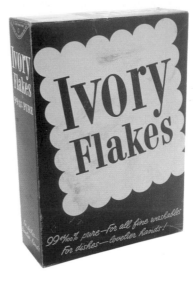

Raymond Loewy Industrial Designer

Raymond Loewy (1893–1986), who said "Never leave well enough alone," brought the idea and name "streamlined" to America. Loewy was born and educated as an engineer in Paris, and after World War I, he moved to the United States. He had a brief career as a fashion illustrator, and in 1923 he designed the trademark for the Neiman Marcus department store. In 1929 Loewy opened his own industrial design firm. His first redesign was for a Gestetner duplicating machine; he gave the machine a sleek shape, straightening the curved legs and removing protruding parts that kept poking users. Loewy designed a car, the 1934 Hupmobile, and he kept improving the design, integrating headlights into the streamlined form. He also designed the 1934 Sears Coldspot refrigerator. Soon he was designing locomotives, Greyhound buses, Studebakers, sewing machines, and Coca-Cola coolers. But his most talked about design was the new, white, 1942 Lucky Strike cigarette package. In 1962, Loewy designed the exterior of Air Force One, President Kennedy's airplane.

Designs on boxes have changed often. In the 1940s and early '50s, the grocery would have stocked this Ivory Flakes box. Box and soap cost thirty cents.

signs were often stored and forgotten in warehouses and manufacturing plants.

Collectors are especially interested in items considered historic "documents" that reflect the times, showing houses, home furnishings, ethnic stereotypes, patriotic emblems like the flag or Uncle Sam, Santa Claus, planes, trains, or cars. Eye-catching lithographed signs and packages made in the 1890s are scarce today, but advertising signs, packages, and figures made since the 1940s are still available. Collectors specialize in everything from enamel-painted (pyroglaze) soda bottles, animated counter displays, Coca-Cola items, or one-pound coffee cans to gas pump globes, beer bottles, cloth dolls, fast-food giveaways, advertising mirrors, or anything related to oysters. Many historical societies and even art museums have added special advertising pieces to their collections to represent an event, a way of life, a period of time, or the work of an artist.

THE HISTORY OF TWENTIETH-CENTURY ADVERTISING

From a Collector's View

Advertising has taken many forms. Trade cards were introduced about 1870 but lost favor by about 1910. Bookmarks were popular giveaways promoting stores and products from 1880 to 1915. The tin advertising tray was first used in the 1880s and is still popular. Giveaways and point-of-sale items—such as signs, furniture, pot-scrapers, puzzles, recipe books, ashtrays, fans, bottle openers, dinnerware, kitchenwares, and even clocks with ads—were first used to promote products in the late 1800s and have remained popular. Stickers on fresh bananas were introduced in 1961 to give brand-name status to the fruit. In the late 1980s, stickers with a PLU (Price Look Up) code were put on fresh fruits and vegetables to accurately identify and price the product and to speed the check-out process. Some were also small ads for brands. Even T-shirts became walking billboards during the 1970s.

Early store giveaways were sometimes worth more than the product. This Abbey *pattern ironstone dish was given away by a cereal company. A note on the back explains that the early 1900s dish is the right size to hold a shredded wheat biscuit.*

The package that holds a product is also the focus of an advertising collector's interest. Bottles, boxes, cans, labels, lithographed tins, paper bags, and other wrappings are saved.

The first national advertising campaign was for Uneeda prepackaged biscuits. The campaign, launched in 1898 by the National Biscuit Company, eventually cost $1 million. It used magazines, newspapers, and store signs and other outdoor ads, and featured a boy in boots and a yellow slicker with

This set of Chiquita Banana football team stickers cost only $1.99 plus some labels in 1984. It is popular with both sports and fruit seal collectors today.

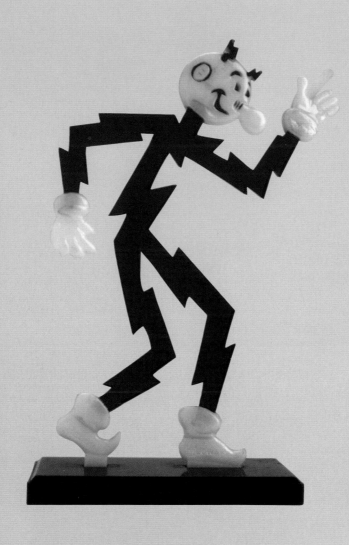

Reddy Kilowatt is obviously a symbol of an electric company. He was first used in 1926. This 5½-inch Lucite and Bakelite figure even has a lightbulb nose.

the slogan "Lest you forget, we say it yet, Uneeda Biscuit."

In the early years of the twentieth century, particularly after World War I, improvements in printing and color in popular magazines launched a new age of advertising that was increasingly sophisticated. Agencies produced eye-catching illustrations and slick copywriting to sell everything from toothpaste and soft drinks to presidential candidates.

Radio, television, and movies changed the look of advertising. Many product premiums were directly related to radio and TV shows or movie stars. From the 1930s to the 1960s, adventure shows offered decoder rings, space guns, or other toys that were linked with the program's plot. In the mid-1980s, many television ads had an "MTV look," featuring obscure references and psychedelic colors.

Collectors in the 1950s began saving unusual or clever advertising, including popular corporate symbols like Tony the Tiger or the Cracker Jack sailor boy. TV commercials were copied on video tape.

Highway Advertising

Within This Vale
Of Toil
And Sin
Your Head Grows Bald
But Not Your Chin
Burma-Shave

Before I Tried It
The Kisses
I Missed
But Afterward—Boy!
The Misses I Kissed
Burma-Shave

It Would Be More Fun
To Go By Air
But We Can't Hang
These Signs Up There
Burma-Shave

Remember Burma-Shave signs? These sets of small wooden signs advertising shaving cream first appeared by the side of the road in 1925. Each sign had one line of a humorous rhyme. They were placed about every one hundred feet or so. They disappeared about 1964.

Mail Pouch tobacco used the painted barn as a huge ad from the beginning of the twentieth century until the 1990s.

National Biscuit Company in 1898 made the first crackers sold in a moisture-proof box, not sold loose from a barrel. This Uneeda Biscuit boy wearing a yellow slicker that keeps out rain was the most famous advertising figure in America for decades.

Stuffed dolls were popular premiums. This is the front half of an Aunt Jemima doll given away by Aunt Jemima Mills Company in the early 1900s. The doll parts were cut out, stitched together, and stuffed.

Collectors looked for signs, posters, and magazine pages that were part of an ad campaign or were used in store displays.

ADVERTISING ICONS

Aunt Jemima

The Pearl Milling Company first used the Aunt Jemima symbol on its ready-mixed pancake flour in 1889. R. T. Davis Milling Company bought the Aunt Jemima trademark in 1890 and changed its name to the Aunt Jemima Mills Company in 1914. Quaker Oats Company bought the company in 1925 and used the symbol. Aunt Jemima's appearance changed through the years. A live Aunt Jemima appeared at the 1893 Chicago World's Fair. She was played by a former slave, Nancy Green, a thin woman who didn't resemble the heftier Aunt Jemima of the 1930s. The familiar Aunt Jemima cook in a bandana was featured as the logo by the early 1900s, and from 1930 to 1951, a large woman named Anna Robinson became the second live Aunt Jemima. In 1968 Aunt Jemima became slimmer and younger. In 1989 she was modernized into a food-industry businesswoman with a new hairstyle, pearl earrings, and a lace collar.

Aunt Jemima cloth dolls were introduced about 1905. In 1931 an 18½-inch composition doll was available. Aunt Jemima dolls made from a fabric that resembled oilcloth were available in 1950. Ceramic salt and pepper shakers were giveaways in the 1920s and '30s, and again in the 1980s. Plastic salt and peppers date from the 1950s. Other Aunt Jemima premiums have been made, but collectors should be careful. Many, including the iron doorstop and plastic figures, have been reproduced. Aunt Jemima packaged syrups and mixes are still made by Quaker, a division of PepsiCo since 2001.

Buster Brown's larger than-life-size head is part of the apparatus that was used to fill balloons at a shoe store in the 1960s and '70s. The plastic head was attached to a tank of helium.

Buster Brown

Buster Brown and his dog, Tige, first appeared in Richard Felton Outcault's cartoon strip in 1902. Outcault dreamed up the idea of licensing cartoon characters to merchants to promote products. He sold the

right to use the Buster Brown name and figures as product trademarks to over fifty different companies. The Buster Brown Gang was featured on radio in 1943 and on television from 1951 to 1954. Three companies—Buster Brown Shoe Company, Buster Brown Apparel, Inc., and Gateway Hosiery (makers of Buster Brown socks)—still use Buster Brown logos. Many old and new Buster Brown collectibles are available, including banks, buttons, clocks, mirrors, playing cards, pocketknives, puzzles, signs, and trays.

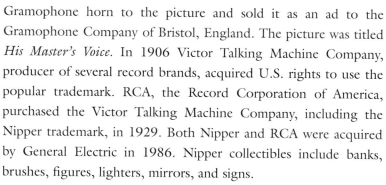

Nipper, the Victor/RCA Dog

The trademark now known as Nipper was based on a painting by Francis Barraud that pictured his fox terrier listening to a recording on a phonograph. Barraud added a Gramophone horn to the picture and sold it as an ad to the Gramophone Company of Bristol, England. The picture was titled *His Master's Voice.* In 1906 Victor Talking Machine Company, producer of several record brands, acquired U.S. rights to use the popular trademark. RCA, the Record Corporation of America, purchased the Victor Talking Machine Company, including the Nipper trademark, in 1929. Both Nipper and RCA were acquired by General Electric in 1986. Nipper collectibles include banks, brushes, figures, lighters, mirrors, and signs.

BRANDS

Some brands have attracted collectors more than others. The most popular include Coca-Cola, McDonald's restaurants, and M&Ms. Some of the others are Planters Peanuts, Anheuser-Busch, Budweiser, Kentucky Fried Chicken, and soft drinks like Pepsi-Cola, Moxie, and Hires Root Beer.

Carter's Ink

Carter, Dinsmore and Company, founded in 1858 in Cambridge, Massachusetts, was named Carter's Ink by 1898. The company made different types of ink bottles and labels that appeal to collectors. Ma and Pa Carter inkwells, a pair of ceramic figures with removable heads, were patented in 1914. Carter's tall Ryto brand cathedral-shaped bottles of cobalt blue glass were made during the 1920s. Carter's Ink advertising icons from the 1940s that are popular with collectors include a group of colorful cats promoting colored inks and Inky Racer, a running black figure that was a logo for Carter's ink eraser. Inky decorated the ink eraser's box. In 1976 the company was purchased by Dennison Manufacturing Company, which merged with Avery in 1991. Carter's ink and stamp pads are now part of the Avery Dennison product line.

Old labeled Carter's Ink bottles can still be found. This bottle with a cork stopper could date from the 1920s.

Coca-Cola

Coca-Cola, a soft drink introduced at an Atlanta soda fountain in 1886, is one of the world's best-known brand names. For more than a century, the company has been promoting the popular soft drink—and creating thousands of ads on bottles, trays, calendars, signs, toys, lamps, and other memorabilia that can be found in shops and sales.

The Coca-Cola company has made metal serving trays since 1897. This 1916 tray pictures Elaine in a yellow summer dress. It is 19 inches high by 8½ inches wide. Reproductions of many trays have been made. (Photo: James Julia)

Coca-Cola written in script was trademarked in 1893. The nickname *Coke*, first used in 1941, was registered in 1945. It is possible to date original Coca-Cola items from the slogans used in the advertising campaigns: *Drink Coca-Cola* (1886), then *Deliciously Refreshing* (1904), *The Pause That Refreshes* (1929), *It's the Real Thing* (1942), *Things Go Better with Coke* (1954), *Things Go Better*

with Coke again (1969), and *Coke Is It* (1982). Many Coca-Cola items have been reproduced, including trays, glasses, lamps, mirrors, and signs. There are also "fantasy" pieces illegally using the Coke logo, including a large brass belt buckle, made in the 1970s, showing a seminude woman.

Heinz

The H. J. Heinz Company traces its history back to 1869. Its first product was horseradish, but within a few years Heinz was selling ketchup, celery sauce, pickles, sauerkraut, and vinegar. The condiments were sold in tin cans, glass jars, and tin or stoneware crocks.

The term *57 Varieties* was chosen for its advertising effect, not because there were fifty-seven products. The Heinz pickle pin, which is still being given away, was introduced at the Chicago World's Fair in 1893. It has been joined by a Heinz ketchup bottle pin, first issued in 2000. Collectors can find thousands of cans, bottles, signs, advertising cards, and other Heinz items. To celebrate 120 years in business in 1989, the company offered a limited edition replica of the turn-of-the-century 14-ounce ketchup bottle. Heinz crocks, cans, and signs have also been reproduced. ◌℘

Opposite Page: Heinz packed ketchup and other condiments in pottery or glass containers. This early Heinz ketchup jug has a colorful paper label picturing tomatoes, peppers, and other vegetables.

Chapter 14

KITCHENWARE

IF YOU WALKED into an American home a century ago, you wouldn't find a television in the living room or a computer in the bedroom, but the rooms would look a lot like the same rooms in your own house—especially if you have an old house with wood floors and you have furnished the house with antiques.

The kitchen, however, would look much different. It's the room that has changed the most from generation to generation since 1900. New appliances were invented, built-in cabinets became standard, and new materials were used for floors, countertops, pots and pans, and kitchen utensils. Electricity and central heating also altered the way kitchens and kitchen gadgets look, and so did changing tastes and attitudes about how the kitchen fits into a family's life.

Remember the history of cooking methods and products when collecting. Large appliances and furniture, such as stoves and Hoosier cabinets, and cookware of all kinds from iron toasting racks to streamlined electric toasters are all collected.

KITCHEN DESIGNS AND FURNISHINGS

Most kitchens a hundred years ago had a stove that burned coal, oil, or wood. There might have been a small wooden icebox to keep food cold. Cabinets were small pieces of furniture that could be moved or mounted on a wall. Food preparation was done at a table with a wooden top. Some families still had to pump water outside; a few had running water pumped into the kitchen sink. Electricity

Opposite Page: In the modern kitchen of the 1930s, coffee could be made in an electric percolator and served at the table. This Hall China pot was made to be attractive and useful.

Hoosier Cabinets

Between the time of freestanding or wall-hung cabinets and the arrival of built-ins came the Hoosier cabinet, a creative piece invented by an Indiana man named J. S. McQuinn. The Hoosier cabinet is a large, freestanding unit with bins for dry ingredients like flour and sugar, a tin (later porcelain) work surface, and drawers and closed shelves for pots, pans, bowls, dishes, and utensils. McQuinn founded the Hoosier Manufacturing Company in Albany, Indiana, in 1899, then moved it to nearby New Castle, Indiana. By the mid-1920s, the factory was producing hundreds of cabinets a day and selling them all over the country. Other manufacturers, most in Indiana, made similar cabinets, and soon the public was calling all of them "Hoosiers." The Hoosier Manufacturing Company closed in 1942. Built-in kitchen cabinets had taken over the market. Hoosier-type cabinets are still popular with collectors.

The Hoosier cabinet was the cook's workstation. It had space for all sorts of baking and cooking needs, including dispensers for flour, sugar, and spices.

was already on its way—changing lighting, refrigeration, cooking, baking, cleaning, washing and drying dishes and clothing, and more.

Collectible early 1900s kitchen furniture includes baker's cupboards and racks, butcher-block tables, stepstools, and possum-belly tables (the kind with flour bins and drawers under the tabletop). Breakfast sets of tables and chairs changed throughout the twentieth century. Early twentieth-century kitchen sets were all wood. By the 1930s, tables had porcelain enamel tops. In the 1950s, Formica-topped, metal-legged tables with plastic-covered padded chairs were common. The kitchen of the 1960s and later had eating islands with pull-up chairs or stools, a corner with built-in table and benches, or any of the modern tables with glass, wood, or plastic tops and matching chairs.

Appliances

Electric or gas-powered appliances also changed the look of the twentieth-century kitchen, and today the old appliances are wanted by those restoring early twentieth-century houses. Electric refrigerators were made by the early 1920s by General Electric, General Motors (Frigidaire), and Kelvinator. They were heavy, with wooden cases and nickel hinges, and were too expensive for the average homeowner. By the mid-1920s, refrigerators came down in price and had a new look created by an exterior

The GE refrigerator's monitor top held cooling equipment. A miniature milk-glass salt and pepper set shaped like Monitor-Top refrigerators was given to new owners to use in the kitchen. There was also a matching clock.

Electric toasters in the 1930s and '40s were continually changed and improved. Some turned the toast to rest against the heater. Others sent it down a long slot to emerge toasted. This Fostoria toaster would flip the toast when the side knobs were turned.

of porcelain over steel. In 1927 General Electric introduced its Monitor-Top model, which sold for a relatively affordable $300. The Monitor-Top was the first refrigerator to sell widely in the United States, and it is the model most sought by collectors today. In 1947 General Electric started mass-producing the two-door dual-temperature refrigerator-freezer still made today, and in the 1960s many manufacturers added icemakers and water dispensers. Styles and colors changed over the decades, and often the color will help date a refrigerator.

Stoves heated by natural gas were found in most American households by the 1920s, and within another decade, electric stoves were also on the market. Some old gas stoves are cast iron, but eventually both gas and electric ranges were coated with enamel, usually white with black trim.

Electric washing machines, which replaced the copper boiler and hand-cranked washer, and electric or gas dryers that replaced the clothesline were inventions of the early 1900s, although it took decades for them to reach most American households. It was in 1937 that Bendix Corporation introduced the first fully automatic washer. The electric-powered household-size dishwasher came into widespread use during the 1950s, and Amana introduced the first microwave oven for home use, the Radarange, in 1967.

Collectors are interested in all sorts of small appliances that were introduced during the twentieth century. There is more interest in the "look" than in the manufacturer. Some collectors are interested in the designer. All kinds of kitchen products are collected: classic toasters, coffeemakers and coffeepots, coffee grinders, mixers, waffle irons, griddles, teakettles, hotplates, bread makers, food processors, can openers, frying pans, pressure cookers, Crock-Pots, fondue pots, popcorn poppers, juicers, milkshake makers, bottle warmers, choppers, chafing dishes, broilers, roasters, water kettles, hotdog cookers, bun warmers, ice cream makers, egg cookers, toaster ovens, and fireless cookers.

Special-use kitchen appliances were the rage in the twentieth century, so what better to own than an electric marshmallow toaster that heated just one marshmallow at a time?

METAL COOKWARE

Pots and pans made of cast iron or enameled tin (often called graniteware) were manufactured before 1900, and they are still made today. Other twentieth-century pots and pans were manufactured of copper, tin, aluminum, brass, stainless steel, chrome-plated steel, and combinations of these materials and others. Since 1960, nonstick coatings like Teflon have been used.

Griswold

The most famous name in cast-iron cookware is Griswold Manufacturing Company, founded in Erie, Pennsylvania, in 1865. By the end of the 1880s, Griswold was known as a manufacturer of high-quality cast-iron griddles, waffle irons, Dutch ovens, and roasters. By the 1920s, it was making cast-iron and aluminum kettles, cake and muffin pans, pots and pans of all sizes, sadirons, trivets, tobacco cutters, and meat grinders.

Griswold's Erie plant closed in 1957, the company was sold, and the brand disappeared. Collectors prefer Griswold products manufactured before the 1940s.

Wagner

Another well-known manufacturer of cast-iron and early cast-aluminum cookware was the Wagner Manufacturing Company, founded in Sidney, Ohio, in 1881. Wagner pre-seasoned iron cookware with pure beeswax, which helped prevent rust and formed a less sticky surface. In 1934 Wagner introduced a brightly finished aluminum alloy it dubbed Magnalite. Both the Wagner and the Magnalite brand names have survived, although the original company is no longer in business.

TWO-IN-ONE APPLIANCES

Some odd combination appliances were invented during the twentieth century. Armstrong came out with a *Perc-O-Toaster* in 1918 that made coffee while it also toasted bread or waffles. Merit-Made used the same idea to create its "moderne" coffeemaker-toaster in the 1930s. Ronson introduced a *Cook 'n Stir* in 1965; it blended and cooked simultaneously.

Griswold made many types of cast-iron pans, including this #8 Tite Top Dutch oven. Iron is durable, and many of the old Griswold utensils are "still cooking."

GLASS KITCHENWARE—PYREX

Corning Glass Works of Corning, New York, introduced Pyrex brand glass baking dishes in 1915. The first Pyrex products included covered casseroles, pie pans, shirred egg dishes, custard cups, an individual baker, an au gratin dish, and a loaf pan. Within two years, Corning added several more shapes and sizes of Pyrex transparent ovenware, and by 1918 some pieces could be ordered with engraved patterns, including *Wreath, Fern and Key,* and *Spray,* and casseroles could be ordered with decorative metal serving holders. Only the *Spray* design lasted past 1922, and it was discontinued in the 1940s.

By the mid-1920s, the Pyrex line ran to more than a hundred items and included oven roasters as well as dishes to be used outside the oven—refrigerator storage containers, serving platters, teapots and coffeepots, and measuring cups with red markings. Corning experimented with a small line of white opalescent and white iridescent casseroles in 1921, but the line was quickly discontinued.

During the 1930s, Corning began producing clear Pyrex mixing bowl sets, coffee percolators with aluminum baskets and stems, reamers, molds, nursing bottles, pie birds, and a short-lived (1936–1937) line of red-decorated casseroles.

In 1947 Pyrex introduced colored, tempered opal-glass kitchenware. Almost all of it had sprayed-on colors, and many had

FLAMEWARE

In the 1930s, Corning's chemists invented another type of clear glassware that the company used to make stovetop cookware marketed as Pyrex Flameware. Products, which were tinted slightly blue, included saucepans and skillets with detachable handles, double boilers, a teakettle and a teapot, coffee percolators, bottles, bowls, refrigerator storage containers, and additional kitchenware.

Pyrex ware was born in 1915 and is still found in most kitchens. This Pyrex Flameware double-boiler was a well-designed cook's delight in the 1930s and is a collector's item today.

The ear-of-corn-shaped pan for baking corn muffins is a nineteenth-century idea. This Wagner Ware cast-iron pan was patented in 1920.

screen-printed patterns. Pieces were made with the same molds Corning used to make its clear ovenware and included all sorts of kitchenware, from butter dishes, refrigerator sets, and baking pans to casseroles, mixing bowls, and salad and snack sets. Production continued into the late 1980s, when Corning moved on to other glass and glass ceramic lines.

Early colored mixing bowls were thicker than later ones and were sold in sets of four bowls, each a different color (blue, red, green, and yellow). Other colors, including pink, turquoise, yellow, and charcoal, were introduced in the mid-1950s, and so were decorative patterns. Especially popular were the nesting bowls with two lips, called *Cinderella* sets, introduced in 1958. The wide lip formed a handy grip and the narrow lip could be used for pouring. The wide grip was added to a line of casseroles, also called *Cinderella*, that featured patterns on either opal or colored glass.

The 1930s kitchen was usually beige and red or beige and green. Jadite, a green glass, was used to make all sorts of kitchen bowls and dishes like this refrigerator leftover jar. Notice the space-saving recessed handle and square shape.

The decorative patterns on Corning's colored kitchenware ranged from simple to abstract, and each was given a name. Some were white on colored glass and others were color on opal glass. Additional colors and patterns were added over the years. Most popular with collectors are the earlier patterns like *Snowflake* (1956) and *Butterprint* (1959). Others to look for include: *Dairy* (1957), *Gooseberry* (1958), *Golden Acorn* (1960), *Early American* (1961), *Golden Honeysuckle* (1962), *Terra* (1964), *Town & Country* (1964), *Rainbow Stripes* (1965), *Americana* (plain colors with a white band, 1966), and *New Dot* (1967). Pyrex dishes are marked in various ways, depending on the type of ware and when it was made, but nearly every piece has the word *Pyrex* and an item number.

In the 1950s Corning scientists developed a ceramiclike glass material that could withstand extremes of hot and cold, and in 1958 the company introduced Corning Ware cooking utensils and dishes that can go from freezer to oven to table. *Corelle,* a line of

This Pyrex bowl is one of four nesting bowls in a Cinderella *set. It is avocado, a color made in the 1960s.*

Alessi—Italian Design for the Home

(Photo: Alessi)

The stainless steel kettle with a blue plastic handle and a red bird whistling on the spout and the corkscrew that looks like a smiling woman with levers for arms were designed for and made by Alessi. The Italian company was founded in 1921 to make metal products for eating and drinking. At first, the products were more or less traditional, but by the 1940s, eye-catching design had become important. In the 1950s, Alessi began showing products at large expositions, and by the 1970s, prominent artists and architects were designing for the company. Beginning in the 1970s, the company created a new type of kitchenware that would change some food traditions and open the way for radical design, such as the Can Can can opener and the Mandarin citrus-squeezer with goblet. In 1979 Alessandro Mendini became Alessi's general design consultant. He was responsible for some of Alessi's most creative and well-known designs, including the famous tea and coffee sets by name artists. Alessi has worked with major designers and architects like Frank Gehry, Michael Graves, Ettore Sottsass, and Philippe Starck to create whimsical, colorful, and useful utensils from metal, ceramics, and plastic.

break-resistant dishes that have the feel of fine china, was first sold in 1970.

OTHER KITCHENWARE

Other collectible kitchenware made of glass, ceramic, and plastic includes: Anchor Hocking's Fire-King glassware, Fry Glass Company's Oven Glass, Hall China Company's refrigerator and oven wares (made for Westinghouse, Sears, Montgomery Ward, Hotpoint, and General Electric), Homer Laughlin's Fiesta Kitchen Craft line of bake-and-serve pieces, McKee Glass Company's kitchenware, Watt Pottery's various patterns of kitchenware, Texas Ware's speckled plastic mixing bowls, and even some early Tupperware.

KITCHEN UTENSILS

Thousands of small kitchen utensils were manufactured during the twentieth century. Some collectors specialize in a specific kitchen tool—eggbeaters, spatulas, corkscrews, or bottle openers. Others might want anything with a Bakelite or green wooden handle.

Bakelite, a phenol formaldehyde resin, an early synthetic plastic, was invented in 1907 by chemist Leo Baekeland. He patented the new material and started the General Bakelite Company in 1910, but it wasn't until 1927 that Bakelite entered the kitchen, bringing color with it. Bakelite handles were made for beaters, knives, mashers, spatulas, peelers, graters, serving spoons, syrup pitchers, and flatware, as well as for tea sets and coffeepots—just about any other kitchen or eating tool. Once Bakelite opened the door to color, manufacturers started painting wooden handles with bright colors.

Early Bakelite was black or shades of brown, but bright reds, greens, and yellows soon followed. So did other brands of phenol formaldehyde resins similar to Bakelite and other plastics, including Lucite, a transparent plastic that can be made in colors.

Collectors must be detectives to identify some utensils. Not many of us use butter curlers or meat axes today, but many utensils, even unfamiliar ones, are marked with a maker's name or a patent date that can help determine age. 🙿

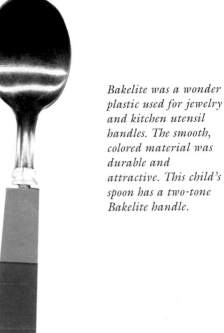

Bakelite was a wonder plastic used for jewelry and kitchen utensil handles. The smooth, colored material was durable and attractive. This child's spoon has a two-tone Bakelite handle.

APPENDIX

Twentieth-Century Metal and Jewelry Designers

This table lists the maker or factory, location, date, mark, and other information about metal and jewelry designers of the twentieth century. Parentheses enclose the birth and death dates of the artist. Other dates given are approximate working dates of the factory or artist. The names of workers or designers connected with jewelry factories are also in parentheses in the third column. One mark, if available, is used for each listing, although the makers often used a variety of marks. Many pieces are unmarked or marked with the seller's, not the designer's or maker's, name.

Workshop or Artist Location	Dates	Artists, Factories, and Related Information	Mark
AUSTRIA			
Carl Otto Czescha (Czeschka) Vienna	(1878–1960)	Metalwork (Wiener Werkstätte)	
Hagenauer Werkstätte Vienna	1898–1956	Metalwork (Carl Hagenauer, Karl Hagenauer, Otto Prutscher, Josef Hoffmann)	
Josef Hoffmann Vienna	(1870–1956)	Jewelry, metalwork (Wiener Werkstätte)	
Otto Prutscher Vienna	(1880–1949)	Jewelry, enamel (Wiener Werkstätte)	
Wiener Werkstätte Vienna	1903–1932	Metalwork, jewelry (C. O. Czeschka, J. Hoffmann, J. Hossfeld, K. Kallert, K. Koch, M. Likarz, K. Moser, O. Prutscher, E. Wimmer, J. Zimpel)	
BELGIUM			
Henri Clemens Van de Velde, Brussels, Berlin	(1863–1957)	Jewelry, metalwork, bronze, silver	
BRAZIL			
H. Stern Rio de Janiero	1945–present	Gold, diamonds, precious gems	

Workshop or Artist Location	Dates	Artists, Factories, and Related Information	Mark
CANADA			
Henry Birks & Sons Montreal	1879–present	Silver, gold, jewelry Founded by Henry Birks	BIRKS STERLING
FRANCE			
Boucheron Paris, Biarritz, London, New York	1858–present	Jewelry	
Edgar Brandt Paris	(1880–1960) 1900–1930	Metalwork, brass, iron, copper	E BRANDT
Cardeilhac Paris	1802–1951	Silver	
Cartier Paris, London, New York	1847–present	Jewelry (Louis-François Cartier; his son, Alfred Cartier; Alfred's sons, Louis Cartier, Pierre Cartier, and Jacques Cartier)	Cartier
"Coco" Chanel Paris	(1883–1971) 1920s–present	Jewelry	CHANEL
Chaumet et Cie Paris, London	c.1780–present	Jewelry	CHAUMET PARIS
Christofle St. Denis	1839–present	Silver, silver plate (Charles Christofle, Henry Bouilhet, E. Reiber, J. M. Olbrich)	
Edward Colonna Paris; New York City; Dayton, Ohio; Canada	(1862–1948)	Jewelry Born in Cologne, Germany; worked in New York (Tiffany's, Associated Artists, 1883–1884), Paris (S. Bing, H. Vever, 1898–1905)	COLONNA
Fouquet Paris	1860–late 1930s	Jewelry Founded c.1860 by Alphonse Fouquet; joined by son, Georges Fouquet (1862–1957), in 1891 (Alphonse Mucha and Charles Desrosiers)	G. FOUQUET

Workshop or Artist Location	Dates	Artists, Factories, and Related Information	Mark
René Lalique Paris	(1860–1945)	Jewelry, silver, glass	LALIQUE
Alphonse Maria Mucha Paris and Czechoslovakia	(1860–1939)	Silver, jewelry	Designed jewelry for G. Fouquet
Gilbert Poillerat Paris	(1902–1988) 1921–1950s	Lamps, ironwork	Items rarely marked
Gerard Sandoz Paris	c.1925–1931	Silver	Jewelry marked with name
Lea Stein Paris	(1931–present) 1957–present	Costume jewelry	LEA STEIN PARIS
Van Cleef & Arpels Paris	1906–present	Jewelry	VCA
Maison Vever Metz, Paris	1821–at least 1982 (c.1982)	Jewelry	VEVER PARIS
GERMANY			
Peter Behrens Munich	(1868–1940)	Metalwork	B
Theodor Fahrner Pforzheim	(1868–1928)	Silver, jewelry	TF
J. P. Kayser Sohn Krefeld-Bochum	1885–c.1910	Pewter (H. Leven, Otto Schulze)	KAYSER ZINN 4477
Kayserzinn (See J. P. Kayser Sohn.)			
Bernd Munsteiner Idar-Oberstein	(1943–present)	Gemstone cutter	
Orivit (See Ferdinand Hubert Schmitz.)			

Workshop or Artist Location	Dates	Artists, Factories, and Related Information	Mark
Ferdinand Hubert Schmitz Köln-Ehrenfeld	(1863–1939) 1900–1905	Pewter, silver Founded Rheinische Broncegieserei in 1894. Became Orivit in 1900. Württembergische Metallwarenfabrik (WMF) took over Orivit in 1905.	
Württembergiche Metallwarenfabrik Geislingen	1853–present	Pewter, silver plate, glass, Ikora metal (Wilhelm Wagenfeld)	WMF
GREAT BRITAIN			
Artificers' Guild London	1901–1942	Silver, copper, metalwork (Nelson Dawson, Montague Fordham, Edward Spender, John Paul Cooper)	
Charles Robert Ashbee London	(1863–1942)	Silver, jewelry Founded Guild of Handicraft in 1888.	
Asprey & Company, Ltd. London	1781–present	Jewelry	
J. W. Benson London	1874–present	Jewelry Merged with Alfred Benson and Henry Webb, c.1897.	
Birmingham Guild of Handicraft Birmingham	1890–present	Metalwork, jewelry, silver (Arthur Dixon [founder], Montague Fordham, Claude Napier Clavering, E. & R. Gittins Co.)	
Bromsgrove Guild of Applied Art Bromsgrove	c.1890–1966	Jewelry, metal (Walter Gilbert, Arthur Gaskin, Georgina Gaskin)	B.G.A.A.
Alwyn C. E. Carr London	(1872–1940)	Silver, enamel, wrought iron (Ramsden & Carr)	
Collingwood & Company London	1817–present	Silver, jewelry	
Comyns, William & Sons London	1848–present	Silver	
J. Paul Cooper Westerham	(1869–1933)	Silver, copper, jewelry (Artificers' Guild)	

Workshop or Artist Location	Dates	Artists, Factories, and Related Information	Mark
Bernard Cuzner Birmingham, London	(1877–1956)	Silver, jewelry (Liberty & Co., Birmingham Guild of Handicraft)	B.C.
Nelson Dawson London	(1859–1942)	Jewelry, silver, metalwork, enamel (Artificers' Guild)	N·D
James Dixon & Sons Sheffield	1806–present	Silver, silver plate, Britannia metal	J.W.D
Christopher Dresser London	(1834–1904)	Designed for many companies	Chr. Dresser
Elkington & Co. Birmingham	1824–present	Silver, silver plate, metalwork, enamel	E & Cº Lᴰ
Alexander Fisher London	(1864–1936)	Silver, jewelry, enamel	AF
R. and S. Garrard London	1802–1952	Silver, gold, jewelry (Robert Garrard, James Garrard, Sebastien Garrard)	GARRARD & CO LTD 112, REGENT STREET LONDON. W.1.
Goldsmiths' & Silversmiths' Co. London	1890–1952	Silver, jewelry (William Gibson, Harold Stabler)	G.& S.Cº Lᴰ
Hennell, Ltd. London	1735–present	Jewelry	Items marked "Hennell"
Charles Horner Halifax	1885–1984	Mass-produced enameled silver, jewelry	C.H.
Hukin & Heath Birmingham	1875–1953	Silver, silver plate	JWH JTH
Hunt & Roskell London	1844–1939	Silver, silver plate, jewelry	H & R Lᵀᴰ
Archibald Knox London	(1864–1933)	Jewelry (Liberty & Co.)	LY & Cº

Workshop or Artist Location	Dates	Artists, Factories, and Related Information	Mark
Liberty & Co. London	1875–present	Silver, pewter Partnered with W. H. Haseler & Co. to produce Cymric line. (B. Cuzner, A. H. Jones, A. Gaskin, A. Knox)	LY&Cº
Margaret Macdonald Glasgow, Scotland	(1865–1933)	Metalwork, jewelry	MARGARET MACDONALD MACKINTOSH
Arthur Mackmurdo Heygate	(1851–1942)	Metalwork	M
Harold Stabler Keswick, London	(1872–1945)	Jewelry, metalwork, silver (Keswick School of Industrial Art, Goldsmiths' & Silversmiths' Co., Adie Bros.)	·HS·
Henry J. Wilson London	(1864–1934)	Metalwork, jewelry (Art Workers' Guild)	HW

HOLLAND

Workshop or Artist Location	Dates	Artists, Factories, and Related Information	Mark
Bonebakker & Sons Amsterdam	1767–present	Jewelry	AB Z 1792
Jan Eisenloeffel Amsterdam	(1876–1957)	Silver (Amstelhoek)	JAN EISENLOEFFEL

ITALY

Workshop or Artist Location	Dates	Artists, Factories, and Related Information	Mark
Bulgari Rome	1881–present	Jewelry (Sotiro Bulgari, Constantine Bulgari, Giorgio Bulgari)	BVLGARI
Buccellati Milan	1919–present	Gold, precious and semiprecious stones, pearls, minerals, watches, sterling silver	MARIO BUCCELLATI ITALY
Paolo De Poli Padua	1905–1996	Enameled jewelry	P. DE POLI MADE IN ITALY

JAPAN

Workshop or Artist Location	Dates	Artists, Factories, and Related Information	Mark
Mikimoto Tokyo	1899–present	Pearls Many other locations after 1913	M

Workshop or Artist Location	Dates	Artists, Factories, and Related Information	Mark
MEXICO			
Hector Aguilar Taxco	(1905–1986) 1939–1966	Silver	
Frederick Davis Mexico City	(1880–1961) 1920s–1960	Silver	
Antonio Pineda Gomez Taxco, Mexico City	(1919–present) 1941–present	Silver	
Bernice Goodspeed Mexico City	(?–1971) 1940–1972	Silver	
Enrique Ledesma Taxco	1950–1979	Silver	
Los Castillo Taxco	1939–present	Silver	
Isidro Garcia Piña Taxco	1943–1986	Silver (*Maricela*)	
Sigfrido Pineda (Sigi) Mexico City, Taxco	(1929–present) 1952–present	Silver	
Matilde Poulat **Mexico City**	1934–1960	Silver (*Matl*)	
William Spratling Taxco	(1900–1967) 1931–present	Silver	
Margot de Taxco (Margot van Voorhies Carr) Taxco, Mexico City	(?–1985) 1948–c.1985	Silver	
Salvador Vaca Teran Mexico City	1930s–1974	Silver	
RUSSIA			
W. A. Bolin (See SCANDINAVIA, W. A. Bolin)			
House of Fabergé Moscow, St. Petersburg	1842–1918	Jewelry, gold (Peter Carl Fabergé)	
Feodor Rückert Moscow	c.1890s–1917	Gold, jewelry	

Workshop or Artist Location	Dates	Artists, Factories, and Related Information	Mark
SCANDINAVIA			
Sigvard Bernadotte Sweden	(1907–2002)	Jewelry, silver dinnerware	
W. A. Bolin Sweden	1791–present	Jewelry (Carl Edward Bolin, William James Bolin, Charles and Henrik Bolin, William Bolin, K. S. Bolin). Founded in St. Petersburg. Moved to Sweden in 1916.	BOLIN
David-Andersen Norway	1876–present	Silver, enamel (Carl Johansgate, G. Gaudernack)	D·A NORWAY STERLING
Nanna & Jorgen Ditzel Denmark	Nanna (1923–2005) Jorgen (1921–1961)	Jewelry	
Hans Hansen Denmark	(1884–1940) 1906–present	Flatware, hollow ware, jewelry	
Georg Jensen Denmark	(1866–1935) 1904–present	Jewelry, silver	HN DENMARK GEORG JENSEN STERLING
Henning Koppel Denmark	(1917–1982)	Jewelry, silver	HK
Erik Magnussen Copenhagen, Denmark New York City, Chicago, Hollywood, U.S.A.	(1884–1960) 1909–1925; 1939–1960 1925–1939	Jewelry	ERIK MAGNUSSEN
Anton Michelsen Denmark	(1809–1877) 1841–present	Jewelry, silver	ANTON MICHELSEN COPENHAGEN GS STERLING DENMARK
Evald Nielsen Denmark	(1879–1958)	Hand-hammered silver	EN
Harald Nielsen Denmark	(1892–1977)	Jewelry, silver	H N
Johan Rohde Denmark	(1856–1935)	Silver	R

Workshop or Artist Location	Dates	Artists, Factories, and Related Information	Mark
UNITED STATES			
Acme Studios Los Angeles; Maui, Hawaii	1985–present	White metal, enamel (Memphis designs)	
Allan Adler Los Angeles	(1916–2002)	Silver, jewelry	ALLAN ADLER HANDMADE STERLING
Alvin Manufacturing Company Alvin Corporation Providence, R.I.	1886–1928 1928–present	Silver	
Aaron Basha New York City	1950s–present	Gold, enamel	AARON BASHA
Bailey, Banks & Biddle Philadelphia	1832–present	Jewelry	BAILEY BANKS & BIDDLE
F. Carlton Ball San Francisco	(1911–1992)	Silver	Items rarely marked
Benedict Manufacturing Company East Syracuse, N.Y.	c.1900–1930s	Copper, pewter, silver plate	BENEDICT KARNAK BRASS
Harry Bertoia Detroit; Los Angeles; Bally, Pa.	(1915–1978)	Hammered brass	Items rarely marked
R. Blackinton & Company North Attleboro, Mass.	1862–present	Jewelry, silver	Ⓡ ⊞ Ⓒ
Bradley & Hubbard Meriden, Conn.	c.1895–1930	Brass	BRADLEY & HUBBARD MFG. CO.
Alexander Calder New York City	(1898–1976)	Costume jewelry	Items rarely marked
Hattie Carnegie New York City	(1886–1956) 1918–1976	Costume jewelry	Hattie Carnegie

Workshop or Artist Location	Dates	Artists, Factories, and Related Information	Mark
Ciner New York City	1892–present	Costume jewelry	CINER©
Charles Clewell Canton, Ohio	c.1899–1955	Copper, bronze	
Betty Cooke Baltimore	(1924–present)	Silver, enamel, wood, pebbles	COOKE
Coro Providence, R.I.	c.1901–1979	Costume jewelry (Coro, Inc., Canada until 1990s)	Coro
Craftsman Workshops Syracuse, N.Y.	c.1900–1915	Copper (Gustav Stickley)	
Margaret Craver Boston	(1907–present) 1930s–1988	Silver	Items marked with "C" in a scalloped circle
Margaret De Patta San Francisco	(1903–1964)	Silver	
Harry Dixon San Francisco	(1890–1967) c.1908–1967	Copper	
William B. Durgin Company (Gorham) Providence, R.I. Concord, N.H.	1853–1935	Silver Merged with Gorham in 1905	WM.B.DURGIN
Eisenberg Chicago	1930–present	Costume jewelry	
Claire Falkenstein San Francisco; Paris; Venice, Calif.	(1908–1997) 1950 1965–1997	Wire, rough glass	
Theodore W. Foster & Brothers Company Providence, R.I.	1873–1951	Jewelry, silver	F. & B.
George Gebelein Boston	(1878–1945)	Silver	GEBELEIN

Workshop or Artist Location	Dates	Artists, Factories, and Related Information	Mark
Gorham Corporation Providence, R.I.	1818–present	Silver, silver plate, bronze, metalwork, jewelry, copper, gold Named Gorham Mfg. Co. in 1842.	martelé
HAR New York City	1940s–1950s	Costume jewelry	©HAR
John Hardy Bali, New York City	c.1975–present	Jewelry	
Miriam Haskell New York City	(1899–1981) c.1924–present	Costume jewelry	MIRIAM HASKELL
Oscar Heyman and Brothers New York City	1912–present	Jewelry	HB
Frances Higgins Chicago	(1912–2004)	Glass jewelry	higgins
Hobé Mt. Vernon, N.Y. New York City	c.1887–present	Costume jewelry	Hobé STERLING DESIGN PAT'D
Yuri Ichihashi New York City	1991–present	Handwoven gold and platinum	Jewelry marked with name
Jaccard Jewelry Company St. Louis	1829–present	Jewelry	MERMOD & JACCARD CO. TRIPLE
Eugene Joseff Joseff of Hollywood Hollywood, Calif.	(1905–1948) 1935–present	Costume jewelry	JOSEFF HOLLYWOOD
Kalo Shop Chicago	1900–1970	Silver, copper, jewelry (Clara Barck Welles)	KALO X 3 2 5
Samuel Kirk Baltimore	1815–present	Silver	S.KIRK & SON
Florence Koehler Chicago	(1861–1944)	Jewelry (Chicago Arts & Crafts Society)	
Sam Kramer New York City	(1913–1964)	Silver	

Workshop or Artist Location	Dates	Artists, Factories, and Related Information	Mark
Kramer Jewelry Creations New York City	1943–1980	Costume jewelry	KRAMER©
Krementz Newark, N.J.	1866–present	Jewelry	KREMENTZ ⅃
Walter Lampl New York City	(1895–1945) 1921–1959	Silver, gold, charms	10K WL
Kenneth Jay Lane New York City	(1930–present) 1963–present	Costume jewelry	KENNETH © LANE
Judith Leiber New York City	(1921–present)	Costume jewelry (Opened own company in 1963)	Judith Leiber
Fred Leighton New York City	(1932–present) c.1965–present	Jewelry	Jewelry marked with name
Ed Levin New York City Bennington, Vt.	(1921–present) 1950–present	Silver	©LEVIN
Paul Lobel New York City	(1899–1983) 1930s–1965	Silver	LOBEL STERLING
Peter Macchiarini San Francisco	(1909–2001) 1937–2001	Silver, mixed metals	MACCHIARINI
Marcus & Company New York City	1892–1950s	Jewelry, copper, silver (Herman Marcus and sons, George Elder and William E. Marcus)	MARCUS&CO
Marshall Field & Company Craft Shop Chicago	1904–1950	Jewelry, silver, brass, bronze	MADE IN OUR CRAFT SHOP MARSHALL FIELD & CO
Marvella New York City	1911–present	Costume jewelry, fake pearls Bought by Trifari in 1982	MARVELLA
Matisse (See Renoir of California)			
John Paul Miller Cleveland	(1918–present)	Gold, silver	JPM

Workshop or Artist Location	Dates	Artists, Factories, and Related Information	Mark
Monet East Providence, R.I.	1937–present	Costume jewelry	MONET
Napier Meriden, Conn.	1922–present	Costume jewelry	NAPIER
Paloma Picasso New York City, Switzerland	(1949–present)	Jewelry (Tiffany's)	©Paloma Picasso
Earl Pardon Saratoga Springs, N.Y.	(1926–1991)	Enamel, stone, wood, wire	Pardon
Potter Studio Cleveland	c.1899–c.1927	Brass, copper, jewelry, silver (Potter & Bentley, c.1928–1933), (Potter & Mellen, 1933–present)	POTTER STUDIO
Frank or Francisco Rebajes New York City	(1906–1990) 1934–c.1967	Costume jewelry	Rebajes
Reed & Barton Taunton, Mass.	1824–present	Silver, silver plate, jewelry	TRADE MARK ® STERLING
Renoir of California Los Angeles	1946–1964	Costume jewelry, copper, enameled copper (Matisse)	Renoir
Nettie Rosenstein New York City	(1890–1980) c.1935–1975	Costume jewelry	Nettie Rosenstein
Roycroft East Aurora, N.Y.	1895–1938	Copper (D. Hunter, E. Hubbard, K. Kipp, Leon Varney)	
Seaman Schepps Los Angeles, San Francisco, New York City	1904–present	Gold, precious and semiprecious stones	seaman schepps
Elsa Schiaparelli Paris, New York City	(1890–1973) 1920s–late 1950s	Costume jewelry	schiaparelli
Jean Schlumberger New York City	(1907–1987) 1946–1956	Jewelry (Own shop from 1946, then joined Tiffany & Co. in 1956.)	SCHLUMBERGER
Selro New York City	1950s–1960s	Costume jewelry	SELRO CORP ©

Workshop or Artist Location	Dates	Artists, Factories, and Related Information	Mark
Shreve & Company San Francisco	1852–present	Jewelry, silver	SHREVE&CO SAN FRANCISCO STERLING
Shreve, Crump & Low Boston	1796–present	Founded in 1796; became Shreve, Crump & Low in 1869.	SHREVE CRUMP & LOW CO. HAND WROUGHT S M C STERLING
Art Smith New York City	(1917–1982)	Silver, silver wire, brass, copper (Opened own shop in 1948)	Art Smith
Spaulding & Company Chicago	1888–present	Silver, silver plate, jewelry (Henry A. Spaulding)	S&C
Henry Steig New York City	(1906–1973)	Silver	STEIG STERLING
Gustav Stickley Syracuse, N.Y.	(1857–1942)	Copper (Craftsman Workshop)	
Arthur J. Stone Gardiner and Boston, Mass.	(1847–1938)	Silver (Stone Associates: Alfred Wickstrom, David Carlson, George Blanchard, Charles Brown, Arthur Hartwell, Herbert Taylor, George Erickson, Herman Glendenning, Edgar Caron, Earl Underwood)	Stone STERLING T
Tiffany & Company New York City	1853–present	Jewelry, silver, metalwork (Charles Louis Tiffany)	TIFFANY&CO 550 BROADWAY
Tiffany Studios New York City	1890–1932	Metalwork, (Louis Comfort Tiffany)	TIFFANY STUDIOS NEW YORK
Trifari New York City	1918–present	Costume jewelry	TRIFARI.
Unger Bros. Newark, N.J.	1872–1919	Silver, jewelry	STERLING 925 FINE
Dirk Van Erp Oakland and San Francisco, Calif.	(1859–1933)	Copper (D'Arcy Gaw, Harry Dixon)	

Workshop or Artist Location	Dates	Artists, Factories, and Related Information	Mark
Nicholas Varney New York City	c.1996–present	Jewelry	
Webster Company North Attleboro, Mass.	1869–1950	Silver (Acquired by Reed & Barton in 1950. Sold to A. J. Reilly in 1974.)	WEBSTER≫W
Frank M. Whiting Company North Attleboro, Mass.	1878–c.1960	Silver	W
Whiting Manufacturing Company North Attleboro, Mass.; Newark, N.J.; Bridgeport, Conn.; Providence, R.I.	1866–present	Silver	WHITING MFG CO NEW YORK
Ed Wiener Provincetown, Mass., New York City	(1918–1991)	Silver	ED.WIENER
James H. Winn Chicago	(1866–c.1940)	Jewelry (Chicago Arts & Crafts Society)	~WINN~
Harry Winston New York City; Geneva; Paris; Beverly Hills, Calif.; Tokyo	(1896–1978) 1932–present	Jewelry, diamonds	H W
Samuel Yellin Philadelphia	(1885–1940)	Ironwork	SAMUEL YELLIN
David Yurman New York City	(1942–present) 1980–present	Jewelry	925 ©D.Y.
Marie Zimmermann New York City	(1879–1972)	Metalwork, jewelry	MAKER MARIE ZIMMERMANN

BIBLIOGRAPHY

Information for *Kovels' American Collectibles* came from many sources, including books and the Internet. This is a list of the books we think are useful for readers who want to know more about a subject. Some of the books can be found in bookstores. Others that are older and out of print are available in libraries or from antiquarian book sources.

GENERAL

Adams, Henry. *Viktor Schreckengost and 20th-Century Design*. Cleveland, OH: The Cleveland Museum of Art, 2000.

Albrecht, Donald, Robert Schonfeld, and Lindsay Stamm Shapiro. *Russel Wright: Creating American Lifestyle*. New York: Harry N. Abrams, 2001.

Barré-Despond, Arlette, ed. *Dictionnaire International des Arts Appliqués et du Design*. Paris: Éditions du Regard, 1996.

Brandstätter, Christian. *Wiener Werkstätte, Design in Vienna, 1903–1932*. New York: Harry N. Abrams, 2004.

Byars, Mel. *Design Encyclopedia*. New York: Museum of Modern Art/ London: Laurence King Publishing, 2004.

Collins, Michael, and Andreas Papadakis. *Post-Modern Design*. New York: Rizzoli, 1989.

de Noblet, Jocelyn, ed. *Industrial Design: Reflection of a Century*. Paris: Flammarion, 1993.

Design since 1945. Philadelphia: Philadelphia Museum of Art, 1983.

Duncan, Alistair. *American Art Deco*. New York: Harry N. Abrams, 1986.

_____. *The Encyclopedia of Art Deco: An Illustrated Guide to a Decorative Style from 1920 to 1939*. New York: E.P. Dutton, 1988.

Eidelberg, Martin, ed. *Design, 1935–1965: What Modern Was*. New York: Le Musée des Arts Décoratifs de Montréal, in association with Harry N. Abrams, 1991.

Fahr-Becker, Gabriele. *Art Nouveau*. Köln, Germany: Könemann, 1997.

Fiell, Charlotte, and Peter Fiell. *Industrial Design A–Z*. Köln, Germany: Taschen, 2003.

Fusco, Tony. *Collecting Art Deco*. New York: House of Collectibles, 2004.

Garner, Philippe, ed. *Encyclopedia of Decorative Arts, 1890–1940*. New York: Van Nostrand Reinhold, 1978.

Heide, Robert, and John Gilman. *Popular Art Deco: Depression Era Style and Design*. New York: Abbeville Press, 1991.

Hiesinger, Kathryn B., and George H. Marcus. *Landmarks of Twentieth-Century Design: An Illustrated Handbook*. New York: Abbeville Press, 1993.

Johnson, J. Stewart. *American Modern, 1925–1940: Design for a New Age*. New York: Harry N. Abrams, 2000.

Koch, Robert. *Louis C. Tiffany's Glass-Bronzes-Lamps: A Complete Collector's Guide*. New York: Crown, 1971.

Kovel, Ralph, and Terry Kovel. *Kovels' Antiques & Collectibles Price List*. New York: Random House. Published annually.

Savage, George, and Harold Newman. *An Illustrated Dictionary of Ceramics*. New York: Thames & Hudson, 1985.

Wilson, Richard Guy, Dianne H. Pilgrim, and Dickran Tasshjian. *The Machine Age*. New York: The Brooklyn Museum, in association with Harry N. Abrams, 1986.

CHAPTER 1: AMERICAN POTTERY AND PORCELAIN

American Studio Ceramics, 1920–1950. Revised ed. Minneapolis: University Art Museum, University of Minnesota, 1988.

Anderson, Ross, and Barbara Perry. *The Diversions of Keramos: American Clay Sculpture, 1925–1950*. Syracuse, NY: Everson Museum of Art, 1983.

Birks, Tony. *Lucie Rie*. Radnor, PA: Chilton Trade Book, 1987.

Chipman, Jack. *Collector's Encyclopedia of California Pottery.* 2nd ed. Paducah, KY: Collector Books, 1999.

Clark, Garth. *American Ceramics, 1876 to the Present.* Revised ed. New York: Abbeville Press, 1987.

_____. *A Century of Ceramics in the United States, 1876 to the Present.* New York: Abbeville Press, 1979.

Evans, Paul. *Art Pottery of the United States: An Encyclopedia of Producers and Their Marks.* New York: Feingold & Lewis Publishing Corp., 1987.

James, A. Everette. *North Carolina Art Pottery, 1900–1960: Identification & Value Guide.* Paducah, KY: Collector Books, 2003.

Kovel, Ralph, and Terry Kovel. *Kovels' American Art Pottery.* New York: Crown, 1993.

_____. *Kovels' New Dictionary of Marks: Pottery & Porcelain, 1850 to the Present.* New York: Crown, 1986.

Lehner, Lois. *Lehner's Encyclopedia of U.S. Marks on Pottery, Porcelain & Clay.* Paducah, KY: Collector Books, 1988.

McCready, Karen. *Art Deco and Modernist Ceramics.* London: Thames and Hudson Ltd., 1995.

Nelson, Marion John. *Art Pottery of the Midwest.* 2nd ed. Minneapolis: University of Minnesota Press, 1988.

Paul, Larry R. *Made in the 20th Century: A Guide to Contemporary Collectibles.* Lanham, MD: Scarecrow Press, 2005.

Perry, Barbara, ed. *American Ceramics: The Collection of Everson Museum of Art.* Syracuse & New York: Everson Museum of Art, in association with Rizzoli, 1989.

Perry, Barbara Stone, ed. *North Carolina Pottery: The Collection of the Mint Museums.* Charlotte, NC: The Mint Museums, in association with The University of North Carolina Press, 2004.

Rago, David, and Bruce Johnson. *Official Price Guide to American Arts and Crafts.* New York: Random House Reference, 2003.

Rago, David, and John Sollo. *Collecting Modern: A Guide to Midcentury Studio Furniture and Ceramics.* Salt Lake City, UT: Gibbs-Smith, 2001.

Random House Collector's Encyclopedia: Victoriana to Art Deco. New York: Random House, 1974.

Reed, Cleota, and Stan Skoczen. *Syracuse China.* Syracuse, NY: Syracuse University Press, 1997.

Rickards, Maurice. *Encyclopedia of Ephemera: A Guide to the Fragmentary Documents of Everyday Life for the Collector, Curator, and Historian.* New York: Routledge, 2000.

Stern, Bill. *California Pottery: From Missions to Modernism.* San Francisco: Chronicle Books, 2001.

Trapp, Kenneth R. *The Arts and Crafts Movement in California: Living the Good Life.* New York: Abbeville Press, 1993.

CHAPTER 2: TABLEWARE

Cunningham, Jo. *The Best of Collectible Dinnerware.* Revised 2nd ed. Atglen, PA: Schiffer, 1999.

Duke, Harvey. *The Official Price Guide to Pottery and Porcelain.* 8th ed. New York: House of Collectibles, 1995.

Eidelberg, Martin. *Eva Zeisel: Designer for Industry.* Montreal, Canada: Le Château Dufresne, Musée des Arts Décoratifs de Montréal, 1984.

Kerr, Ann. *Collector's Encyclopedia of Russel Wright Designs.* Paducah, KY: Collector Books, 2002.

Rosson, Joe L. *Official Price Guide to Pottery and Porcelain.* 9th ed. New York: House of Collectibles, 2005.

Venable, Charles, Ellen P. Denker, Katherine C. Greier, and Stephen G. Harrison. *China and Glass in America, 1880–1980.* Dallas, TX: Dallas Museum of Art, in association with Harry N. Abrams, 2000.

CHAPTER 3: TILE

Karlson, Norman. *American Art Tile, 1876–1941.* New York: Rizzoli International Publications, 1998.

———. *The Encyclopedia of American Art Tiles.* 4 vols. Atglen, PA: Schiffer, 2005.

Taylor, Joseph A., ed. *California Tile: The Golden Era, 1910–1940, Acme to Handcraft.* 2 vols. Atglen, PA: Schiffer, 2003.

CHAPTER 4: BRITISH ART POTTERY

Bergesen, Victoria. *Encyclopaedia of British Art Pottery, 1870–1920.* London: Barrie & Jenkins Ltd., 1991.

Cunningham, Helen C. *Clarice Cliff and Her Contemporaries: Susie Cooper, Keith Murray, Charlotte Rhead, and the Carlton Ware Designers.* Atglen, PA: Schiffer, 1999.

Eyles, Desmond. *The Doulton Burslem Wares.* London: Barrie & Jenkins Ltd., 1980.

_____. *Royal Doulton, 1815–1965: The Rise and Expansion of the Royal Potteries.* London: Hutchinson & Co. Ltd., 1965.

Godden, Geoffrey A. *The Concise Guide to British Pottery and Porcelain.* London: Barrie & Jenkins Ltd., 1990.

_____. *Encyclopaedia of British Porcelain Manufacturers.* London: Barry & Jenkins Ltd., 1988.

_____. *Encyclopaedia of British Pottery and Porcelain Marks.* New York: Bonanza Books, 1964.

Hayward, Leslie. *Poole Pottery: Carter & Company and Their Successors, 1873–1998.* Somerset, England: Richard Dennis, 1998.

Welsh, JoAnne P. *Chintz Ceramics.* Revised & expanded 3rd ed. Atglen, PA: Schiffer, 2000.

CHAPTER 5: POTTERY AND PORCELAIN FROM EUROPE AND JAPAN

Eliëns, Titus M., Marjan Groot, A. Krekel-Aalberse, Frans Leidelmeijer, Timo de Rijk, and M. Singelenberg-van der Meer. *Dutch Decorative Arts, 1880–1940.* Kingston, NY: Batteldore Ltd., 1997.

Fiell, Charlotte, and Peter Fiell. *Scandinavian Design.* Köln, Germany: Taschen, 2002.

Forsythe, Ruth A. *Made in Czechoslovakia.* Book 2. Marietta, OH: Antique Publications, 1993.

Mauriès, Patrick. *Fornasetti: Designer of Dreams.* Boston: Bulfinch Press, 1991.

McCalsin, Mary J. *Royal Bayreuth: Collector's Guide.* Book 2. Marietta, OH: The Glass Press, 2000.

Röntgen, Robert E. *Marks on German, Bohemian, and Austrian Porcelain, 1710 to the Present.* Atglen, PA: Schiffer, 1997.

Vingedal, S. E. *Porslinsmärken: En bok om porslins-, fajans- och andra keramikmärken.* Stockholm, Sweden: Forum, 1977.

Zühlsdorff, Dieter. *Keramik-Marken Lexikon: Porzellan und Keramik Report, 1885–1935, Europa (Festland).* Stuttgart, Germany: Arnoldsche, 1994.

CHAPTER 6: GLASS

Edwards, Bill, and Mike Carwile. *Standard Encyclopedia of Carnival Glass.* 10th ed. Paducah, KY: Collector Books, 2006.

Florence, Gene. *Anchor Hocking's Fire-King & More: Identification & Value Guide.* 3rd ed. Paducah, KY: Collector Books, 2006.

_____. *Collectible Glassware for the 40s, 50s, 60s.* 8th ed. Paducah, KY: Collector Books, 2005.

Florence, Gene, and Cathy Florence. *Collector's Encyclopedia of Depression Glass.* 17th ed. Paducah, KY: Collector Books, 2005.

_____. *Elegant Glassware of the Depression Era: Identification & Value Guide.* 11th ed. Paducah, KY: Collector Books, 2005.

_____. *Hazel-Atlas Glass: Identification & Value Guide.* Paducah, KY: Collector Books, 2004.

Frantz, Susanne K. *Contemporary Glass: A World Survey from the Corning Museum of Glass.* New York: Harry N. Abrams, 1989.

Grover, Ray, and Lee Grover. *Contemporary Art Glass.* New York: Crown, 1975.

Hartmann, Carolus. *Glasmarken Lexikon, 1600–1945: Signaturen, Fabrik- und Handelsmarken, Europa und Nordamerika.* Stuttgart, Germany: Arnoldsche, 1997.

Jackson, Lesley. *20th Century Factory Glass.* New York: Octopus Publishing Group, 2000.

Revi, Albert Christian. *American Art Nouveau Glass.* Camden, NJ: Thomas Nelson & Sons, 1968.

Truitt, Robert, and Deborah Truitt. *Collectible Bohemian Glass, 1880–1940.* Kensington, MD: B&D Glass, 1995.

_____. *Collectible Bohemian Glass, 1915–1945.* Kensington, MD: B&D Glass, 1998.

Welker, John, and Elizabeth Welker. *Pressed Glass in America: Encyclopedia of the First Hundred Years, 1825–1925.* Ivyland, PA: Antique Acres Press, 1985.

CHAPTER 7: FURNITURE

Clark, Michael, E., and Jill Thomas-Clark. *The Stickley Brothers: The Quest for an American Voice.* Salt Lake City, UT: Gibbs Smith, 2002.

Collins, Philip. *Pastime: Telling Time from 1879 to 1969.* San Francisco: Chronicle Books, 1993.

Deneberg, Thomas Andrew. *Wallace Nutting and the Invention of Old America.* New Haven, CT, & London: Wadsworth Atheneum Museum of Art, in association with Yale University Press, 2003.

Edwards, Robert L. *Arts & Crafts Furniture of Charles P. Limbert*. Watkins Glen, NY: American Life Foundation, 1982.

Emmerling, Mary Ellisor. *American Country: A Style and Source Book*. New York: Clarkson N. Potter, a division of Crown Publishers, 1980.

Fiell, Charlotte, and Peter Fiell. *1000 Chairs*. Köln, Germany: Taschen, 1997.

Finegan, W. Robert. *California Furniture: The Craft and the Artistry*. Chatsworth, CA: Western Furnishings Manufacturers Association and the Association of Western Furniture Suppliers, in cooperation with Windsor Publications, 1990.

Gray, Stephen. *Gustav Stickley after 1909*. New York: Turn of the Century Editions, 1990.

Hamilton, Charles F. *Roycroft Collectibles*. Tavares, FL: SPS Publications, 1992.

Jenkins, Emyl. *Emyl Jenkins' Reproduction Furniture: Antiques for the Next Generation*. New York: Crown Publishers, 1995.

Kaplan, Wendy, ed. *Designing Modernity: The Arts of Reform and Persuasion, 1885–1945, Selections from the Wolfsonian*. New York: Thames and Hudson, 1995.

Limbert, Charles P., and Company. *Limbert Arts and Crafts Furniture: The Complete 1903 Catalog*. New York: Dover Publications, 1992.

Miller, R. Craig. *Modern Design in the Metropolitan Museum of Art, 1890–1990*. New York: The Metropolitan Museum of Art and Harry N. Abrams, 1990.

Oda, Noritsugu. *Danish Chairs*. San Francisco: Chronicle Books, 1996.

Rouland, Steve, and Roger Rouland. *Heywood-Wakefield Modern Furniture*. Paducah, KY: Collector Books, 1995.

Shenton, Alan, and Rita Shenton. *The Price Guide to Collectible Clocks, 1840–1940*. Woodbridge, Suffolk, England: Antique Collector's Club, 1985.

Smith, Bruce. *Greene & Greene Masterworks*. San Francisco: Chronicle Books, 1998.

Sprigg, June. *Shaker Design*. New York: Whitney Museum of American Art, in association with W. W. Norton & Company, 1986.

Winchell, Terry. *Molesworth: The Pioneer of Western Design*. Salt Lake City, UT: Gibbs Smith, 2005.

CHAPTER 8: LAMPS AND LIGHTING

Feldstein, William, Jr., and Alastair Duncan. *The Lamps of Tiffany Studios.* New York: Harry N. Abrams, 1983.

Fiell, Charlotte, and Peter Fiell, eds. *1000 Lights, 1879 to 1959.* Cologne, Germany: Taschen, 2005.

_____. *1000 Lights, 1960 to Present.* Cologne, Germany: Taschen, 2005.

Hibel, Carole Goldman, John Hibel, and John Fontaine. *The Handel Lamps Book.* Pittsfield, MA: Fontaine Publishers, 1999.

May, Martin M. *Great Art Glass Lamps: Tiffany, Duffner & Kimberly, Pairpoint, and Handel.* Atglen, PA: Schiffer, 2003.

Neustadt, Egon. *The Lamps of Tiffany.* New York: Fairfield Press, 1970.

Uecker, Wolf. *Art Nouveau and Art Deco Lamps and Candlesticks.* New York: Abbeville Press, 1978.

CHAPTER 9: SILVER AND OTHER METALS

Carpenter, Charles H., Jr. *Gorham Silver, 1831–1981.* New York: Dodd, Mead & Company, 1982.

Darling, Sharon S. *Chicago Metalsmiths.* Chicago: Chicago Historical Society, 1977.

Drucker, Janet. *Georg Jensen: A Tradition of Splendid Silver.* Expanded & revised 2nd ed. Atglen, PA: Schiffer, 2001.

Loring, John. *Magnificent Tiffany Silver.* New York: Harry N. Abrams, 2001.

Rainwater, Dorothy T., and Judy Redfield. *Encyclopedia of American Silver Manufacturers.* Revised 4th ed. Atglen, PA: Schiffer, 1998.

Stern, Jewel. *Modernism in American Silver: 20th Century Design.* Dallas, TX: Dallas Museum of Art/New Haven, CT: Yale University Press, 2005.

CHAPTER 10: JEWELRY

Cirillo, Dexter. *Southwestern Indian Jewelry.* New York: Abbeville Press, 1992.

Davidov, Corinne, and Ginny Redington Dawes. *The Bakelite Jewelry Book.* New York: Abbeville Press, 1988.

Goddard, Phyllis M. *Spratling Silver, A Field Guide: Recognizing a William Spratling Treasure.* Altadena, CA: Keenan Tyler Paine, 2003.

Greenbaum, Toni, essay and catalog, and Martin Eidelberg, ed. *Messengers of Modernism: American Studio Jewelry, 1940–1960.* Paris: Montreal Museum of Decorative Arts, in association with Flammarion, 1996.

Meilach, Dona Z. *Art Jewelry Today.* Atglen, PA: Schiffer, 2002.

Miller, Judith. *Costume Jewelry (DK Collector's Guides).* New York: DK Publishing, 2003.

Modernist Jewelry of Claire Falkenstein. Long Beach, CA: Long Beach Museum of Art, 2004.

Romero, Christie. *Warman's Jewelry Identification and Price Guide.* 3rd ed. Iola, WI: Krause, 2002.

Wasserstrom, Donna, and Leslie Piña. *Bakelite Jewelry: Good, Better, Best.* Atglen, PA: Schiffer, 1997.

CHAPTER 11: TOYS AND DOLLS

Coleman, Dorothy S., Elizabeth A. Coleman, and Evelyn J. Coleman. *The Collector's Encyclopedia of Dolls.* Vol. 2. New York: Crown Publishers, 1986.

Herlocher, Dawn. *200 Years of Dolls: Identification & Price Guide.* 2nd ed. Iola, WI: Krause, 2002.

Hoffman, David. *Kid Stuff: Great Toys from Our Childhood.* San Francisco: Chronicle Books, 1996.

Izen, Judith. *Collector's Guide to Ideal Dolls: Identification & Value Guide.* 2nd ed. Paducah, KY: Collector Books, 1999.

Jacobs, Flora Gill. *Dolls' Houses in America: Historic Preservation in Miniature.* New York: Charles Scribner's Sons, 1974.

Kennedy, Paul, ed. *Warman's Barbie Doll Field Guide: Values & Identification.* Iola, WI: Krause, 2003.

Long, Patricia. *The Barbie Closet: Price Guide for Barbie & Friends Fashions and Accessories, 1959–1970.* Iola, WI: Krause, 2000.

O'Brien, Karen, ed. *O'Brien's Collecting Toys: Collector's Identification and Value Guide.* 11th ed. Iola, WI: Krause, 2004.

Rich, Mark. *Toys A to Z: A Guide and Dictionary for Collectors, Antique Dealers, and Enthusiasts.* Iola, WI: Krause, 2001.

Richardson, Mike, and Sue Richardson. *Christie's World of Automotive Toys.* Osceola, WI: MBI Publishing Company, 1998.

Santelmo, Vincent. *Complete Encyclopedia to GI Joe.* 3rd ed. Iola, WI: Krause, 2001.

Stephan, Elizabeth, ed. *O'Brien's Collecting Toy Cars & Trucks: Identification & Value Guide.* 3rd ed. Iola, WI: Krause, 2000.

Walsh, Tim. *Timeless Toys: Classic Toys and the Playmakers Who Created Them.* Kansas City, MO: Andrews McMeel Publishing, 2004.

Zillner, Dian, and Patty Cooper. *Antique & Collectible Dollhouses and Their Furnishings.* Atglen, PA: Schiffer, 1998.

CHAPTER 12: PRINTS, PHOTOS, AND PAPER EPHEMERA

Guptill, Arthur L. *Norman Rockwell Illustrator.* New York: Watson-Guptill Publications, 1975.

Holland, William R., Clifford P. Catania, and Nathan D. Isen. *Louis Icart: The Complete Etchings.* Revised 3rd ed. Atglen, PA: Schiffer, 1998.

Ivankovich, Michael. *Collector's Value Guide to Early Twentieth Century American Prints.* Paducah, KY: Collector Books, 1998.

Mulligan, Therese, and David Wooters, eds. *A History of Photography, from 1839 to the Present.* Köln, Germany: Taschen, 2005.

CHAPTER 13: ADVERTISING AND PACKAGING

Kovel, Ralph, and Terry Kovel. *Kovels' Advertising Collectibles Price List.* New York: Random House Reference, 2005.

_____. *The Label Made Me Buy It: From Aunt Jemima to Zonkers—The Best-Dressed Boxes, Bottles, and Cans from the Past.* New York: Crown Publishers, 1998.

CHAPTER 14: KITCHENWARE

Celehar, Jane H. *Kitchens and Gadgets, 1920 to 1950.* Des Moines, IA: Wallace-Homestead Book Company, 1982.

Franklin, Linda Campbell. *300 Years of Kitchen Collectibles.* 5th ed. Iola, WI: Krause, 2003.

Mauzy, Barbara. *Pyrex: The Unauthorized Collector's Guide.* Atglen, PA: Schiffer, 2004.

Photo Credits

About Mimi's Gems
P.O. Box 458
Methuen, MA 01844

Antique Bear Shop
Susan Edwards
www.antiquebearshop.com

Antiques At Time Was
P.O. Box 3330
Ashland, OR 97520

April's Attic
www.cyberattic.com/AprilsAttic

Atlanta Antique Gallery
3550 Broad Street, Suite A
Chamblee, GA 30341

Bertoia Auctions
2141 DeMarco Drive
Vineland, NJ 08360

Brunk Auctions
P.O. Box 2135
Asheville, NC 28802

Cincinnati Art Galleries
225 East 6th Street
Cincinnati, OH 45202

Collectors Auction Services
RR2 Box 431 Oakwood Road
Historic Oil City, PA 16301
(out of business)

Collectors of Crackle Glass
101 Cypress Street
Massapequa Park, NY 11762

Cottone Auctions
15 Genesee Street
Mt. Morris, NY 14510

Craftsman Auctions
333 N. Main Street
Lambertville, NJ 08530

Deco Days
www.deco-days.com

Deco Dog's Ephemera
Jan's Early Attic
P.O. Box 33
Bloomfield, NY 14443

Dmitry Levit Asian Art
127 Paradise Road
Swampscott, MA 01907

Doyle New York
175 East 87th Street
New York, NY 10128

Droog Design
Staalstraat 7a
1011 JJ Amsterdam
The Netherlands

Erie Art Museum
411 State Street
Erie, PA 16501

Fantasy Jewels
P.O. Box 5697
Baltimore, MD 21210

Fighting Bear Antiques
375 South Cache
Jackson, WY 83001

Fontaine's Auction Gallery
1485 West Housatonic Street
Pittsfield, MA 01201

Garth's Auction, Inc.
P.O. Box 369
2690 Stratford Road
Delaware, OH 43015

Glasshound
www.glasshound.com

Green Valley Auctions
Rt. 2, Box 434-A
Mt. Crawford, VA 22841

Hake's Americana & Collectibles
1966 Greenspring Drive
Suite 400
Timonium, MD 21093

Henry/Peirce Auctioneers
1456 Carson Court
Homewood, IL 60430

Heritage Galleries
3500 Maple Avenue
Dallas, TX 75219

Hi+Lo Modern
www.hiandlomodern.com

Jackson's Auctioneers & Appraisers
2229 Lincoln Street
Cedar Falls, IA 50613

James D. Julia, Inc.
203 Skowhegan Road
Fairfield, ME 04937

Jitterbug Jewelry
1056 Green Acres Road, Suite 102
Eugene, OR 97401

Joy Luke Auction Gallery
300 East Grove Street
Bloomington, IL 61701

Limited Edition Collectibles
6240-M Glen Valley Terrace
Frederick, MD 21701

Los Angeles Modern Auctions
  (LAMA)
P.O. Box 462006
Los Angeles, CA 90046

Mark's Treasure Chest
1060 Phillip Street
Baden, PA 15005
www.trocadero.com/tasmark

McMasters Harris Auction
  Company
5855 John Glenn Hwy.
P.O. Box 1755
Cambridge, OH 43725

Michael Ivankovich Antiques &
  Auction Co., Inc.
P.O. Box 1536
Doylestown, PA 18901

Mike Schultz
Reverse Time Page
www.uv201.com

Morphy Auctions
2000 North Reading Rd.
Denver, PA 17517

Myers Fine Art & Antiques
  Auction Gallery
1600 4th Street North
St. Petersburg, FL 33704

Neal Auction Company
4038 Magazine Street
New Orleans, LA 70115

Noel Barrett Antiques
P.O. Box 300
Carversville Road
Carversville, PA 18923

One of a Kind Antiques
36D Plains Road
Essex, CT 06426

Perrault Rago Gallery
333 North Main Street
Lambertville, NJ 08530

Phillips, de Pury & Co.
450 West 15th Street
New York, NY 10011

Rago Arts and Auction Center
333 North Main Street
Lambertville, NJ 08530

Randy Inman Auctions, Inc.
P.O. Box 726
Waterville, ME 04903

Replacements, Ltd.
1089 Knox Road
P.O. Box 26029
Greensboro, NC 27420

Robert C. Eldred Co., Inc.
1483 Route 6A
East Dennis, MA 02641

Ruby Lane
www.rubylane.com

Samuel T. Freeman & Co.
1808 Chestnut Street
Philadelphia, PA 19103

Shapiro Auctioneers
162 Queen Street
Woollahra NSW 2025
Australia

Skinner, Inc.
357 Main Street
Bolton, MA 01740

Sloans & Kenyon
7034 Wisconsin Avenue
Chevy Chase, MD 20815

Sotheby's Auctions
1334 York Avenue (at 72nd Street)
New York, NY 10021

Toy Car Collector
www.toycarcollector.com

Treadway Gallery, Inc.
2029 Madison Road
Cincinnati, OH 45208

Village Doll & Toy
P.O. Box 705
Adamstown, PA 19501

Waddington's
111 Bathurst Street
Toronto, Ontario M5V 2R5
Canada

Waiapo Webstore
Wailuku, HI 96793
www.waiapo.com

Williemouse
Fresno, CA 93704
www.cyberattic.com/stores/
    williemouse

Woody Auction
P.O. Box 618
Douglass, KS 67039

Wright
1140 West Fulton
Chicago, IL 60607

Yester-Years Boutique
2675 E FM 696
Lexington, TX 78947

Zanotta Spa
Via Vittorio Veneto 57
Milan 20054
Italy

Index

Chase Brass & Copper, 288, *288*, 291

Chase, Waldo, 383

Chaumet et Cie, *422*

Chein, J., & Company, 324, *367*

Chelsea Keramic Art Tile Works, 3, 99

Cheney Building, 285

Cheri-Glo, 184

Chicago Institute of Design, 199

Chicago Stock Exchange, 285

Chihuly, Dale, *202*, 203

Child, Julia, 68

Chinese Teal, 119

Chintz, 83, *85* 116, 117, *117*, 118, 128, *180*

Chip 'n' dip set, x, 67, 68

Chipped ice, 156; Handel, 256

Chippendale, xvii

Christiansen, Ole, 338

Christmas, 66, *66*; Christmas plates, 108

Christofle, *272*, *422*

Christy, Howard Chandler, 392

Chrome, xix, 219, 221, 244

Chromolithography, 377

Cincinnati Art Pottery Company, 2–3

Cinderella sets, 415

Ciner, 306, *430*

Cintra, 157

Citroen, *367*

CKO mark, *323*

Clapsaddle, Ellen, 392

Classique, *259*

Clay Glow Tile Company, 95

Claycraft Potteries, *101*

Clement Massier Pottery, 25

Cleminson Clay, *48*

Cleveland Institute of Art, 71

Cleveland School artists, 126

Clewell Pottery, *16*

Clewell, Charles, *430*

Cliff, Clarice, 83, *85*, 117, *118*, *122*

Clifton Art Pottery, *16*

Cliftwood Art Potteries, *16*

Clip, 298, 299, 306, 320

Clock cases, chrome, brass, copper, Bakelite, Formica, celluloid, glass, 249

Clocks, 248–251; animated alarm, 249; art deco, 251; battery-operated, 249; Big Ben alarm, 252; Bulle, 249; digital, *251*; eight-day windup, 249; electric, 251; figural, 251; mystery, 248; Nelson, *250;* neon, *251*; radio, 252; Sabino, 251; Tambour, 248; windup, 249

Clues to Dating American Dinnerware, 82

Cluthra, 157

Coalport, 114

Coat rack, *247*

Cobbler's bench, xvii

Co-Boys, 131

Coca-Cola, 398, 404, 405–407; coolers, 398; reproductions, 407; slogan, 405; trademarks, 405; tray, *405*

Cocktail, bars, 218; party, ix, 66, 67; shakers, ix, 66

Cocteau, Jean, 304

Coin Dot, 172

Cole Pottery, 40

Cole, Fern, 294

Collier's, 381

Collingwood & Company, *424*

Colombo, Joe, 247

Colonel Sanders, 404, *404*

Colonial Furniture of New England, 234

Colonial Revival and Other Revivals, 234–237

Colonial Revival style, 206, 270

Colonial Williamsburg, xvii, 83

Colonna, Edward, *422*

Commercial wares, 1, 3

Compagnie des Cristalleries de Saint-Louis, *167*

Compiègne, Cristalleries de, *158*, *166*

Compote, 70, *204*

Comyns, William & Sons, *424*

Conant Ball Company, *219*, 222

Confusing Cameo, *158*

Console, 70, *204*

Consolidated Lamp and Glass Company, 178, *179*

Continental Can Company, *175*

Cook 'n Stir, Ronson, 414

Cook Pottery Company, 57, *63*

Cookbooks, *389*

Cooke, Betty, 310, *430*

Cookie jars, xviii, 55

Cooper Union, 27

Cooper, J. Paul, *424*

Cooper, Susie, 83, 118, *118*, *122*

Co-Operative Flint Glass Company, *175*

Copeland, Elizabeth, 292

Copier, Andries Dirk, *191*

Copper Craftsmen, 285–287

Copper, 281, 413

Coralene beading, 151

Corbett, Bertha, 392

Cordey China Company, 58

Coreano bowl, 188

Corelle, 415

Corgi, *367*

Corn King, 80; Corn Queen, 80

Corn Popper, 340

Cornelison Pottery, 37

Cornelison, Webster, 37

Corning Glass Works, 158, *168*, *169*, 200, 415

Corn-on-the-cob sets, 66, 68

Coro, 306, 312, *430*

Corporate symbols, 401

Cosmo Manufacturing, 330, *367*

Costume jewelry, 298, 304–311

Coty, 161

Country of origin, 148

Coupe soup, 70

Cowan, 3, 13–14, *13*, *16*, 27, 71, 126, 276, 292

Cox, Paul, 9, *34*

Coxon, Jonathan, 60

Cracker Jack, 396, 401

Craftsman Workshops, 208, 253, *287*, 296, *430*

Doll Makers, American, *358*

Dollhouse, 363–365, *363*, 364; Bliss, *365*; furniture, 363–364

Dolls, American Girl, 357, *358*; American Presidents, 353; Aunt Jemima, *402*; Baby Brother Tender Love, 345; Ballet, 354; Barbie, 345–346; Beloved Belindy, 353; Betsy Wetsy, 348; Bye-Lo Baby, 345, 346–347; Cabbage Patch Kids, 357; Camel with the Wrinkled Knees, 353; Campbell Kids, 347; Celebrity, 347–348; Christie, 345; Cissette, 352; Cissy, 352; Crissy, 348; cloth, 398, 352; crying, 348; Dionne Quintuplet, 347, 352, *352*; Francie, 345; French Province, 353–354; Ginny, 356, *356*; Googly-eyed, *147*; Hush a Bye Baby, 354; Just Me, 356; Kelly, 345; Ken, 345; Krissy, 345; Lenci, 351, *350*; Madame Alexander, 346, 351–252, *352*; Magic Skin Baby, 348; Mary Hartline, 348, *348*; Midge, 345; Nancy Ann Style Show, 354; P.J., 345; Patti Play Pal, 348; Poor Pitiful Pearl, 345, *345*; Raggedy Ann and Andy, 353, *353;* Real People, 354; Saralee, 348; Scarlett O'Hara, 352; Shirley Temple, *347,* 347, 348; Skipper, 345; sleepy-eye, 348; Sprites, Pixies and Fairies, 354; Stacie, 345; Steffie, 345; Storybook, 354; Strawberry Shortcake, 357, *357*; Tickle Me Elmo, 343; Toni, 348; Tutti, 345

Domex Floor & Wall Tile Company, 99

Donruss, 396

Doranne of California, *48*

Dorfan Company, 335, *368*

Double Fabric Tire Corporation, 326

Doulton and Company, 2, 105, 106–107, *106*, 122

Dow, Arthur Wesley, 383

Dowst Brothers Company, 330, 364, *368*; Dowst Manufacturing Company, *368*

Drerup, Karl, *293*, 294

Dresser, Christopher, *425*

Dreyfuss, Henry, xx, 252

Drip-o-later, 70

Droog Design, 234, *235*, 264

Duchess of Windsor's charm bracelet, 299

Duffner & Kimberly, *259*

Dugan Glass Company, *170, 173*

Dumler & Breiden, 56

Dunbar Furniture, Inc., 222, *222*

Duncan and Miller Glass Company, 178–180, *178*

Duncan, David Douglas, 388

Duncan, George, 178; James, 180

Duplo, 338

Durand Art Glass Shop, *168*

Durand, Victor, *168*

Durant Kilns, *16*

Durgin, William B., Company, *430*

Dutch ovens, 414

Eagle mark, 314

Eames, Charles and Ray, 222, 223, 247; ESU storage unit, *223*; LCS plywood chair, *222*; LCW (Lounge Chair Wood), 223

Earthenware, 110, 143, 145

Ebeling & Reuss, 86, 128

Ebony, 177, 184, 217

Eckhardt, Edris, *34*, 197, *198*, 199, *199*, 294

École de Nancy, 159

Econolite Corporation, *263*

Economy Tumbler Company, 182

Edgerton Art Clay Works, *17*

Edgerton Pottery, *17*

Edmond Etling & Company, 260

Edward Miller & Company, 253, *259*

Edwin Bennett, *15*

Edwin M. Knowles China Company, 79

Eegee's, *358*

Effanbee, *358*

Egyptian, 126, 217

Eisenberg, 306, *309*, 312, *430*; Eisenberg Ice, 309; Eisenberg Original, 309, *309*

Eisenloeffel, Jan, *426*

Eisenstaedt, Alfred, 388

Ekenäs, *192*

Electrolux vacuum cleaner, 291

Electronic Games, 343–344; Atari 2600 computer system, *343*, 343; Donkey Kong, 343; Game Boy, 343; Intellivision, 343; Nintendo, 64, 343, 345; Odyssey, 343; Pac-Man, 343, *343*; Pong, 343; Sony PlayStation, 343; Super Mario Brothers, 343; Zork, 343

Elegant Hand-Pressed Glassware, 174, 177–184

Elijah Cotton, 117

Elkington & Co., *425*

Ellis, Harvey, 211

Elton Sunflower Pottery, *122*

Elvis Presley, 347

Emerald Green, 177

Emeralite Company, *265*

Emmerling, Mary, 240

Empire Floor & Wall Tile Company, 99, *103*

Enamel, 281, 291–294

Enameled metal, x, 199

Encyclopedia of Ephemera, 389

Energizer Bunny, 404

Enesco Corporation, 54, 128

Enfield Pottery and Tile Works, *102*

Englund, Eva, *192*

Enterprise (ESD), 54

Epsom Glass Industries, *165*

Erickson Glassworks, 197

Ernst Plank, *372*

Gallimore William Wood, 100
Gamble House, 212
Gambone, Bruno, 138, *138*; Guido, 138
Games, Candyland, 345; Clue, 345; Dungeons & Dragons, 345; electronic, 343–344; Monopoly, 345; Pictionary, 345; Rubik's Cube, 345; Scrabble, 345; The Game of Life, 345; Trivial Pursuit, 345; Twister, 345; Wiffle Ball, 345
Garden City Pottery, *49*
Gardiner, H. Marshall, 386; W. H., 386
Garella family, 351
Garrard, R. and S., *425*
Garton Toy Company, 336, *368*
Gas pump globes, 398
Gaspari, Luciano, *195*
Gates Pottery, 7
Gateway Hosiery, 404
GDA (Gerard, Dufraisseix, and Abbot), 129
Gearhart, Frances, 383
Gebelein Silversmiths, Inc., *277*
Gebelein, George, *430*
Gehry, Frank, 418
Geisha Girl, 147
Gem Clay Forming Company, 71, *71*
Gendron Wheel Company, 336, *368*
General Bakelite Company, 418
General Electric, 251, 381, 404, 410, 413
General Housewares Corporation, 55
General Mills, 335
General Motors, 410
Geometric designs, 116, 143
Georg Fischer, *368*
George Borgfeldt & Company, 86, 128, 346, *358*
George Carette, *367*
George Duncan and Sons, 180
Georgene Novelties Company, 353, *353*, *358*

Gerald, Dufraisseix, and Abbot, 129
German Pottery and Porcelain, 130–135
Gesetzlich Geschutzt (Ges. Gesch.), *89*
Gilbert, A. C., 337, 368
Ginori, Richard, 86, *86*, 137, *137*, 224
Gladding, McBean and Company, 41, 43, *49*, 74, *102*
Glasfabrik Johann Loetz-Witwe, 162, *164*
Glass, agate, 157; animals, 182; blown, 180, 182, 184; art, 155, 178, 182; Bohemian, 161; cire perdue, 156, 161; cut, 161, 174, 177, 180; dime-store, 174; engraved, 161; enameled, 156, 161, 188; elegant, 177, etched, 180, 188; flashed, 170; frosted, 156; fused, 200; gold, 199; hammered, 156; iridescent glass, 155, 156, 157, 162; kitchenware, 415–418; lime, 174; machine-made, 174; marbles, 177; millefiori, 157; Mosser, *185*; Muranese, 182; Murano, 194; novelties, 171; opalescent, 170–172; post-World War II, 1945–1969, 186; pressed, 177; Radiance, 182; Reuben, 178; Ruby, 184; satin, 170; soda, 174; stretch, 181; studio, 197–203; table-ware shape name, *204*; tank, 174
Glassmakers, Bohemian 161–162; Dutch, *190–193*; Scandinavian, *190–193*
Glazes, crackle, 149; crystalline, 37, 107; lavalike, 130, 138; luster, 100, 111, 113; rainbow, 148; transmutation, 107; USPA approved glaze, *89*; volcanic, 138
Glidden Pottery, 51, *51*

Gnomes, 131
Goblet, *204*
Godey's Lady's Book, 44
Goebel, 130, 131–132, *153*
Goetz, Otto, 128
Gold Lustre, 157
Goldberger Doll Manufacturing Company, Inc., *358*
Goldscheider (Germany), 130
Goldscheider of Austria, *125*
Goldsmiths' & Silversmiths' Co., *425*
Golf Ball glass pattern, 182
Goodspeed, Bernice, 314, *427*
Gorham Corporation, 267, 270, *271*, *272*, *430*, *431*; marks, 271
Gorham, Jabez, 270
Goss china, 106, *106*
Goss, William Henry, 106
Gouda pottery, *134*, 135–136
Goupy, Marcel, *166*
Graham, Bill, 391
Grain-painted cast iron, 244
Gramophone Company, 404
Grand Feu Pottery, *17*
Grand Rapids companies, 237
Graniteware, 414
Grape and Cable, 172
Grape scissors, 65
Graves, Jennie, 356
Graves, Michael, 230, 268, 418
Gravy boat, 70
Gray, A. E., & Company, 83, 118
Gray, Eileen, *217*
Gray, William E., Company, 257–258
Gray-Stan, *165*
Great American Tea Company, 77
Green Giant (Sprout), 347
Green Hornet, 360
Green, Nancy, 403
Greene & Greene, *213*
Greene, Charles, 212; Henry, 212
Greenwood Pottery Company, 57, *63*
Gregory, Waylande DeSantis, 27, *27*, *34*

Hislop, James White, 95
Hispano Moresque Tile Company, *102*
Hitchcock, 240
Hobbs, Brockunier & Company, 170, 171
Hobé, 306, 312, *431*
Hobnail, 172
Hochschild Kohn and Co., 331
Hocking Glass Company, *175*
Hoffmann, Josef, 120, *421*
Höglund, Erik, *186*
Hollywood Deco, 218
Holmegaard Glassworks, 147, 187, *187, 190*
Holt Howard, 53, *54,* 54–55, 128
Holt, Grant, 54
Homer Laughlin China Company, 25, *63,* 67, 71, 72, 77, *77,* 80; Fiesta Kitchen Craft line, 418
Honesdale Decorating Company, *169*
Hoosier Manufacturing Company, 410
Hopi, 313
Hopkins, Edna Boies, 385
Horner, Charles, 296, *425*
Horseshoe design mark, 238
Horsman, E.I., & Aetna Doll & Toy Company, *358*
Horsman, Ltd., *359*
House of Fabergé, *427*
Houston, James, 158
Hoving, Walter, 268
Howard, John and Robert, 54
Howard Pierce, *49*
Howell Company, 245
HS marks, *272, 277, 287*
Hubbard, Alice, 211; Elbert II, 211; Elbert, 210, 211, *211*
Hubley Manufacturing Company, *328,* 329–330, *369*
Hukin & Heath, *425*
Huldah, Cherry Jeffe, 131
Hull Pottery Company, *18,* 52, *52,* 54, 55

Hummel, Berta, 131
Hummel, fakes, 148; figurines, 56, 130, *130,* 131; marks, 131
Hummel, Goebel, *130*
Humphrey, Maud, 382
Humpty Dumpty Circus, 364
Hunt & Roskell, *425*
Hunt, Peter, 242, *242*
Hupmobile, 398
Hutschenreuther, 86, 130
Hyatt, John W., 347
Hyde, Helen, 385
Icart, Louis, 378–381, *379*
Ice lip, *204*
Icebox, 409
Ichihashi, Yuri, 304
Ideal Novelty and Toy Company, 340, *347,* 348, *359,* 360, 362, *362, 369*
IG mark, *173*
Iittala glassworks, 188, *188, 190*
Imperial Geddo, 57
Imperial Glass Company, *169, 173,* 178, 181, *181,* 197
Imperial Jewel, 181
INARCO (International Artware Corporation), 54; mark, *53*
Indian Arts and Crafts Boards, 312
Indian trade jewelry, 312
Indiana Glass Company, *175, 185*
Indiana Jones, 340
Industrial designer, xix, xx, xxi
Inky Racer, 405
International Artware Corporation, 54
International Exhibition of Modern Jewelry, 303
International Molded Products, 88
International Silver, 267, 291
International style, 214, 230
Internet, x, xxii, xxiii
IOGA mark, *61*
Iowa State Pottery, *18*
Irish Belleek, 60, 62
Ironstone, 66, *66,* 81
Ironwork, artistic, x, 281

Iroquois China Company, 79
Irving and Casson, 237
Islamic influence, 194
Italian Design, 418
Italian furniture designers, ix, 224
Italy, 128, 137–140
Ives Corporation, 332, 335, *369*
Ivrene, 158
Ivy ball, *204*
Jaccard Jewelry Company, *431*
Jackdaw of Rheims, 108
Jacobsen, Arne, *226,* 227
Jadite, *416*
Jaeger cement mixer, *326*
Jalan Pottery, *18*
James Dixon & Sons, *425*
James Kent, 117
James Macintyre and Company, 111
James, Richard, 341
Japan, 83, 86, 148, *153;* mark, made in, 148, 149, *347*
Japanese Pottery and Porcelain, 147–153
Japanese, ceramics, 2; marks on ceramics, 148; style, 270
Japonisme, 285, 385
Jarvie, Robert Riddle, *277,* 286, *287*
Jasperware, 119
Javanese batik-printed textiles, 136
Jeannette Glass Company, *175*
Jefferson Glass Company, 170, 171
Jefferson Lamp Company, *259*
Jeffery, Charles Bartley, 294
Jelly belly, 306
Jenkins Glass Company, *175*
Jensen, Georg, *279,* 280, 316, *316, 428*
Jensen, Georg, Inc. U.S.A. mark, 280
Jensen, Georg, Silversmiths, 147, 187, 279, 280
Jensen, Georg, store, 140, 227, 280
JEP mark, *369*

Lalique, glass, *160,* 161, *166,* 178, *184,* 251, 260; René, 161, *166,* 295, *423*

LaMar, 23

Lambeth ware, 107

Laminated wood, 227

Lamperti Design Studios, *263*

Lampl, Walter, 302, *432*

Lamps, Aladdin, 253, 258, *258, 265;* animated-action, 263; electric, 253, 256, 258; Emeralite, 253, 257–258; floor, 254; Greenalite, 258; halogen, 263, 264; Handel, 253, 254–255, 256, *256;* kerosene, 258; lava, 263; Lily, 254; Moss, 263; motion, 263; nude dancing-lady, 258; oil, 180, 254; pole, 260; Saturn, 260; Tiffany, xii, 254; TV, 263; whale-oil, 254

Lampshades, glass, 253

Lancaster Colony Corporation, 180

Lancaster Glass Company, *176*

Landberg, Nils, *192*

Lane Company, *237*

Lane, Kenneth, 306, *307,* 312, *432*

Lange, Dorothea, 388

Lanternier, 129

Larkin, John, 210; Soap Company, 151, *152,* 210

Larson, Lisa, *143*

LaSa, 23

Lasenby, Arthur, 280

Laughlin Brothers Pottery, 2, 77

Laughlin, Shakespeare, 77

Laurel Pottery, 80

Lawson Time, Inc., 251

Lazzell, Blanche, 385

Le Corbusier, *244*

Le Verre Français, *158*

Leach, Bernard, 106, 120, *120, 123*

Lead crystal, 187

Lead free, *89*

Lead Lustre, *180*

Leaded glass, lampshades and windows, 157

Lebolt & Company, *277*

LED (light-emitting diodes), 263, 264

Ledesma, Enrique, 314

Lee, D. H., Company, Inc., *359*

Lee, Thomas, 238

Leeds China Company, 55

Leerdam (N. V. Glasfabriek Leerdam), *191*

Lefton, George Zoltan, Company, 53, 54

Lego, blocks, 336, 338, *338;* Company, *370*

Legoland theme park, 338

Legras & Cie, *158, 167*

Lehmann, 324; Ernest, *370*

Lehr, 174

Leiber, Judith, 312, *432*

Leibovitz, Annie, 388

Leigh Potters, 71

Leighton, Clare, 119; Fred, *432*

Lenci pottery, 139, *139*

Lenox, Inc., 57, 60, *60, 63,* 72, 86, 88, 136, 181; Walter Scott, 60

Lesney Products, 332, *370, 371*

Lessell Art Ware Company, 23; John, 23, *23*

Levin, Ed, 310, *432*

Lewis, Edward Gardner, 13

Libbey Glass Company, *176,* 194

Liberty & Company, *165,* 280–281, *280,* 296, *426*

Liberty Works, *176*

Lichtenstein, Roy, 133, 391

Light-emitting diodes (LED), 263, 264

Lightolier, *265*

Limbert, Charles P., 212, *212*

Limelight, 181

Limited (Ltd.), *89*

Limited editions, 108, 133

Limoges china, 81, 129; China Company (American Limoges), 71

Limoges, France, *66,* 292

Lincoln, Abraham, 268

Lindner pottery, 56

Lindshammar Glasbruk, *192*

Lindstrand, Vicke, *187, 192*

Linemar, *339*

Lineol, *370*

Lines Brothers Ltd., *370*

Lionel Manufacturing Company, 335, *370*

Lipper & Mann, 54

Lithographs, 377

Little Red Riding Hood, 52

Little Women, 352

Littlefield, Edgar, *35*

Littleton, Harvey, 200, *201,* 203

Lloyd, Loom, 243; Manufacturing Company, 243

Lo Ball decal, 197

Lobel, Paul, 310, *432*

Lobmeyr, J. & L., 162, *164*

Loetz, *158,* 161, 162, *163,* 182

Loetz, Widow Johann, Glassworks, 162

Loewy, Raymond, xx, 188, 398

Longwy, 130

Lonhuda Pottery, 3

Lord Nelson, 117

Los Angeles Pressed Brick Company, *102*

Los Castillo, 281, 314, *314, 427*

Losanti, *2*

Lotus ware, 57

Louie Glass Company, *176*

Louis Amberg & Son, *358*

Louis Marx & Company, 324, 335, 340, *359,* 360, *370*

Low Art Tile Works, 3, 99

Luce, Jean, *167*

Lucite, 248, 306, *306, 400,* 419

Lucky Strike cigarette package, 398

Ludwig Moser & Söhne, *165*

Lukens, Glen, 28, *28,* 32, *35*

Lum, Bertha, 385

Lundgren, Tyra, *193*

Lundin, Ingeborg, *193*

Lunéville, *158*

Lunning, Frederik, 316

Ruskin Pottery, 113, *113, 123*
Russia, *153*
Rustic furniture, 238, 240
Ryto, 405
S.E.G. mark, *12*, 13
S.E.T. Co., *104*
Saarinen, Eero, *220*, 247; Eliel, 227, *272*
Sabino, Marius-Ernest, *167*, 260
Saf-Handle teapot, 77
Sahar, 181
Saint-Louis glass, *158*
Salem China Company, 71, *71, 80*
Salt and pepper shakers, xviii, 53, *411*
Salviati & C., *195*
Samson Import Company, 54
Samsonite, 222
San Jose Pottery, *103*
Sandoz, Edouard Marcel, 129, *129*; Gerard, *272, 423*
Sandwich servers, 70, *204*
Santa Catalina Island Company, 43
Santa Claus, 341, 398
Santa Monica Brick Company, *103*
Sarpaneva, Timo, *191*
Satsuma, *149*, 149–151
Saturday Evening Girls Club, 12, *12, 21*
Saturday Evening Post, 382
Sawyer, Charles, 386
Scandinavian Modern, 221, 228
Scandinavian, ceramics, 140–147; furniture, ix, 206, 226–228, 242; glassware, 186–189, 197; silver jewelry, 314–317; studio potters, 143
Scarpa, Tobia, *195*
Scavini, Enrico and Elena, 351
Scheier, Edwin and Mary Goldsmith, *30*, 31, *36*
Scheurich, Paul, 56, *132*
Schiaparelli, Elsa, 306, 312, *433*
Schlumberger, Jean, 302, *302, 433*

Schmitz, Ferdinand Hubert, *424*
Schneider, Charles, *158, 167*; Frères et Wolf, *167*; S.A. des Verreries, *167*
Schoenhut & Company, 364, *364, 372*
Schoop, Hedi, 44, *45*
Schreckengost, Don, 71, *71*, 72; Paul, 71, *71*; Viktor, xx, xxi, *36*, 71, *71, 72*, 126
Schuco, *372*
Scott, Herbert, 249
Scribner's Magazine, 381
Scripto Corporation, 44
Seagrove Pottery, 40
Seagull, 144
Seaman Schepps, 301, 304, *433*
Sears, Roebuck & Company, xxi, 72, 80, 81, 206, 219
Sebring Pottery, 71
Seguso Vetri d'Arte, *195*
Seguso, Archimede, *195*
Seibel, Ben, 72, 137
Selchow & Richter Company, *372*
Selro, 307, *433*
Seneca Glass Company, *176*
Serpaut et Tharaud, 129
Sèvres china, 130; Sèvres China Company, *64*
Sgraffito, 26, 31, 37, 105
Sgrafo pottery, 56
SH mark, *372*
Shafford Company, 54
Shaker furniture, 240–242, *241*
Sharkskin, 217
Shaw, Evan K., 78
Shawnee Pottery Company, 54, 55, *55, 80*, 80–81
Shawsheen Pottery, *21, 104*
Sheerer, Mary G., 9
Shelley china, 83, 114, *114,* 116–117; Joseph, 116; Percy, 116
Shirayamadani, Kataro, 7
Shire, Peter, 230
Shmoos, *78*
Shoshone Furniture Company, 238

Shoson, Ohara, 385, *385*
Shreve & Company, *434*; Shreve, Crump & Low, *272, 434*
Shure, Nathan, 330
Shwayder Brothers, 222
Sicard, Jacques, *24, 25*
Sicardo, *24, 25*
Silhouette dinnerware, 197
Silicon ware, 107
Silver, English, 280; guilds, 280; marks, American and European 272; overlay, 7, 184; plate, 267, 270
Simon, by Hasbro, 343
Simonds, Elgin, 207
Sinel, Joseph, xix
Singer and Sons, *225*
Singer, Susi, *36*
Sintesi task light, 264
Skawonius, Sven-Erik, *193*
Skrufs Glasbruk, *193*
Slovakia, 129, 318
Smed, Peer, *278*
Smell test, 320
Smith Fife and Company, 57
Smith, Art, *303*, 310, *434*
Smith, L. E., Glass Company, *176, 185*
Smoking stands, 218
Snack plate, 66
Snack set, *67*
Snail Room, 206
Snap-Lock beads, 340
Snow Babies, 133
Soleil, *158*
Sophie Newcomb College, 9
Sottsass, Ettore, 140, *141*, 230, 231, *231*, 304, 318, 418
South Beach Furniture, 243
Southern folk pottery, 37–40
Southern Potteries, Inc., 74
Souvenir spoons, 270
Souvenirs, 106
Sowden, George James, *231*
SP mark, *104*
Space guns, 401
Space-related dinnerware patterns, 83

Wileman & Company, 116
Wileman, Henry, 116
Wilhelm Kralik & Söhn, *158,
162, 165*
Wilkinson, A. J., pottery, 117
Wilkinson, Arthur J., & Co.,
117
Willets Manufacturing Company,
57, 62, *64,* 136
Willets, Daniel, 62; Edmund R.,
62; Joseph, 62
Williams, A. C., Company, *373*
Williamsburg reproductions, 236
Willow, 147, 148
Wilson, Alexander, 4
Wilson, Henry J., *426*
Wimmer, Jonathan and Louise,
200
Winfield Pottery, *50*
Winn, James H., *435*
Winston, Harry, *435*
Winter, Edward, *290, 292;*
Thelma Frazier, 32, *36,* 292
Winton, Don, 44
Winzeler, Howie, 342
Wirkkala, Tapio, 132, 187, 188,
188, 191
WMF (Württembergische
Metallwarenfabrik), *168*
Wolverine Supply &
Manufacturing Company, 324,
373
Wood, Arthur, & Sons, 117
Wood, Beatrice, 28, 32, *33, 36*
Wood, Grant, 382
Wood, Red gum tree, 242

Woodblock prints, 377, 378,
383–385
Wooden pins, 306, 321
Woodward, Ellsworth, 9
Woolley, Ellamarie and Jackson,
294
Woolworth Company, F.W.,
80–81
Worcester Royal Porcelain
Company, 85
Works Progress Administration,
199
World War I, 66, 83, 106, 125,
126, 140, 151, 159, 211, 215,
298, 323, 327, 351, 381, 391,
398, 401,
World War II, 67, 74, 85, 95,
116, 128, 130, 131, 144, 148,
174, 186, 187, 219, 228, 247,
260, 271, 280, 301, 306, 312,
317, 326, 327, 329, 340, 351,
354, 391, 395
Wormley, Edward, 222, *222*
WP mark, *104*
WPA, 199
Wreath with letter N mark, 152
Wright, Frank Lloyd, *209,* 210,
214, 214–215, 216, 268, *269,*
337
Wright, L. G., Glass Co., *185*
Wright, R. John, Dolls, Inc., *359*
Wright, Russel, Associates, 137
Wright, Russel, xviii, xx, 67, 72,
79, 88, *88,* 137, 197, 218,
219, 222, 251, 288, 291, *291*
Wrigley, William, 43

Wrigley's Spearmint Gum, *325;*
Wrigley man, *397*
Wristwatches, 302
Württembergiche
Metallwarenfabrik, *424*
Wyandotte Toys, *373*
Wyeth, Andrew, 382
Wyman, Claire, 294
Yam, 342
Yamato, 197
Yellin, Samuel, 281–285, *435*
Yellin, Samuel, Metalworkers, **282**
Yellow Kid, 338, 348
Yonezawa, *373*
Yoshida, Hiroshi, 385
Yoshida, Toshi, 385
Yoshiya of Japan, *340*
Young, James B., 268
Ypsilanti Reed Furniture
Company, 244
Yuenglings ice cream, 396
Yugoslavia, *153*
Yuri Ichihashi, *431*
Yurman, David, 304, 309, *435*
Zane Pottery, *22*
Zanesville Art Pottery, *22*
Zanesville Tile Company, *104*
Zanini for Ace/Los Angeles, *318*
Zeisel, Eva, xviii, xx, 72, *72,* **137,**
197
Zenith Plastics, 247
Zimmermann, Marie, *278,* **282,**
283, 435
Zircon, 181
Zsolnay, 72
Zuni silver jewelry, 313, *313*